ADVENTURES IN NATURE
COSTA RICA

Ree Strange Sheck

Ree Strange Sheck

**AVALON
TRAVEL**
publishing

Adventures in Nature: Costa Rica
2nd EDITION

Ree Strange Sheck

Published by
Avalon Travel Publishing, Inc.
5855 Beaudry St.
Emeryville, CA 94608, USA

Printing History
Second edition—February 2001
5 4 3 2 1

Please send all comments,
corrections, additions,
amendments, and critiques to:

Adventures in Nature: Costa Rica
AVALON TRAVEL PUBLISHING
5855 BEAURDY ST.
EMERYVILLE, CA 94608, USA
e-mail: info@travelmatters.com
www.travelmatters.com

ISBN: 1-56691-242-3
ISSN: 1531-4162

Editors: Jeannie Trizzino, Marisa Solís
Copy Editor: Carolyn Perkins
Index: Lynne Lipkind
Graphics Coordinator: Erika Howsare
Production: Karen McKinley, David Hurst
Map Editor: Mike Balsbaugh
Cartography: Mike Morgenfeld, Doug Beckner, Kathleen Sparkes—
    White Hart Design

Front cover photo: Reventazón River; © Leo de Wys Inc./Bob Krist
Back cover photo: Arenal Volcano; © Nicholas DeVore III—
    Photographers/Aspen, Inc.

Distributed in the United States and Canada by Publishers Group West

Printed in the United States by Publishers Press

CONTENTS

ABOUT THIS BOOK

Adventures in Nature: Costa Rica is a guide to Costa Rica's most exciting destinations for active travelers who are interested in exploring the country's natural wonders. Along with the best places for hiking and birding and prime spots for exploring rain-forest canopy or the altiplano, author Ree Strange Sheck recommends outfitters and local guides that can provide gear and lead you to the more remote parts of the country. She also points out places to eat and stay that will help you enjoy local cultures and cuisine.

Like all Adventures in Nature guides, this book emphasizes responsible, low-impact travel. Restaurants, accommodations, and outfitters that are particularly eco-friendly—those that strive to operate in ways that protect the natural environment or support local ecotourism efforts—are highlighted in most chapters.

ACKNOWLEDGMENTS

I first visited Costa Rica in 1968, a country that became my home from 1990 to 1998. For the more than 10 years that I have researched and written this book, which evolved from *Costa Rica: A Natural Destination* to *Adventures in Nature: Costa Rica,* I thank my daughter Claren Sheck-Boehler for her unfailing support. Continuing love and gratitude go to my son, Curt, whose death in 1984 was the beginning of a new journey for me, a journey that led me back to Costa Rica and to this book.

For this edition, special thanks go to Nora Schofield, whose assistance in countless ways was invaluable as I struggled to meet deadlines, to my sister Ruth Hamilton, who lightened my load by her presence and good humor on one leg of the travels, and to Alex Segura, Lizbeth, John Aspinall, Deborah Kushner, and Pat Brandenburg. I am grateful for the support of family: Rayburn, Vetha, Rosie, Sonny, Virgil, Gayle, Robert, Bobbie, Jeff, Julia, and Lauren.

To the naturalist guides I have been privileged to travel with and to learn from, to tour operators, to owners of private nature reserves and hotels visited, thank you for gracious attention. Thanks go to rangers at parks, reserves, and wildlife refuges for taking time to talk or walk with me; I have profound respect for these guardians of the forest who often live and work under difficult circumstances.

I am grateful to the many readers of this book who have sent suggestions and shared their own discoveries with me, and to the editorial, graphics, and production staff at Avalon Travel Publishing who work hard to produce a fine book.

I express my appreciation to the people of Costa Rica for their generosity of spirit, for smiles, for helping me get on the right bus or the right road, for neighborliness that transcends international boundaries.

I am forever grateful to those in Costa Rica and abroad whose efforts have helped preserve the extraordinary richness of Costa Rica's tropical ecoystems and to those who continue this work today.

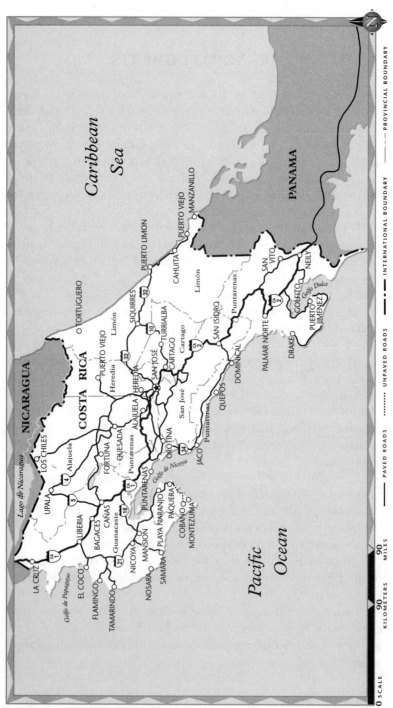

CHAPTER 1

Why Costa Rica?

Costa Rica touches the heart and mind, not through elegant boulevards, towering cathedrals, or an imposing place in history, but through its incredible natural beauty and a gracious people disposed to peace, kindness, and a generosity of spirit. No one feels a stranger here for long.

It is one of the most biologically diverse countries in the world—a treasure house of flora and fauna unequaled in so small an area. Casual tourist and dedicated nature traveler alike come under the spell of a natural wonderland studded with tropical forests, rushing rivers, exotic animals, uncrowded beaches, high mountains, and awesome volcanoes.

Struggling to explain why increasing numbers of people are making their way to this small Central American country, one observer simply said, "The greatest tourist attraction in Costa Rica is Costa Rica."

With more than a century of democracy under its belt in a region with a history of political strife, Costa Rica boasts "teachers, not soldiers." The country has had no army since 1948. It lays claim to one of the highest literacy rates in the world and a national health-care system that covers all its citizens. The people's cultural inclination toward modesty, simplicity, and friendliness, along with

1

the country's political commitment to peace, create a climate of trust for travelers.

And what a place to travel! Visitors can walk among rain-forest giants, see green turtles nesting, get a ringside view of one of the most active volcanoes in the world, ogle the keel-billed toucan, and hear the howler monkey. Pristine beaches beckon on both the Caribbean and Pacific coasts. Trees alive with their own miniforests of bromeliads, lichens, and mosses assume mysterious forms in the high cloud forests; orchids grow wild amid lush vegetation that tumbles down along road cuts.

Travelers can enjoy world-class white-water rafting, sunning on deserted beaches, bicycle touring, surfing, snorkeling, fishing, bird-watching, hiking, diving, climbing to the forest canopy, and kayaking or ballooning.

A small country, a little smaller than West Virginia or Nova Scotia, Costa Rica abounds with plant and animal species: North American, South American, and those endemic to the area. It is known around the world for its national park system, now protecting about 11 percent of the country, which encompasses some 1.4 million acres (570,000 ha). Added to land in other reserves, that brings the total to about 33 percent of its territory under some status of protection—an enviable record for any country, remarkable for a developing one. That commitment to conservation makes it possible for resident and tourist alike to encounter the natural world in a special way. An agouti and I once surprised each other on a park trail; a paca (known locally by the marvelous name of *tepezcuintle*) amazed me by rushing from bushes to plunge into a pool at the base of a waterfall where I had been swimming. Giant blue morpho butterflies can turn any ordinary day into a mystical experience. There is the chance of coming face-to-face with a white-faced monkey or catching a glimpse of a scarlet macaw. Tropical trees towering to 150 feet (46 m) and delicate, tiny flowers blooming in a high Andean-like climate open us to not only the magnificence of the universe but also the interrelationship of all living things.

This guide is offered as a companion for your journey in Costa Rica, to help you touch and be touched by the land and its people on paths that are most comfortable for you. It includes information about national parks and privately owned nature reserves, beaches, and volcanoes, as well as information about towns and villages. With each destination are suggestions for ways you can experience it, as well as helpful information on what you will find at the end of the trail: a private room and bath with hot water or a bunk in a dormitory atmosphere with a shared bath and cold water. There are sections to let you know whether you can fly in or drive in or whether access is by foot, boat, or horseback; what to bring along and how to call home; where and when you might see a quetzal; and which beaches turtles choose for nesting.

Find your own adventure and sense the heartbeat of this special place, from the quiet rhythm of its rural landscape to busy San José. Your experience will be your own. Just bring an open heart to contain it.

LAY OF THE LAND

Costa Rica is a small country, but its varying geography creates a constantly changing panorama for travelers. The chain of mountains that forms a backbone down the length of Costa Rica starts in the north with the Guanacaste Cordillera (*cordillera* is the Spanish term for mountain range), continuing through the Tilarán Cordillera (location of Monteverde and Arenal), and Central Cordillera (Irazú, Poás, Braulio Carrillo). The southern Talamanca Cordillera is the highest in the country.

The Pacific coastline is almost 780 miles (1,254 km); the Caribbean, only 132 miles (212 km). Hilly peninsulas jut out from the Pacific coastline; there are two large gulfs, many small coves and bays, and two major commercial ports: Puntarenas and Puerto Caldera. On the Caribbean, a natural harbor exists only in the Moín-Limón area. The largest area of lowland plains in the country, which stretches back from the northern coastline almost to Limón, makes up about one-fifth of Costa Rica.

Costa Rica lies in the tropics about 10 degrees north of the equator, about the same latitude as the southern tip of India. Because Costa Rica is a small country, you might expect the climate to be relatively uniform, but the rugged mountain chain's effect on factors such as wind, rain, and temperature creates many microclimates.

Some rules of thumb, however, can be helpful. In general, temperatures are moderate, varying more with altitude than time of year—most people are surprised to learn that frost and ice can occur on some of the loftier peaks. Temperatures are somewhat higher on the Pacific side than on the Caribbean at the same elevation. (There are more clouds on the Caribbean watershed year-round than on the Pacific.) At sea level on either side, the annual average is above 75°F (24°C). Some of the highest peaks in the Central Mountain Range and Talamanca Mountains average 54°F (12°C), though temperatures can fall below freezing.

Though the warmest months are March, April, and May, temperature variation is much greater from night to day than from season to season: the difference in daily temperatures averages 14°F to 18°F (8°C to 10°C). From November to January, cold air from the north can funnel down from the mountains of North America. Though much weakened by the time they get to Costa Rica, the breezes bring a bite to the air. This is one of the few places in the world where polar air gets this close to the equator.

Arenal Volcano, active since 1968

4

VOLCANOES

Volcanoes are a hot topic. Some 112 craters, including the two on Coco Island, mark the Costa Rican landscape. They range from extinct to dormant to active, and from a mere remnant rising 328 feet (100 m) above the Tortuguero Plains to majestic peaks more than 11,000 feet (3,350 m) high that still fuss and fume along the country's spine.

If you have never heard a volcano breathe, consider a visit to 5,358-foot (1,633-m) Arenal, one of the most active volcanoes in the world. Hearing the huff of its breath one unforgettable morning made me one with primitive peoples; the mountain became a living being. When it hurled fiery blocks high into the air, not a doubt remained: Arenal was angry. It has been angry enough to kill people since beginning its current phase of activity in 1968, including volcano-watching tourists in August 2000. Be prudent when you visit any active volcano.

Activity at Poás and Rincón de la Vieja has caused the national parks associated with them to close occasionally since 1989. Other volcanoes with some level of activity include Irazú, Miravalles, and Turrialba. Vulcanological and seismological institutions constantly monitor active sites.

Spring and fall have little meaning here; the seasons are called *verano* (summer) for dry season months, generally from December through April, and *invierno* (winter) for wet months, generally from May through November. The country's most prevalent rainfall pattern is in the range of 79 to 158 inches (2,000 to 4,000 mm). Precipitation can come in the form of a tropical downpour—a gully-washer complete with impressive lightning and thunder—or a steady rain. The downpour is called an *aguacero;* a continuous rain for several days is a *temporal.*

On the Pacific side, particularly from the central to the northern area, September and October are wettest, with the length of the wet season increasing the farther south you go. Rainfall amounts vary from less than 59 inches (1,500 mm) in the northwest and central part to more than 190 inches (4,800 mm) in the south.

On the Atlantic side, the rainy season can begin in late April and end in January, with December and July the wettest months. When it's rainy in the rest of the country in October, the southern Caribbean can be sunny. Annual rainfall averages are higher here than on the Pacific side. Heaviest rainfall is inland on the eastern (windward) face of the northern mountains: it may exceed 355 inches (9,000 mm) per year. Elsewhere in the lowlands, annual rainfall averages from 118 inches to about 200 inches (3,000 to 5,000 mm).

HISTORICAL HIGHLIGHTS

Travelers often ask what has led this country on a path that sets it apart from its Central American neighbors. Different it is. Costa Rica is a country without an army in a world that counts tanks, missiles, and nuclear warheads as the measure of a nation's power. The national hero is not a general but a young, barefoot *campesino* (farmer). Schoolchildren, not soldiers, parade on Independence Day. While other countries debate the issue, Costa Rica abolished the death penalty more than a century ago.

Located in a region where violence has too often been the order of the day, Costa Rica lives in peace. Costa Ricans like to say they have gained through evolution what other countries try to attain through revolution. A brief look at its history, economy, and political and social systems sheds light on some of the questions most often asked.

When Christopher Columbus dropped anchor off Costa Rica in 1502, near the present-day port of Limón, he still thought he had found a new route to the East and believed he was on the southeast coast of Asia, near Thailand. Even today, some people confuse Costa Rica with another Caribbean locale, Puerto Rico.

Stories about great wealth to be found here began at that time. The indigenous peoples Columbus encountered offered gifts of gold, and Spanish explorers began to refer to the area as *costa rica,* or "rich coast." Later expeditions touched along the Caribbean and then the Pacific coasts, but it was not until the 1560s that the first

Ree Strange Sheck

Indigenous treasures in the National Museum

permanent European settlement took root. Cartago, in the Central Valley, became the capital of what would become a province under the Captaincy General of Guatemala.

The first Spanish inhabitants of this new land found neither mineral wealth nor a large indigenous population that could be used as forced labor. The indigenous peoples they did find were not keen on servitude. Resistance ranged from warfare to retreat into the forested backcountry. Though definitive numbers on the indigenous population at the time of the conquest are not available, a range of 300,000 to 500,000 individuals is commonly cited. By 1522, Spanish colonial authorities reported only 27,000 individuals, probably an underestimate but still indicative of greatly reduced numbers resulting from intertribal conflicts, wars with the Spanish, illness introduced from the Old World, intermarriage, and sale of natives as slaves to other countries. By 1801, the number was 8,000.

So even though traditional Spanish colonial systems of forced indigenous labor existed in Costa Rica, colonizers were effectively reduced to small landholdings that they and their families could mostly work themselves. Communication was hampered by rugged terrain and lack of roads and made more difficult by seasonally heavy rains. Efforts went into survival rather than commerce, with the agrarian society based on subsistence farming and ranching.

Throughout the colonial period, Costa Rica was a poor, neglected outpost of the Spanish Empire. The poverty and isolation gave rise to a simple life, strong individualism, hospitality, and a certain spirit of equality that cut across existing social class lines, contributing to the beginnings of rural democracy.

Even the name Costa Ricans call themselves, *ticos*, is said by some to come from a colonial saying: "We are all *hermaniticos* (little brothers)." (Diminutive endings of *-ito* and *-ico* are used in everyday speech. For example, you may hear *pequeñito* for "small" rather than *pequeño*.)

The Latin American wars for independence from Spain were far removed from this solitary enclave. When victory finally came in 1821, Costa Rica received word about a month later. A popular story is that a messenger on a mule delivered the official victory letter. Costa Rica joined the Central American Federation for a time but declared itself an independent republic in 1848.

A war that did have an impact on the country came in 1856, when William Walker, a U.S. adventurer who had gained control of the armed forces of Nicaragua and dreamed of controlling all of Central America, invaded Costa Rica. The strong national identity forged during colonial isolation brought volunteers from around the country to defend the nation. In a battle that lasted only a few minutes, the well-armed invading force was routed at Hacienda Santa Rosa in Guanacaste. The site of the confrontation is now protected in Santa Rosa National Park. When you visit there, remember how remote it was at the time; the ragtag citizen army of 9,000 marched 12 days from San José to get there. The army pursued Walker's forces into Nicaragua, where a second battle occurred.

In the fighting at Rivas, a brave young *campesino* from Alajuela named Juan Santamaría volunteered to set fire to the Walker stronghold, losing his life in the act. He became the national hero for his part in this crucial battle. Walker's dream ended in 1860 before a firing squad in Honduras.

The first true popular elections came in 1889, which is why Costa Rica claims more than 100 years of democracy. The president at the time tried to cancel the promised vote in order to name his successor, but the elections were held when country people invaded San José and demanded their say.

By this time, the exportation of coffee was ending Costa Rica's isolation. Soon bananas thrust the country further into international commerce. The population grew, frontiers expanded, and transportation routes carried produce out and the world in.

Costa Rica's own brief "revolution" came in 1948, when Congress annulled the presidential election to keep the opposition candidate from taking over. It was a short but savage civil war in which more than 2,000 people died. The leader of the revolt was José Pepe Figueres, who took control of an interim government for 18 months before the elected opposition candidate assumed office. Figueres abolished the army; military facilities were converted into schools, a prison, and the National Museum. The Constitution of 1949 set up a government of checks and balances.

Succeeding governments have spent money on roads, schools, hospitals, electricity, and running water instead of arms. Compromise and negotiation are the key words in resolution of conflict.

HAGA FILA: GET IN LINE

Waiting your turn is a surviving piece of the "everyone is equal" mentality born in colonial times. No one is exempt. In fact, the more important a person is, the more essential it is that this tenet be respected. I observed this for myself one lunchtime when I noticed the Costa Rican president entering a downtown San José McDonald's. It was almost as if a ritual—understood by all the players—were being performed as he took his place in line to order and looked for an empty table. That president was Oscar Arias, winner of the 1987 Nobel Peace Prize.

The same decorum is expected when waiting at a bus stop, store counter, grocery store, or public telephone.

Citizens do, however, continue to take to the streets to protest or pressure the government for action.

Today large landholdings exist alongside small farms; wealth exists alongside poverty. But there is still a genuine faith in peace as a force, in democracy, and in fundamental human dignity. Social, economic, and political mobility is possible. The national character is still tied to the land. Even in urban centers, Costa Ricans tell you that their strength is in the hard-working, loyal *campesino* and the land. It will be interesting to see how this idealization of the past holds up as more and more *campesinos* become *peónes* (day laborers) and the pressures on the land increase. You can be sure of one thing: it will be a Costa Rican solution.

POLITICAL SYSTEM

Governmental power is divided among executive, legislative, and judicial branches, with a Supreme Election Tribunal in charge of elections. The decentralized form of government reflects Costa Ricans' aversion to a concentration of power.

A president is elected every four years by secret ballot and cannot be reelected. Two vice-presidents are elected at the same time. Numerous checks and balances were written into the 1949 constitution, under which the country is governed, to prevent abuse of power, especially by a strong president. The unicameral Legislative Assembly is considered to have more power than the president. Its 57 deputies are also elected every four years and may not serve consecutive terms. Seats are allocated according to population in each of the country's seven provinces. Municipal elections take place at the same time as national elections. These are the two important levels of government.

Magistrates of the Supreme Court of Justice are named by the legislature for staggered eight-year terms. These magistrates name justices at the provincial level.

To safeguard against electoral fraud, a kind of fourth branch of government is set up as an autonomous body. This Supreme Election Tribunal oversees everything from voter registration to counting of votes. It also oversees registration of political parties and keeps an eye on political campaigns for misconduct. As a further check, six months before the election, command of the Civil and Rural Guard, essentially police forces, passes from the president to the tribunal.

Campaigning can be dirty, but election day itself is a party. Even children turn out to help get people to the polls, wave party flags, and shout slogans. Do not, however, mistake fanfare for frivolity. *Ticos* take their voting seriously. Women have had the vote since 1949, and the minimum voting age is 18. Even those who cannot read and write are entitled to cast a ballot. Women have been elected to high office, both in the legislature and as vice-president.

Political parties come and go; the two principal ones today are the National Liberation party and the Social Christian Unity party. Factions split off and coalitions form. The Communist Party is recognized but does not carry much weight at the polls.

Costa Rica has a large bureaucracy. The government produces electricity, runs the telephone service and the national banking system, builds houses, and distills liquor, along with doing all the other things one expects a government to do. About 14 percent of the country's workers on fixed salaries are employed in the public sector.

SOCIAL WELFARE AND EDUCATION

The Social Security system, referred to by *ticos* as the *Caja* and identified by the initials CCSS, was instituted in 1941 by the same president who helped enact a labor code that set minimum wages and guaranteed workers the right to organize. Though complaints about inefficiency and the level of care are common, no one denies the vital role Social Security has played in improving health care. Infant mortality rates here are among the lowest in Latin America. Life expectancy at birth in the early part of the 20th century was 40 years; today it is 76 years. When the system started, coverage was limited, but now practically all citizens have access to care.

Rural health-care programs geared to both prevention and treatment touch the lives of the poor even in remote corners of the country. Scenarios may include a medical center staffed by para-

Litter patrol by a primary class in Dominical

Ree Strange Sheck

medics and visited regularly by doctors and nurses. I was once visiting a rural highland school when the doctor came for his scheduled community visit. He used one room of the two-room school for consultations. In a coastal Caribbean village, a young mother told me the doctor came by boat once a month. Poor urban neighborhoods are also targeted.

As you travel around the country, you'll see clinics in small towns and a growing number of regional hospitals. The Red Cross (*Cruz Roja* in Spanish) is a strong, highly respected organization in Costa Rica, working closely with health-care agencies and providing ambulance service.

Housing, another focus of social programs, has been particularly emphasized in recent years. Both urban and rural public projects have been implemented in an attempt to meet a serious housing shortage.

Costa Rica and schools are practically synonymous. The country was among the first in the world to mandate free, compulsory, tax-supported education (1869); children must attend school through the ninth grade. More than 22 percent of the national budget goes to education. The literacy rate is an impressive 95 percent.

In rural areas the schoolhouse may be one room, with six grades divided between morning and afternoon classes. Continuing on to secondary school can mean real commitment for students, for while primary schools are abundant, secondary schools are centered in areas with larger populations. Two young people on a mountain road explained to me that they were on their way to the nearest bus stop for a 30-minute ride to school in Turrialba. The daily walk to the bus stop was 90 minutes each way, with the return trip after dark. About 40 percent of secondary-school-age students do not attend school.

Most visitors ask about the rationale behind school uniforms for primary and secondary students. This, too, harks back to egalitarian roots. The idea is to minimize differences between social classes. Private schools also have uniforms. Many private primary and secondary schools do exist, an option for those who complain about inferior levels of instruction at public schools.

Costa Rica has four state universities in the Central Valley, with branches in outlying areas. University education is not free, but tuition is generally low (although rising), and scholarships are available. Technical and vocational schools outside the San José metropolitan area also put higher education within reach of more students as well as promote other regions in the hope of stemming the flow of people into the heavily populated Central Valley. The number of private universities has mushroomed.

Debates on the quality of education and even what constitutes an education rage here as elsewhere. Resources are stretched thin. Urban areas have an advantage because of backup facilities (such as libraries) and easier access to educational support; it is often difficult to retain teachers in small, isolated areas. The overall picture, however, has some positive hues. For the most part, schools remain the nucleus around which a sense of community forms, especially in rural areas. Dedicated teachers do exist, often working with few of the materials that teachers in the United States or Canada take for granted. Innovative projects include a growing program to provide computers to classrooms and initiation of English-language training in primary schools. Bilingual materials in the surviving indigenous languages (Maleku, Cabecar, Guaymí, and Bribrí) have been incorporated into the curriculum on reserves for indigenous peoples, including history and legends that have passed down through oral tradition.

While some historians question aspects of the rural democracy thesis (such as whether the colonial social structure was egalitarian, whether there was universal poverty, or whether landholdings were uniformly small), no one seems to debate the importance of early emphasis on public education to the democratic process—a major difference from its neighbors. Until universal suffrage came with the 1949 constitution, literacy was a requisite for voting. Enlightened education policies enfranchised the populace and gave them power at the polls.

ECONOMY

Starting from a base of subsistence agriculture in colonial times, Costa Rica moved into the world economy only in the latter half of the 19th century with exportation of coffee to Europe, followed soon by banana exports. A Costa Rican journalist, lamenting his country's economic dependence on agricultural exports, once said to me in the last decade, "What makes it worse is that the country produces *postres* (desserts)—coffee, bananas, sugar, and chocolate. When importing countries are in an economic bind, demand for these things drops first."

That situation, however, is changing dramatically. Investment in nontraditional products for export and to cut dependence on the *postres* is paying off. In 1988, for the first time nontraditional exports edged past traditional ones (bananas, coffee, meat, sugar) in dollar value. In 1999, tourism topped the foreign-income-earned list, followed by electronics and textiles (*maquila* operations). Export of fresh flowers, ornamental plants, pineapples and melons, frozen fish, and pharmaceutical products are among other nontraditional items filling out the menu. Check the label of the next shirt or pair of pants you buy—it could very well say "Assembled in Costa Rica." The country has become one of the largest brassiere manufacturers in the world. A good percentage of the hair dryers imported by the United States come from Costa Rica.

Some of Costa Rica's current economic problems have roots in the crisis of 1979 to 1982, when the country went through one of the worst economic crunches in its history. World prices for its traditional crops collapsed at the same time that petroleum costs soared. Since Costa Rica imports all its oil, the dynamics were devastating. The country had borrowed heavily from eager banks, with the money used largely, as one Costa Rican put it, "to maintain our accustomed standard of living." It has been difficult to cut the social programs citizens take as their due. National spending still outstrips income earned from exports and taxation, while juggling foreign-debt payments demands enormous energy.

The U.S. Caribbean Basin Initiative, which provides preferential customs treatment to many products from the region, has been a stimulus to Costa Rica's economy; the United States is the country's biggest business partner, but multinational companies from Europe and the Far East have also set up shop. The nation's stability, a large and educated middle class that provides a stable workforce, competitive labor costs, and national and international incentives draw foreign firms and spawn joint ventures with Costa Rican companies.

Debate continues regarding the privatization of state-owned companies that dominate sectors of power generation, telecommunications, banking, petroleum, insurance, and manufacture of liquor. It seems only a matter of time before competition wins out in some of these sectors.

The average annual per-capita income is $2,719 (U.S. per capita is $25,000) and the minimum hourly wage is just under $1. Unemployment is less than 6 percent and inflation about 10 percent.

POPULATION PATTERNS

The Central Valley, home to many of the country's 3.6 million people, has been the center of population since colonial times. As was the pattern in other Central American countries, settlement centered in the highlands. Early Spanish colonists in Costa Rica shunned the hotter, rainier coastlands in favor of this mountain valley and its rich volcanic soil. This New World enclave continued in relative isolation until the 19th century. As late as 1700, Cartago,

POPULATION

Costa Rica	**3,558,697**
Province	
San José	1,284,500
Alajuela	638,177
Cartago	398,691
Heredia	298,116
Guanacaste	279,266
Puntarenas	396,136
Limón	275,811

Source: Dirección General de Estádistica y Censos, January 1, 1999, census figures

with a population of 2,535, was the country's only permanent urban center. In 1821, when Costa Rica and its 60,000 residents gained independence from Spain, 90 percent lived in the Central Valley. About 5 percent had ventured out toward Esparza (not far from Puntarenas) and Bagaces (16 miles [26 km] south of present-day Liberia) to raise cattle, and another 5 percent were indigenous peoples living in dispersed settlements on their traditional lands in the north and south.

A small bean introduced into Costa Rica around the beginning of the 19th century ended up transforming the life of this agrarian society, pushing the frontier farther and farther away from the Central Valley. Coffee was its name. The export of coffee led to the opening of a road to Puntarenas, since the first loads went to Panama, then to Chile, and finally to Europe via the Strait of Magellan. To transport the beans to the port of Limón for more direct European market access, a railroad was built, paving the way the beginning of large banana plantations on the Caribbean.

Blacks brought to work on the railroad and plantations, mainly from Jamaica, added another ethnic group and an English-speaking component. The African American population today is about 3 percent. The estimated population of indigenous peoples is about 1 percent; the estimated East Asian population, mainly Chinese, is 3 percent.

As Central Valley land values rose, small farmers sought new territory. Satellite towns took shape around colonial centers, but Costa Rica still had an abundance of unoccupied land at the beginning of the 20th century.

In 1938, banana activity moved to the southern Pacific coastal region from the Atlantic; roads followed, and so did settlement. With the opening of the Pan-American Highway south of the Central Valley to San Isidro de El General in 1946, the trickle of pioneers who had braved the high, chilly climate of Cerro de la Muerte on foot or horseback became a flood of immigrants looking for new land, following the transportation route as it made its way to Panama in the 1960s. (The Pan-American Highway is called the Inter-American Highway in Costa Rica, as it is throughout Central America.)

Immigrants added to Costa Rica's population. Italians, for example, developed San Vito, and Quakers from the United States settled Monteverde. New transportation routes helped drain some of the population pressure in the central region. In 1956, Costa Rica had one million inhabitants; by 1976, two million. The limits of settlement extended to the Plains of San Carlos and Sarapiquí, to Guanacaste and Tilarán, to the Nicoya Peninsula, and to the San Isidro de El General and Coto Brus regions.

Today Costa Rica is facing the pressures of a growing population with little remaining public land. Most of what exists is in reserves set aside for indigenous peoples, forest reserves, national parks, and wildlife refuges. Since one of the frontier legacies is a belief that every *campesino* has a right to a piece of land to work, pressure on this protected land is going to be enormous.

As you travel on the road from the capital to San Isidro de El General, remember that most settlement along here dates from the middle of this century. As you drive over the highway from San José to Limón through Guapiles, look at what has developed in the 1990s. If you sense a frontier spirit as you get to know outlying areas, you will understand why.

17

TRAVEL STRATEGIES

The first-time visitor to Costa Rica can feel overwhelmed by the banquet of choices: tropical forests to explore, steaming volcanoes to photograph, beaches to comb, mountains to climb, rivers to raft, flowers to smell along the way. Hire a guide? Take a tour? Travel independently?

If it's your first trip, you may choose to stay a day or two in San José. It has crazy traffic and crowded sidewalks, but it also has museums and parks and is the center of Costa Rican culture and government. You can stay in San José itself or choose among some wonderful small hotels and inns not far from the airport, near Alajuela, Heredia, Atenas, or Grecia. Some travelers start their experience from Liberia, landing at the country's second international airport.

Wherever you make your initial base, sign up for a trip with a naturalist guide for a good introduction to the tropical world. The guide knows where the crocodiles hang out, what time scarlet macaws fly over the trail, what tree the hummingbirds nest in, and which orchids are in bloom.

Costa Rica's essence is tied to its rural roots. Its people and its natural resources are the biggest part of what it has to offer. Privately owned reserves provide excellent opportunities for adventures in nature: whether your bliss is tromping along muddy trails through a jungle miles from nowhere, viewing plant and animal life from a shady veranda, or strolling along a quiet beach. Some reserves employ bilingual biologist guides; others offer local people with varying commands of English who are naturalists by life experience. Accommodations range from bunk beds to first-class hotels with hot water and fine dining. Few national parks, reserves, and wildlife refuges offer a place to stay, but nearby lodges generally offer day visits to the neighboring reserves.

Though distances may seem short in miles, travel by car or bus can take longer than you think: many paved roads are potholed, and unpaved roads can be slow going. A network of buses reaches into areas once remote, and major car-rental companies have offices in San José, with branches at other locations. Many hotels transport guests to and from other locales, sometimes cheaper than renting a

COUNTRY AT A GLANCE

Population: *3.6 million*

Area: *19,730 square miles (51,100 sq. km)*

Capital: *San José*

Population: *330,131 in the canton of San José; greater metropolitan area, 52% of the country's people (about 1.8 million)*

Elevation: *3,809 feet (1,161 m)*

Provinces: *Alajuela, Cartago, Guanacaste, Heredia, Limón, Puntarenas, San José*

Official language: *Spanish*

Official religion: *Roman Catholic (82 percent of population)*

Government: *Constitutional, democratic republic; elections every four years*

President: *Miguel Angel Rodríguez (1998-2002)*

Flag: *Five horizontal stripes—blue, white, red (wide), white, blue*

Currency: *Colón*

Main exports: *Electronics, bananas, coffee, textiles*

Time: *Central Standard, no daylight saving time*

Electric current: *110 volts*

Telephone country code: *506*

Latitude: *10° north of equator; longitude 84°15′ west*

Highest point: *Mount Chirripó, 12,529 feet (3,819 m)*

Seasons: *Rainy, May–November; dry, December–April*

car. Increased in-country flights make it easier to experience a variety of destinations during your stay.

When is the best time to visit? The dry season—December to April in most of the country—draws greatest numbers of travelers and has highest rates; however, June through August (marketed as the Green Season) are increasingly popular months: rates, especially in beach areas, are lower. Remember that even in the wet season, rain will not fall all day every day. It usually begins in early afternoon in the Central Valley and other highland areas and later in the afternoon in the Pacific lowlands, while drumming steadily at night in the Atlantic lowlands and valley bottoms. October, generally the rainiest month for most of the country, tends to be a beautiful month on the Caribbean side.

Each season has its beauty and its particular cares. In wetter times plant life is profuse, with a vibrant greenness that seeps into the soul. In the dry season a subtler background is a perfect canvas for orchids, bougainvillea, and *reina de la noche* (queen of the night), with its large white or pink trumpet-shaped flowers, as well as for deciduous trees that flower only then.

As for accommodations, I emphasize small and midsize lodges and hotels, many owner-operated, because I believe they give the traveler a sense of place and are more in keeping with the wonderful smallness and variety of the country itself, facilitating the connection with both people and nature.

Vacations have to do with moving you beyond the ordinary. Let your dreams come true in Costa Rica: climb a mountain, be pampered on a cruise, tramp along trails in a tropical forest, ford rivers with water that reaches to the hood of the car, stay up all night trying to photograph a volcanic eruption, or take off on horseback to explore the countryside. Sit on a beach, walk in a cloud forest, see birds and animals you know only from *National Geographic* specials, and bathe under a waterfall. Meet a warm and gracious people. Walk softly, aware of your own impact on the culture and environment.

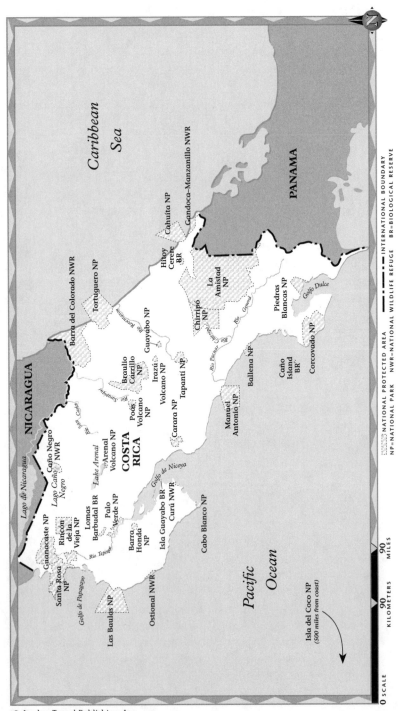

Caribbean
Sea

PANAMA

Gandoca–Manzanillo NWR

Cahuita NP

Hitoy
Cereré
BR

Barra del Colorado NWR

La
Amistad
NP

Tortuguero NP

Piedras
Blancas NP

Golfo Dulce

Río Reventazón

Chirripó
NP

Guayabo NP

Río General

Braulio
Carrillo
NP

NICARAGUA

Irazú
Volcano NP

Río Pacuare

Caño
Island
BR

Corcovado NP

Lago de Nicaragua

Río Sarapiquí

Poás
Volcano
NP

Tapantí NP

Ballena NP

Caño Negro
NWR

Río Infiernito

Arenal
Volcano NP

Carara NP

Lago Caño
Negro

COSTA
RICA

Manuel
Antonio NP

Lake Arenal

Guanacaste NP

Rincón
de la
Vieja NP

Lomas
Barbudal BR

Palo
Verde NP

Golfo de Nicoya

Santa Rosa
NP

Río Tempisque

Barra
Honda
NP

Isla Guayabo BR

Curú NWR

Golfo de Papagayo

Cabo Blanco NP

Las Baulas NP

Ostional NWR

Pacific
Ocean

Isla del Coco NP
(500 miles from coast)

NATIONAL PROTECTED AREA   INTERNATIONAL BOUNDARY
NP=NATIONAL PARK   NWR=NATIONAL WILDLIFE REFUGE   BR=BIOLOGICAL RESERVE

0 SCALE

90
KILOMETERS

90
MILES

© Avalon Travel Publishing, Inc.

CHAPTER 2

Conservation and Responsible Tourism

In pre-Columbian times, the area now known as Costa Rica was inhabited by small, dispersed indigenous groups whose impact on the land was small. Spanish colonial settlement was also limited in both size and location, being focused in San José, Cartago, Alajuela, and Heredia. Even then, however, there are records of governmental action to control the burning of fields and forests. After Costa Rica gained independence from Spain, the frontier began a retreat pushed by roads and the development fanning out from them. Environmental controls reflected the concerns of an agrarian society: laws maintained forested watersheds and forests along main riverbanks. Population growth and expansion of towns and agricultural activities in the 20th century made it clear that forest and the incredible life in it, left unprotected, would not long survive.

Today the combination of public and private initiatives that keeps Costa Rica on the cutting edge of conservation strategies has earned international acclaim. The national park system is perhaps the best known of these strategies, but the stage is crowded with other players, including large and small private reserves, biological corridors, carbon credits (see "Carbon Credits," page 39), "eco" labels, ecotourism, biological prospecting, reforestation incentives, and private conservation organizations. Dedicated individuals, both

HOW MANY SPECIES?

Mammals	209
Birds	850
Reptiles	220
Amphibians	163
Freshwater fish	130
Arthropods (insects, spiders, and crabs with segmented bodies and jointed limbs)	366,000
Plants	13,021
Trees	1,500
Orchids	1,400

Source: INBio

Costa Rican and foreign, working in public and private sectors have made the difference.

In 1998 Costa Rica passed the Biodiversity Law, one of the first laws of its kind in the world. Its intent is to protect sustainable use of the country's biological resources while fulfilling the three basic principles of the 1992 Biological Diversity Convention held in Río de Janeiro: conservation, sustainable use of biodiversity, and fair and equitable distribution of the benefits derived from such use.

At stake are Costa Rica's richly diverse ecosystems, which are estimated to contain half a million plant and animal species: about four percent of the species that exist on the planet. This small country is considered one of the 20 most biodiverse in the world. There are more butterflies here than in the United States, nearly as many bird species as in all of North America, and almost half its number of plant species. Here and around the world, species are being lost before they have even been identified, much less studied for their importance to humanity. Plants are gone before their medicinal value is known. Disappearance of a species of flora or fauna can cut a link in a food or reproductive chain that directly affects other species. Preservation of this biological diversity holds importance far beyond national boundaries.

Successes so far have not come without struggle; much remains to be done. Some of the challenges and achievements for conservation and responsible tourism follow. A common theme runs throughout: conservation of nature cannot be separate from the human community. Sustainable development is the watchword.

NATIONAL PARKS, RESERVES, AND WILDLIFE REFUGES

Today, nationally designated protected areas cover about 33 percent of Costa Rica. Almost half of this area is in national parks (11 percent), biological reserves (0.5 percent), and wildlife refuges (3.4 percent); the rest (with varying degrees of protection) is in forest reserves (5.5 percent), protected zones (3.5 percent), wetlands and mangroves (1.5 percent), reserves for indigenous peoples (6.4 percent), and a few other areas (1.2 percent). All are part of 11 conservation areas in the National System of Conservation Areas, referred to by its Spanish acronym SINAC. The conservation areas (listed in Appendix B) were created to facilitate the regional protection of ecosystems and cultural resources as well as the sustainable use of natural resources.

The cornerstone of the wildlife areas is the national parks. Although "paper parks" had been created earlier, the national park system did not come into existence until the late 1960s. The park system grew from four in 1970 (Cabo Blanco, Poás, Santa Rosa, Tortuguero) to 17 in 1978, and today includes more than 30.

While preservation was the necessary initial step, a challenge to parks and protected areas today is not only to conserve biodiversity but also to put people into the conservation equation. Population pressures are increasing at a time when public land available for new settlement is practically gone. Neighbors who receive some benefit from those protected lands will be more inclined to preserve them.

This is where SINAC comes into play. The conservation areas encompass not only wildlife areas but surrounding private lands.

Each has offices to coordinate conservation efforts within its area and to work with communities in buffer zones. Participation by private entities is fundamental. The Arenal Conservation Area, for example, has assisted local communities in organic vegetable farming, ecotourism trails and lodges, medicinal plant nurseries, tree nurseries, handcrafts, and reforestation projects.

In some conservation areas, private lands are promoted for scientific research: community members are trained to work as parataxonomists or naturalist guides, to start a butterfly farm, or to raise pacas (a paca is a type of large rodent). They work as caretakers and environmental education teachers in protected areas. These activities tie livelihoods directly to conservation.

Preservation of land as a park, refuge, or reserve is one thing. Protecting its biological integrity over the long haul is another, and this challenge is one that faces not only parks but all public and private reserves. It requires manpower, scientific study, and money. Poaching is a problem: hunting, nest-robbing, trapping of tropical birds to sell as pets to national or international buyers, and extrac-

The tapir, a relative of the horse, is threatened by hunting and habitat destruction.

tion of plants such as orchids. In the short term, prevention requires constant surveillance, both costly and difficult in rugged terrain. In the long term, education and development of alternative sustainable economic activities are the best solution.

Squatters sometimes pose a dilemma, especially for private reserves, but national parks have also been a target. A well-known example is the invasion of Corcovado National Park by gold miners, at its worst in the 1980s. I saw for myself in 1985 the destruction of mountainsides and streams caused by mining inside the park. In interviews with miners, it was clear that forest preservation came in a poor second to earning a living the way they knew how. They saw no direct economic benefit from keeping Corcovado pristine.

For some protected areas, forest fires pose a threat, particularly in the dry season; these fires are sometimes intentionally set by hunters to flush out game. The rich marine life at Isla del Coco is threatened by illegal fishing and overharvesting. Illegal harvesting of trees in protected areas is a danger that can increase as forests outside of preserved areas diminish.

Budgets for public parks, reserves, and refuges continue to be tight, with personnel stretched thin. Most lack sufficient staff to patrol adequately, much less meet needs of visitors. While infrastructure for tourists at most sites is still limited, some visitor centers are now in place and more are in the works. The most-visited parks have management plans that incorporate guidelines on tourist capacity to prevent the places from being loved to death. Substantial improvement has been made in printed information available for visitors, usually in a bilingual format. Some information is free (especially trail maps). Attendants at entrance booths are not always good salespeople, so be sure to ask for a booklet or brochure.

Another challenge facing parks is lack of funds to purchase inholdings (private land taken by parks which has never been paid for), which amount to perhaps 15 percent of total park land. Some private owners, who have waited for years to be paid, demand resolution—either pay or give back the land.

For wildlife refuges, an innovative strategy incorporates private reserves into the national system. Landowners who comply with requirements receive benefits: exemption from the territorial tax, assistance in case of problems with squatters, free technical help on

WANT TO BE A PARK VOLUNTEER?

If you are open to a different kind of vacation, are 18 years of age or older, and speak at least basic Spanish, the National Parks Service may have a deal for you. As a volunteer in parks, you can work alongside rangers or in the San José office—minimum 30 days, which allows you to volunteer at two different sites.

Depending on skills and interests, you could work on an archaeological dig, help fight forest fires, protect nesting sea turtles, cook, or maintain trails. Extra hands and minds are always needed in environmental education and to assist visitors.

Some volunteer jobs can be hard work; others not so demanding. Hours can be long, and living conditions are generally rustic. You pay $10 per day, which covers food and lodging; transportation costs are out of your pocket. Laundry? Count on hand washing your own clothes, and bring your own sheets. Some stations have no electricity, with outside contact only by radiophone. Both men and women are welcome, and there is no upper age limit.

What does a volunteer get out of all this? A rare opportunity to experience Costa Rica's parks in a way no tour or day visit can offer, to learn, and to contribute to conservation efforts. Parks are understaffed and for the most part work within severe budget constraints.

Consult the website for more information: www.minae.go.cr/ asvo. If you're interested, write for an application and state when you can come. E-mail correspondence is quickest—about one month for the exchange of letters to arrange your stint: asvo89@racsa.co.cr. If you use snail mail, allow three months: contact ASVO, Programa de Voluntariado para el Servicio en las Areas Protegidas Silvestres, Apartado 11384-1000, San José, Costa Rica. The office is in the Ministry of Environment and Energy, Calle 25, Avenida 8/10, San José, tel./fax 506/233-4989; open weekdays 8 A.M. to 4 P.M.

wildlife management, and the prestige that comes with being a government-recognized wildlife refuge—the latter a marketing edge for private reserves involved in tourism. The refuge status does not preclude development but regulates it, gaining wildlife habitat without displacing landowners or removing land from productive private use. The owner can still raise livestock, live there, build a hotel, restaurant, or shop, or permit scientific research. This seems a useful approach to protecting habitats not found within the parks, reserves, and government refuges at little cost to government.

Continued scientific study of species—not just the superstars like monkeys, jaguars, frogs, sloths, orchids, and fig trees but insects and lichens and grasses—are essential for sound ecological management of preserved areas. Fortunately, Costa Rica draws large numbers of scientific researchers, and internationally known organizations such as the Organization for Tropical Studies, Tropical Science Center, and the National Biodiversity Institute along with Costa Rican universities are also at work here to increase knowledge about tropical ecosystems. Incorporation of that information into management plans of preserved areas is critical. Preservation is not just about protecting scenery for the public to enjoy; it has to do with protecting the whole ecosystem.

PRIVATE RESERVES

As governments struggle with budget constraints that affect habitat and biodiversity protection, private reserves offer an excellent alternative. The Costa Rican Network of Natural Reserves began in 1995 as an initiative by private landowners to protect important habitats and species. More than 95 private reserves are already members of the network, representing more than 150,000 acres (60,000 ha). Many function as important buffer zones around national parks, reserves, and refuges.

The network provides legal and technical assistance to its members and organizes education and training workshops, recent ones having to do with carbon sequestration (read about this conservation strategy in the "Carbon Credits" section), squatters, and bioprospecting. An increasingly important actor in the legal arena, the

BOSQUE ETERNO DE LOS NIÑOS: A CHILDREN'S RAIN FOREST

Once upon a time, there was a teacher from the United States who came to Monteverde, Costa Rica, to do biological research. Her enthusiasm for the rain forest and her concern about its destruction found its way into a small primary school far away in rural Sweden. There, some nine-year-old students wondered whether they could do something to save the trees, the waterfalls, and the many animals that lived in the tropical forest. With their teacher, they decided there was. They wrote a play and presented it for their parents, sold handmade cards, gave from their allowances. That money was sent to the Monteverde Conservation League, a local group working hard to protect threatened rain forest. The donation bought 15 acres (6 ha).

The idea of a rain forest saved by children spread to schools in Sweden, England, Japan, Germany, and the United States; now more than 40 countries have lent a hand. These children ask for donations instead of birthday presents, collect materials for recycling, and sponsor "green days." The result is Bosque

network has played key roles in the Biodiversity and Forestry Laws and taxation issues that affect private reserves. Members are helping establish similar networks in other Central American countries, looking to focus on how private natural reserves can be developed as both economically and environmentally sustainable.

Who are the members? Some are nongovernmental organizations that use their private reserves for research, education, or tourism. Well-known examples are the Monteverde Cloud Forest Preserve operated by the Tropical Science Center; La Selva and Las Cruces Biological Stations, which belong to the Organization for Tropical Studies; and Bosque Eterno de los Niños, which belongs to the Monteverde Conservation League.

Eterno de los Niños (Children's Eternal Forest), the first international children's rain forest.

Since it began in 1989, BEN, as it is often called, has grown to protect more than 56,800 acres (23,000 ha) of trees and wildlife. Living in this lush habitat are quetzals, monkeys, barenecked umbrella birds, ocelots, jaguars, and tapirs. Long vines trail to the forest floor. A Children's Nature Center and research stations, where people study life in the tropical forest, are also open to visitors. Maybe you can come.

As children learn about this Costa Rican forest, they begin to think in a new way about their own environments. Parents and others join the campaign and learn. Whatever your age, you can help BEN. Long-term rain forest protection is more than buying land. It means patrols by forest guards, environmental programs with neighboring schools and communities, planting trees, and research. Send contributions to Monteverde Conservation League, Apartado 10581-1000, San José, Costa Rica. For information on tax-deductible gifts, contact the league: 506/645-5003, fax 506/645-5104; acmmcl@racsa.co.cr; www.monteverde.or.cr. (See Chapters 7 and 10 for more on BEN.)

Others own private reserves oriented principally to ecotourism, though they may also incorporate research and education. These encompass both individuals and communities who see tourism as a way to bring in income and maintain their forest, river, and beach habitats.

Some individuals with private reserves inherited land or bought it simply to prevent habitat destruction, expecting virtually no economic benefit. In reality, farmers who maintain natural forest on their farms have private reserves. Within this broader definition, the network estimates that some 8,000 owners hold about 617,000 acres (250,000 ha) within Costa Rica.

Whatever the category, these reserves face threats from hunters and squatters just as public protected areas do, but management osts come out of owners' pockets. The value of the .er biological resources is one issue the network ue goes far beyond cost per hectare. What about roles л of biodiversity and watershed, in carbon fixation, in geι. ɔ, in production of water and energy, in preservation of scenic bι auty?

This issue, confronted by this group of farmers, biologists, and lodge owners, is one that faces politicians, businesspeople, and all of us who share the planet. What are the costs of conservation? Who is paying them now? Who should pay them? What are the benefits? Who is receiving them?

I recommend that your travels in Costa Rica include a private reserve. You will experience firsthand its contributions to conservation and quality of life. For information, contact Red Costarricense de Reservas Naturales, 506/256-6050, fax 506/258-4268, reservas @racsa.co.cr.

NATIONAL BIODIVERSITY INSTITUTE

Individuals from science, government, and industry are beating a path to the door of INBio, the National Biodiversity Institute, in Santo Domingo de Heredia near San José. Here work is underway to systematically inventory the estimated half million species in the country, to look for and promote sustainable uses of these resources, to organize and manage the information, and to transfer that accumulated knowledge in ways that increase biological literacy at all levels and sectors of society.

INBio was set up as a private nonprofit organization so it could be apart from political whims and be more flexible than a governmental entity. Its activities require a close integration with many public and private institutions, both national and international.

Advances to date are impressive in technology transfer, training of technical and scientific personnel in Costa Rica, development of innovative information management strategies (such as bar coding of data for even the tiniest of microorganisms), and improved infrastructure within Costa Rica to permit more laboratory work in country.

Ree Strange Sheck

Cataloging Costa Rica's species at the National Biodiversity Institute

Species Inventories

Years of research in Costa Rica by national and international investigators have been incorporated into INBio's program; scientists willingly collaborate in this mutually beneficial project. INBio also uses its own unconventional brand of field researcher in an enormously popular and productive program. Men and women are chosen for intensive training to be collectors and initial catalogers of species. These parataxonomists, in turn, serve as vital links with the community, sharing the information being revealed about that environment. Many are neighbors to protected areas. As you visit parks and reserves, you may be lucky enough to come across one of these dedicated young people. Though they hold no Ph.D.s, they are becoming respected specialists. They have discovered as many as 400 to 500 new species of insects, mollusks, and microorganisms in a single year.

Counting species is one thing. Knowing enough about them to protect them and manage their use for the public good is another challenge. What does a species eat? What does it produce? Where is it found? How does it reproduce? How tolerant is it to changes? Where else can it grow? What is it good for? Answers to these and other questions require studies over time and collaboration with researchers from other countries where this species exists. INBio says that only 17 percent of the estimated half-million species in Costa Rica have been described.

Bioprospecting

The premise is that tropical countries can conserve their species in the wild to the extent that the biodiversity generates enough intellectual and economic benefits to cover costs of conserving it. How? Pharmaceutical, medical, nutritional, biotechnological, cosmetic, and agriculture industries are interested in prospecting rights in Costa Rica's conservation areas—looking for chemical substances in plants, insects, mollusks, bryophytes (such as mosses and liverworts), and microorganisms that they might be able to use. Companies sign contracts with INBio, with money up front as well as a promise of a percentage of royalties from any product developed as a result of what is found here. Ten percent of the research contract payments go to the Ministry of Environment and Energy (MINAE) to be reinvested in conservation. If a product is developed, 50 percent of royalties go to MINAE for use by SINAC, the system of conservation areas, and the other half continues to finance INBio's activities.

Research into new products takes years, especially in medical research. The average drug takes about 14 years to get from the plant or microorganism sample to the pharmacy shelf. Though perhaps one in 10,000 samples collected is significant, arrival of an important new drug on the shelf could be a golden egg for INBio and the conservation areas. But the strategy already shines: since 1991 when bioprospecting began, more than $2.5 million in direct financial contributions have gone to INBio, the conservation areas, MINAE, and national universities.

Information and Technology Transfer

Part of INBio's plan is to facilitate training so that professionals in Costa Rica can carry out more and more of the detailed chemical

LOOK WHO'S INTERESTED IN BIODIVERSITY

Pharmaceutical companies have been working with INBio since 1991, searching for veterinary and human drugs, including a cure for Alzheimer's disease. Cosmetic companies are interested: a Swiss perfume company receives biological data on plants with interesting scents, using the data to create similar scents in their laboratories. Forest scents can also be used in household products. Agriculture is interested: a natural nematocide can be derived from the seeds of a dry-forest tree, with enormous implications for the environment.

analyses on organisms. Foreign universities currently carrying out much of this work help train Costa Ricans to do the job. A portion of proceeds from prospecting supports scientific and technological infrastructure here.

INBio shares information about natural history and taxonomy with schools and universities, assists lawmakers, takes part in natural resource-management events, trains conservation-area personnel, and publishes field guides and other literature about biodiversity. A new "Biodiversity Garden" called INBioparque aims to increase the bioliteracy of Costa Ricans and international visitors (see Chapter 5). You can check for yourself at www.inbio.ac.cr or contact INBio at 506/244-0690, fax 506/244-2816; askinbio@quercus.inbio.ac.cr.

FOREST PROTECTION

Forest was the natural cover of this tropical land for about two million years, and until this century it continued to dominate the landscape. However, commercial logging and clearing of land for agriculture and settlement have taken a heavy toll. Costa Rica lost 26 percent of its forest cover between 1963 and 1989. Though trees

Ree Strange Sheck

No longer standing tall—logs waiting at a sawmill near San Miguel

are still being cut in primary forest, private and government efforts and national and international attention are focused on integrating conservation and sustainable development to preserve what remains. A 1997 satellite survey suggests a turnaround in the past 10 years, with reforestation outpacing deforestation. The reported 40 percent forest cover, however, includes not only natural forest and regenerating forest but tree plantations. The other side of the picture is that logging is also up: the concern is that extraction of more individual trees from a forest affects the ecological quality, the genetic bank, of that forest, even though the forest cover remains the same.

One issue is how to move beyond the familiar "frontier" mentality in which forests were seen as something to be conquered in order to carve out farms and ranches. Not much value was given to a tree, except its logged value. In fact, not so many years ago thousands of hectares of forest here were burned simply to clear the land; the trees were not even logged.

Legal Considerations

In Costa Rica, statutes forbid tree cutting in erosion-prone areas such as steep slopes, hilltops, and riverbanks. While they came too late to save some of the almost-perpendicular denuded slopes you will see on your travels, they should protect what's left.

The Forestry Law passed in 1996 encourages people to see forests as valuable resources from which they can receive economic benefit, rather than as obstacles to development. Under the previous law, those who developed tree plantations were granted subsidies and tax concessions. Sounds good, but what actually happened is that in too many cases, natural forests were felled to make room for plantations. In effect, the government paid people to deforest.

THE FIG AND THE WASP

There are at least 65 species of fig trees in Costa Rica, adapted to a variety of habitats. Each is pollinated by a different species of wasp. After the female wasp pollinates the fig, she lays eggs inside the fruit. The wasp depends on the fig, and the fig depends on the wasp. Remove either and the cycle of survival is broken. Complex relationships between flora and fauna are not fully understood, but what is understood points dramatically to nature's intricacies. Maintaining a rich animal mix is crucial to preservation of diverse plant species. Animals are more important to seed dispersal in tropical forests than in temperate ones, where wind is the primary agent.

Reforestation counts, but preservation of natural forests is crucial. Replacing a primary forest of mixed species with one or two types of trees will not maintain the diversity: the fig wasp is not going to make it in a teak plantation. While reforestation projects on already cleared lands are essential—erosion control and watershed protection alone merit the effort—they are not going to replace what has been lost.

These subsidies have stopped. The current approach offers incentives to keep natural forests standing. Forest Protection Certificates pay landowners for the environmental services provided by the forest they are conserving, such as carbon fixation and protection of biodiversity, watershed, and scenic beauty. While money from an environmental fuel tax introduced in 1996 to compensate landowners has not all found its way to the program, real promise for funding lies in Joint Implementation projects with highly industrialized countries (see "Carbon Credits," next page).

Critics of the new Forestry Law pointed to loopholes that could still favor deforestation; some enforcement regulations have already been changed as a result. Environmentalists are watching to see how the law works out in reality. Proper enforcement in line with the intent of the law is the key.

Some Reforestation Strategies

The government estimates that between 988,400 and 3.7 million acres (400,000 to 1.5 million ha) of deforested land could be recovered. Diverse strategies to reestablish forest cover are in use. Tree plantations do have a place, especially where established on already cleared or degraded land. Natural regeneration moves cleared land from scrub vegetation to secondary forest and over time can result in a primary forest.

Some exciting work in reforestation focuses on planting native species of trees to connect existing forests, large and small. These biological corridors allow seasonal migrations of species as well as genetic maintenance of populations such as the jaguar, puma, and tapir. They help ensure survival of the biodiversity that is jeopardized in isolated units.

Research in Monteverde has shown the importance of small forest fragments in the survival of the region's biodiversity: fragments contain species absent in the large private reserves there, and they are feeding sites for altitudinal migrants, species that seasonally move between higher and lower elevations, such as the quetzal and three-wattled bellbird. More than 42 species of Neotropical migrant birds were tallied in these fragments. As a result of this research, the Monteverde Conservation League has worked with local farmers to help them reforest, connecting forest patches to each other and to the larger protected areas.

On an even grander scale, international initiatives call for corridor connections throughout Central America, the ambitious Mesoamerican Biological Corridor to stretch from southern Mexico to Panama.

CARBON CREDITS

Costa Rica was in the forefront a few years ago in debt-for-nature swaps that reduced foreign debt while providing money for in-country conservation projects. Now this tiny, progressive country is at the front of the line to try to cash in on carbon credits, a novel concept proposed as a way to help industrialized countries reduce their emissions of carbon dioxide gas.

The carbon-credit idea grew out of the 1992 Río de Janeiro Earth Summit, where goals were set for industrialized countries to reduce greenhouse gas emissions to 1990 levels. Then in 1995 at the United Nations Climate Change Convention, a Joint Implementation program was proposed under which industrialized countries would be allowed to mitigate their emissions by channeling money into conservation, reforestation, and alternative energy generation projects in developing countries. Under a Joint Implementation agreement, a country such as Costa Rica could receive compensation from an industrialized country for absorbing and storing carbon dioxide in forests.

How would Costa Rica do that? One way is to protect existing forests, reforest cleared land, or develop commercial forest plantations: trees absorb carbon dioxide, which is one of the gases that contribute to global warming, and they store carbon and release oxygen. Worldwide deforestation accounts for 17 percent of carbon dioxide released into the atmosphere. Another way is to promote wind farms or hydroelectric plants, "clean" ways to generate energy.

While the rest of the world debates whether this should or will be a way for countries to meet emission requirements, Costa Rica has issued its first carbon bonds. The first buyer was Norway, which purchased 200,000 tons worth of carbon bonds for $2 million. The tons

of carbon it bought will be sequestered for 25 years through reforestation and forest conservation programs in an area where hydroelectric projects with Norwegian interests are being built. In another
project, a company building a hydroelectric plant in the Central
Volcanic Mountain Range pays Environmental Service Payments to
forest and tree-plantation owners with land along the watershed of
the river that feeds a series of small dams. Forests in this watershed
soak up rainfall and retain it, helping provide water to the river in
times of little or no rainfall. How much does a landowner receive?
About $35 per hectare ($14 an acre) annually over a five-year period.

Trading of carbon bonds on the stock market? Not so far-
fetched, really. Nitrogen oxide and sulfur oxide are already traded
in Chicago right alongside pork bellies as a result of the Clean Air
Act of 1990. Watch out for the carbon bonds, known in financial circles as CTOs (Certifiable Tradable Offsets).

GREEN SEALS

Eco-labeling is another conservation strategy bearing fruit in Costa
Rica. Green seals of approval are the result of negotiated environmental standards among industry, environmental advocates, and
government. Rather than mechanisms such as boycotts, which hard-
en the line between conservationists and industry, this approach
favors working together toward environmentally sound solutions. A
company that meets standards is certified and may mark its products with a seal, a marketing advantage to environmentally aware
consumers in Europe and the United States. Remember to look for
these seals when you shop.

An ECO-O.K. Banana Project begun in 1992 has been credited
with virtually stopping deforestation to plant bananas. For certification, plantations must protect rivers, watershed, and worker health
and safety. Requirements promote greenways along rivers and roads
and preserve forest patches. Reforestation is encouraged.

So far, plantations enrolled in the program have planted thousands of trees (some purchased from community nurseries), modified packing plants to provide primary treatment of waste water that
formerly contaminated rivers, and reduced worker exposure to

fungicides. Some have stopped—and others reduced—the use of herbicides. The plastic bag placed around each bunch of bananas as it grew often ended up in a river and made its way to the ocean, where it killed wildlife and harmed habitat. All plastic waste is now collected and mostly recycled on these farms.

Environmental education with banana zone schools is a component, and environmental workshops for plantation managers and workers are offered. ECO-O.K.-sponsored research looks at the effects of plantations on wildlands and watersheds to help identify conservation priorities. Research has already shown that patches of remaining forest within plantations are critical habitat for migratory birds. ECO-O.K. was begun by two conservation groups, U.S.-based Rainforest Alliance and Costa Rica's Fundación Ambio, tel/fax 506/222-3182, ecook@expreso.com. So far, about 25 percent of banana production in Costa Rica has received certification—it is a work in progress.

Other important eco-labeling programs in Costa Rica involve the Smart Wood program, which encompasses both plantation reforestation and natural forest restoration, and coffee, which promotes a return to coffee grown traditionally, in shade, in order to limit erosion and provide wildlife habitat.

To see a list of certified companies under these programs check out www.rainforest-alliance.org. Other international certification programs are also underway but those described here incorporate important in-country educational components. The following section describes the tourism certification program.

RESPONSIBLE TOURISM

Tourism has come to play an important role in the economic life of Costa Rica: since 1993 it has reigned as the number-one foreign-income earner edging out coffee and bananas and holding its own against rising income from the burgeoning electronics industry. Growth continues, though in 1999 tourism dropped to second in income earnings after electronics, due in large part to the opening of a huge microchip plant in the Central Valley.

Enormous change has come quickly with the tourism boom that

began at the end of the 1980s: in number of visitors, size and number of hotels, growth of tourism-related businesses, and types of tourists and what they expect.

The lifeblood of the tourism industry until now has been the traveler focused on the natural world—the ecotourist. By definition, the ecotourism industry seeks to make a low impact on the environment and local culture while simultaneously helping to create jobs and to conserve wildlife and vegetation. Its ends are responsible tourism that is ecologically and culturally sensitive. While other types of tourism are developing in the country today, the measuring stick by which they are evaluated is that set by ecotourism. The tourism industry, the many conservation groups located around the country, government agencies, community groups, and travelers themselves play important roles in determining the impact tourism has on resources and culture.

Big or Little?

In less than 10 years, large chain-operated hotels have moved in to join the traditionally small hotels and lodges, often owner operated, that had dominated the industry. Though the prospect of thousands of additional hotel rooms in a single development causes concern, the issue is not simply small hotels versus big but more one of overall impact and appropriateness to landscape and culture. Are ten 30-room hotels on the beach inherently better than one 300-room hotel? My bias for smaller has already been stated, but the answer is not simple. As this kind of question is debated in the country, issues enter in such as environmental impact studies, water resources, infrastructure, carrying capacity related to natural resources, and the impact on communities and their way of life.

Sustainable Tourism

A mechanism to help travelers choose environmentally responsible businesses is being put in place. The green seal program is managed by the Costa Rican Tourism Institute (ICT), in cooperation with other government agencies, nonprofit organizations, and international entities. While the program has been designed for all tourism-related companies, the first stage encompasses only lodging: hotels, inns, B&Bs, and lodges. Later stages address tour operators, cruise ships, and car rental agencies. Participation in the program is entirely voluntary and so far is offered at no cost to businesses other than providing necessary information.

The Sustainable Tourism Certification Program (CST) encompasses proper stewardship of natural and cultural resources, improvement in quality of life of local communities, and economic success that contributes to national development. Businesses are rated on a scale of 1 to 5, with 5 considered outstanding in terms of sustainability. Don't confuse this system with the star-rating system. The symbol for sustainability is leaves. Some aspects considered for certification include the degree of harmony with the physical setting, consumption of water and electricity, disposal of wastes, use of biodegradable products, the relationship between hotel guests and staff, and social/economic integration in the host community—benefits the community receives, contribution to local infrastructure, promotion of local culture (via information to guests and social contact), and safety.

Since studies indicate that the majority of tourists to Costa Rica are environmentally concerned, ICT believes the rating system will influence travelers' choices about where to stay. Tourism operators will respond by upgrading their operations to climb the green ladder. Up-to-date information is posted on the bilingual website www.turismo-sostenible.co.cr. You can search by categories such as type (mountain, beach, city), location, size, and number of leaves.

I encourage travelers to support businesses that participate in this program. By mentioning the importance you place on the green seal in choosing where to spend your time and money, you help determine the success of this countrywide initiative toward responsible tourism. Remember, though, that the program is new and that scarcely one-third of the applicants have received their ratings. It is another important work in progress.

The program has implications far beyond the tourism industry; for example, businesses get points for using recycled materials, large containers instead of small ones, biodegradable cleaning products—suppliers will be looking for these products, which affects manufacturers, and so goes the chain toward sustainability. Other countries in Central America and the Caribbean already are looking at implementing the certification program. Once again, this small country is way out front.

In conjunction with other government entities, ICT also administers a Blue Flag *(Bandera Azul)* to rate beaches, taking into account factors such as water quality (both ocean and drinking water), public bathrooms, and amount of trash on the beach. Blue flags fly only on beaches that meet the standards. Heavily visited beaches are checked monthly, others bimonthly.

OTHER WAYS TO TRAVEL RESPONSIBLY

Before you arrive, learn something about Costa Rica and its people (known as *ticos*). Don't be like the traveler who expressed a desire not only to see volcanoes and beaches but to get into the Amazon. No Amazon here. Look at a map, read a book, talk to someone who has been, look on the web.

Avoid whizzing through the country as if you were on a cross-country road race. Allow time to begin to know something about a place, to feel it, before you move to the next destination. Talk to local people. Take a public bus. Eat at a local restaurant, and while you are there, soak up what is happening around you, get a feel for how *ticos* interact with each other. Share something of yourself.

Being an ecotourist is more than following a list of rules, though there are helpful guidelines. It is about awareness and a way of thinking that center on respect, learning, and personal responsibility. All tourism has an impact—be aware of your own.

When you observe animals in the wild, do it from a distance that *they* consider safe—watch for alarm signals that let you know you are getting too close. Be careful around nesting birds—scaring them away can open their eggs and hatchlings to predators. Don't feed animals in the wild, even those captivating white-faced monkeys at Manuel Antonio National Park, the ones that come begging. Altering their diets can have harmful effects. Instead, watch to see them eat what the forest provides. Don't harass an animal in order to get that perfect photo and don't permit a guide to do it for you.

Other simple guidelines include: stay on trails; don't collect things (seeds, flowers, rocks, shells), speak softly and tread quietly— be aware of your impact on others. Ask permission before you photograph another person. Keep your garbage-generating level low, and pack out what you pack in. Be responsible with use of water, especially in drier areas such as Guanacaste, and especially in dry season. Lend a helping hand to show appreciation for all the human and financial resources that protect the natural resources you enjoy during your travels. Support one of the private, nonprofit conservation organizations that abound in Costa Rica. Donate money or volunteer your time or expertise to a project. Many hotels and lodges contribute to local community efforts—schools, libraries, youth activities—ask if you can help, too.

Most of all, keep your travels simple. Make time to hear the message of a place, to learn what it has to teach. Be aware of others as fellow travelers in this time and place.

Climb to a platform in the upper layer of the forest.

Jack Ewing

CHAPTER 3

Nature Adventure Options and Tour Companies

Nature and adventure options in Costa Rica can run the gamut from solitary encounters with the natural world to shared experiences in organized groups. Choose the medium that's right for you. If it is your first visit to Costa Rica, and especially to the New World tropics, consider hooking up with a naturalist guide during a visit to a park or private reserve early on—the rest of your trip will be richer for it. A good guide can make you aware of what to look and listen for and expose you to mind-expanding stories about intricate relationships among tropical species.

What can you do here? The sky, literally, is pretty much the limit. If your tastes run to aerial views, get the big picture from a hot-air balloon, ultralight, helicopter, or small plane. Oceans on both coasts offer snorkeling, diving, surfing, kayaking. River rafting is popular, both for pros and beginners—many people try it for the first time here. The watery world encompasses kayaking, wind surfing, cruises, and wildlife-viewing boat trips. Landlubbers take heart. There is plenty for you: hiking, biking, bird- and butterfly-watching, beachcombing, horseback riding. People of all ages take to the canopy, whether viewing the upper level of the forest from a gondola, platform, or hanging bridge, or whizzing through it via a system of harnesses, cables, and pulleys. For more demanding adventure travel, do some serious mountain climbing or survival training. If you want to lend a helping hand, try ecological volunteer work. Spend some time with a local community discovering land and people. Visit volcanoes, hot springs, cloud forests, tropical dry forests, parks and reserves, animal rehabilitation centers, botanical gardens.

This summary of activities is designed to whet your appetite and help refine your ideas of what you want to do in Costa Rica. With each activity find a sample of Costa Rica-based tour operators that specialize in that activity. Following the activity categories, find a brief description of community tourism projects and a sample of U.S. companies that organize tours to Costa Rica follows. Though prices vary from season to season, these high-season rates offer an idea of what to expect. The list of each company's offerings is a glimpse of possibilities; it is not all-inclusive.

See the destination chapters for more-detailed descriptions of ways to experience the country in each region, including local tour operators. See Appendix A for for transportation options.

HIKING, BIRD-WATCHING, GENERAL NATURE TRAVEL

Travelers are in for a veritable smorgasbord of habitats to explore: rain forest, cloud forest, dry tropical forest, *páramo* (a subalpine habitat with grasses and shrubs—no trees), mangrove, swamp, oak forest, savanna, riparian forest. Most visitors make their way to at least one volcano and a park or reserve, and many choose a beach experience. Here are some Costa Rican operators that specialize in general nature travel to diverse habitats. They offer an excellent way to see a variety of plant and animal species and to learn from the good guides they provide. If you opt for traveling alone without a guide, use common sense, stay on trails, and let someone know where you are headed and when you will be back. Rescue teams search for lost tourists every year. Most searches have happy endings; a few don't.

Whether in a group or alone, bring binoculars, a camera, a hat (don't let sunburn spoil your trip), and respect for the environment. Slow down. Pay attention.

Rates quoted below for half-day or full-day trips are per person and for multiday trips are per person, double occupancy, excluding international airfare, unless otherwise noted.

Arenas Tours, Avenida 7, Calle 13, San José, 506/221-6839, fax 506/257-7735, arenas@ticanet.com. One-day tours are a specialty. A nine-hour Quetzal Expedition Search to Cerro de la Muerte is $75. Morning at Poás Volcano and afternoon at the handcraft center of Sarchí is $62, or combine Poás with a stop at La Paz Waterfall, a wildlife-viewing boat trip on the Sarapiquí, and return through Braulio Carrillo National Park, $79. Combine a visit to Irazú Volcano with Cartago on a five-hour tour for $38, or extend it to include a stop at Lankester Gardens and the Orosi Valley for $62. A new tour allows those on a tight schedule to combine a nature hike, a boat trip, and a beautiful beach in a one-day venture from San José: take a boat trip on the Tárcoles River for viewing crocodiles and good birding (unlike some other tours, food is not used to lure wildlife to the boat); then hike in a private reserve at Punta Leona and enjoy a white-sand beach, $79.

Camino Travel, downtown location, Calle 1, Avenidas 1/ Central, 506/257-0107; main sales office 506/234-2530, fax 506/ 225-6143; caminotr@racsa.co.cr, www.caminotravel.com. The downtown office, open weekdays, offers travelers a one-stop travel shop. Services include hotel reservations, tour reservations, and purchase of bus tickets and domestic airline tickets. Rent a car, with a driver or a private guide if you wish—pay the same as if you book directly. Contact Camino for trip planning before arrival as well.

A seven-day, six-night Costa Rica Verde trip goes to Poás and Arenal Volcano National Parks, hot springs, the Peñas Blancas River for a wildlife float trip, Monteverde, and Dundee Ranch for horseback riding and a visit to Carara. The cost includes an English-speaking guide, lodging, specified meals, entrance fees, and in-country transportation, $913 double occupancy. Fly-and-drive packages include a meet-and-greet service at the San José airport to orient travelers: drive to the Turrialba area (rafting, biking, or visit to Guayabo National Monument), continue to La Fortuna area (volcano, hot springs, rafting, horseback riding options), and then travel to the central Pacific region (with optional visits to Manuel Antonio or Carara National Parks). The budget version is $469; the superior version is $806. Ask about visiting farms and rural families living around conserved areas, another arm of sustainable tourism. Groups visit rural schools where students show and tell about the agricultural products their parents produce and share their own drawings; a built-in donation funds materials and supplies specified by the school.

Costa Rica Expeditions, Avenida 3, Calles Central/2, San José, 506/222-0333, fax 506/257-1665, ecotur@expeditions.co.cr, www .expeditions.co.cr. This company pioneered natural history travel in Costa Rica and has a team of excellent naturalist guides. It offers one-day Tropical Forest Adventure tours to Poás Volcano, Tapantí National Park, or Cerro de la Muerte (quetzals and *páramo*) for $99, including transportation, guide, lunch, and park fees. Another one-day option is to internationally known La Selva Biological Station for $119. Choose your own destination for a day trip and hire one of Costa Rica Expedition's superb naturalists as your private guide, $119 for the guiding service for up to eight person for eight hours. If you also need transport for that day, inquire about costs.

Costa Rica Expeditions has fixed-departure multiday packages. For example, the 10-day Costa Rica Explorer takes in Tortuguero, Arenal, the Reventazón River (for white-water rafting), Poás, and Monteverde, $1,798. New is an adventure program attractive for young adults and their active parents or grandparents. This nine-day River and Rain Forest trip includes a hike in quetzal country, comfortable tent camping near Corcovado, viewing the canopy from a platform, hiking in scarlet macaw country, a two-day rafting trip with camping beside the Pacuare River; $1,698, double occupancy, including in-country travel, lodging, guides, park fees, taxes, and some meals. The company also offers white-water tours and owns three lodges: Tortuga Lodge at Tortuguero, Corcovado Lodge Tent Camp, and Monteverde Lodge; packages are available. It has received numerous awards for conservation and ecotourism.

Costa Rica Sun Tours, 200 meters south of Agromec, La Uruca, San José, 506/296-7757, fax 506/296-4307, suntours@racsa.co.cr., www.crsuntours.com. Sun Tours offers several day trips from San José. The 12-hour Arenal Volcano Night Tour includes time at Tabacón for a swim in the hot springs, as well as volcano-viewing time for $74. Others include Guayabo National Monument or Cerro

de la Muerte, $110 each for two persons; Carara N
Irazú/Lankester Botanical Garden/Orosi
Volcano/Sarchí, $54. The company also ope
horseback riding, rafting, boat trips, turtle nesting
cruises in the Gulf of Nicoya, and park tours from the Arenal area,
Guanacaste, Jacó Beach, Manuel Antonio, and Monteverde.

The Tropical Adventure program has multiday trips such as a
three-day hike at Chirripó, a day of mountain biking, or two days of
biking and rafting. Eight- and nine-day nature and adventure programs cover the country. The Southern Rainforest Odyssey includes
Cerro de la Muerte and the chance of seeing the resplendent quetzal, lovely Wilson Botanical Gardens, Tiskita Rainforest Reserve, and
Corcovado for $1,465 including in-country transport, lodging, speci-
fied meals, and taxes. Ask about Best of Costa Rica (Corcovado,
Tiskita, Arenal, Monteverde, Carara) and Coast to Coast
(Tortuguero, southern Pacific rain forests, and Corcovado). Sun
Tours has a number of multiday tours to the two private nature
reserves it operates, Arenal Observatory Lodge and Tiskita Jungle
Lodge.

Expediciones Tropicales, Calle 3b, Avenidas 11/13, San José,
506/257-4171, fax 506/257-4124, expetrop@racsa.co.cr, www.costa-
ricainfo.com. For day trips this company stands out: its half- and
full-day offerings are used by many other tour companies. The Irazú
Volcano tour is $35, but it can be combined with Lankester Gardens
and the Orosi Valley with lunch at a nice restaurant for $42. The
Carara tour guarantees a full four hours at the famous park with
lunch every day except Saturday at nearby Punta Leona, which I
highly recommend for the natural beauty of its private forest over
the Saturday lunch site at Jacó (which by the way is where several
companies regularly dine). A half-day tour to Grecia and the handcraft center at Sarchí is $29, or combine that with a visit to Poás
Volcano and lunch for $54. For those without much time, an 11-
hour tour takes in Poás, the La Paz Waterfall, and rafting on the
Sarapiquí River, returning through Braulio Carrillo National Park
for $79. A San José City tour is $24.

Expediciones Tropicales offers an eight-day fly-and-drive package that includes Arenal, Monteverde, and a coastal destination
south of Jacó at $439 each for two persons. A two-day Arenal, hot

rings, and Caño Negro tour is $199; one-day Arenal and hot springs tour is $74. A two-day Monteverde tour is $260. The company also rents vans for up to eight persons, plus guide and driver, and publishes a country map distributed free at the office and through hotels.

Horizontes Nature Adventures, Calle 28, Avenidas 1/3 (just north of Pizza Hut on Paseo Colón), San José, 506/222-2022, fax 506/255-4513, horizont@racsa.co.cr, www.horizontes.com. With a well-deserved reputation for quality nature-based tourism, Horizontes offers personalized service to individuals and small groups interested in travel for nature observation, conservation, education, soft adventure, and connections with local people. The staff designs custom trips, taking into account physical abilities, budget, length of visit, and time of year; they want to make sure clients don't take off on a trip that's too long or too tough. High-quality bilingual guides are chosen according to each client's specific interests and needs.

Horizontes has a wide array of packaged programs from which travelers may choose, including both single- and multiday tours. Horizontes has received international recognition for its leadership in ecotourism.

Jungle Trails, Calle 38, Avenidas 5/7 near Centro Colón, San José, 506/255-3486, fax 506/255-2782, jungletr@racsa.co.cr. Staff customize one-day trips or multiday expeditions throughout the country, taking into account travelers' interests and budgets. Jungle Trails creates an itinerary suited to travel independently or with a guide. Its team of guides includes biologists, many of whom have taught or are teaching at Costa Rica's universities, with specialists in botany, ornithology, ecology, and other branches of biology. The small company is committed to personalized attention and has experience with all modes of travel, from hiking to flying. Jungle Trails continues with its program to plant a tree in San José for every tour sold. The native species of trees are purchased from Arbofilia (the Association for the Protection of Trees), a grassroots ecological organization.

Rain Forest Tours, office in Moravia (San José suburb), 506/296-7074, tel/fax 506/236-6105, info@rainforesttours.com, www.rainforesttours.com. Specializing in custom-made itineraries for couples, families, and very small groups, Rain Forest Tours aims to provide a personal and adventurous trip open to community interaction. It features a few set packages: a three-day Tortuguero Canals and Sarapiquí tour travels via both the Tortuguero canals and the San Juan River, including not only the riches of Tortuguero National Park but those at premier La Selva Biological Station and a ride on the Rain Forest Aerial Tram near Braulio Carrillo National Park, $575; a five-day Caribbean tour includes hiking, horseback riding, tree climbing, a wildlife canoe trip, and two days on the beach, $475. The custom trips revolve around personal interests, time, preferred level of comfort, and budget.

ADVENTURE TRAVEL

An increasing number of more demanding adventure options are available, which can range from tough hikes through less-traveled terrain, camping adventures, and waterfall rappelling to multiday horseback trips and classes in wilderness skills.

Coast to Coast Adventures, near the church in Lourdes de Monte de Oca (San José suburb) 506/280-8054, fax 506/225-6055, info@ctocadventures.com, www.ctocadventures.com. The two-day biking trip starts at Cerro de la Muerte, 4,644 feet high (2330 m), and descends through hills and farming and coffee communities, with either overnight camping or a hotel stay; the next day to the Pacific coast and beaches at Manuel Antonio, $250. Or bike, hike, and raft 145 miles (234 km) from coast to coast, from Manuel Antonio to Cahuita (camping and small hotels), including the thrilling descent from Cerro de la Muerte on dirt roads and single-track trails; the 15-day challenge is $1,980, double occupancy. A seven-day Hidden Valleys adventure involves two days of mountain biking on dirt roads and single-track mountain trails, three days of hiking through remote rain forest with a local indigenous guide, and two days of rafting on the Pacuare, $1,425. A two-day horseback ride goes into quetzal land, with time for a hike to a waterfall and a tour through a dairy cooperative, $250. Ask about trips to El Nido del Tigre (Tiger's Nest), a forest reserve Coast to Coast Adventures protects along the Pacuare, with the assistance of local people. From this remote white-water base, guests can hike, ride horses, go mountain biking or tree climbing/rappelling. Eat under the stars and sleep in spacious tents on fixed platforms along the river.

Adventure unlimited awaits at **Jungla Expeditions,** based in Turrialba 20 meters south of Palí Super Market, 506/556-9525, fax 506/556-6225, jungla@racsa.co.cr, www.jungla.net. Choose backpacking, rafting, river and sea kayaking, mountain biking, horseback riding (day or overnight), trekking, or canyoning. What is canyoning? It uses adapted mountain-climbing equipment to allow you to descend into rugged canyons, often moving alongside waterfalls, $105. A specialty is white-water kayak trips, with 21 rivers on the list—from lowland jungle rivers to high-elevation mountain streams. Kayak instruction at all levels is offered. Trekking trips can be a one-day hike to the top of Turrialba Volcano or multiday trips to little-visited areas of the Talamanca Mountains, the highest in the country. Mountain bike near Pacuare, Turrialba Volcano, or Irazú for $40 to $95 per day. On backpacking trips, tents are provided. Jungle Store can outfit for any adventure. Get a 10 percent discount with this book.

Ocarina Expeditions, San Pedro Montes de Oca (San José suburb), 506/283-2854, fax 506/253-4579, ocarina@racsa.co.cr, www .ocarinaexpeditions.com. Specializing in outdoor adventure, this company combines a number of activities in one tour, and activities range from moderate to demanding. Terrific one-day tours are to Barva Volcano from San José, $65, and to the Río Celeste at the base of Tenorio Volcano, where the river is a sublime, mineral-induced blue and cascading waterfalls and hot springs are surrounded by forest, $59 (leaves from La Fortuna).

The eight-day Mountain & Caribbean Sports Adventure includes mountain biking, whitewater rafting, tree climbing, rappelling, kayaking, and horseback riding, $1,275. The four-day Rincón de la Vieja tour includes rain forest hiking, camping in two-person tents, visiting hot springs, and hiking to waterfalls and the volcano rim. The cost is $450 from San José. The 12-day Mountain and Jungle Trek includes hiking to Savegre Waterfall in quetzal country, trekking in Chirripó National Park, and exploring Corcovado National Park from La Palma to Sirena to Carate. Ocarina arranges transportation (bilingual drivers) and a private bilingual guide for anywhere in the country.

Rainforest Outward Bound School, Quepos, tel/fax 506/777-1222, 506/777-0052, voice-mail 800/676-2018, crrobs@racsa.co.cr; www.crrobs.org. Courses run from days to weeks, depending on the season and activities. All are geared to learning through adventure experiences at personal, cultural, and environmental levels; course service projects focus on rain forest conservation and neighboring communities. The Multi-Element Courses include rain forest trekking, rafting, climbing, a homestay, caving, and conservation and beach activities. Intensive courses are devoted to surfing (or boogie boarding) or white-water river exploration; you can combine an Outward Bound adventure with learning Spanish (month-long courses). Adult Adventure is for those who have reached voting age; one has the intriguing title of Life/Career Renewal. A sample 15-day itinerary includes trekking through varied habitats (with overnights in remote shelters or tents), cave exploration, village homestays, a 12- to 24-hour solo experience in the wilderness, tree climbing, community service project, beach time, rafting (with overnight camps); from $1,695, excluding international airfare.

AIR TOURS

Balloons, ultralights, small planes, or helicopters expand air options. Remember that air travel is subject to weather conditions, which can be especially fickle in rainy season. So do not schedule yourself tightly. The view from above is fantastic, from shoreline to folded hills and craggy peaks, from remote forest devoid of roads to the patchwork of farms and cities.

Costa Rica Serendipity Adventures, office in Turrialba; 506/556-2592, 877/507-1358 (in U.S.), fax 506/556-2593, costarica @serendipityadventures.com, www.serendipityadventures.com. Experience the country by hot-air balloon. Two private charter flights are offered, each $900 for up to five persons: the Naranjo option goes over coffee fields and mountain villages; an Arenal option soars near the volcano. Another trip features the Turrialba Valley, with trees in touching distance of the basket and white water below; flight is for a minimum of two for $500. All pilots are U.S. FAA-licensed commercial pilots.

Serendipity also offers multiday custom trips that can encompass rafting, sea kayaking, mountain biking, canyoning, tree climbing, rappelling, camping, and horseback riding. A sample eight-day itinerary includes cloud forest, an active volcano, hot springs, caves, Duckie river float, ballooning, horseback riding, tree climbing in a 700-year-old strangler fig, mountain biking, white-water rafting, hiking for $6,900 for two, international airfare excluded.

Pitts Aviation, Skytours and Aircharter Services, Tobias Bolaños airport in Pavas, San José, 506/296-3600, fax 506/296-1429, skytours@racsa.co.cr, www.pitts-aviation.com. Tours in small aircraft give travelers a bird's-eye view of some of the country's greatest attractions. It's all set to music that complements the symphony of nature played below. Each passenger has use of a pair of quality binoculars and a stereo headset along with a description of the route and tips on what to look for along the way. "Give your soul wings," says company advertising. Dance on the Volcanoes circles active volcanoes with views of glacial lakes, rain forest, waterfalls, and ribbons of white sand along the Pacific, 1.5 hours, $119 per person. On Jungle Spirit, fly over Poás Volcano to the sounds of Beethoven's *Fifth,* to Tortuguero, where breakfast awaits, and a two-hour boat ride through the jungle-lined canals; the half-day trip is $179. A four-day Whistlestop Tour flies over volcanoes, with stays in the Guanacaste region and both the Caribbean and Pacific coasts— Quepos/Manuel Antonio and Tortuguero— for $1,250 per person. In-country and international charter flights are available.

Skyline of Costa Rica, Dominical, 506/771-4582, fax 506/771-8841, selvamar@racsa.co.cr. Ultralight flights (pilot and one passenger) take off from the Punta Uvita/Ballena Bay local airstrip south of Dominical on the Pacific coast. Flights range from 20 minutes to three hours. Flying slow and low, see rain forest, coral reefs, the ocean, mountain peaks, estuaries and rivers. Here are some options: Ballena National Marine Park (20 minutes), or add another 10 minutes and go to the vast mangrove swamps and the mouth of the Térraba River; with 40 minutes, the flight includes views of Nauyaca, Santo Cristo, and Cristo Rey Waterfalls and a view of Chirripó and the coastline from Quepos to the Osa Peninsula. Rates range from $55 for 20 minutes to $180 for 90 minutes. Ask about photography flights.

Ree Strange Sheck

Small planes can get you to remote places.

Tropical Heli-Tours, 506/220-3940, fax 506/290-3044, fly@heli-tour.com. Helicopter tours from one hour to more than four hours depart from the Pavas airport in San José. FAA certified, the company also offers charter flights anywhere in the country. Here's a sample of daily tours with per person prices based on two passengers; the per person price goes down with each additional person. A 2.5-hour flight to Quepos and back passes over Orotina, Tárcoles River (crocodile country), Carara National Park, and along the Pacific coast from Jacó to Manuel Antonio National Park, $480. A Central Valley route, less than an hour, flies over Irazú, Poás, and Barva Volcanoes, $260.

CANOPY EXPERIENCES

The upper level of foliage in the forest, the canopy, long an unexplored frontier, passed quickly from being the subject of research by a handful of dedicated biologists who struggled to gain access to its secrets to being high on the must-do list of natural history

me places you climb trees in the canopy using tech-
ped by those early researchers; in others you can be
no-sweat bosun's chairs to a platform more than 100
feet (30 m) above the forest floor. Swing high speed from tree to
tree via cables, harness, and pulley, or stand on hanging bridges at
canopy-level, surrounded by a beauty so diverse that time stands
still. Or view this New World from a cable car. A movement is under
way to establish and enforce safety standards for canopy tours and
other tourist adventure activities that are currently unregulated.

If you are interested in the canopy walkways, two stand out: Sky
Walk in Monteverde and Rainmaker outside Manuel Antonio.
Consider platform experiences at Corcovado Tent Camp, Hacienda
Barú at Dominical, and Rara Avis, south of Puerto Viejo de
Sarapiquí near Horquetas. The Rain Forest Aerial Tram near
Braulio Carrillo is the high-tech offering, about an hour from San
José. Pulley and harness operations abound, some also with plat-
forms where you can spend a little time. The Original Canopy Tour
has operations in Monteverde, Rincón de la Vieja, Tortuga Island,
Iguana Park, and San Carlos. Chiclet Trees Tour operates near Jacó.
Canopy Safari is run by Outdoor Expeditions near Quepos. In fol-
lowing chapters, find information on all of these and more.

CRUISES

Day trips by yacht or sailboat through the Gulf of Nicoya to Tortuga
Island or other destinations on the Pacific are popular. Passengers
are wined and dined during the daylong outing, with time for swimming, snorkeling, or just relaxing. Some day trips offer historical
perspectives, and one looks to the stars. Multiday trips are available.
Companies mentioned here meet safety standards, but it's always
good to check out locations of life jackets.

Calypso Tours, in Edifico Las Arcadas, Avenida 2, Calles 5, San
José, 506/256-8787, 800/566-6716 (U.S. number), fax 506/256-
6767, info@calypsotours.com, www.calypsotours.com. Sail to
Tortuga Island on the catamaran *Manta Raya*, with two hot tubs on
deck and an underwater viewing window; $99 includes
air-conditioned bus, continental breakfast, and lunch (with chilled

white wine) on the island. Other $99 cruises include one on the yacht *Calypso* to Punta Coral Private Reserve on the Nicoya Peninsula in front of Negritos Island Biological Reserve. Walk nature trails to see monkeys and parrots, or kayak, snorkel, or swim. Chilled white wine accompanies lunch to live marimba music. A tropical sky cruise on the *Manta Raya*, also $99, is led by a bilingual astronomer. Stargaze on the way to Punta Coral, where you have a torchlight gourmet dinner, and a look through a star-finder reflecting telescope. Return to San José about 1 A.M. Sail on the *Lohe Lani* on a four-hour harbor cruise from Puerto Caldera to Puntarenas and San Lucas Island, where prisoners once lived, and Guayabo and Pan de Azucar Islands, sanctuaries for sea birds; $150 per person. A multiday Pacific coastal eco-tour is $150 per day.

Temptress Adventure Cruises, 506/220-1679, 800/336-8423 (U.S. number), fax 506/220-2130, info@temptresscruises.com, www.temptresscruises.com. Cruise on the *Temptress*, a 99-passenger, 185-foot boat, all outside cabins, private baths, and air conditioning. Voyages include walks with naturalist guides and activities such as

Cruising the Pacific coast on the Temptress

uba diving, sea kayaking, or swimming. The seven-
᠆ᠴy starts in Puntarenas and travels to Curú Wildlife
᠆ᠴuge, Tortuga Island, Corcovado National Park, Coiba Island in
Panama (coral reef here), a reserve on the Golfo Dulce, Golfito,
Drake Bay, and Manuel Antonio National Park. From mid-
December to mid-April, the rates for a middle category cabin are
$2,495 for seven nights. Off-season rates are lower. Naturalist guides
are excellent, and the food is superb.

FISHING

To try your hand at some of Costa Rica's world-class sportfishing, look
for regional hot spots and companies in following destination chapters.
On the Pacific coast, anglers seek sailfish, marlin, tuna, and dorado;
check out locations such as Playa del Coco, Ocotal, Flamingo, Punta
Leona, Quepos, Dominical, and Drake Bay. On the Caribbean, fish for
tarpon, snook, wahoo, dorado, Atlantic sailfish, and blue marlin: check
out areas such as Barra del Colorado, Cahuita, Puerto Viejo, and
Gandoca-Manzanillo. Catch and release of billfish is the name of the
game. Of fresh water species, rainbow bass (*guapote*) is a favorite, along
with snook and catfish. Several mountain lodges offer trout fishing. If fly
fishing is your passion, some charter operators specialize in big-game fly
fishing. Costa Rican fishing licenses are required; most hotels and guides
provide a license as part of the fishing package. Ask. The Costa Rica
Tourist Board has published a brochure called "The World's Best
Fishing," with information on seasons, species, and top locations;
800/343-6332 (U.S. number).

Costa Rica Outdoors Travel Division, office located in Santa
Ana, 506/282-6743, 800/308-3394 (U.S. number), fax 506/282-
6514, jruhlow@racsa.co.cr, www.costaricaoutdoors.com. Custom fishing trips are planned by Jerry Ruhlow, who has been fishing and
writing about fishing in Costa Rica since 1982. He promises an itinerary within a couple of days after learning when you are coming
and what you want to do. The company also arranges nonfishing
activities such as surfing, diving, snorkeling, rain forest tours, and
golf. It offers private day tours in an air-conditioned van: perhaps
Cartago, Lankester Botanical Garden, Irazú or Poás Volcanoes, a
coffee plantation, or the artisan centers at Sarchí.

HORSEBACK RIDING

Many private reserves and lodges offer horseback riding, and stables are found in areas such as Manuel Antonio, Monteverde, Dominical, Turrialba, and Puerto Viejo de Sarapiquí. Horseback tours go to volcanoes and waterfalls, and riders can accompany cowboys for a day. Destination chapters include information on these and more. Be sure to check out Los Inocentes in Guanacaste, and Finca Los Caballos Nature Lodge outside of Montezuma (see index). A couple of U.S. companies that offer horseback riding tours are listed under "International Companies with Nature Tours to Costa Rica." See "Adventure Travel" above for multi-activity tours that include horseback rides.

MOTORCYCLING

Motorcycle touring has arrived in Costa Rica. Operators rent motorcycles, offer escorted tours, and some provide support for do-it-yourself adventures. These tours are for experienced motorcyclists with valid licenses. Tours combine a chance to experience challenging terrain with some of the country's spectacular scenery and top destinations.

Harley Tours, 506/289-5552, fax 506/289-5551, matour@racsa.co.cr, www.mariaalexandra.com. See the country on a Harley Davidson. On Ride by Your Own tours, travelers rent a Harley and follow one of the company's suggested tours, from one to multiple days, or follow a custom itinerary that includes hotel reservations, airport transfers, the works. Natural Paradise is an eight-day vacation with five days of riding that gets you to Puerto Viejo de Sarapiquí, Poás and Arenal Volcanoes, hot springs, Lake Arenal, and Hermosa Beach; depending on type of motorcycle, rates begin at $1,420 from San José, including a support van and tour guide. Several one-day tours take in Poás Volanco, Irazú Volcano, or Braulio Carrillo National Parks, starting at $126. Nontour motorcycle rentals are also available. Minimum age for rental is 25 years, and the driver must have a valid motorcycle license.

Motoadventure, 506/228-8494, fax 506/228-2568, U.S. fax 510/352-8050, motoadve@racsa.co.cr, www.motoaventura.com. Honda XR400R is the vehicle of choice for an seven-day tour that heads to Turrialba Volcano, Irazú Volcano, the colonial city of Cartago, Carara National Park, to the beach at Jacó, sampling parts of enduro trails along the way. The cost is $2,395 per person, including Honda rental, fuel, lodging, meals, support vehicle to carry luggage, a bilingual guide, and even a Motoadventures T-shirt. Other tours are from one to seven days, all inclusive except airfare. Trip planning includes optional activities for nonriders, such as mountain biking, rafting, sightseeing.

MOUNTAIN BIKING

Costa Rica's terrain offers terrific mountain-biking opportunities, with tours that take in volcanoes, forest, beaches, and rural villages.some tours combine biking with adventures in kayaking, rafting, fishing, and hiking. Operators provide logistical support and equipment on adventurous multiday tours that include overnight stays in lodging from rustic to luxurious. Some lodges have mountain bikes for rent to guests and can suggest local tours, noted in the destination chapters.

Aguas Bravas, in San José 506/292-2072, fax 506/229-4837; in La Fortuna 506/479-9025; info@aguas-bravas.co.cr, www.aguas-bravas.co.cr. Half-day and full-day mountain bike routes for each level are arranged at the Aguas Bravas Arenal Outdoor Center in La Fortuna. All tours include transportation, bikes, and bilingual guide. A half-day trip is $45; a full day in either the Arenal Volcano area or a Sarapiquí jungle is $65. A two-day trip takes in hot springs, an active volcano, a lake, and tropical forest, $295.

Bi.Costa Rica Bike Tours, 506/380-3844, tel/fax 506/446-7585, bicostarica@yellowweb.co.cr, www.yellowweb.co.cr/bicostarica. Small groups (six-rider maximum) explore the country's diverse ecosystems with expert guides. Lodging is in small, luxurious country inns, most offering swimming pools for relaxation after the daily ride. Luggage is shuttled daily in the support vehicle. Riders average 30 miles (48 km) a day, and tours include other adventures: hiking, swimming in the pool at the base of a waterfall, sunset cruise, sea kayaking, white-water rafting, caving, and fishing. One-day tours to such sites as Tapantí National Park and the Orosi Valley are $85 including breakfast, lunch, and park fees. The one-day trip to Poás Volcano, Grecia, and Sarchí is also $85. Two-day trips are in the Arenal area or to Carara and Jacó. A three-day trip cycles on the Osa Peninsula with a visit to Corcovado. The nine-day Rain Forest, Volcanoes, and Beaches tour, starting in San José, is $1,595. Ask about the nine-day Bike the Beaches trip. Ruta Conquistadores, a coast-to-coast tour, is from $995 to $1,475, depending on lodging and level of support. Custom tours are also available.

Calypso Tours, 506/256-8787, 800/566-6716 (U.S. number), fax 506/256-6767, info@calypsotours.com, www.calypsotours.com. A one-day trip in the Orosi Valley—Cachí, Tapantí National Park, and church ruins at Ujarrás—is $79. A two-day trip that begins at Irazú Volcano and goes to Orosi Valley, overnight in Turrialba is $249.

Rock River Lodge, at Lake Arenal northwest of Tilarán, tel/fax 506/695-5644, rokriver@racsa.co.cr, www.rockriver.mastermind.net. Explore unusual mountain-biking routes. The three-day Volcano Trail for intermediate bikers goes all the way to Orosi Volcano near Nicaragua for $100 per day. A Quipilapa trail goes to Miravalles, and two- to five-hour day tours go to Cañas for a swim in the Corobicí and to a waterfall for swimming in the Tenorio River.

RAFTING AND KAYAKING

Costa Rica's wealth of sea and river resources makes it an ideal destination for both rafting and kayaking. The Pacuare River is among the five wildest and most scenic rivers in the world, with class III–V rapids and virgin forests. The Reventazón River is rated as the third-best river for world-class kayaking. The General River has more than 100 class III and IV rapids in its first 40 miles.

The Caribbean and Pacific coasts, as well as Pacific gulfs, offer terrific sea-kayaking opportunities; the hundreds of rivers that flow into the two oceans offer river kayak experiences from sublime to spectacular, many through remote tropical rain forest. In following destination chapters, find local companies and hotels and lodges in

PROTECTING RIVERS AND PEOPLES

Fundación Ríos Tropicales is a private nonprofit foundation whose mission is to preserve, protect, and restore watersheds of the Pacuare and Reventazón Rivers and the well being of surrounding communities. These rivers have been threatened by deforestation, sedimentation, contamination, and hydroelectric projects. Some of the hydro projects are proposed; some are already being built. The foundation was begun in 1994 by Ríos Tropicales, a leading white-water rafting and kayaking operator.

Volunteers are needed to present environmental education programs on river and watershed conservation and restoration in rural schools near the targeted rivers—Spanish language skills, a two-month commitment, and basic elementary education teaching experience are required. Other volunteer programs focus on staff assistance or research, helping compile data related to the Pacuare River. Requirements and benefits can be found at www.riostro.com. For information about volunteer work or contributions, contact the foundation at frt@riostropicales.com, or contact Ríos Tropicales, 506/233-6455, fax 506/255-4354, info@riostro.com. Send tax-deductible donations to Fundación Ríos Tropicales, Interlink #124, P.O. Box 526-770, Miami, FL 33152.

each area that offer kayak opportunities. A real rafting/kayaking hot spot is in the Turrialba area. Check out Chapter 6 for local companies that offer a terrific variety of rivers to explore.

All of the following specialists in rafting and/or kayaking have trained, bilingual guides and good equipment. There are trips for beginners, with instruction given. You can raft or kayak at any time of year in Costa Rica, though a few specific rivers may have limitations, particularly from August to December.

Standard rafting trips include one-day trips Reventazón, which offers rapids and calm stretch spectacular landscapes, $69 to $90. Another po float trip on the Corobicí River near Cañas (clas viewing, especially birds and monkeys, $70 to $85 ing trip on the Pacuare River is about $90. All companies offer multiday trips that may include hiking, biking, or camping.

Aguas Bravas, in San José, 506/292-2072, fax 506/229-4837, in La Fortuna 506/479-9025, info@aguas-bravas.co.cr, www.aguas-bravas.com. Aguas Bravas organizes white-water rafting from San José, La Fortuna, and Sarapiquí, with trips on the Sarapiquí, Toro, and Peñas Blancas Rivers. The Peñas Blancas, just 30 minutes from Arenal Volcano and relatively new to the white-water scene, offers a half-day trip through class II–III rapids for $37. The class IV–V upper Sarapiquí is $80 ($50 from Sarapiquí), but there are beginners' trips on the Sarapiquí, some especially for bird-watching. For kayaking on the Sarapiquí River, one-day tours are available for both beginners and experienced, $60 to $80. Lessons are available. Custom packages can encompass the Sarapiquí and Arenal areas, Monteverde, and the Caribbean, including kayaking, rafting, biking, surfing, hiking, snorkeling or diving, and horseback riding. Ask about camps for 10- to 17-year-olds, either weekend or seven-day programs that offer hiking, horseback riding, compass reading, rafting, biking, and learning how to have fun in nature without harming the ecosystem. The company's White-Water Center is in the Sarapiquí area between La Vírgen and Puerto Viejo. Its Aguas Bravas Arenal Outdoor Center is in La Fortuna.

Aventuras Naturales, 506/225-3939, 800/514-0411, fax 506/253-6934, avenat@racsa.co.cr, www.toenjoynature.com. The two-day Pacuare River rafting trip (class III–IV) is great for seeing wildlife and enjoying the thrill of white-water rafting. Overnight is in the company's rustic, two-story Pacuare Jungle Lodge. Each of five screened bungalows has beds with orthopedic mattresses and private bath, but no electricity—dine by candlelight, $249 per person. Hiking in Aventuras Naturales' forest reserve is added on the three-day Pacuare trip, with waterfalls and trails into the mountains to the land of the Cabecar, an indigenous people, $324. Multiday trips include rafting, hiking, and biking. One 10-day adventure

White-water excitement

package offers hiking in Monteverde, a visit to Arenal and thermal springs, a canopy experience, biking, kayaking on the Sarapiquí, white-water rafting, overnight at Pacuare Jungle Lodge, which now has a platform-and-cable canopy option, and exploring Tortuguero canals, $1,820 per person. The company operates the Fleur de Lys Hotel in San José. Custom packages are available, as are hiking and biking tours.

Costa Rica White Water, Avenida 3, Calles Central/2, San José, 506/222-0333, 506/257-0766, fax 506/257-1665, ecotur@expeditions.co.cr, www.expeditions.co.cr. The first white-water company in Costa Rica, the company prides itself on quality and safety. Rafts are custom-made by Demaree inflatable self-bailing boats. Trips are on the Pacuare and Reventazón. One-day Reventazón tours for experienced rafters run daily with a minimum of four: either the Pascua run (class III–IV) or the more rugged Guayabo Run (class IV–V) is $85. First-time rafters run the Tucurrique section of the Reventazón, which the company describes as "exciting but forgiving rapids in a tropical setting," $69. A two-day trip on the Pacuare

includes beautiful hikes and overnight camping on the ı
Costa Rica White Water is a division of Costa Rica Expeɑ
pioneer in natural history travel that can arrange your enɩ   ⸗
(see under "Hiking, Bird-Watching, General Nature Travel").

Ríos Tropicales, Calle 38, Paseo Colón/Avenida 2, San José,
506/233-6455, fax 506/255-4354, info@riostropicales.com,
www.riostropicales.com. This company is recognized internationally for its efforts in conservation, reforestation, and environmental education; the owners are authors of *The Rivers of Costa Rica.* A
three-day Pacuare trip offers rafting (class III–IV) and hiking,
with overnights in private bungalows high on the river bank in a
1,000-acre (405- ha) private reserve belonging to Ríos Tropicales
—electricity from hydropower. On the second day, trail guides
lead a five-hour hike into Garcia's Indian Village; day three is
back on the river for more waterfalls, rapids, and wildlife, $305.
One-day Sarapiquí tours, one of them more a scenic float trip
and the other with moderate rapids (class III) are each $70. The
four-day General River trip (class III–IV) is a thriller, $440. Ríos
Tropicales has both sea and white-water multiday kayak trips. A
four-day Curú trip includes hiking at the wildlife refuge, beach
camping, and an estuary trip, $600. The nine-day Golfo Dulce
tour (for advanced kayakers) starts and ends at Golfito and
includes the Esquinas River area, Puerto Jiménez, camping
where dolphins play, an Osa Peninsula beach where squirrel
monkeys, scarlet macaws, toucans, and other wildlife are regular
visitors, and Pavones, which has some of longest left-breaking
waves in world, $1,370. Ríos Tropicales has an outdoor store,
with equipment for camping, hiking, climbing, and water sports
as well as kayak gear rental to experienced paddlers: Calle 22 Bis,
Avenida 3, 506/255-0618.

SCUBA DIVING AND SNORKELING

Both the Pacific and southern Caribbean coasts of Costa Rica draw snorkelers and divers. The southern Caribbean still has some of the best coastal diving, though sedimentation from deforestation and agriculture is damaging reefs: Cahuita, Puerto Viejo, and Gandoca-Manzanillo areas are top spots. Although Pacific soft and hard coral formations are not large, the underwater geography includes volcanic rock formations, rock pinnacles, canyons, and tunnels—ideal for marine life. The Pacific islands are also hot spots: in the northern Pacific, Santa Catalina (west of Pan de Azúcar Beach) and Murciélagos (off the Santa Elena Peninsula). To the south, Caño Island (off the Osa Peninsula) is a prime destination. Coco Island, 330 miles (532 km) offshore, is legendary for snorkeling and diving. When diving is best varies, influenced by factors such as rainfall, winds, and river runoff. Here are some generalizations: Osa Peninsula—November through April; Guanacaste—the water is calmer May through November; Isla del Coco—June through August; southern Caribbean—anytime, but September and October can be quite clear here when the rest of the country is not.

Wherever you snorkel or dive, abide by rules aimed to protect the waters and wildlife. Don't walk on or disturb coral. Do not feed the fish—find spots to see them in their natural environment. Don't go out with operators who use feeding to attract fish. Listings of dive centers are in regional sections: look at areas such as Ocotal, Playa Hermosa, Flamingo, Drake Bay, Cahuita, Manzanillo, Caño Island, and Coco Island.

Okeanos Aggressor, in Plaza Colonial in Escazú, 506/289-3333, 800/348-2628 (U.S. number), fax 506/289-3737, info@okeanos.net, www.okeanos.net. Sail aboard the *Okeanos,* a 110-foot (33.5-meter) yacht, to Coco Island, more than 330 miles (532 km) off the coast of Costa Rica. Water visibility is typically 80 to 100 feet (24 to 30 m), with water temperatures of 78° to 82° F (26° to 28°C). Ten-day tours with seven full days of diving start from $2,995; nine days, with six days of diving, from $2,795, both based on double occupancy. See hammerhead and white tip sharks, dolphins, manta rays, reef fish, eels—200 species of fish. The island is a national park and a World Heritage Site. Rent photo equipment or take classes on board.

SURFING

Grab your board and head for either coast. Surfing on the Caribbean coast is seasonal: January to March and July to October, with most popular sites from Limón south. Find good quality surf all year in north Pacific areas and in the central Pacific zone, while the south Pacific, with what is considered one of the longest lefts in the world at Pavones, is best from July to November. And remember, the water is warm year-round. Look in destination chapters for local lodges, hotels, and operators that offer surfing. The Costa Rica Tourist Board has a brochure entitled "Take a Break Point," with descriptions of 37 favorite surfing spots, 800/343-6332 (U.S. number).

Calypso Tours, 506/256-8787, 800/566-6716 (U.S. number), fax 506/256-6767, info@calypsotours.com, www.calypsotours.com. A six-day cruise on the catamaran Lohe Lani combines sailing with surfing on an adventure that begins in Puntarenas and can range as far south as Pavones near the border with Panama, depending on weather and ocean conditions. Some surfing spots along the beach are accessible only by boat—they don't even have names. The cost is $150 per person per day and is limited to six surfers, departures January through June.

WINDSURFING

Lake windsurfing is tops here while ocean windsurfing is just beginning. Summer months are best. At its northern end, Lake Arenal is considered one of the top five windsurf spots in the world; the average wind velocity is 25 miles per hour, and it blows year round, although winds from September to November are not predictable. Other good surfing lakes are Coter Lake, north of Arenal, and the Cachí Reservoir in the Orosi Valley. See destination chapters for hotels and lodges in these areas that offer windsurfing tours or packages. For those who want to try ocean windsurfing, summertime offshore winds in northwestern Costa Rica are beginning to draw windsurfers.

COMMUNITY TOURISM PROJECTS

As you travel, be aware of communities that operate small hotels, lodges, and reserves. These projects channel tourism income to local peoples who live near protected areas—sustainable development at work—and give you an opportunity to get to know individuals and families who share their traditional way of life with visitors. The goals of these groups include providing an alternate source of income, creating opportunities for their children to stay and work on the land, and demonstrating that environmental protection can be profitable. Facilities range from rustic to comfortable; English-language skills also vary. Some communities offer a wide range of activities and have their own private forest reserves.

COOPRENA, tel/fax 506/259-3605, 506/259-3401, cooprena@racsa.co.cr, www.agroecoturismo.net.. Some 10 community projects are under this umbrella, most of them operated by cooperatives. All accept volunteers. Activities can include horseback riding, hiking, bird-watching, agricultural tours, beach activities, canoeing, and fishing. Look for descriptions of these in following chapters: CoopeSanJuan R.L. near Aguas Zarcas (between La Fortuna and Puerto Viejo de Sarapiquí), Albergue EcoVerede near Monteverde, Albergue La Catarata near La Fortuna, CoopeOrtega R.L. near the Tempisque River and Palo Verde National Park, Albergue Heliconias Ecolodge near Bijagua at the base of Tenorio Volcano, CoopeSilencio R.L. south of Quepos on the Savegre River, CoopeMangle R.L. on the banks of the Terraba and Sierpe Rivers near Ciudad Cortés, CoopeUnioro R.L. on the Osa Peninsula near Corcovado National Park, and Ecopavones R.L. at Langostino Beach south of Golfito.

INTERNATIONAL COMPANIES
WITH NATURE TOURS TO COSTA RICA

Many tour companies In the United States and Canada offer trips to Costa Rica. Here are a few of those that specialize in nature and adventure travel.

Costa Rica Connection, 800/345-7422, fax 805/543-3626, tours@crconnect.com, www.crconnect.com. A nine-day New Tropical Forests and Manuel Antonio tour does a great loop that takes in Arenal Volcano, hot springs, the cloud forest at Monteverde, and Manuel Antonio National Park with its beautiful beaches, $1,095 per person, double occupancy. Another takes in Corcovado, Arenal, and Monteverde plus the private reserve at Tiskita, $1,350. An eight-day option combines Arenal with Manuel Antonio, with some options for mountain biking, river trip, kayaking, and fishing, $615. Join a small group for 11 days to discover Costa Rica's tropical forests, visiting Lankester Botanical Garden, Braulio Carrillo and Tortuguero National Parks, Tiskita on the south Pacific, Arenal, Monteverde, and Carara, $1,795, international airfare excluded. The Tropical Adventure program has short adventures: a three-day hike at Chirripó, a day of mountain biking, or two days of biking and rafting. Also available are sportfishing, diving, and surfing. Ask for the "Costa Rica Trip Planner."

Cross Country International, 800/828-8768, fax 914/677-6077, xcintl@aol.com, www.equisearch.com. Horses are the preferred mode of transport for these adventures in the northwest region of Guanacaste. Four- or five-day riding trips start at beautiful Sugar Beach, go on to Pirates Bay, Playa Grande (a turtle-nesting beach), Tamarindo, and Junquillal, and end at Nosara. Join the tour at Tamarindo or Liberia, $1,500.

Earthwatch, 800/776-0188, 617/926-8200, info@earthwatch.org, www.earthwatch.org. This nonprofit organization teams up interested volunteers from age 16 to 85 with university scientists and cultural experts worldwide to work on field research expeditions around the world. No special skills are required, though they are welcomed. Contact Earthwatch about projects in Costa Rica.

Geo Expeditions, 800/351-5041, 209/532-0152, fax 209/532-1979, info@geoexpeditions.com, www.geoexpeditions.com. A 12-day fixed-departure tour experiences Tortuguero canals, volcano-viewing, relaxing in nearby thermal waters at Arenal, visiting tropical cloud forests at Monteverde, hiking in Corcovado, and snorkeling at Caño Island; from $2,195, excluding international airfare. A 10-day natural history tour, led by first-class naturalist guides, focuses on

Poás and Tortuguero parks, Monteverde, Arenal Volcano, and rafting on the Reventazón. December through March fixed departures are $1,698. Custom-designed tours are available.

Geostar Travel, 800/624-6633, 707/579-2420, fax 707/579-0604, jbhopper@sonic.net, www.GeostarTravel.com. Specialties are bird-watching, botanical, and natural history tours. Naturalists lead 10-day trips to sites such as the Monteverde Cloud Forest Preserve, Arenal Volcano, and Tortuguero and Corcovado National Parks. Activities include hiking in tropical forests, white-water rafting, wildlife river trips, bathing in thermal waters, bird-, butterfly-, and turtle-watching, and volcano-viewing, $1,698, excluding international airfare.

Hidden Trails, 604/323-1141, 888/987-2457, fax 604/323-1148, hiddentrails@hiddentrails.com, www.hiddentrails.com. Horseback riding is the forte. An eight-day mountain and beach tour (rides on four days) starts out at the Los Angeles cloud forest and continues on to Arenal, Fortuna Waterfall, and to beach rides at Bolaños Bay on the Pacific; there's time for a canopy tour, hot springs, hiking, diving, sportfishing, canoeing, mountain biking, $1,295 from San José. Ask about a new nine-day route (riding on six days) that heads from San José north to the Ciudad Quesada area (hot springs, Juan Castro Blanco National Park, canopy tour, hiking), Sarapiquí area (floating or rafting), and Cahuita on the Caribbean (fishing, snorkeling). Equestrian naturalist guides accompany riders, $1,695. Nonriding guests are welcome.

Holbrook Travel, 800/451-7111, 352/377-7111, fax 352/371-3710, travel@holbrooktravel.com, www.holbrooktravel.com. Choose from an array of all-inclusive natural history tours. Via Verde is a nine-day exploration of Arenal and Monteverde, with guided hikes, boat rides, canopy tour, bathing in hot springs, and visits to a butterfly garden and the artisan center of Sarchí; from $1,097, land only. The nine-day Introduction to Costa Rica Birding goes to hot birding spots such as La Selva, Monteverde, and the Palo Verde area, $1632, land only. White-water rafting, river camping, hiking, snorkeling, biking, and a float trip are part of the 10-day Adventure in Costa Rica, from $1,868. In association with the Caribbean Conservation Corporation, Holbrook offers Turtle Tagging in Costa Rica, one- to three-week volunteer programs at Tortuguero. Ask about family trips and custom tours. Holbrook Travel owns Selva Verde Lodge near Puerto Viejo deSarapiquí. **Mariah Wilderness Expeditions,** 800/462-7424, 510/233-2303, fax 510/233-0956, rafting@mariahwe.co, www.mariahwe.com. Their 16-page "Costa Rica Trip Planner" is chock-full of possibilities: modules by regions with possible activities allow travelers to home in on where to go—for example, a three-day rafting trip, a two-day hiking option, etc.; then staff ties them together for a custom tour. Several fixed itineraries exist, including a nine-day Tropical Cloud Forest-Manuel Antonio adventure that travels to Arenal Volcano, Monteverde, and Manuel Antonio, with activities such as hiking, experiencing hot springs, exploring a recent lava flow, nature hike, canopy tour, swimming, snorkeling, sea kayaking; from $1,115 exclusive of international airfare. For the active adventurer, try an eight-day option that includes white-water rafting, hiking at Arenal, and sea kayaking, scuba diving, fishing, snorkeling, or mountain biking at a Pacific beach; from $1,085.

Overseas Adventure Travel (OAT), 800/493-6824, 800/955-1925, www.oattravel.com. Excellent naturalist guides lead small groups (16-person max) on 11-day trips to explore a variety of habitats, where you can enjoy hikes, rafting, wildlife boat trip, volcano watching, horseback riding, relaxing on a white-sand beach, hot spring bathing, thermal mud bath, river trip to observe crocodiles, cruising on a yacht, and guided walks at private nature reserves. Areas include Sarapiquí, Arenal, Caño Negro, Chachagua, Rincón de la Vieja, Punta Leona, and Punta Coral. Eat with a local family, visit a rural school, and experience a local cantina. Real Affordable Costa Rica starts at $1,790, including round-trip airfare from Miami; a three-day extension to Tortuguero National Park is available, $350. The cost includes a donation to support ecological research and community projects in Costa Rica. OAT is a member of Grand Circle Foundation, a nonprofit organization that contributes to cultural, community, and environmental projects in the country.

Preferred Adventures Ltd., 800/840-8687, 612/222-8131, fax 612/222-4221, paltours@aol.com, www.preferredadventures.com. Customized individual adventures and natural history travel are featured as well as a raft of exciting nature tours and some special-interest tours. With the Roger Tory Peterson Institute of Natural

History, it offers a 10-day trip to top birding destinations for $1,995, excluding international airfare. The nine-day Best of Costa Rica visits Tiskita Jungle Lodge, Arenal Volcano, Monteverde, and Carara National Park, with an optional trip to Corcovado National Park, from $1,350; extend for three days in Tortuguero for and additional $234. Costa Rica Coast to Coast reaches from Tortuguero on the Caribbean to Corcovado and a southern rain forest on the Pacific, from $1,395. A helpful catalog lists popular one-day trips along with longer itineraries. Preferred Adventures has developed its own excellent Nine Commandments of Ecotourism, which it shares with travelers, and contributes both financially and otherwise to a number of conservation projects in Costa Rica.

Remarkable Journeys, 800/856-1993, 713/721-2517, fax 713/728-8334, cooltrips@remjourneys.com, www.remjourneys.com. A diverse array of attractive, active tours is available, accompanied by bilingual guides. Nine-day Paddles and Pedals emphasizes white-water rafting, sea kayaking, overnight campout, and mountain biking, while exploring the Pacuare River, Pacific coast, and Nicoya Peninsula from Sámara to Mal Pais near Cabo Blanco Nature Reserve, $1,525 from San José. A Costa Rica Adventure offers eight days of white-water rafting, rain-forest hiking, biking, horseback riding, canoeing, and kayaking, $1,200 from San José. Or if trekking is your thing, consider Hidden Valleys of Costa Rica: mountain bike through the Orosi Valley to Turrialba, hike in the Talamanca Mountains, camp near a settlement of indigenous peoples, and white-water raft, $1,425.

Specops, 800/713-2135, 719/686-9388, thegroup@specops.com, www.specops.com. Adventure and outdoor-skills vacations for the active traveler are offered by Special Forces veterans, former soldiers who were trained in learning the culture, customs, and language of a society and in entering and departing an area without leaving a trace of ever being there Transformation of these skills to adventure tourism aims to have travelers experience nature firsthand without negatively impacting the environment. The 12-day Big Adrenaline Rush offers white-water rafting, bungee jumping, canopy tour, surfing, scuba diving, windsurfing, skiing, and high-speed casting. Instruction includes wilderness first aid, map reading, jungle survival, rope management, tides and currents, small boat handling, windsurfing, surfing, $2,760. Shorter versions are available: Introduction to Survival Traveling and Fun, five days; and one without the white-water rafting. Survival Trekking in the Osa Peninsula teaches outdoor skills and survival techniques, from $1,700. Ask about a photo safari.

Wildland Adventures, 800/345-4453, 206/365-0686, fax 206/363-6615, info@wildland.com, www.wildland.com. The company's aim is to help individuals, families, and groups experience natural habitats and discover local cultures in enriching ways. The eight-day Tropical Trails Odyssey travels to Monteverde and the Osa Peninsula and includes waterfalls, beaches, tropical forests, and lodging on the classy side, from $1,895. The 12-day Mountain and Jungle Trek integrates trekking, camping, hiking, photography, wildlife viewing, bird-watching, and rain-forest exploration with stays in the Savegre cloud forest, Chirripó (the highest mountain in Costa Rica), and adjacent to Corcovado National Park, from $1,850, in-country transportation only. Try Caribbean Highland and Jungles, which goes to Monteverde, Arenal, and Poás Volcanoes, the Reventazón River, and Tortuguero, from $1,598. Ask about special itineraries for families and honeymooners. Trips support the company's nonprofit Travelers Conservation Trust, which contributes to numerous conservation projects in countries where Wildland Adventures sends travelers.

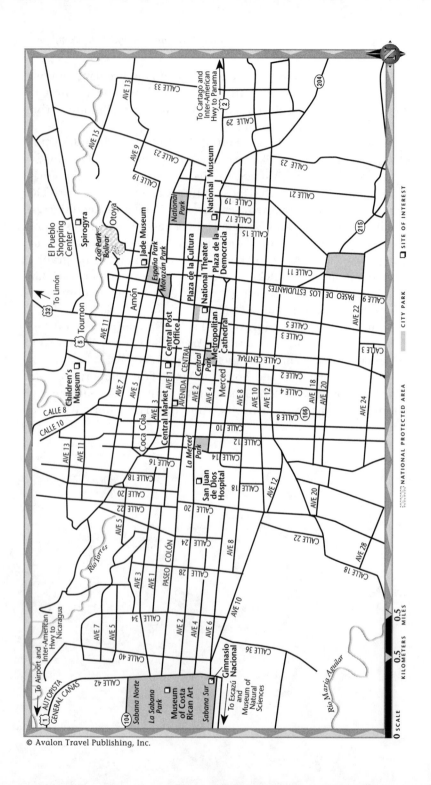

© Avalon Travel Publishing, Inc.

CHAPTER 4

San José and Environs

San José is the capital of Costa Rica. Founded in 1737, it is the center of government, theater, and art, as well as air pollution and congestion. This capital city has beautiful parks and museums, along with a few street beggars. Be prepared for fierce traffic, honking horns, worthwhile museums, good restaurants, crowds, charming small hotels, friendly people, and small slices of the natural world in an urban setting.

Even from its crowded downtown streets, you can manage a view of surrounding mountains, green against the sky. Poás, Irazú, and Barva Volcanoes help define the horizon. Squawks of colorful parakeets flying overhead or gathered in trees are as common downtown as the calls of street vendors. Policemen on foot, bicycle, and horseback patrol to counteract increased theft—be alert. See Appendix A for safety tips.

Downtown San José is taking on a new look thanks to significant public works projects. Some sidewalks have been widened, and electric cables have gone underground in selected areas. People once again stroll along Central Avenue in the heart of the city thanks to a 10-block-long pedestrian boulevard that invites exploration and accesses some of San Jose's most interesting and historic sites. Tucked along the boulevard are old-fashioned street lamps, shade

Ree Strange Sheck

Morazán Park in downtown San José

trees, potted shrubs, benches, and sculpture. For pure magic, stroll toward Calle 4 and listen to a group of retired *tico* musicians play Latin rhythms with heart. Passersby stop, couples dance, toes tap, and young and old smile and applaud. The band plays Tuesday through Friday from about noon to 4 P.M., unless it rains.

LAY OF THE LAND

Here are navigation tips for getting around downtown. *Avenida* (pronounced ah-vay-NEE-dah) means "avenue" and avenidas run east and west. *Calle* (CAHL-yay) means "street," and calles—you got it—run north and south. Get your bearings early because when you ask for directions, answers come in terms of so many meters to the north, east, south, or west. A city block is about a hundred meters long, so when a helpful person tells you to go "*200 metros al norte*," it means two blocks north. *Metros* is pronounced "MAY-tros."

The defining streets are Calle Central and Avenida Central. Look at the San José map and you will see that odd-numbered streets are east of Calle Central, even-numbered streets to its west. Odd-numbered avenues are north of Avenida Central, even-numbered, south. Thus if you go north from Avenida Central, you cross in succession Avenidas 1, 3, and 5. West from Calle Central, you encounter Calles 2, 4, and 6. Few buildings have numbers posted. A typical address is Calle 1, Avenidas 2/4, which means the place is on Calle 1 in the block between Avenida 2 and Avenida 4. Look for calle and avenida numbers at intersections—sometimes you can find one. The Costa Rica Tourism Institute (ICT) map of the country has a San José map on the back. You can buy city maps at gift shops and bookstores.

If you can't walk to your destination, it is usually easier to take a taxi or hop onto a public bus than to maneuver through unfamiliar territory (many one-way streets) in a rented car. With the fierce traffic, it's hard to realize that the era of the automobile began here only in the 1950s. It is not uncommon to see carts scattered among cars even now, though they are generally pulled by people rather than by the oxen more typical of rural areas. In early morning, walk along Avenida 1 to the Central Market, Calles 6/8, or Borbón Market, Avenida 3, Calles 8/10, to see carts being loaded and unloaded.

In recent years San José has paid attention to its parks, and it shows. **Morazán** and **España Parks** start at Calle 5 near Avenida 3, a place to join *ticos* eating sack lunches and watching schoolchildren play. Enjoy bird-watching even here: blue-gray tanagers, a few parrots and parakeets, and a woodpecker or two. The elaborate bandstand in Morazán reverberates with music on special occasions. The yellow and green metallic school building nearby was built in the 1890s, its plates designed by Alexandre Gustave Eiffel of Eiffel Tower fame and shipped from Belgium by boat for assembly here. **National Park**, Avenida 3/Calle 15, is another good place to escape crowds, while **Central Park** in front of Metropolitan Cathedral, Avenida 2/Calle 2, is a people place. San José's moderate temperature makes sitting outside and seeing the sights pleasant: the average high is 77°F (24.9°C); low, 61°F (16.3°C).

Plaza de la Cultura, Avenida Central, Calles 3/5, is an event. A mime, juggler, marimba band, Andean music group, or magician may be there, drawing clusters of onlookers. It is the stage for civic and political events, and on its periphery artisans display wares.

Looking for handcrafts? Predominant are jewelry, wooden items, furniture, T-shirts, leather goods, carved and painted gourds, pottery, artwork, and distinctive paper products made from plants such as bananas, coffee, rice—sustainable development at work. The **Central Market,** watching over the corner of Avenida Central and Calle 6 since 1880, is a city block in size. Stalls and shops offer everything from souvenirs, rubber boots for muddy trails, and flip-flops for the beach to vegetables and tropical fruits. Find flower stalls, pharmacies, candles, cold cuts, live chickens, and typical eateries. Be ready for crowds and watch your belongings. Open daily early until late.

The **Mercado Nacional de Artesanía** is a nonprofit center that trains artisans and helps market products for more than 700 artists from around the country. Stop by the colorful center at Calle 11, Avenidas 4/6, open weekdays 9 A.M. to 6 P.M., Saturday 9 A.M. to 5 P.M. **Galería Namu,** Avenida 7, Calles 5/7, is a must—only Costa Rican art here, with a real commitment to indigenous and women artists, especially primitive art by country women. Information sheets go with most pieces. The gallery is open weekdays 10:30 A.M.

Sculpture of campesinos *"standing present" in the heart of San Jose*

Ree Strange Sheck

to 6:30 P.M. and Saturday noon to 6 P.M. Check out the website at www.galerianamu.com. For one-stop shopping **Boutique Annemarie,** Hotel Don Carlos, Calle 9, Avenidas 7/9, is one of the best. More than 400 paintings are on display, along with one of the most complete selections of handcrafts around. It's open daily 9 A.M. to 7 P.M. **La Casona,** Calle Central, Avenidas Central/1, has two floors crowded with shops, open 9:30 A.M. to 6 P.M., closed Sunday. **Suraska Gallery,** Avenida 3, Calle 5, and **La Galería,** Calle 1, Avenidas Central/1 are two that show off handcrafts and elegant jewelry as the works of art they are. They are open weekdays 9 A.M. to 6 P.M., and Suraska is also open Saturday 9 A.M. to 4 P.M.

For general shopping, head west from the Plaza de la Cultura on Avenida Central to find **La Gloria** department store, Calles 4/6. For sunscreen or aspirin, pharmacies abound. Look for a sign that says "Farmacia." **Second Street Books** at Calle 7 between Avenida 1 and Avenida Central, 506/256-8251, has a marvelous selection of natural history books along with interesting history, cultural studies, and fiction volumes, magazines, newspapers, and used books, open daily 9 A.M. to 6 P.M. **Librería Lehmann,** Avenida Central, Calles 1/3, also has books and magazines, and **Librería Universal,** Avenida Central, Calles Central/1, has books, posters, maps, film, photo developing, and department-store items.

IFSA photo shops (Kodak products) usually offer one-day print developing; one is at Avenida Central, Calle 5, across from Plaza de la Cultura. Fuji film and same-day developing is on Avenida 1, Calle Central/Calle 1. If disaster strikes with camera or lenses, don't despair. Try **Equipos Fotográficos Canon,** Avenida 3, Calles 3/5, 506/223-1146, open weekdays 8 A.M. to noon and 1 to 5:30 P.M., Saturday 9 A.M. to 1 P.M.

NATURE AND ADVENTURE ACTIVITIES

Though nature and adventure travelers often shun cities and quickly head for the hills, San José is where many begin their journeys because of its proximity to Juan Santamaría International Airport. The city is the major transportation hub, so many multiday tours start

PEDESTRIAN SAFETY

One of the most dangerous things facing a traveler in downtown San José is crossing the street. The pedestrian's job is to keep out of a driver's way—whatever the driver may decide to do. The tico's gentle nature seems to give way to rampant individualism behind the wheel. Cars turning right do not yield to pedestrians. Expect no mercy if the light change finds you in the middle of the street. To meet the challenge, follow a Costa Rican woman who is hanging onto at least two small children. Go when she goes. If you don't see the light turn green at a wide street like Avenida 2, wait a full cycle and be ready to sprint across when it next turns green.

One other word of caution: back up on corners where buses make turns on narrow streets; you could actually be hit by the bus while standing on the sidewalk. The downtown pedestrian walkway on Avenida Central keeps getting longer. It's great.

and end here, and top natural history and adventure destinations are near enough for half-day or one-day trips to volcanoes, white-water rivers, rain forests, and bird, butterfly, and botanical attractions, making it a good base of operations. In the city itself are small, interesting museums related to natural history, as well as historical and cultural museums that give perspective to what this country is about.

VISITOR INFORMATION

The **Costa Rican Tourism Institute** office, 506/222-1090, beneath Plaza de la Cultura, Calle 5, Avenida Central/2, has information on city and countrywide buses. Loads of brochures, notebooks with photos of lodges and hotels, and a bulletin board crowded with tourist information let you to browse on your own, or staff can help. At an interactive Conservation Areas module, choose an area you want to visit to look at a map, hotels, restaurants, species you might see, and parks information. Pick up a free map. Open 9 A.M. to 5 P.M. weekdays.

GETTING THERE

San José is the center of the country as far as transportation goes. Most travelers arrive at Juan Santamaría airport less than half an hour from downtown. Airport taxis can deliver you to your hotel for about $12. If you don't have more luggage than you can carry, you can walk to the bus stop in front of the airport and take a bus—no facilities for large luggage. The Inter-American Highway that runs from the northern border with Nicaragua to the southern border with Panama comes through San José, so if you arrive in Costa Rica by car or bus, the road will bring you.

NATURE AND ADVENTURE
SIGHTS IN SAN JOSÉ

Small nature centers in San José offer good introductions to flora and fauna of the country; museums give insight into history and culture. Some of the best are described below. A base of operations in the capital city offers a multitude of half-day and full-day trips to top nature/adventure destinations. National parklands with easy access are Irazú and Poás Volcanoes, Tapantí, and Braulio Carrillo, as well as Guayabo National Monument, the only archaeological park. Package tours by air bring Tortuguero and Barra de Colorado National Parks into the picture. A cruise in the Gulf of Nicoya or a tour to Carara National Park takes you to the Pacific. Exploring historical and biological treasures of the Central Valley is possible with tours to the Orosi Valley, Lankester Botanical Garden (for orchids), Zoo Ave (bird sanctuary) or the Butterfly Farm, the colonial capital of Cartago with its religious shrine, and the handcraft city of Sarchí. One-day tours take you rafting or kayaking on the country's waterways and hiking on Barva Volcano. Look for descriptions of these sights in following chapters.

NATURE SIGHTS IN SAN JOSÉ

Insect Museum

This small museum has a dazzling display of butterflies, bees, exotic-looking beetles and walking sticks, poisonous spiders, the large *bala* ant found in the Atlantic zone, and a 162-pound wasp nest from near San Isidro de El General. Scientifically, among the most important collections are bees and wasps, leafhoppers and their relatives, beetles, and dragonflies. Learn about mimicry in insects, tropical diseases transmitted by insects, and insects important to agriculture.

Details: In the basement of the Music Arts Building (Facultad de Artes Musicales) on the University of Costa Rica campus in San Pedro; 506/207-5318. If the entrance at the bottom of the stairs is locked, ring the bell. Open 1 to 5 P.M. weekdays; admission $2.

Museum of Natural Sciences

Though some specimens appear a bit moth-eaten, exhibits show many of the mammals and birds to be found in Costa Rica, along with insects, reptiles, and crustaceans. It may be your only chance to see the harpy eagle, an endangered species, even if it is stuffed. There are also mineralogy, anthropology, and paleontology sections.

Details: At Colegio La Salle, across from the southwest corner of La Sabana Park; 506/232-1306. Take a taxi or Sabana-Estadio bus from downtown and ask to be let off at Colegio La Salle for the Museo de Ciencias Naturales. Open weekdays 8 A.M. to 4 P.M., Saturday 8 A.M. to noon, Sunday 9 A.M. to 4 P.M.; admission $1.25 adults, $1 children.

Serpentarium

You may not encounter a single snake during your forays into the natural world, so here is a chance to see some: the boa constrictor, coral snake, brightly colored tree viper, and fer-de-lance. More than 45 species of reptiles and amphibians (including tiny poison-dart frogs) are here, along with a photographic exhibit of Costa Rican wildlife. Learn how to distinguish between venomous and nonvenomous snakes. A bilingual biologist is on hand; most signs are in English and Spanish.

Details: Avenida 1, Calles 9/11, on the second floor, 506/255-4210. Open weekdays 9 A.M. to 6 P.M., weekends and holidays 10 A.M. to 5 P.M; admission $4.

Spirogyra Butterfly Garden

This small garden showcases hundreds of butterflies of some 30 species. In one of the last remaining forested areas in San José, this oasis is a visual feast of trees and flowering plants. Learn about butterflies from egg to metamorphosis to feeding habits and defense systems. A video is followed by a self-guided tour on paths through a dazzling area of flowering plants that provide nectar and are host plants on which butterflies lay eggs and caterpillars feed.

Spirogyra is much more than a butterfly garden. Men and women from six small rural groups are trained here to raise butterfly pupae for export; Spirogyra also markets for them. Almost one-fourth of group members never finished elementary school; they all live in areas where employment opportunities are scarce; farming is the main activity. The project goal is to increase the socio-economic level of these rural people through use of renewable natural resources. The $20 or so per week they can make is a big difference to family incomes, and members and even their communities have changed their views about the larvae, formerly seen as pests, and the host plants that they considered weeds. Their evolving status as butterfly "experts" lessens chances they will have to migrate from their homes to earn a living.

Details: One block east and 1.5 blocks south of El Pueblo Shopping Center; 506/222-2937, parcar@racsa.co.cr, www.infocostarica.com/butterfly. Open daily 8 A.M. to 3 P.M., admission $5 for adults, $2.50 for children. You can even purchase butterfly pupae online.

Zoológico Nacional Simón Bolívar

Though quite humble compared with big city zoos in the States, here you can see species found in Costa Rica. Observe white-faced and spider monkeys in close proximity so you can more easily identify them in the forest. Simón Bolívar has a tapir, which you are not likely to see in the wild, and members of the cat family such as the ocelot, margay, and mountain lion. (The pen for the tapir seems to be long-term temporary and is sad—a new enclosure is on the drawing board). Iguanas and agoutis share a sunken exhibit area, and you can see a porcupine, a kinkajou, and crocodiles. A well-done herpetological aquarium displays five of Costa Rica's colorful poison-dart frog species. There are macaws, owls, and parrots, and free-flying birds hang out here,

Details: Avenida 13, Calles 7/11. The zoo is open daily 9 A.M. to 4:30 P.M.; admission $1. On weekends it tends to be jammed with local folks, and on weekdays schoolchildren come as part of an ongoing education program. Bolívar Zoo can use financial help—especially to free that tapir of its depressing cement pad. Ask about donations through Fundación Pro-Zoológica, 506/233-6701, fax 506/223-1817, fundazoo@racsa.co.cr.

CULTURAL SIGHTS IN SAN JOSÉ

Jade Museum

Here is a marvelous collection of jade objects, pre-Columbian ceramic and stone works, and archaeological and ethnographic displays. It encompasses more than 7,000 pieces, of which some 2,000 are exhibited: jade pendants, ear ornaments, beads, small jade jars, pre-Columbian pottery, and striking stone sculptures. This is the only museum in the world dedicated to jade, a semi-precious stone that was believed by early cultures to have curative properties. The pendants are breathtaking, carved or with delicate figures outlined on the stone. An added attraction of the museum are views through expanses of windows on all four sides—an unparalleled view of San José and surrounding mountains and volcanoes.

Details: Avenida 7, Calle 9, 11th floor of Instituto Nacional de Seguros (the National Insurance Institute), 506/287-6034. Open weekdays 8:30 A.M. to 3 P.M.; admission $2.

Museos

This three-level museum beneath Plaza de la Cultura was established by the Central Bank of Costa Rica. The **Pre-Columbian Gold**

Museum contains a spectacular collection of gold objects dating from A.D. 500. Included are more than 2,300 pieces of gold jewelry, armored plates, religious items, and even gold tweezers. Find out how indigenous peoples worked gold, using wax and solid casting methods. The **Numismatic Museum** displays collections of coins and bills dating back to the 16th century. Changing expositions of pre-Columbian pottery and contemporary art fill out the menu. The museum shop sells original art, books, and reproductions of collection pieces.

 Details: *Calle 5, Avenidas Central/2, 506/243-4202. Open 10 A.M. to 4:30 P.M., closed Monday; admission $4.*

Museo del Niño (Children's Museum)

It may be for children, but this museum, housed in a former prison, delights all ages with its hands-on exhibits (biology, astronomy, electricity, natural history), television and radio studio, art galleries, and life-sized mechanical talking figures (including astronaut Franklin Chang of Costa Rica). More than 32 exhibition rooms are chock-full of learning experiences, many of them interactive. Visit a dairy farm here, and in an arboretum look at Costa Rican tree species and learn about their uses.

 Details: *Follow Calle 4 past Avenida 9 to what appears to be a yellow castle and you're there; 506/223-2734. Open weekdays 8 A.M. to 3 P.M., weekends 10 A.M. to 5 P.M.; admission $2.50 for adults, $1.50 for children.*

Museum of Costa Rican Art

Housed in what was the airport terminal when La Sabana Park was the international airport (Charles Lindbergh landed here), this beautiful building houses a permanent collection of some of the country's finest artists. It is usually not crowded, and you can roam from room to room at leisure. In case you wondered, the airport moved in 1955.

 Details: *Calle 42, where Paseo Colón ends at La Sabana Park, 506/222-7155. Open daily 10 A.M. to 4 P.M., closed Monday; admission $3. Take a Sabana-Cementerio or Sabana-Estadio from downtown.*

National Museum

An exhibit on modern history joins pre-Columbian art, natural history, and religious art in this 19th-century building that was converted from a military fortress after the army was abolished The exhibits are rather somber in appearance but well worth a visit. Bilingual labeling is progressing, making displays more accessible to non-Spanish-speaking visitors. Rooms open onto an inviting covered veranda and a manicured courtyard, which has a terrific view of the city and adjoining Plaza de la Democracia. Dedicated in 1989, the plaza commemorates 100 years of democracy in Costa Rica.

Details: *Avenidas Central/2, Calle 17, 506/257-1433. Open 8:30 A.M. to 4:30 P.M., closed Monday; admission $1, free for children.*

National Theater

This is a must-see. Inaugurated in 1897, this architectural and artistic gem is beloved by Costa Ricans. Start-up funds for the building came from coffee growers through a voluntary tax on every bag of coffee exported. Later a tax on all imports was levied to complete construction. The reason? A famous European opera star appearing in Guatemala had refused to perform in Costa Rica for lack of an adequate performing space, one of a number of snubs from touring music and theater groups. National honor resulted in this neoclassical treasure. Early in the 20th century, a Spaniard reporting on his visit described San José as "a small village around a grand theater." Today's visitors continue to be impressed by its beauty: the statuary, paintings, ornate ceilings, marble columns with bronze capitals, a regal staircase with ornaments laminated in gold, and the center of it all, a grand three-tiered, horseshoe-shaped auditorium. Attend a performance if you can, or take a tour.

Details: *Avenida 2 side of the Plaza de la Cultura, at Calle 3. Theater tours daily 9 A.M. to 5 P.M.; admission $2.50.*

Pueblo Antiguo

The site recreates the ambiance of an earlier Costa Rica, from 1880 to 1930, portraying life of city, country, and coasts: reconstructed rural houses, a milking barn, train station, traditional *trapiche* (for

TAKING THE BUS

Thousands of people ride buses in San José every day. You can, too. Fares are inexpensive. Hotel staff or the ICT office can tell you where stops are. Wait your turn in line and pay as you enter. Though correct change is not necessary, don't pay with a large bill. The fare should be posted on the front window.

If there is no vacant seat, hang on. Men and women passengers relinquish seats to pregnant women, parents with a small child or two in tow, the handicapped, and frail, elderly persons. Men sometimes surrender seats to females. Microbuses cost more but are quicker, and a seat is guaranteed.

Buses are great for people-watching, eavesdropping, and catching glimpses of local people's everyday lives. When it's time to get off, push a button, pull a cord, or yell "parada" (bus stop) so the driver will know to let you off at the next scheduled place. Carry money or passports in a safe place.

extraction of cane juice), *pulpería,* ranchitos, and a mini-plantation of banana and coffee.

Details: *In Parque de Diversiones, one mile (two km) west of Hospital Mexico, 506/296-2212. Open weekdays 9 A.M. to 5 P.M., weekends 9 A.M. to 9 P.M.; admission $2. Inquire about weekend programs in English and night tours with music and food.*

GUIDES AND OUTFITTERS

A half-day city tour usually includes the National Theater, at least one museum, and perhaps a drive through the University of Costa Rica campus and past historic landmarks. Here are a couple of good options.

Expediciones Tropicales, Calle 3b, Avenidas 11/13, 506/257-4171, fax 506/257-4124, expetrop@racsa.co.cr, www.costaricainfo.com, drives by Sabana Park, the Supreme Court complex, and the University of Costa Rica and visits the National Theater and a museum for $24. There's time for shopping in handcraft stores in Moravia, known for its leather goods. Ask about the night tour of Pueblo Antiguo.

For something a bit different, try a walking tour with **Caña Dulce,** 506/258-3535, fax 506/222-0201, canadulc@racsa.co.cr, www.costaricaculturaltours.com. This company specializes in cultural tourism. For about $5 go on a guided walk through España, Morazán, and National Parks and the historic neighborhoods of Aranjuez, Amón, and Otoya, with their turn-of-the-century architecture and many restored homes, some now small hotels. Its City Tour by Night, including historic buildings, wine, *bocas*, music, and Costa Rican coffee, is $30. A six-hour San José Cultural City Tour takes in Sabana Park, the art museum, Atlantic train station, National Monument, Costa Rican Cultural Center, National Theater, traditional neighborhoods, and a traditional Costa Rican lunch.

For half-day and one-day tours to other sites, check out tour operators listed in Chapter 3.

LODGING

Not a comprehensive list of hotels, this represents a range of prices with emphasis on smaller places and interesting options. Rates are for high season; most have reduced rates from May through November. For a list of hotels that have received the Certificate for Sustainable Tourism, a "green seal" for good management of environmental, social, and cultural resources, from the Costa Rican Tourism Institute, check out www.turismo-sostenible.co.cr, or send an e-mail to info@turismo-sostenible.co.cr. Read about this program in Chapter 2.

San José has a growing number of hotels affiliated with international hotel chains. Since the emphasis of this book is on smaller and owner-operated hotels, you will not find detailed information on the chain hotels here. Here are a few you can check on through their respective companies: **Aurola Holiday Inn, Best Western Irazú,**

RATES AND RESERVATIONS

All rates, listed in U.S. dollars, were valid at the time of publication. They do not include the 13 percent sales tax or 3 percent tourism tax unless specified. These are high-season rates, which usually last from December to April; green-season rates are often less. Some hotels have higher rates for Christmas and Easter weeks.

Reservations are recommended. When calling from outside Costa Rica, use the country area code, 506, before the number. Inside the country, do NOT use the 506 code. Because mail service can be slow and unreliable, it's better to phone, fax, or e-mail.

Costa Rica, Marriott Hotel and Resort, Hotel Camino Real, Hotel Radisson Europa, Meliá Cariari Conference Center & Golf Resort, Meliá Confort Corobicí, San José Palacio, Sheraton Herradura Hotel & Spa.

Many of the hotels and inns that follow, in alphabetical order, were once lovely old homes in residential areas whose use changed as the city grew—historic zones such as Barrio Amón, Otoya, and Aranjuez. These are in the greater San José metropolitan area. Look also at Chapter 5 for options with easy access to San José, close to the airport.

Britannia Hotel, Avenida 11, Calle 3, 506/223-6667, fax 506/223-6411, tel/fax 800/263-2618, britania@racsa.co.cr, www.centralamerica.com/cr/hotel/britania, is in a 1910 Victorian mansion I have long admired. Great care was taken in its restoration and conversion into an exquisite 24-room hotel. The entrance is grand. Large rooms have hardwood or carpeted floors, air conditioning, tiled baths with tubs and showers, cable TV, writing desks, pretty comforters with matching window treatment, and wallpaper wainscoting. The Cellar Bar and Restaurant, with a varied menu and good food, opens onto a light-filled atrium. Standard rooms are from $89 for a double, deluxe rooms from $105.

Fleur de Lys Hotel, Calle 13, Avenidas 2/6, one block from the National Museum, 506/223-1206, fax 506/257-3637, florlys@racsa .co.cr, www.hotelfleurdelys.com, is in a renovated three-story Victorian built more than 60 years ago. Its 19 unique rooms, named for flowers, are all tastefully furnished—soft colors, warm woods, cable TV, telephones, and hair dryers. Some original tile and hardwood floors remain; rooms are carpeted. Fresh flowers brighten comfortable sitting alcoves; skylights bring sunshine in. An intimate restaurant specializes in French cuisine. Book tours at an in-house travel agency. Doubles start at $75; suites, at $85; breakfast is included.

In Aranjuez, one of San José's oldest districts, **Hotel Aranjuez,** Calle 19, Avenidas 11/13, 506/256-1825, fax 506/223-3528, aranjuez@racsa.co.cr, www.hotelaranjuez.com, has 28 rooms with the flavor of a pleasant Costa Rican home. Amenities in rooms include typical Costa Rican bedspreads, bamboo chairs with bright cushions, hair dryers, cable TV, and solar-heated water. Lounge areas and tropical gardens invite relaxation. Doubles with shared bath are $29; with private bath, starting at $35. Rates include breakfast buffet, taxes, and parking. No credit cards are accepted. Owner operated, this neat, small hotel is a real bargain.

In Barrio Amón, **Hotel Don Carlos,** Calle 9, Avenida 9, 506/221-6707, fax 506/255-0828, hotel@doncarlos.co.cr, www.doncarlos.co.cr, has character—another favorite. Find patios with fountains, a sun deck, personal service, sculpture, gardens with orchids and tropical birds, walls covered with original art, most rooms with a small balcony, terrace, or view of an interior courtyard garden. All 32 rooms have cable TV—and free e-mail is available for guests. The Pre-Columbian Lounge and Restaurant offers typical Costa Rican fare with live guitar and piano music at lunchtime and happy hour. Boutique Annemarie is one of the city's best. The main lobby's remarkable mural of San José at the turn of the 19th century, made of 272 hand-painted tiles, draws guests and non-guests. Murals along the wall on Avenida 9 are created around phrases of one of Costa Rica's beloved writers, Aquileo Echeverría. Don Carlos Tours offers natural history trips with a bilingual naturalist guide, rafting, and city tours, and handles reservations for domestic airlines and car rental. Doubles are $70 to $80, including continental breakfast; parking is free.

In Los Yoses, **Hotel Don Fadrique,** Calle 37, Avenida 8, 506/224-7583, fax 506/224-9746, fadrique@intercentro.net, is in a residential area but only minutes away from downtown by bus or on foot. The 20 large rooms, with views of tropical gardens, fountains, and a spreading mango tree, have ceiling fans, telephones, cable TV, and safes. A fine collection of Costa Rican art adorns the walls. Breakfast and dinner are served in the restaurant. An in-house tour agency specializes in adventure tours such as rafting, kayaking, and mountain biking. Doubles are $65, including breakfast.

Hotel Europa Centro, Calle Central, Avenida 5, 506/222-1222, fax 506/221-4609, europa@racsa.co.cr, has been around almost 90 years. Always comfortable and convenient, the grand old lady right downtown has new luster. The 72 refurbished rooms are spacious and have cable TV, air conditioning, large closets, and direct telephones; some rooms open onto balconies overlooking a pretty outdoor swimming pool. There is a restaurant with an international menu, a cozy downstairs bar, gift shop, and travel agency. Doubles or triples are $50.

A personal favorite is **Hotel Grano de Oro,** Calle 30, Avenidas 2/4, 1.5 blocks south of Paseo Colón, 506/255-3322, fax 506/221-2782, info@hotelgranodeoro, www.hotelgranodeoro.com. Inner patios bright with tropical plants and intimate courtyards peaceful with the music of the fountains weave the gracious turn-of-the-century mansion and attractive additions into a harmonious whole. Each of 35 rooms has a direct-dial telephone, satellite TV, and minibar; most have bathtubs—spotless, with charming brass and porcelain fixtures. All rooms are nonsmoking. Service is superb. Enjoy hot tubs on the rooftop garden terrace, and stop in the excellent small gift shop. Try delicious, creative fare in a charming ambiance at Restaurante Grano de Oro—great bocas, tropical cocktails, delicacies such as stuffed palm heart pie, scrumptious desserts. Eat inside or on a delightful patio, where tropical birds drop by to feed on flowering and fruiting plants. Doubles range from $80 to $110; suites, from $130. The hotel is a member of Small Distinctive Hotels of Costa Rica.

Hotel Kekoldi, Avenida 9, Calle 3b, in Barrio Amón, 506/223-3244, fax 506/257-5476, kekoldi@racsa.co.cr, www.kekoldi.com, is colorful, from bed coverings to multicolored murals that bring sea views right into San José. The 14 rooms, with Bribri names, have telephones and safes. The house, more than 85 years old, seems young in spirit. Under German management, Hotel Keloldi also arranges a variety of tours and keeps brochures and trip descriptions, with photos, on hand to help guests choose their destinations. Doubles start at $45, including continental breakfast.

A friendly bed-and-breakfast near Morazán Park, **Hotel La Amistad Inn,** Avenida 11, Calle 15, in Barrio Otoya 506/258-0021, fax 506/221-1409, wolfgang@racsa.co.cr, www.centralamerica. com/ cr/hotel/amistad, is a seven-minute walk from Plaza de la Cultura. Each of 23 rooms has cable TV, direct telephone, ceiling fan, free in-room safe, and queen-sized beds with orthopedic mattresses; three suites have refrigerators. Owner/operator Wolfgang Hilbich is always improving things—he has an Internet café for guests and a key-card security system. His tours have pick-up at the door. Doubles are $46, including taxes and a great German-style breakfast. Ten luxury rooms and three apartments should be open by your arrival, starting at $65.

In pretty Los Yoses, **Hotel Le Bergerac,** a half block south of Avenida Central on Calle 35, 506/234-7850, fax 506/225-9103, bergerac@racsa.co.cr, www.bergerac.com, offers roses on the table, balconies and gardens, a sun terrace, fountains, spacious rooms, Monet prints on the walls, and personalized service. French Canadian owners pay attention to detail. The two-story establishment, with the flavor of a fine French inn, has 18 airy rooms (in three buildings connected by gardens and archways) with framed, padded headboards, ceiling fans, cable TV, direct-dial telephones, hardwood floors, and baths with dark forest-green fixtures. Open to a central garden and its musical fountain is the gourmet dinner restaurant, well-known Ile de France, open to the public from 6 to 10 P.M., closed Sunday. Alexis Travel offers highly personalized service to guests. Doubles range from $68 to $88, breakfast included.

Hotel Petit Victoria, Calle 28, Avenida 2a, 506/233-1812, fax 506/222-5272, Victoria@infoweb.co.cr, is a two-story Victorian house more than 120 years old. It has elaborate tile floors in the reception area and wood floors in some of the high-ceilinged rooms. Rooms are more humble than the outside elegance: some are smallish; all are simply furnished and have cable TV. Owner Guglielmo tells interesting stories to do with the history of the house. Across the street is Sala Garbo, with top movies and art films. The restaurant, open 24 hours a day, is open to the public, serving reasonably priced, tasty food, and regional specialties. Doubles are $55, taxes and continental breakfast included.

Hotel Rosa del Paseo, Paseo Colón, Calles 28/30, 506/257-3225, fax 506/223-2776, rosadelp@racsa.co.cr, www.online.co.cr/rosa, encompasses a restored century-old residence. The 18-room hotel has beautiful antique pieces, stenciled friezes, charming alcoves and front bay windows, some of the original painted-tile floors, and stained glass. Older rooms have high ceilings (when did you last stay in a room with a transom?), a wardrobe, desk, and large baths with tubs. A pretty garden, where complimentary tropical breakfast is served, ties the house to a two-story addition. A computer is available for guest use. The restaurant serves light meals for lunch and dinner. Rooms range from $70 to $90, some with air-conditioning, one with a hot tub. Owners Paula and Fernando run an in-house tour agency and have an excellent tourist information center. Packages are available.

Hotel San José, Avenida 2, Calles 17/19, 506/256-2191, fax 506/221-6684, has a great location just east of the National Museum. Its 20 rooms and two two-room suites have telephones, safes, and TV; parking is available. Double rooms are $35; suites, $45, breakfast included.

Hotel Santo Tomás, Avenida 7, Calles 3/5, 506/255-0448, fax 506/222-3950, info@hotelsantomas.com, www.hotelsantomas.com, is in a renovated circa-1910 mansion where a coffee plantation once flourished. Each of 20 rooms is different but all feature high ceilings, reproduction Louis XV furniture, orthopedic queen-size beds, ceiling fans, telephones, and cable TV. Persian rugs decorate gleaming hardwood floors. Corridors have original tile floors; the comfortable parlor area sets a nice tone. A former courtyard is now an appealing place to start the day (a complimentary tropical breakfast of fruits and pastries served on glass-topped tables) or to wind down with a drink from the bar after a day of sightseeing. The staff arranges tailored tours; e-mail access is available. Parking is nearby at a discount. Doubles begin at $60.

Toruma Youth Hostel, Avenida Central, Calles 29/31, 506/234-8186, fax 506/224-4085, recajhi@racsa.co.cr, www.hostels.com/cr, has 19 spic-and-span rooms (105 beds). There's a small gift shop, laundry area, and a TV in the lobby. Toruma stores luggage and has safe deposit boxes. Rates are from $10 in dormitory-style rooms; in private rooms with shared baths, from $26 per person, double occupancy. Nonmember rates are $2 more. A continental breakfast is included. Ask about reduced rates elsewhere in the country for hostel members.

FOOD

San José has many fine restaurants: French, Italian, Thai, Chinese, German, Spanish, Peruvian, Mexican, and Japanese cuisine as well as typical food. American food chains have downtown locations: Burger King, Hardee's, Kentucky Fried Chicken, McDonald's, Mister Pizza, Pizza Hut. San José has good ice-cream shops. **Helados Pops** has two near the plaza: Avenida Central, Calles 1/3 and Avenida Central, Calle 11. **Helados Monpik** is at Avenida 4, Calle Central.

A 13 percent sales tax is included in your restaurant bill, usually along with a 10 percent service charge (tip). Some restaurants close Sunday or Monday.

Try **Café Britt** in the National Theater, Avenida 2/Calle 3, 506/221-3262, for all kinds of coffee, milkshakes, pastries, sandwiches, and executive lunches. The café has windows opening on to the Plaza de la Cultura, and patio dining is sometimes available: open 9 A.M. to 6 P.M. weekdays. At **Café Ruiseñor** in Los Yoses, find quiches, creative sandwiches, memorable pastries, cappuccino, and reasonably priced daily specials. Patio dining is popular, and both floors have nice views of the tree-lined boulevard in front. Open weekdays 7:30 A.M. to 7:30 P.M., on weekends only lunch is served.

Churrería Manolo, Avenida Central, Calles 9/11, 506/223-4067, has superb typical Costa Rican breakfasts with *gallo pinto* (black beans and rice), eggs, rolls, and sour cream. *Churros* are long, thin, addictive, doughnut-like filled pastries for sale at the front. Another Manolo's is at Avenida 1, Calles Central/2.

El Balcón de Europa, Calle 9, Avenidas Central/1, 506/221-4841, offers excellent Italian food. Try the *piccatine or spagetti carbonara* or great cheeses and desserts. The basket of fresh breads served when you sit down is worth the price of the meal. Fantastic, historic photos of yesteryear and interesting proverbs from around the world decorate walls. It opens at 11:30 A.M., closed Saturday.

Head for **Chalet Tirol,** above San Rafael de Heredia, 506/267-7371, less than half an hour from downtown for superb French food and excellent service. The Tyrolean-style restaurant is in a mountain setting, so allow time to walk among the trees and along the stream. When the weather is nippy outside, warm fires welcome inside.

El Pueblo, Calle 3 past Avenida 13, turning right across from the newspaper *La República,* is a Spanish-style complex with gift shops, galleries, nightclubs, and restaurants. Here are some good places to eat: **La Cocina de Leña** features traditional food far beyond rice and beans—plantain ceviche, black bean soup, *olla de carne*—served in quaint surroundings. **El Fogón de Leña** offers regional specialties from Guanacaste, Limón, and the Central

Quiet breakfast at Hotel Grano de Oro

97

Valley. **La Estancia** is for steak lovers. **Rías Bajas** has seafood specialties and attentive waiters.

Esquina del Café, Avenida 9, Calle 3B, 506/257-9868, in a restored 100-year-old house in historic Barrio Amón, has one of the best executive lunches around, $4 for main dish, salad, fruit drink, and coffee. Breakfast is good here, too. The regular menu goes from filet mignon and fajitas to sea bass, spaghetti, sandwiches, and soups. Coffee is serious business, with beans from top Costa Rican plantations: find espresso, cappuccino, café latte, Irish coffee. Check out the gift shop for beans, coffee mugs, pottery, or coffee paper.

The restaurant of **Gran Hotel Costa Rica,** Avenida 2, Calle 3, 506/221-4000, offers the ambiance of an outdoor terrace, live marimba music, and patio dining in the heart of San José next to the National Theater. Watch the world go by from breakfast on.

Hotel Grano de Oro, Calle 30, Avenidas 2/4, has delicious, unusual fare inside or on a peaceful patio—even blue-gray tanagers stop by. Consider an enchilada pie, shrimp thermidor, spaghettis, sea bass specialties, mussels, chicken in creamy coconut sauce, scrumptious salads, a garden sandwich. Leave room for piña colada cheesecake or a chocolate extravaganza called Pie Grano de Oro. The drink menu alone is worth stopping in.

La Bastille, Paseo Colón, Calle 22, 506/255-4994, is an old favorite with Costa Ricans and visitors—43 years of history. Dimly lit and somehow distanced from the noise and traffic outside, the restaurant-gallery specializes in Swiss-French cuisine: paté, escargot, meat fondue, crèpes Suzette, and pistachio ice cream with chocolate sauce are on the menu. Beef and fish dishes are superb.

Las Orquídeas, 7.5 miles (12 km) north on Limón highway is a getaway place on the road to Braulio Carrillo, with nice atmosphere, good food, good service, and Costa Rican cuisine. The typical plate with *gallo pinto*, plantains, and your choice of meat is superb. Flowers are glorious. It's a great place to escape the hubbub of San José and yet is only 15 minutes from downtown.

Le Chandelier, 100 m east and 100 m south of ICE, San Pedro, 506/225-3980, is an exquisite French restaurant. Dishes are also a feast for the eyes; expect superb attention. Come here for a memorable lunch or an elegant evening; closed on Sunday.

Le Monastère Restaurant, San Rafael de Escazú, 506/289-4404, serves fine French food in a 1940s monastery with spectacular views from the hillside setting, a chapel, great Belgian beer, and a wine cellar. Take the Santa Ana Road from Escazú and watch for the sign near Multicentro Paco, turn left, and follow the green crosses. Open for dinner only, closed Sunday. No athletic clothes are allowed.

Restaurant Ambrosia, in La Calle Real Shopping Center in San Pedro, 506/253-8012, is an easy taxi or bus ride from downtown San José. A retreat from urban rush, the dining room is intimate. The menu links myth with culinary delights—maybe Osiris soup or Orion tenderloin. Natural, fresh ingredients are emphasized. Open for lunch and dinner only; on Sunday, lunch only.

Restaurante El Chicote, north side of Sabana Park, 400 m west of ICE, 506/232-0936, has excellent baby beef and seafood (fresh lobster, New Zealand mussels); it is traditionally a favorite with Costa Ricans for good dining, lunch and dinner.

Restaurante Italiano Il Ponte Vecchio, San Pedro near Hispanidad Fountain, 506/283-1810, serves gourmet Italian cuisine in a picturesque setting. Open for lunch and dinner; closed Sunday.

Restaurante Tin-Jo, Calle 11, Avenidas 6/8, 506/221-7605, offers Chinese, Japanese, Indian, and Thai food. Try any of the dishes served in a nest of taro for a real treat. Tin-Jo has a vegetarian menu and serves jasmine and brown rice and organic vegetables.

Spoon, Avenida Central, Calles 5/7, 506/221-6702, is a reasonably priced, pleasant place with a menu for every appetite, whether for a full dinner of heart-of-palm or chicken lasagna or something lighter, such as quiche, sandwiches, crepes, or soups. Empanadas (light pastry filled with meats or vegetables or cheese) are good. Desserts are displayed in glass cases. Eat in or carry out. Open daily 9 A.M. to 9 P.M.

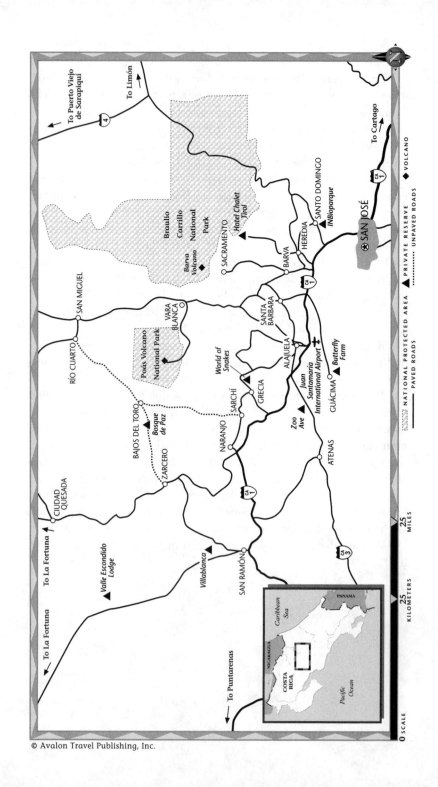

© Avalon Travel Publishing, Inc.

CHAPTER 5

Central Valley—West: Alajuela, Heredia, San Ramón Areas

Since colonial times, the Meseta Central (Central Valley) has been Costa Rica's population center. This chapter focuses on the historically rich northeast part of the Meseta, which encompasses two of the four colonial cities of Costa Rica: Alajuela and Heredia. (The other two are San José, described in Chapter 4, and Cartago, in Chapter 6.) Each of these colonial cities had its own character and strong sense of identity. That is still true today. Though younger, the towns of Grecia, Naranjo, Atenas, and San Ramón also have their history, and their own identity.

As you travel to or through these places, remember that this land was once covered with forest. Imagine what travel must have been like on foot or horseback up and down these mountains and across rivers now spanned by bridges. Life here was hard; it helped forge the national character. Beauty, not hardship, is the sensation travelers experience today. Protected forests remain, but the landscape is also painted with coffee fields, sugarcane, small farms, picturesque villages, and pastures for dairy cows. Rural houses have flowers, a porch to sit on when work is done, a few banana and coffee plants, fruit trees, and perhaps beans, squash, and corn—a link back to agrarian self-sufficiency.

LAY OF THE LAND

This region is close enough to Juan Santamaría International Airport, where most international travelers arrive, to make it a convenient base of operations from day one. Many find it an attractive alternative to staying in San José on arrival or departure. Top natural history destinations are here, as are charming small inns and lodges, many of them set in protected forest, extensive tropical gardens, or an agricultural landscape.

Alajuela, capital of the province of Alajuela, is a pleasant town (population 52,395), a stone's throw from Juan Santamaría airport and 10.5 miles (17 km) northwest of San José. It was the home of Juan Santamaría, the country's national hero. A statue honors him as a symbol of the Costa Ricans' desire for peace and freedom. **Juan Santamaría Cultural and Historical Museum,** 506/441-4775, one block north of the Central Park, documents the campaign against William Walker and his filibusters in which the young farmer lost his life; open 10 A.M. to 6 P.M., closed Monday; free admission. See a collection of more than 200 orchids at the museum. Stop by Central Park, a veritable orchard of mango trees. Blue-gray tanagers are among birds that flock to eat ripe fruit.

Heredia (population 29,935), the other colonial town in this area, was founded in 1706. Capital of the province by that name, it is known as the city of flowers and is home to the National University. Visit the 1796 church and the nearby tower of an old fort that remains in pretty gardens. On Sunday morning or Thursday evening, listen to a band play *paso dobles,* boleros, tangos, mazurkas, and waltzes in Central Park, a 150-year tradition. Heredia is 7.5 miles (12 km) north of San José and east of the airport. It is the jumping-off place for visits to the Barva sector of Braulio Carrillo National Park.

The other towns in the region are even smaller, but if you take time to sit in their central plazas, eat a meal in a local restaurant, or saunter down their streets, you can capture some of the flavor of Costa Rican friendliness. **Atenas,** founded in the 16th century, is a lovely, small town (population 6,475) in an area known for the quality of its fruits, 26 miles (41 km) northwest of San José. *Ticos* travel to Atenas on weekends just to buy fresh produce. Explore nearby attractions on day trips from local lodges. This area is easily accessible from the airport and on a road that leads to Pacific beaches, such as Punta Leona, Jacó, and Quepos, and to Carara National Park. **Grecia** (population 16,842) has what may be the only metal church in Latin America, the iron pieces shipped from Belgium in the 19th century, brought from Limón to Alajuela by train, and then transported the final 13 miles (21 km) by oxcart; open daily.

Many travelers stop in **Sarchí** (population 10,604), an artisan center 35 miles northwest of San José, where even

Ree Strange Sheck

Artisans at work in Sarchí

trash cans and bus stops are decorated with bright, colorful paintings. The most famous product is the painted oxcart. Sarchí was a stopping place for caravans that carried coffee to Puntarenas for shipping, spurring an industry in cart repair and cart production. When motorized vehicles took over, cart makers switched markets. Watch local artisans paint delicate freehand designs. In addition to carts—from miniatures to full size—find salad bowls, wooden fruit, mobiles, jewelry, and more. Sarchí-style chairs are famous. Factories and shops are around every turn along the two-mile (three-km) road from South Sarchí to North Sarchí. Two are Fábrica de Carretas Joaquín Chaverri and COOPEARSA, a cooperative. Plaza de la Artesanía has dozens of stores exhibiting arts and crafts.

San Ramón (population 13,909) is a center for the rich agricultural land you see as you travel along the Inter-American Highway. Here is the intersection that takes travelers north to major private reserves and to La Fortuna and Arenal. Watch for killer speed bumps as you travel through the residential outskirts. Signs warn, *"Reductor de velocidad"* ("Speed reducer").

NATURE AND ADVENTURE ACTIVITIES

Natural history and adventure activities include the Barva sector of Braulio Carrillo National Park and Póas Volcano National Park, where there are opportunities for hiking, wildlife viewing, and volcano exploration. A number of excellent private nature reserves offer lodging as well as rain or cloud forest tours with bilingual naturalist guides, canopy tours, and hiking.

Some of the best wildlife breeding, exhibition, and reintroduction programs in the country are here, where visitors can learn about birds, snakes, orchids, and butterflies from those who work with and study them.

FLORA AND FAUNA

Birds and butterflies are highlights in this region, though you may see small mammals and hear the sounds of howler monkeys as you visit private reserves or parks. Iridescent colors of hummingbirds (Trochilidae family) delight and mystify observers. Among names early Spanish explorers gave to these small New World birds was *joyas voladores* (flying jewels). And indeed they are. Since the colors of hummingbird plumage are structural rather than pigmented, the play of light on them creates different hues. Hummers may appear dark and without color, while at other times they glitter with dazzling flashes of red, green, purple, blue, or turquoise.

Costa Rica has at least 57 of the 330 species of hummers known to exist from Alaska to Tierra del Fuego (21 in the United States and Canada). Observe lengths and shapes of bills as clues to which flowers provide their nectar. Hummingbirds are important pollinators of tropical plants, and these plants' flowers have developed features that allow access to hummers while excluding other species. Many flowers are tubular and trumpet-shaped, and many bloom at branch tips, which facilitates feeding from a hovering position. Try to get a glimpse of the bird's tongue as it feeds—the tongue can measure twice as long as the bill itself. Hummers are attracted by color, not scent.

High-energy creatures (up to 80 wing beats per second), hummingbirds need protein as well as nectar, which they get from flying insects, spiders, and tiny insects in some of the flower tubes. They must feed about every 10 minutes during the day. At night they slow their metabolism to conserve energy, going into a torpor state in which the heartbeat slows from as many as 1,260 beats per minute to 50 per minute.

After mating, the female assumes total responsibility for building the nest, sitting on the eggs (usually two), and feeding the young, which remain in the nest about three weeks.

VISITOR INFORMATION

There are no information centers per se, but staff at any of the nature and adventure sites described below are glad to answer questions. And the owners and managers at the lodgings listed are excellent sources of information.

GETTING THERE

Public buses go from San José to these destinations (see Appendix A). You can also travel between many of these sites by bus. If you are driving, the Inter-American Highway is the major lifeline here, though smaller roads crisscross the area. Distances are relatively short: Alajuela, for example, is only a half hour from San José, five minutes from the airport. The farthest, San Ramón, is about an hour from the capital.

NATURE AND ADVENTURE SIGHTS

Barva Sector, Braulio Carrillo National Park
To walk in this lofty place is to experience the mystical silence of the cloud forest. Barva Volcano, the highest part of the park, is also one of the highest summits in the Central Volcanic Mountain Range; its three peaks are known as Las Tres Marías. The volcano is not extinct—it just rests. Its last period of activity is thought to have been about 5,000 years ago.

Trails are lined with large-leafed poor-man's umbrella and tiny blossoms of trees and shrubs; there is a veritable banquet of bromeliads. Exquisite rain-fed lakes shimmer in volcanic craters. The trail from the ranger station to Barva Lagoon, 1.8 miles (three km) of breathtaking beauty, climbs gently in spots and is almost level in others. The air is a bit thin—it's about 9,500 feet (2,900 m) elevation. Flock after flock of mixed species of birds feed along the path; tiny flowers and colored leaves found at this elevation demand attention. The view from the *mirador* (view point) above the crater lake is worth the short climb, sparkling in sunshine and magically shrouded in mists. Linger a bit on the chance of seeing a magnificent hummingbird feed in nearby flowers. From Barva Lagoon, it's 1.5 miles (2.5 km) to Copey, a shallow lake that becomes isolated ponds in dry season. A third lake, Danta, is the largest and least accessible.

Park rangers report that quetzals stay year-round but are seen more often between January and March when they are nesting. They are among more than 80 bird species, including the three-wattled bellbird, black guan, and volcano hummingbird. Mammals are not seen as often as in lower sections of the park, though tracks of jaguar and tapir are found. Agoutis, mountain lions, tayras, porcupines, coyotes, and two-toed sloths live here. Keep an eye out for smaller things, like scarabs; some 21 species of beetles are registered.

Barva lies at the upper end of an important migration corridor that joins Braulio Carrillo with lowland forest protected by La Selva Biological Station near Puerto Viejo de Sarapiquí, extremely important for migrating species of birds, butterflies, moths, and perhaps bats. Research shows that the corridor ecosystem is home to 17 species of threatened birds; 81 species of North American migratory birds depend on this habitat during migration or for wintering. Braulio Carrillo National Park was established in 1978. For information on the lower part of the park, see Chapter 8.

Camping is permitted at the station and bunks can sometimes be rented. Bathrooms and a covered picnic area are at the entrance; covered picnic shelters are in the forest off the trail. In addition to rain gear, bring a jacket. Temperatures range from 37°F to 68°F (3°C to 20°C).

Details: *19 miles (30 km) north of San José through Heredia and Sacramento; telephone hotline 506/192, 506/261-2619, fax 506/261-0257, www.minae.go.cr/accvc/braulio. Take a Sacramento bus from the Central Market in Heredia and continue by foot 2.5 miles (four km) to the park. By car, it's four-wheel-drive country from Sacramento to the ranger station—one terrible road in rainy season. Bring a jacket and rain gear. Open 8 A.M. to 4 P.M., closed Monday; admission $6, camping $2. Among tour agencies in San José that provide good tours to the Barva sector are Jungle Trails and Ocarina Expeditions (see Chapter 3); some area lodges also offer tours.*

Bosque de Paz Rain/Cloud Forest

This Forest of Peace has centuries-old trees, waterfalls, orchids, valleys, mountains, and rivers. Birds are abundant: frequently seen are the resplendent quetzal, red-headed barbet, emerald toucanet, black guan, collared trogon, green violet-ear hummingbird, and golden-browed chlorophonia—286 species identified so far. More than 17 miles (28 km) of well-built trails take visitors into the forest. See species such as the black-faced solitaire, ruddy-capped nightingale-thrush, red-faced spinetail, and eight of the country's 12 breeding species of warblers, including the endemic flame-throated warbler. Monkeys are here, too: spider, howler, and white-faced capuchin.

The short, easy Natural Garden Trail is between two rivers whose pools offer crystal-clear water for bathing. Forest Canopy Trail, 1.8 miles (three km), allows observation of the crowns of ancient trees. The Waterfall and Poás Volcano Lookout is for those in good physical condition. Benches along some trails allow perfect places to absorb the peace for which this place is named. Federico Gonzáles-Pinto, his wife, Vanessa, and son, Federico Jr., owners of Bosque de Paz, believe that intimate contact with nature transmits peace, and they offer their piece of heaven as a sanctuary. The hospitality they and their local staff provide in this rain and cloud forest is unsurpassed.

Bosque de Paz goals of conservation, research, and education are quietly and powerfully evident. Documentation of research done here is available to guests. The 1,730-acre (700-ha) private biological reserve serves as an important corridor between two national parks: Poás and Juan Castro Blanco. To protect more land, most earnings now go toward forest purchase. Guests can help by contributing a per-tree amount. The reserve straddles the Continental Divide, with elevations from 4,943 to 8,202 feet (1,400 to 2,500 m). While Bosque de Paz is open to one-day tours, the fortunate spend the night. The farmhouse has two cozy rooms and nine charming new rooms in a two-story addition, each with two double beds, décor enhanced with Costa Rican pottery, and forest views from windows and wide terraces. From the farmhouse dining room, where food is plentiful and delicious, Costa Rican fare with rich flavors, look out at the butterfly garden and watch for some of the 20 or so species of hummingbirds found here. Doubles are $105 per person, including lodging, meals, guided trail walks, and taxes; airport transfers are available. Reservations are necessary.

Optional tours for overnight guests include hot springs at Tabacón, Arenal or Poás Volcanoes, little-visited Juan Castro Blanco National Park, and La Selva Biological Station; or guests may enjoy white-water rafting or a boat trip to view wildlife.

Details: About 14 miles (22.5 km) north of Sarchí, between Poás Volcano and Juan Castro Blanco National Park; 1.5 hours northwest of San José, 506/234-6676, fax 506/225-0203, info@bosquedepaz.com, www.bosquedepaz.com. Day tours are $79, including transport from San José, guided walk, snack, and lunch; without transport, $35. From Sarchí, follow the road northeast toward Bajos del Toro and watch for signs.

Butterfly Farm

Owners Joris Brinkerhoff and María Sabido have created a beautiful opportunity to observe, learn about, and photograph butterflies and tropical flowers in this private reserve. An introductory video focuses on butterfly stages of life, habits, and habitats, while live specimens waft through the room and dozens of eye-catching species vie for your attention through a glass wall. An enclosed garden of native plants is home to about 1,000 breeding butterflies, some 70 species.

A two-hour guided tour touches on butterfly defense mechanisms, predators, host plants, and reproduction. It's a hands-on experience for those who choose to touch pupae, feel caterpillars, and spot butterfly eggs. See the cracker butterfly: listen for the noise that explains its name. Observe morphos, clearwings, sweethearts, swallow-tails, tigers, zebras, and the large owl eyes of the caligo. After the tour, stay as long as you like to observe or photograph the butterflies.

The Butterfly Farm began in 1990, growing out of a butterfly export company that Joris, a former Peace Corps volunteer, and María began in 1983 as a way of promoting sustainable development and protecting natural resources. It was the first commercial butter-fly farm in Latin America. From one client in England in 1984, business has expanded to clients in France, Germany, Italy, the United States, Canada, and Singapore, shipping about 12,000 pupae per month, more than 50 species. The Butterfly Farm produces only a small percentage of what it exports; most pupae come from small producers—some 120 rural families get all or part of their liveli-hood from this activity. On export days, see sorting and packing.

While survival rate of eggs in the wild is 2 percent, here it is 90 percent. Eggs develop into larvae that feed for an average of one month before forming pupae, the stage for export. Butterflies emerge from pupae in 7 to 10 days and, since transport to clients takes three days, timing is of the essence.

Some of the butterflies bred here are released to replace ones originally taken from the wild, and flora that butterflies need have been planted on the farm to create a natural butterfly refuge. Check out the Butterfly Farm website for natural history of butterflies, pho-tos, and curriculum suggestions for butterfly education.

The gift shop and snack bar, which has a view of Poás, Barva, and Irazú Volcanoes, weather permitting, has loads of butterfly handcrafts and literature, along with other natural history offerings. Look for an amazing poster of the alphabet created by patterns on butterfly wings.

Details: *La Guácima de Alajuela, 506/438-0400, fax 506/438-0300, info@butterflyfarm.co.cr, www.butterflyfarm.co.cr. Admission is $15 for adults, $7 for children 5 to 12 years old, under 5 free. Open daily 9 A.M. to 5 P.M. The last full tour begins at 3 P.M. Excellent two-hour guided tours are continuous throughout the day. A four-hour package includes transport from San José; $20, with departures at 7:20 A.M., 10 A.M., and 2 P.M. The public bus from San José to La Guácima stops about three blocks from the farm. From Alajuela, take a La Guácima Abajo public bus and ask to be let off at La Finca de Mariposas, a 40-minute ride. Driving from San José, the easiest*

IS IT A BUTTERFLY OR A MOTH?

Here are some general rules of thumb for telling the difference, though exceptions keep it challenging. Both belong to an order of insects called Lepidoptera.

- Butterflies generally have bright colors; moths have more neutral colors.
- Butterflies have straight, clublike antennae; moths usually have curved or fuzzy antennae.
- Butterflies rest with wings closed; moths rest with wings open.
- Butterflies have slender bodies; moth bodies are hairier and fatter.
- Butterflies form a hanging chrysalis; moths form a cocoon, usually found on the ground.
- Butterflies fly during the day; moths like to fly at night.

route is via the San Antonio de Belén exit off the Inter-American Highway and to La Guácima, about six miles (10 km). From Alajuela, cross the Inter-American and go to La Guácima through Ciruelas.

Chalet Tirol Hotel and Private Reserve

It looks like an Alpine village in its 5,900-foot (1,800-m) mountain setting: 10 picturesque wooden chalets with red roofs and window boxes. Across from the village square, with requisite fountain, is the churchlike Salzburg Café Concert Dinner Theater, site of musical performances that include International Music Festival artists in July and August. A sloped-roof restaurant with exquisite French cuisine and a building housing 14 suites round out the scene.

The rustic chalets, my personal favorite, face each other across a garden of tropical flowers. Double doors open onto back porches and forest, some to a small stream. Downstairs living areas have

Charming Chalet Tirol in mountain setting near Heredia

Ree Strange Sheck

carved wooden chairs, cloth-covered tables, and knickknacks that add a homey touch. Up narrow wooden stairs is a cozy bedroom under the rafters. These rooms were hand-painted and decorated by María Batalla, co-owner with husband Alvaro. Spacious suites, added later, have wood-burning fireplaces, each room with a different decor. Chalets and suites have telephones and TV. Chalets and junior suites are $90 for two; the honeymoon suite is $120.

Chalet Tirol's award-winning French restaurant offers gracious service and a charming atmosphere—good music, fires in the fireplaces. For more casual dining, try the pizza parlor, with its wood-fired oven.

Here in this cloud-forest setting, ride horses, play tennis, and explore paths in the 38-acre (15-ha) private forest to see ferns, bromeliads, orchids, mosses, toucanets, motmots, hummingbirds, and trogons. Or venture to Braulio Carrillo National Park with a guide. Tirol's A Walk in the Clouds tour begins with a tractor-trailer ride to the upper reaches of the park and continues with a guided hike in cloud forest—sightings perhaps of resplendent quetzals, sooty robins, redstarts, violet-sabrewing hummingbirds, or white-faced monkeys. Then it's back via hotel transport to a gourmet lunch; $60 with transportation from San José, $45 without transport. Horseback Riding in the Clouds, led by a local Spanish-speaking cowboy, goes by a rural school and across dairy farms to a viewpoint of the Central Valley and into cloud forest; $48 with transport from San José, $35 without, box lunch included.

Something new is the **BIOPLANET** Institute, taking shape beside Chalet Tirol. This exhibition-education project focusing on biodiversity incorporates some of the extraordinary Whitten Entomological Collection of more than one million tropical forest insects and other arthropods. The Whitten collection, exhibited previously in Costa Rica as Jewels of the Rain Forest, is a marvel—highly recommended, $10 per person.

The Batalla family also operates Dundee Ranch Hotel near Orotina.

Details: 45 minutes north of San José; 506/267-6222, fax 506/267-6229, info@chalet-tirol.com, www.chalet-tirol.com. From Heredia, continue past Universidad Nacional and follow the road until it ends; turn right and follow signs to San Rafael; the hotel is a mile beyond Castillo Country Club.

INBioparque

This ambitious project is a work in progress, but enough is finished already to recommend this center of education and information, a project of Costa Rica's internationally recognized National Biodiversity Institute (INBio). A private, nonprofit organization, INBio works to achieve conservation of natural resources through research, education, and search for sustainable uses of nature's bounty. It is involved in inventory of species, research, training, and a link with companies doing bioprospecting, which look to flora and fauna as sources for drugs, agricultural products, cosmetics, etc. (see Chapter 2.)

INBioparque is geared to share the ABC's of biodiversity with Costa Ricans and international visitors through interactive displays, videos, exhibits, and trails through different habitats. Visit the Parataxonomist House for a glimpse of how specially trained locals live and work in the field as they collect specimens in parks and reserves—the dirty boots, the insect boxes, the pressed plants. Another module focuses on contamination of the environment as part of natural resource management. Move to the large map on the floor and choose a conservation area to find out about its resources. Another INBioparque goal is to serve as a gateway to the national parks and reserves, which play a key role in conserving the country's biodiversity. An information office has data on these conserved areas—services available, trails, even lodging possibilities near them.

After visiting the bio-exhibits, experience different habitats on the four trails through the grounds: tropical rain forest, tropical dry forest, forest native to the Central Valley, and an aquatic habitat. Walk through a butterfly garden. Visitors can have a basic 2.5-hour guided tour through exhibits and trails for $3 or take a self-guided tour using a pamphlet, $1.50. Ask about other options, such as a tour without the trail walk or longer trail walks.

Hungry? The restaurant serves breakfast and dinner, delicious Costa Rican food prepared to the specifications of well-known Hans van der Wielen, owner of nearby Bougainvillea Santo Domingo Hotel. *Details: 15 minutes north of San José; 506/244-4730, fax 506/255-4790, inbioparque@inbio.ac.cr, www.inbio.ac.cr/inbioparque. Open daily 7:30 A.M. to 4 P.M.; admission $18 for adults, children $9. Inquire about discounted rates for families of four or more persons. Transport is provided from San José: $10 adults, $5 children. From San José, head north through Tibas to Santo Domingo de Heredia. INBioparque is 500 meters north and 250 meters west of the local cemetery. From Heredia, head southeast toward San José and watch for signs in Santo Domingo.*

Poás Volcano National Park

Stand at the edge of a multicolored crater almost a mile (1.3 km) in diameter, look down 984 feet (300 m), and watch geyserlike eruptions that leave no doubt this mountain still has something to say.

Of the five craters on this 8,884-foot (2,708-m) giant, two get the most attention: the large active crater responsible for more recent lava, rocks, ash, and steam, and the extinct one that now cradles beautiful Botos Lake. The lookout at the edge of the active crater affords a spectacular view of a greenish hot-water lake. The earlier you go, the better chance you have of an unimpeded view. Clouds that drift in as the day progresses can obscure the bottom. Don't give up easily, however, if it is socked in—glimpses come and go. While you wait for a column of mud and water to shoot into the air, notice the fumaroles and look for small measuring devices scattered around the crater. Costa Rica has fine volcanological and seismological observatories whose staffs keep close watch at Poás and other sites around the country.

Depending on wind direction, you may get a good whiff of sulfur—a 1994 eruption, the last important one so far, increased production of sulfurous gas. Emissions sometimes damage vegetation both in the park and nearby; look for evidence of the acid rain, especially on the huge leaves of the *sombrilla de pobre* (*Gunnera insignis*) lining the walk to the crater—known in English as poor man's umbrella.

Trails lead through shrubs, dwarf forest, and cloud forest covered with epiphytes. Because of volcanic activity, hunting, and deforestation outside the park, few larger mammals remain. Coyotes, rabbits, weasels, frogs, and toads are common, and at least 79 bird species are at home here. A park ranger reported he has seen quetzals fly over the road between the park entrance and administration building in early morning. Hummingbirds are everywhere; you might also spot an emerald toucanet, brown robin, black guan, or masked woodpecker. At the picnic area, watch for yellow-thighed finches and sooty robins.

The trail to Botos Lake, named for the Botos people who lived on the north slope when the Spaniards arrived, begins near the active crater viewpoint; it's an easy 20-minute climb to the extinct crater. At this altitude, though, take your time, enjoy the tangled shrub or dwarf-forest vegetation, and hear the tantalizing song of hidden birds. Amphitheater seating beside this rain-replenished lake offers a vantage point for bird observation and for remembering that the crater walls around you, now tranquil and forest-covered, were once witness to fiery emanations. My favorite trail is Escalonia, which begins at the picnic area. Trees soar overhead, bromeliads abound, and trail markers full of poetry salute the forest's magnificence.

The visitor center's first floor houses an exhibit and restrooms. On the second floor are a restaurant operated by Café Britt and a private insect exhibit and hummingbird observation area, admission about $.50. There is a path for the physically impaired, and a ramp enables wheelchair access to the crater viewing area. Created in 1971, the park is now 16,076 acres (6,506 ha) in size. Bring a jacket and rain gear (especially May to November; rainfall is 138 inches (3,500 mm). Temperatures average between 50°F and 57°F (10°C and 14°C), but bright, sunny days can be 70°F (21°C).

Details: 90 minutes from San José, 23 miles (37 km) north of Alajuela; telephone hotline 506/192, 506/442-7041, fax 506/441-0308, accvccr@racsa.co.cr, www.minae.go.cr/accvc.PNPoas. Open daily 8 A.M. to 4:30 P.M. (closes at 3:30 P.M. May to November), admission $6. A public bus leaves San José daily at 8:30 A.M. and leaves the park at 2:30 P.M. (see bus info in Appendix A). By car from Alajuela, go either through San Pedro de Poás and Fraijanes or through Heredia and Vara Blanca. Parking costs a little extra, but it goes to the Red Cross. San José agencies and local lodges offer Poás tours: check to see how much time a tour allows there—some give barely time to peer into the crater; others allow more and include a naturalist guide.

Villablanca and Los Angeles Cloud Forest

Villablanca was built to resemble a small village: an 1800s colonial settlement centered on the *casa grande* (big house), the dwelling for the family that owned the land. The landowners in this case are former Costa Rican president Rodrigo Carazo and his wife, Estrella, who bought the site in 1989.

Individual *casitas* (little houses) where workers would have lived serve as charming guest cottages. They have the look and feel of adobe, with rough white plaster and blue trim. Some are suites with separate sitting rooms. All have corner fireplaces with *bancos* on each side, rocking chairs in front of the hearth, and writing desks. Colorful comforters on beds and bright rugs lend a cozy look. Nights can be cool here, so the comforters and fireplaces are not merely decorative. The big house contains a dining room, bar, small library, and sitting areas. Upstairs are five rooms. Double rooms are

$99. There's also a dormitory-style building (shared baths) for student groups. Meals are buffet-style.

The 48 *casitas* and four family villas have small gardens in front and a 2,000-acre (800-ha) forest out back. The Los Angeles Cloud Forest is wet, exuberant, and green. Two easy one-mile (two-km) trails are walkways of wooden planks covered with wire to prevent slipping. The forest is home to about 280 bird species, including bare-necked umbrella birds, tawny-capped euphonias, black guans, great curassows, chachalacas, and hummingbirds, along with three species of monkeys, sloths, raccoons, squirrels, *tepezcuintles*, ocelots, and snakes. Tree ferns are magnificent. A guided walk on these trails is $24. A more difficult 3.7-mile (six-km) trail is open for solo walks. The cloud-forest elevation is about 3,600 feet (1,100 m). Driest months are March to May; go prepared for rain.

A Canopy Fair allows visitors to travel through tree crowns, viewing the forest from seven platforms in five trees. After a guided walk to the site, visitors climb to the first platform, at 33 feet (10 m), and move to other platforms via cable. The highest platform is 72 feet (22 m); the longest distance between platforms is 345 feet (105 m). Cost is $39. From a *mirador* about a mile from the main house you can see Arenal Volcano, Lake Nicaragua, and the Plains of San Carlos, on a clear day.

Visit the farm's cultivated land (coffee, sugarcane, vegetable crops) and dairy operation that provides the dining room's milk and cheese. Rent a horse to explore the farm or the forest. Villablanca can arrange car and driver to destinations such as Tabacón, Poás, Arenal, and Sarchí. Day visitors are welcome. A one-day tour from San José includes guided forest walk Canopy Fair, or horseback ride, transfers, and lunch. These activities are also available by reservation to those who come on their own.

Details: 12 miles (19 km) north of San Ramón, 50 miles (80 km) northwest of San José; 506/228-4603, fax 506/228-4004, info@villablanca-costarica.com, www.villablanca-costarica.com. By car from San Ramón, turn off just past km 8 at the guard station. Villablanca/San José transfers available, $30 per person, as are transfers from San Ramón, $15.

Valle Escondido Lodge

Combine fantastic forest treks in a private forest preserve with walks through acres of ornamental plants grown for export, and come back to attractive quarters with a magical view of a valley and green, green mountains that appear and disappear in the mists. The 31 rooms open onto a covered terrace, complete with rocking chairs and, in the evenings, large frogs. Rooms are spacious and bright, with beautiful polished hardwood furniture. Bathrooms have big lighted mirrors and bidets; doubles are $80.

Valle Escondido ("Hidden Valley") is 272 acres (110 ha), about half of which is a private reserve of primary and secondary forest. Elevation here is from 1,772 to 2,034 feet (540 to 620 m); the temperature ranges from 68°F to 86°F (20°C to 30°C).

Owner Marco Hidalgo grows and exports ornamental plants to Italy, the Netherlands, and Belgium—guests can visit greenhouses, fields of plants such as shefleras, palms, crotons, and *itabo* (a standard along Costa Rican byways) and packing sheds. One greenhouse is exclusively for orchids.

An abundance of mountain streams flow through the reserve, accessed by some 12 miles (20 km) of hiking trails on the other side of the plantations. The tall forest's understory is a natural tropical greenhouse with heliconias and fascinating tree roots. I watched one masked tityra feed another. An aracari, a member of the toucan family, frustrated my attempts to photograph him but allowed wonderful glimpses. Near one trail is a huge tree with enormous buttresses where bats live. You might see monkeys, a sloth, coatis; ask for the bird list, which includes red-legged honeycreepers, green-crowned brilliants, buff-throated saltators, and golden-crowned spadebills.

If horseback riding is your thing, six miles (10 km) of trails suitable for horses await. Take off through the farm to the forest and along rushing mountain rivers to incredible viewpoints, $20 each for two persons. Rainforest tour is $20; rates drop with additional persons. Guests can also fish in the pond or walk through treetops on hanging bridges.

Optional tours are to Arenal and hot springs at Tabacón, only an hour away, for $70, or to Caño Negro, a full day for $90, including lunch, transport, and boat ride on the Río Frío. Other possibilities are La Fortuna Waterfall and Venado Caverns.

The restaurant, a short walk downhill from the rooms, offers an international menu with Italian specialties—a feast for the eyes as well as the palate. Take binoculars to the dining room to enjoy birds in the back garden while you eat. The restaurant is open to the public, a five-minute drive from the highway turnoff. A swimming pool and hot tub have fantastic mountain views.

Day visitors are welcome for the rain forest or ornamental plant tour. A two-night package includes lodging, meals, walking tour, ornamental plant visit, horseback riding, Arenal-Tabacón tour, and San José transfer, $335 per person, double occupancy. A two-night package is $171.

Details: 56 miles (90 km) northwest of San José, 20 miles (32 km) north of San Ramón; 506/231-0906, fax 506/232-9591, hotel@valleescondido.com, www.valleescondido.com. Transfers arranged. If you drive, head north off of the Inter-American at San Ramón and watch for the hotel's sign on the right. From La Fortuna, go south through La Tigra and watch for the sign at San Lorenzo. Or take the San Ramón-La Fortuna public bus and get off at the sign: the hotel is almost a mile (1.6 km) down the road.

World of Snakes (El Mundo de las Serpientes)

Here in the hills of Grecia is a terrific snake exhibition and breeding and research center. More than 40 species (also including caimans, iguanas, and frogs) are in large outdoor enclosures, about 5 feet high (1.5 m) with solid walls on the bottom half and reinforced glass and mesh screens on the upper half to allow spectacular, safe observation even for the squeamish. See the endangered ringed tree boa, colorful eyelash vipers, false corals, bushmasters, tropical rattlesnakes, even a Burmese albino python. Most species are natives, but visitors also find beautiful and interesting snakes from Vietnam, Australia, New Guinea, Brazil, Mexico, and Africa.

The project, begun by Robert Meidinger, an Austrian-born herpetologist, focuses on protecting Costa Rica's snakes as well as endangered species from other countries. The exhibition area is a key player on the educational front. A one-hour tour explains these animals' role in the ecosystem, their habits and behavior. It teaches how to distinguish venomous from nonvenomous snakes and how to behave in an encounter with a snake. Prevention of both habitat destruction and indiscriminate killing of snakes is a goal. Already, educational efforts at the local level are paying off. Some snakes that would have been killed are brought here: venomous ones are kept and nonvenomous ones are sometimes released on farms whose owners welcome them: snakes are natural predators to rodents.

World of Snakes has a breeding program that allows sale of snakes in compliance with CITES regulations. So instead of dealing with poachers and contributing to an illegal animal trade, buyers can obtain captive-bred snakes legally. Snakes for this project were captured according to wildlife regulations; all foreign species came with CITES documents.

The project's research phase aims to expand basic knowledge about snakes—mainly species description, range, habitats, and ecological importance—to lesser-known topics such as behavior and reproduction patterns. Knowledgeable, enthusiastic guides tell you that only 19 of the 138 species of snakes in Costa Rica are poisonous; their tales of breeding and behavior characteristics are fascinating. Colors and markings of some of these tropical snakes are outstanding; see for yourself how expert some species are at camouflage. Visitors are allowed to touch certain species under careful supervision.

Details: *One mile (1.5 km) south of Grecia on the old road to Alajuela; telephone/fax 506/494-3700, snakes@racsa.co.cr. Open daily 8 A.M. to 4 P.M.; admission $11 adults, $6 children (under six years free). To get there, go about two blocks past the back of Grecia's metal church and turn east 1.2 miles (two km) toward Tacares and Alajuela. It is across from Poró sawmill (Aserradero El Poró). A stop here can be combined with a visit to Sarchí or Poás Volcano.*

Zoo Ave, Wildlife Conservation Park

Walkways wind through beautifully landscaped grounds home to more than 800 birds representing 100 species (80 of them native), four monkey species, a crocodile named Cornelius that measures about 10 feet (3 m), boa constrictors, tapir, green iguanas, and turtles, along with a few non-native species. Educational signs in English and Spanish and large, well-done enclosures make visiting Zoo Ave a treat. Birds include scarlet, great green, and blue and gold macaws; chestnut-mandibled and keel-billed toucans; the resplendant quetzal; ornate-hawk eagle; long-tailed manakin; scarlet-thighed dacnis; six parrot and five parakeet species; and many more birds often so elusive in the rain forest. Get close-up photos of macaws, which preen and squawk right beside the path, and of nimble spider monkeys as they move from tree to tree in a near-natural setting. New is a gigantic mural showing all the birds of Costa Rica in their actual size.

This is the best zoological park in the country. It occupies 10 acres (4 ha). The remaining 25 acres (10 ha) are being reforested with native trees that provide food and nesting sites for wild birds. Zoo Ave is operated by the nonprofit Nature Restoration Foundation, created by Dennis and Susan Janik, who started Zoo Ave in 1990.

Behind the scenes is an animal hospital, where injured and orphaned animals are cared for until they can be returned to the wild—Zoo Ave is an officially recognized wildlife rescue center. Those who cannot be released become part of the breeding program. Former pets also find a home here. Since 1990, 18 species of rehabilitated birds have been successfully released into the wild as well as 11 species of captive-born birds; other released animals include foxes, anteaters, sloths, porcupines, raccoons, iguanas, caimans, and turtles. All adult monkeys here were once pets; although they cannot survive in the wild, the goal is to release their offspring. Sixty-five native monkeys are bred and maintained in large areas where they have room to move and interact with each other.

Seventy native species are currently in captive breeding programs. Not all are in immediate danger of extinction but all are species whose wild populations are at historically low levels. Some face a loss of genetic diversity in parts of the country: the goal is to release animals into these genetically isolated populations. Endangered scarlet macaws and great green macaws are bred here. I felt privileged to see a pair of two-month-old great green macaws in the bird nursery. As few as 30 to 35 pairs are breeding in the wild in Costa Rica.

In 1998 Zoo Ave built a biological station at San Josecito in the Golfo Dulce area, bordering Piedras Blancas National Park (see

Chapter 14). It is the release site for captive-born scarlet macaws and other birds and reptile species. The plan is to release 10 to 20 scarlet macaws each year for the next 15 to 20 years in an attempt to reestablish a wild population in the park, where they have been locally extinct for about 40 years.

On a stroll through Zoo Ave grounds see released animals that choose to stay: chachalacas, toucans, owls, crested guan, white-fronted parrots, great currasows, and a collared aracari (which has paired with a wild bird).

Ultimate success of release programs depends on enforcement of wildlife protection laws, habitat restoration and/or protection, and educational programs. Some 16,000 schoolchildren learn during class visits to Zoo Ave. To help, look for a donation box near the exit or contact the Nature Restoration Foundation, c/o Zoo Ave, Dept. 280, P.O. Box 025216, Miami, FL 33102, or through Zoo Ave's addresses below.

There is a small snack bar, but visitors are welcome to bring a lunch and spend the day. Leave enough time—observing wildlife is quite a different thing from seeing wildlife.

Details: Located in La Garita de Alajuela, 30 minutes from San José and less than 15 minutes from Alajuela; 506/433-8989, fax 506/433-9140, info@zooave.org, www.zooave.org. Open daily 9 A.M. to 5 P.M.; admission $9 for adults, children $1. A taxi from Alajuela is about $3. By bus, in Alajuela, take La Garita or Dulce Nombre bus (every 30 minutes), both of which pass in front of Zoo Ave. By car, from the Inter-American, take the Atenas/Punta Leona exit west of Juan Santamaría International Airport (watch for a large Zoo Ave sign), turn right, and continue 1.2 miles (two km) to Zoo Ave.

GUIDES AND OUTFITTERS

Tour companies in San José offer day tours and packages to most of the sites listed here. Private reserves have their own guides, but parks do not; so if you go on your own, you can arrange for a naturalist guide through one of the agencies in Chapter 3.

CAMPING

Camping is permitted at the Barva Sector of Braulio Carrillo National Park. Facilities include a covered picnic area and bathrooms. Bring your own gear. Park admission is $6, camping $2 per person per day. For information and reservations, call the parks' telephone hotline 506/192, 506/261-2619, fax 506/261-0257. For a description of Barva, refer to "Nature and Adventure Sights."

LODGING

Delightful **El Cafetal Inn** is in Santa Eulalia de Atenas, 506/446-5785, fax 506/446-7028, cafetal@racsa.co.cr, www.cafetal.com. The spectacular two-story house with rounded glass corner alcoves overlooks the Colorado River Valley and fields of coffee and sugarcane, with views of Alajuela, Heredia, and Poás, Barva, and Irazú Volcanoes. Lee and Romy Rodríguez greet you at the door and treat you as an honored guest throughout your stay. It's a classy place—shiny marble floors, soothing waterfall in the two-story atrium, light and airy rooms, deep cushions on wicker furniture, and lots of floor-to-ceiling windows. Meals are a treat. Romy dons the chef's hat and cooks with a flair. Eat at the poolside restaurant down a path through coffee plants: try La Negrita coffee grown on the farm. Choose from among 21 tours: Poás Volcano; orchid, butterfly, iguana, and coffee farms; Los Chorros Waterfall, Grecia/Sarchí, Tortuga Island, and Carara; go to San José for a city tour and Alajuela for a night mariachi tour. Try white-water rafting or sportfishing. There are ten rooms, doubles start at $87 including full breakfast and taxes. El Cafetal is 20 minutes from the international airport. Routes go through Atenas toward Santa Eulalia de Atenas, or from the Inter-American Highway, turn just west of the Grecia-Sarchí intersection.

    Finca Rosa Blanca Country Inn, outside Santa Barbara de Heredia, 506/269-9392, fax 506/269-9555, info@finca-rblanca.co.cr; www.finca-rblanca.co.cr, is 30 minutes from San José and 15 minutes from the airport. The white two-story building with its domed tower room soars above surrounding coffee plantations. Enormous windows open to dramatic views of the Central Valley, Irazú Volcano, picturesque towns, and landscaped grounds. Inside, rich-colored tropical hardwoods gleam in floors, ceilings, and doors. A curved, cushioned *banco* (long seat) in the atrium-like, two-story living area faces a unique freestanding fireplace. Each of six bedrooms is unique. El Campo is famous for its mural: the actual landscape visible from the window continues onto the wall in a painting done by local artists. Down a spiral staircase from the glass-walled tower bedroom of Rosa Blanca Suite is an unforgettable rain-forest bathroom where a waterfall drops over stones into a two-person pool for bathing. Two separate villas have two bedrooms, a sitting area with distinctive arched windows, and kitchen. A huge deck affords panoramic valley views. Murals and hand-painted Talavera tiles add accents. Doubles are $155 to $240, including breakfast. Enjoy a romantic four-course evening dinner for $26, with dishes that include produce from an organic garden.

The spectacular pool is spring fed, no chemicals. Explore the grounds (where more than 200 fruit trees attract birds), walk a trail where butterflies await, visit the river, or ride horses—perhaps to Barva. Glenn and Teri Jampol and staff arrange special tours and have a van and English-speaking driver available. Glenn initiated a profit-sharing system with the local employees, and the hotel is helping create a library for the small primary school nearby. Guests can help purchase books.

Juan Bo Mountain Restaurant and Cabins, nine miles (15 km) from Poás Volcano National Park, 506/482-2099, is a tiny jewel at the edge of a dairy farm, about 1.2 miles (two km) north of Vara Blanca on the road to San Miguel. The mountain view is spectacular and the dining room warm and cozy, full of good smells and outstanding food. Owner Tatiana offers two charming cabins that feature polished wood floors, brightly upholstered bamboo furniture, and big windows; double $50. Only a 10-minute walk from the cabins are 140 acres (57 ha) of virgin forest with rivers, waterfalls, and verdant vegetation. If you can't stay, this is a delightful stop for a meal, hot coffee or *agua dulce,* and fresh tortillas or dessert. Juan Bo is 90 minutes from San José.

La Providencia Ecological Reserve is near the entrance to Poás Volcano National Park, cellular 506/387-3957, fax 506/232-2498—mark faxes "for Amalia." The farm has 740 acres (300 ha) of primary forest. Forest denizens include quetzals, ocelots, coyotes, armadillos, emerald toucanets, peccaries, hummingbirds, and tayras. Giant ferns abound; find magnificent oak forests, one of which is white because of acid rain from the volcano. Elevation is 8,200 feet (2,500 m). Visitors are welcome for both day tours, $20, and overnight stays. Not much English is spoken here.

Six rustic wooden cabins (generator electricity) spaced on the hillside start at $42 for a double; a *casita* sleeps up to 10. In the small restaurant, hearty, typical meals are cooked on a wood stove, milk comes fresh from the dairy, and homemade cheese is served. Breakfast is $6, lunch or dinner $10, including wine or beer. A three-hour horseback ride ($20) takes visitors on the slopes of the volcano through primary and secondary forest and to waterfalls, *páramo* (with its subalpine vegetation), and view points. Owner Max Blanco, who has owned La Providencia for 30 years, has put in a trout lake for fishing. Bring warm clothes and rain gear. To get there, turn left at the green gate to Poás park and follow a gravel road for 1.5 miles (2.4 km).

A delightful hotel in a garden setting, **Orquídeas Inn,** 506/433-9346, fax 506/433-9740, orchid@racsa.co.cr, www.hotels.co.cr/orquideas, is 10 minutes north of Alajuela on the road to Poás and Grecia. The 18 rooms in the original inn feature arched windows that let in lots of light, with colorful bedspreads, fresh flowers, and glass-topped tables with antique Singer sewing-machine bases. The inn's expansion to an adjacent property has added 12 rooms and suites, most in the luxury class. Owners Fred and Darlys McCloud cook up some mean Buffalo-style chicken wings, available in the Marilyn Monroe Bar. Guitarist/composer/singer Rolando and daughter Leidy give a great evening performance most weekends. Relax in one of two swimming pool areas with views to Barva Volcano and walk along paths bordered by eye-catching tropical plants on this 10-acre (four-ha) estate. Staff arrange van and driver for custom tours apart from a long list of day trips that include Poás, Sarchí, Los Chorros Waterfall, Zoo Ave, Zarcero, Arenal Volcano, and Tabacón hot springs. Ride horses. Double rooms are from $39 to $79; rooms away from the road are quieter. Suites are from $99 to $200; a geodesic dome suite with kitchenette, $130. Breakfast is included; dine in company of free-flying toucans that have made the Orquídeas home. No children under 10.

Charming **Poás Volcano Lodge,** at Vara Blanca, 10 miles (16 km) from the volcano, telephone 506/482-2194, fax 506/482-2513, poasvl@racsa.co.cr, www.arweb.com/poas, is an invigorating 6,234 feet (1,900 m) high. The large farmhouse has an English-manor flavor. A sunny sitting room has a sunken conversation area and fireplace. Two rooms with shared bath and a master suite with private bath, king-size bed, and double glass doors opening onto a terrace are in the main building. Six rooms in two other buildings hint of English or Welsh cottages. Each room is different, with creative use of wood and rock walls; all windows open to a landscaped garden. Poás dominates the horizon. Rooms with shared bath $55, rooms with private bath start at $65, and master suite $100, including country breakfast. Light lunches or dinners served on request.

Take guided bird-watching walks in forest patches on the large farm, with a chance to observe such species as the golden-browed chlorophonia, black-faced solitaires, hummingbirds, and quetzals; epiphytes flourish. Horseback riding is available, and the lodge is 10 minutes from three-tiered Peace Waterfall.

Tuetal Lodge is north of Alajuela in Tuetal Norte, 10 miles (six km) from the airport, tel/fax 506/442-1804, tuetal@racsa.co.cr, www.islandnet.com/~tuetal. Owners Arnold and Carolyn Wiens offer six pleasant rooms, with cable TV and solar-hot water, that open onto tropical gardens. Doubles with kitchenettes are $45, $40 without. The lodge is on 7 acres (2.8 ha), with a pretty swimming pool. Breakfast is served in a pleasant restaurant. Tours arranged. No credit cards.

An upscale country inn on a lush plantation, **Vista del Valle Plantation Inn,** 506/381-0881, airport 506/450-0800, fax 506/451-1165, mibrejo@racsa.co.cr; www.vistadelvalle.com, is 20 minutes from Alajuela and the airport. Palms embellish tropical gardens around the swimming pool, hot tub, main house, and five cottages. Beautiful hardwoods, glass, and stone complement the high ceilings and open floor plan of the two-story house, where two guest rooms have a balcony with views to garden, mountains, and coffee and citrus plantations. The rate for doubles is $110. Charming cottages have an openness to the outdoors, wide verandas and some kitchenettes, from $120 to $145. A full breakfast is included. With prior notice, owners Johanna and Mike Bresnan provide other meals. Ask them about their work with the local community.

Explore paths that wind through the gardens, plantation, or 25-acre (10-ha) private forest reserve—see a 300-foot (90-m) waterfall. Tours by horseback are $15 per hour. The inn furnishes a van and bilingual driver to guests for $28 per day and offers tours to Sarchí, Poás and Barva Volcanoes, Butterfly Farm, Zoo Ave, Tabacón and Arenal, Orosi Valley, and Los Angeles Cloud Forest. Half-day trips are from $50; full-day excursions, from $95. Rafting trips are arranged. The inn is 20 minutes from the airport and has complimentary transfer.

Xandari Plantation, three miles (five km) from Alajuela, 506/443-2020, 800/686-7879, fax 506/442-4847, hotel@xandari. com, www.xandari.com, is a classy tropical paradise designed by owners architect/designer Sherrill and artist Charlene Broudy. The 16 white villas against the backdrop of forested mountains and coffee plantations are stunning. Spacious high-ceilinged rooms with touches of stained glass, dramatic art, custom-designed furniture, sculpture, refrigerator, bar sink, fresh flowers, and tropical plants open onto large private outdoor terraces with spectacular daytime views and romantic sunsets. Health-conscious meals include fruits and vegetables from the plantation's gardens.

Hike on two miles (three km) of scenic trails, experience the magic of bathing in a secluded river pool, go bird-watching, meditate, have a picnic by any of five waterfalls, or ride horses along country roads to small villages. The hotel has two 60-foot-long lap pools, a library, open-air exercise rancho, hot tub, and therapeutic massage. Villas are $150; with kitchenettes, $215; breakfast and airport transfer included (15 minutes from airport). There is a considerable low-season discount. Tours arranged.

FOOD

As you move through this area, you will find lots of small roadside restaurants that serve good local food. In the Poás area, strawberries flourish in the fields, and signs advertising *fresas* show where you can buy some. Strawberry milkshakes are terrific. Around La Garita de Alajuela, restaurants that specialize in corn dishes *(maiz)* are along the road. In Sarchi, the handcrafts town, try one of the restaurants in Plaza de la Artesanía or the one adjoining the Joaquín Chaverri store and factory. The lodging places listed here have excellent food.

The restaurant at Dutch-owned **Bougainvillea Santo Domingo Hotel,** 506/244-1414, serves superb international cuisine in a stylish country inn setting—tablecloths, stemware, bone china. It is in Santo Domingo de Heredia with free hourly shuttle service from San José, 15 minutes away. The hotel is surrounded by 10 acres (4 ha) of gardens.

The heavenly smells that greet you on entering **Juan Bo Mountain Restaurant,** 506/482-2099, set the stage for a memorable meal including soups, vegetarian sandwiches, flavorful beef dishes, and great desserts. Peaceful dairyland in this high-country setting is front stage, with rich forest beyond. Try the *campesino* drink *agua dulce* here, and homemade tortillas. Juanbo is nine miles (15 km) from Poás. Open Monday through Friday 11 A.M. to 8 P.M., opens earlier on Saturday and Sunday.

La Casa del Café, 506/449-5152, is at the intersection of roads from Alajuela and Grecia on the way to Poás Volcano. Set amid fields of coffee on the Doka Estate, the coffeehouse menu offers its coffees and espresso, and you can buy coffee beans here. Find out what a *cocomo* drink is. Stopping here allows you to get leisurely views and photos of the countryside, hard to do otherwise because of narrow, winding roads and traffic.

La Colina, on the Inter-American west of the San Ramón intersection, serves top-quality Costa Rican dishes. The *gallo de picadillo de papa* (tortilla with potato filling) or *gallo de arracache* is great for a snack, even for breakfast. The *torta de yuca* is a treat. Any chicken dish is excellent, or try the *casado* with meat, rice and beans, and plantains. Order *agua dulce con leche* and coconut *cajeta*.

For Italian fare, try the restaurant at **Hotel Valle Escondido,** 506/231-0906, open daily 7 A.M. to 8 P.M. Also find Costa Rican fare —several *yuca* specialties as well as a scrumptious heart-of-palm salad. Only a mile (1.5 km) from the turnoff, 20 miles (32 km) northwest of San Ramón, it's a good stop if you are heading toward La Fortuna from this area.

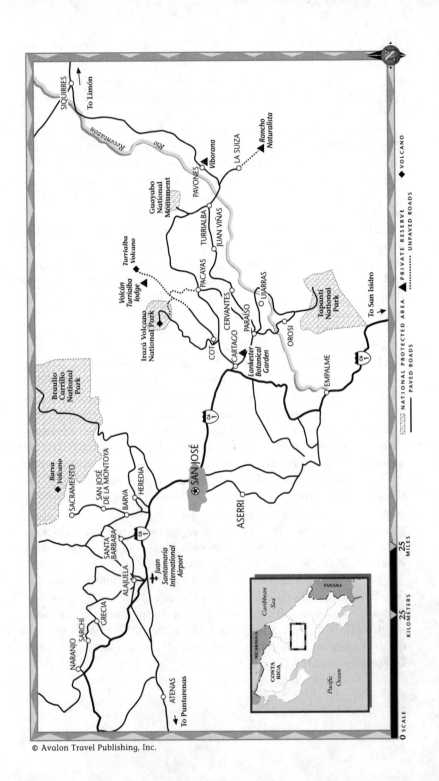

© Avalon Travel Publishing, Inc.

CHAPTER 6

Central Valley—East: Cartago, Orosi Valley, Turrialba Areas

Though the Central Valley (Meseta Central) has been the center of population in the country since colonial times, you will still find rural flavor and mostly small towns. In this higher eastern valley across the Continental Divide from San José is Cartago, the first capital of Costa Rica; in the eyes of the people this region is still the religious center since the basilica honoring the country's patron saaint, Our Lady of the Angels, is here, as well as the country's oldest churches.

Mountains, rivers, lakes, and valleys lie along what once was the main road between the Central Valley and the Caribbean port of Limón. When the faster highway opened through Braulio Carrillo National Park, traffic lessened, though travelers to Cerro de la Muerte and points south still start through Cartago. The area has superb adventure and natural history destinations.

LAY OF THE LAND

Huge sugarcane plantations, at times expansive fields of pink when abloom, and fields of coffee climb up and down the slopes. Volcanic soils produce beautiful vegetables below the craters of

Irazú and Turrialba Volcanoes. See blue-gray fields of cabbage and white-blossomed fields of potatoes; 90 percent of the country's potatoes come from here, which is why people from Cartago are called *paperos* (potato farmers). In rainy season see plastic tents covering onions laid in fields to dry. Roadside stands, especially on weekends, display some of the largest cauliflower in existence along with other produce. Dairy cattle dot pastured hillsides. Rushing rivers, waterfalls, volcanoes, and forested slopes round out the landscape.

Though nature/adventure destinations are day trips from San José and the western part of the *meseta,* many travelers choose Turrialba or Orosí Valley areas as a base of operations as they explore the region's mountains, rivers, and trails. If you don't have a car, public buses and taxis can get you from place to place.

You can visit **Cartago** (population 33,068), 14 miles (23 km) southeast of San José, on your way to Irazú, Turrialba, or the Orosi Valley. Its main attractions, other than being an extremely pleasant town, are remnants of the colonial heritage and the basilica for the country's patron saint. Now capital of Cartago Province, the town was founded in 1563. On Avenida 2/Calle 2, ruins of a stone church, **Ruinas de la Parroquia,** surround a peaceful garden. During the colonial period this parish church, founded in 1575, was reconstructed several times, having been almost destroyed by an 1841 earthquake. But it was a 1910 quake that brought rebuilding efforts to a halt. In front of the ruins a colonial cobblestone street is exposed.

Two blocks farther on Avenida 2 is **Basílica de Nuestra Señora de los Angeles,** the most famous church in the country, which honors La Negrita, Costa Rica's patron saint: Our Lady of the Angels. It is built over the rock where the tiny stone image of a black Virgin first appeared to Juana Pereira, a young wood gatherer, in 1635. (See the rock downstairs to the left of the altar. The image is above the altar.) Cases along walls in the anteroom contain countless tokens celebrating miracles attributed to her. Outside, behind the basilica, the faithful and the hopeful come to holy water that flows from a spring. On August 2 all roads lead to Cartago, as half a million pilgrims gather at the shrine for the Day of Our Lady of the Angels, many having come on foot over long distances.

Ree Strange Sheck

Basílica de Nuestra Señora de los Angeles in Cartago

The road from Cartago to Turrialba is spectacular as it winds up and over the mountains. Agricultural lands around **Juan Viñas** are among the most beautiful in Costa Rica. Fields of sugarcane wave across this top-of-the-world setting. Then comes the winding descent into the Turrialba Valley. A back door snakes through San Isidro de Coronado and Rancho Redondo, dairy country, and oak forests often shrouded in mist. I was once on this road on Corpus Christi Sunday. Flowers strewn in the road marked the path of religious processions in village after village. In one, a milk cow stood in the middle of the road eating the flower petals while worshippers sang in a nearby church.

The town of **Turrialba** (population 33,013), center of a rich agricultural region, is increasingly a destination for nature and adventure travelers. No need for an alarm clock here—at 6 A.M., three strong blasts of the town's fire alarm do the trick. Once you're up, there's plenty to do. Kayakers and white-water rafters use the town as a base for forays on the Reventazón and Pacuare Rivers. Its location is ideal for those interested in archaeology, agriculture, and nature. Turrialba is 40 miles (64 km) from San José.

131

CATIE (east of Turrialba on the main highway), 506/556-6431, fax 506/556-1533, www.catie.ac.cr, is an agricultural education, extension, and research center. Studies focus on agroforestry, dairy and beef livestock, cacao, coffee, plantains, spices, fruit trees, and *pejibaye* (peach palm). Students from more than 34 nations hold master's degrees from its programs in agriculture and natural resources. Tours include a forest walk or a chance to learn about plant collections, the seed bank, and agroforestry projects; reservations are required. CATIE is the Spanish acronym for Tropical Agronomic Research and Education Center.

The other center of nature and adventure tourism is between Cartago and Tapantí National Park in the Orosi Valley, where you find big rivers, lakes formed by hydroelectric projects, fantastic scenery, forests, small towns, and small lodges that offer genuine Costa Rican hospitality. From Paraíso, southeast of Cartago, roads go east and south for magnificent views of both Orosi and Ujarrás Valleys and the lake formed by Cachí Dam; the Río Macho hydroelectric plant here provides 33 percent of the Central Valley's drinking water. The east road leads to ruins of the 17th-century church of **Ujarrás.** Stop at the *mirador* (viewpoint) overlooking Ujarrás. South of Paraíso is the town of **Orosi** and its 18th-century church, the oldest house of worship still in use in the country. Beside it is a small museum of religious art, open daily, housed in what was a Franciscan monastery.

NATURE AND ADVENTURE ACTIVITIES

Rafts, kayaks, and canoes are as familiar here now as the traditional oxcart. Experience some of the best white-water in the country. Mountain biking is popular on rural roads and to both Irazú and Turrialba Volcanoes. The only hot-air balloon company in Costa Rica is based in Turrialba. Nearby Talamanca Mountains, highest in Costa Rica, offer unparalleled trekking options.

Tapantí National Park has rushing, boulder-strewn rivers, picture-book waterfalls, hiking trails, and abundant birdlife. Guayabo National Monument, the country's principal archeological site is a must, not only for the ruins but for also for the surrounding premontane rain forest. Top private reserves offer excellent birding, hiking, and horseback riding. Visit a well-known botanical garden. A newer addition is fishing in trout ponds.

FLORA AND FAUNA

Orchids, hummingbirds, Montezuma oropendolas, eyelash vipers, the big-leafed plant known as poor man's umbrella, agoutis, a wealth of butterflies—nature's bounty is around every turn.

People tend to think of **orchids** related to Lankester Botanical Garden; however, orchids in the wild are common. More than 1,400 orchid species are found in Costa Rica. From tall terrestrials that wave in the breeze to tiny miniatures, orchids add amazing richness to the biological landscape. Orchids growing on branches and trunks of trees are not parasites; that is, they do not take their nourishment from the tree. They are epiphytes, using the tree only as a means of support. Eighty-eight percent of all orchids are epiphytic, while 12 percent are terrestrial. The national flower is an orchid, the *guaria morada* (*Cattleya skinneri*), a showy species chosen in 1939 because it grows easily around the country and was a part of the national folklore.

Miniatures can be so tiny that it is difficult to pick out the three sepals and three petals—one of which has been modified into the lip—that are characteristic of orchids. They can measure as little as one inch (three cm), including roots, foliage, and flower. At the other extreme, some orchids have a stem up to 16 feet (five m) long.

Orchid pollination has bizarre twists. Some orchids have developed flowers that look like certain bee or wasp species. A male bee or wasp attempts to copulate with the flower and goes away carrying pollen. Some orchids produce oils sought by certain bees as food for larvae; in the process bees move pollen from one flower to another. Flowers may last only a day; others last weeks if not pollinated.

VISITOR INFORMATION

Best sources of information are the parks and private reserves, lodges, and tour companies. As you travel in Costa Rica, you will note that tourism information signs frequently are posted at tour company offices.

GETTING THERE

From San José, head east through San Pedro or Zapote following road signs for Cartago and Irazú Volcano; if the Orosi Valley and Tapantí National Park is your destination, continue to and through Paraíso, where road signs have improved to the point that I can almost get through without getting lost in Paradise. For Turrialba and Guayabo, watch for signs in Paraíso. Check Appendix A for buses to this area. To get from Cartago to Orosi, catch the bus just southeast of the church ruins; it runs every 90 minutes.

If the Caribbean is on your itinerary, you can travel this older road one way and take the newer, faster highway through Braulio Carrillo National Park the other way; the routes join at Siquierres.

Alternate routes exist to Turrialba from the Cartago area—look at your map. From Cartago, head for Cot (which was a ceremonial center for the Cotos people; farmers still work fields with oxen), and instead of turning for Irazú continue on through Pacayas and Pastores to Santa Cruz, watching for waterfalls on the skirts of Turrialba Volcano. At Santa Cruz, turn to Turrialba. This road is passable even in rainy season. From Santa Cruz, a jolting road goes on to Guayabo National Monument.

NATURE AND ADVENTURE SIGHTS

Guayabo National Monument

Guayabo is the blue morpho butterfly, the yellow flash of a Montezuma oropendola flying through tall trees, flowing water, patches of profuse pink impatiens, and ancient carved stones. It is the quiet of centuries-old ruins hidden in the rain forest.

Created in 1973 as Costa Rica's only archaeological park, Guayabo protects the remains of a city that flourished and disappeared before the Spaniards arrived. People may have occupied the area as early as 1000 B.C.; at its peak Guayabo is estimated to have had 300 to 500 residents, though perhaps as many as 10,000 lived in surrounding villages, supplying labor and revenue to this religious and political center. There was little new building after A.D. 800, and the site was abandoned by 1400. Some theorize that wars, habitat deterioration, and disease contributed to the abandonment.

Visitors today see *calzadas* (cobbled roads), stone-lined water-storage tanks, open and covered aqueducts that carried water through the site, and *montículos* (mounds) with stone-covered bases. Park information signs depict conical houses made of wood and palm leaves, believed to have been built on the mounds. Trails lead through forest past open tombs, plundered before the park was established. Stylized forms of a jaguar and caiman decorate a striking monolith; 63 petroglyphs depict birds and animals as well as art whose meaning is still unknown. Many mysteries of people and place remain.

A conservation and excavation project begun in August 1989 increased the excavated area to half of the almost-50-acre (20-ha) archaeological site. Among items found are golden bells, carved stone tables, roasted corn kernels, beautiful pottery, a copper-and-gold frog, and a sacrificial stone. Some pieces are exhibited at the National Museum in San José.

Guayabo protects the only remaining primary forest in Cartago Province, accounting for 22 percent of the 538-acre (218-ha) park; other forest is rich, naturally regenerating secondary forest. More than 80 varieties of orchids and other epiphytes adorn trees; toucans are present, as are hummingbirds, woodcreepers, chachalacas, woodpeckers, and brown jays (*ticos* call them *piapias* and say they are the scouts of the forest, their warning cries signaling that an intruder is near). Notice long, hanging nests built by oropendolas, colony dwellers (Icterid family of orioles and blackbirds) in which up to 10 males mate with up to 30 females in a colony, nests often established in a single tree. Listen for the melodious songs and harsh calls that emanate from a group of these spectacular, large black and chestnut-colored birds, which have pale blue on their cheeks, orange-tipped bills, and yellow in the tails. Mammals include sloths, kinkajous, coatis, rabbits, squirrels, and armadillos.

COFFEE, ANYONE?

Coffee, which originated in Ethiopia and Arabia, was Costa Rica's number-one export until this decade. Though today it's the fourth-largest foreign exchange earner after tourism, electronics, and bananas, a drop in the price of coffee still sends a shudder through the country. Most is sold to Germany, the United States, and Great Britain.

Grown in nurseries for about one year, coffee plants are transplanted to the field, where they begin to bear commercially after two years. Some growers harvest from coffee trees for 15 to 20 years and then prune them way back for 20 more years of production.

Planting is in May and June. Harvest time depends on elevation: October to January in areas around San José, June to November in Turrialba and Coto Brus. Pickers are paid by the cajuela (basket). All ages take to the fields for the harvest; Costa Ricans are joined by thousands of temporary workers from Nicaragua. Each berry, which turns from green to red when ripe, contains two seeds: the coffee beans. Pulp must be removed and the beans dried before they can be roasted and exported.

Walk on Sendero de los Montículos, an interpretive trail that leads through the archaeological site to a *mirador* with a fantastic view of the ruins below, mountain peaks, and Turrialba's valley. Another viewpoint overlooks excavation of a road that ran from Guayabo to an outlying area. Some theorize that stone roads were part of a network all the way to Mexico. Explore Los Cantarillos nature trail, which offers either a short or longer loop down to the Lajitas River. Rainfall averages 138 inches (3,500 mm), with driest months February and March. Average temperature is 68°F (20°C), and elevation is 3,150 to 4,265 feet (960 to 1,300 m).

A small visitor center is opposite the park entrance. A nearby camping area has tent sites, bathrooms, and potable water.

Bird-friendly coffee? The switch from shaded coffee plants to unshaded that began in the 1970s—aimed at increasing coffee production—is seeing a reverse, and not just because of environmentalists and bird lovers concerned about decreased habitat for avifauna, especially migrating songbirds. Costs to the farmer and the environment went up with the cutting of trees—sun-tolerant hybrids require more chemical pesticides and fertilizers, and more contaminated soil was washed into streams for lack of tree roots to help hold it firm. Even the U.S. Agency for International Development has gone back to promoting shade-grown coffee. Research shows that shaded farms can support 150 species of birds. Increasingly, organic coffee is touted, and various organizations have "green seal" coffee certification programs: one is the ECO-O.K. seal from Rainforest Alliance (see Chapter 2) that mandates minimal chemicals, growing coffee under trees that keep soil and bird life in place, processing that does not release acid from beans directly into streams, and safe working conditions.

Details: 12 miles (19 km) northeast of Turrialba; from San José, 40 miles (65 km); telephone hotline 506/192, 506/290-1927, fax 506/232-5324, in Turrialba tel/fax 506/556-9507, accvccr@racsa.co.cr. Open 8 A.M. to 4 P.M., closed Monday, admission $6, camping $2 per person. Turrialba taxis make the trip. See Appendix A for bus information. Lodges and private reserves arrange Guayabo tours, and day trips are available from San José.

Irazú Volcano National Park

Indigenous peoples who lived on the mountain's slopes named it Iztarú: "mountain of trembling and thunder." Indeed Irazú

Volcano has a history of showing off. Its awesome power is evident long before you reach the impressive craters. Notice the devastation from the most recent major eruptions, 1963 to 1965. Whole areas were buried in mud, floods were significant, and volcanic rock still peppers the countryside. But as you travel the paved road to the park, credit the volcano for the rich soils that now produce cabbages, potatoes, onions, and grasslands for dairy cows.

Highest peak in the Central Volcanic Range and highest volcano in Costa Rica, Irazú reaches 11,260 feet (3,432 m). It has been known to send ash as far away as the Nicoya Peninsula; steam clouds have billowed 1,640 feet (500 m) high, and debris has shot up 984 feet (300 m). The rumbling giant tossed boulders weighing several tons from its innards in 1963, and its tremors rattled buildings miles away.

Today, with Irazú in a sometimes-restless resting phase, visitors can go to the top of a lunar landscape that muffles its fiery nature. But thin streams of steam or gas and occasional tremors remind us that Irazú is not dead; it only sleeps. Walk along the rim of the main crater, which has a 3,445-foot (1,050-m) diameter; peer down to a bright green lake almost 1,000 feet (300 m) below. Volcanic grays and blacks are highlighted by swatches of reds and oranges in the steep sides. The other principal crater, linked by a trail, is Diego de la Haya, 2,264 feet (690 m) across. The Playa Hermosa crater, now extinct, resembles a beach of gray ash surrounded by stunted vegetation.

Tenacious plants dot largely empty areas around the craters; some bravely sport bright flowers. On slopes where the green of secondary growth testifies to nature's powers of recovery, old, barren branches rise like ghostly fingers above the new forest. Animal life is scarce at the park because of both human and volcanic activity. Where cougar and jaguar once thrived, today you can see rabbits, coyotes, armadillos, and red-tailed squirrels. Hummingbirds are numerous; you might spot a volcano junco, sooty robin, ruddy woodcreeper, or acorn woodpecker. On the road to the entrance, oak giants are festooned with red bromeliads—not parasites—but the bright orange epiphytes are parasitic *matapalos*. Notice the small, thick, hard leaves of many plants here, which are adapted to

Ree Strange Sheck

Irazú Volcano, highest volcano in Costa Rica

the strong winds and sudden changes in temperature at this high elevation.

For clearest views and a hundred-to-one shot at seeing both oceans, go early. Whatever time of day you visit, take a jacket. Average temperature is 52°F (11°C); lowest recorded temperature, 26°F (-3°C). Frost is possible December through February. Annual rainfall is 85 inches (2,158 mm).

A cement pedestrian boulevard leads from the visitor area at the entrance to the crater areas. Hike around Playa Hermosa for a view of craters, moonscape, and visitor center. This viewpoint is accessible by car: go straight instead of taking the right fork to the visitor center. A short walking trail goes to communication towers on the other side of the craters; get directions from park rangers.

One of the country's most visited parks, Irazú is the birthplace of rivers that flow into major waterways: Chirripó, Reventazón, Sarapiquí, and Río Grande de Tárcoles Rivers. Now part of the Central Volcanic Mountain Range Conservation Area, the park, 5,706 acres (2,309 ha) in size, was created in 1955. The visitor center is operated under a concession to Café Rey; it contains a gift shop, restrooms, and snack bar. In addition to coffee, cappuccino, hot chocolate, soups, pastries, and tamales to eat, you can buy batteries and film and even rent a poncho. Picnic tables in front are full on weekends.

Details: 20 miles (32 km) northeast of Cartago, 33 miles (53 km) from San José; telephone hotline 506/192, 506/290-1927, fax 506/232-5324, accvccr@racsa.co.cr, www.minae.go.cr/accvc. Open daily 8 A.M. to 3:30 P.M.; admission $6, minimal parking fee. Irazú is often combined with visits to Lankester Botanical Garden, Cartago, or the Orosi Valley. By car, follow signs from Cartago through Cot. Bus service from San José operates on weekends only; see Appendix A.

Lankester Botanical Garden

Established in the 1950s by English naturalist Charles Lankester to preserve local epiphytes, beautiful Lankester Garden was bought in 1973 by the American Orchid Society and the Stanley Smith Foundation of England and donated to the University of Costa Rica. Thousands have walked these paths to see the orchids—more than 800 species of local and foreign orchids, from tiny miniatures to flowers with stalks more than 15 feet (five m) high. Though peak months for orchids to bloom are February through May, there are enough in flower to dazzle visitors at any time of year.

Well-maintained trails lead over brooks, under arbors, and to greenhouses, through a breathtaking display of flowers and trees that attract more than 100 species of birds and many butterflies. You may be surprised to find a cactus and succulent garden here. Though most Costa Rican cacti grow in tropical dry forest, some live as epiphytes in the rain forest. Palms, bromeliads, bamboo (40 varieties), heliconias (35 varieties), gingers, anoids, and ferns abound. Plaques along one trail graphically depict the loss of natural forest in Costa Rica since 1940. A small loop trail is accessible for visitors in wheel chairs.

Some of the 26-acre (10.7-ha) garden is in secondary forest, which has grown up on abandoned pasturelands. Research and education go hand in hand with plant production at the garden, so you may see schoolchildren on a field trip, adults taking short courses, or scientists at work.

Guided tours through greenhouses and grounds are $2, weekdays only. But a descriptive brochure and trail map allow self-guided explorations any day. Allow one to two hours to enjoy the 26-acre (10.7 ha) garden. Visit the gift shop, where you'll find wonderful books on orchids and natural history, a video about the garden, and snacks. Bring insect repellent in rainy season. Elevation is 4,943 feet (1,400 m), and daytime temperature is 64° to 75°F (18° to 24°C). Average annual rainfall is 39 to 51 inches.

Details: *2.5 miles (four km) east of Cartago toward Paraíso; 506/552-3247, fax 506/552-3151, lankeste@cariari.ucr.ac.cr. Open daily 8:30 A.M. to 3:30 P.M. except Christmas and New Year's Day and Thursday and Friday of Holy Week; admission adults $4, children $.65. Coming from Cartago, watch for entrance on the right. Take the Paraíso bus from Cartago and ask to be let off at the entrance to Jardín Botánico Lankester. Walk one-half mile (one km) to reception. Or take a taxi from Cartago.*

Rancho Naturalista

Fields of cane and coffee spread out below this mountain retreat, while Irazú and Turrialba Volcanoes dominate the skyline across a vast valley. Tropical forest is steps away from the lodge. Tranquility is the key word.

The private reserve, belonging to the Erb family and managed by daughter Lisa, caters strictly to nature travelers. Enthusiastic, knowledgeable guides lead visitors on trails and farm roads to look for the birds, butterflies, and moths that abound here. Lisa herself is a terrific guide. More than 400 bird species have been seen here, 200 from the balcony of the main lodge! You may spot a blue-crowned motmot (notice the telltale tick-tock motion it makes with its racquet-tipped tail), a scarlet-thighed dacnis, or a green honey-creeper; and you're likely to see toucans, manakins, trogons, tanagers, and a world of hummingbirds.

If you have yet to see the gorgeous morpho butterfly, this is your chance. Several of the six Central American species of this butterfly live near the lodge. The blue flash of one of these beauties against the forest's green is a gift. The Erbs don't claim to have all

12,000 of Costa Rica's species of moths, but they believe they have enough to keep you occupied. Just ask, and they'll put up a sheet and plug in a lamp outside at night to attract them. The variety is awesome.

A neighbor down the road has a *trapiche*, an old-style sugarcane press, which guests can visit. Horses are available at no extra charge. Explore roads in the 125-acre (50-ha) farm, outside the farm on neighboring roads, or along the Tuis River.

With a one-week stay, get a complimentary all-day field trip to a different elevation. Popular choices are Tapantí National Park or Irazú Volcano. Other optional tours include Lankester or CATIE, or you can go white-water rafting or visit the Cabecar Indian Reserve.

The main house has five comfortable bedrooms, two of them with private baths. Nearby are three duplex cottages with forest or valley views, private baths. Meals are family style; food is plentiful and delicious, from filet mignon to Mexican and Costa Rican cuisine.

Rancho Naturalista is at 2,953 feet (900 m), in the transition zone between premontane wet forest and premontane rain forest. Daytime temperatures are in the 70s (21°C to 26°C), nights in the 60s (15°C to 20°C). Afternoon rain is common, especially May through November; rubber boots are recommended. Trails on the ranch are well maintained; shelters and benches along the way are ideal spots to sit and wait for nature to reveal its treasures. Sit surrounded by magnificent forest in late afternoon and look down at the Hummingbird Pools: observe snowcaps and purple-crowned fairies, among others, bathe in the waters of the mountain stream—magic time.

Seven nights at Rancho Naturalista, with meals, lodging, guided walks, and a day trip is $877 per person. Split a week's stay between Rancho Naturalista and the Erb's property on the Pacific, Tarcol Lodge (see Chapter 13). Nightly rate, including meals and guiding, is $135. Packages also combine Rancho Naturalista with other top destinations.

Details: *1.7 miles (2.8 km) southeast of Turrialba up a dirt road from Tuis; 506/531-1516, 800/593-3305, Mark@ranchonaturalista.com, www.ranchonaturalista.com. Transfers provided free with a three-night stay.*

Tapantí National Park

"Dripping forest" is not a scientific term, but it describes this park in the Talamanca Mountain Range. Inside the forest, raining or not, the air is moist, plants seem wet, the earth smells fresh. Sounds of water are pervasive: 150 rivers and rivulets run here, important sources for hydroelectric projects. Average rainfall is 256 inches (6,500 mm)—that is 21 feet, friends!—though it has on occasion reached 315 inches (8,000 mm). Even in the drier months of January through April, wise travelers bring rain gear. Average temperature is 68°F (20°C), and elevation is from 4,000 to 8,400 feet (1,220 to 2,560 m).

Tree crowns form a leaky umbrella under which grow delicate ferns (including 18 species of tree ferns), orchids, bromeliads, lianas that tempt one to take a swing, mosses, and multicolored lichens. Along the road and on forest slopes grows a plant with immense leaves and a tall reddish flower that Costa Ricans call "poor man's umbrella." I have, in fact, seen its leaves used in the countryside by people caught in the rain.

Tapantí is a favorite with bird-watchers. Among more than 260 species identified here are ones everybody wants to see: quetzals, hummingbirds, toucans, parakeets, parrots, great tinamous, and squirrel cuckoos. Endangered mammals among the 45 resident mammal species are jaguar, ocelot, and tapir; you're more likely to see squirrels, monkeys, raccoons, opossums, coyotes, agoutis, and red brocket deer. There are porcupines, silky anteaters, otters, and, among the 28 amphibian species, lots of toads. Reptile species also number 28, so be on the lookout for lizards and snakes, including the venomous eyelash viper, also commonly known as the palm viper. Butterflies are everywhere: watch for the blue morpho.

The new visitor center is a good starting place to orient yourself to the 15,024-acre (6,080-ha) park via exhibits and conversation with a friendly ranger; buy a park brochure that includes a trail map, and visit the gift shop. Trails lead through the extravagance of rain-forest vegetation: Oropendola Trail, an easy loop, begins about a half-mile (one km) from the visitor center. For a longer hike, ask rangers about continuing on Sendero Pantanoso, which dips down near the Río Grande de Orosi, whose swift, cold waters rush over and around impressive boulders. Bring a picnic and enjoy the covered shelters while you soak up the scenery. The map indicates the best swimming area in the river: brace yourself for cold water. Sendero Natural Arboles Caídos (Fallen Trees Trail) is more rugged; Sendero La Pava (Guan Trail) also leads to the river.

At the parking and picnic area near the end of the public road, climb a short trail to a covered *mirador* to look across at a gorgeous waterfall and down the river valley to glorious interplays of light and clouds along the forested mountains.

Rooms are sometimes available in park buildings, about $6 per person, shared bath. Meals can be arranged. Ask about camping near the visitor center.

A wildlife refuge by 1982, Tapantí became a national park in 1992 and is within the Amistad Pacific Conservation Area.

Details: 31 miles (50 km) southeast of San José, 17 miles (28 km) southeast of Cartago; telephone hotline 506/192, tel/fax 506/551-2970. Open daily 7 A.M. to 5 P.M.; admission $6. By car from Cartago, continue through Paraíso, Orosi, and Purisil. Watch for "Tapantí" signs. A bus can get you part way: in Cartago, catch the Orosi bus that leaves every hour from the south side of the church ruins, and then take a taxi for the last 7.5 miles (12 km). Park personnel can radio for a taxi for return trip. Or take a taxi from Cartago or Paraíso. Day tours are offered from San José and by area lodges and tour agencies.

Viborana

Minor Camacho Loaiza is a man with a mission. His small, well-done serpentarium is a center for education, research, conservation, and community outreach—all to do with snakes. He, his wife, and their daughter built the information center and an exhibition area with large, attractive, natural-looking enclosures for some of Costa Rica's showiest snake species: boa constrictors, fer-de-lance, corals and false corals, gorgeous golden-yellow eyelash vipers, and the bush-master, largest New World venomous snake, to name a few.

More than 2,000 schoolchildren came in the first four years, learning the difference between venomous and nonvenomous snakes, the role of snakes in the environment, and what to do to keep from being bitten. Minor's thesis is that venomous species are increasingly moving into agricultural areas due to factors such as destruction of natural habitats and abundance of prey among crops.

He takes his show on the road to educate farm workers and indigenous peoples, those most in danger of snakebite. He claims that the fer-de-lance, or *terciopelo,* is responsible for 76 percent of snakebites in the country and for 90 percent of the deaths. He recently participated in filming of a *National Geographic* special on the fer-de-lance.

You are invited to come—not to *see* snakes but to learn: you will get an informative talk, including what to do if you come upon a snake, a tour of the exhibition area, a chance to photograph snakes, and a demonstration of venom extraction. Minor is an expert when it comes to handling snakes, and he does interact with some of the species.

Viborana is set in a flower garden that brings butterflies and birds, so bring binoculars. Minor says he has seen 60 species of birds in a morning. Since this is strictly a private effort, donations are welcomed to help with educational programs.

Details: *Seven miles (12 km) east of Turrialba, about 1,312 feet (400 m) past the turnoff for Pochotel; cellular 506/381-4781, fax 506/556-0427. Open daily 9 A.M. to 5 P.M.; admission $4. From Turrialba take the road toward Siquirres; a Turrialba taxi will get you there. Area lodges offer tours.*

Volcán Turrialba Lodge

Phenomenal vistas, flashy tropical birds, a lodge loaded with rustic charm, eager-to-please local staff, and cappuccino served in speckled blue-and-white metal camping cups—there's no place like Volcán Turrialba Lodge. Advertised as the lodge with a volcano in the front yard, it is not only a mere three miles (five km) from the crater of Turrialba Volcano but its southwestern horizon is defined by the forested back side of Irazú Volcano. Hummingbirds at feeders by the dining room and darting from flower to flower in the gardens put on a spectacular show: among them are breathtakingly beautiful species such as fiery-throated, volcano, and magnificent hummers.

From the 9,186-feet (2,800-m) lodge on the working dairy farm and private forest reserve, take off on hiking, horseback riding, and biking adventures, which at this altitude are not for couch potatoes. A horseback ride to Turrialba Volcano, the third highest mountain in Costa Rica at 10,919 ft. (3,328 m), through *páramo* vegetation takes you to the rim, where you leave the horses and descend into the crater—a four-hour trip. Guests in good shape can consider a hiking or biking option. A three-hour bird-watching special is through tree-studded pastures, along mountain streams, and into the forest. On my hike I observed, up close, golden-browed chlorophonias, a quetzal, collared redstarts, a zeledonia, emerald toucanets, sooty robins, long-tailed silky flycatchers, sooty-capped bush-tanagers, and a black and yellow silky flycatcher, among others. More than 70 species are on the bird list.

Another hiking, biking, or horseback trip takes in old lava flows, and a three-hour hike goes through rain forest and cloud forest, along old lava flows, and into upper Braulio Carrillo National Park. There is a 208-acre (84-ha) primary forest on the farm where ocelots, river otters, quetzals, coatis, porcupines, coyotes, and kinkajous live.

About eight years ago, owner Tony Lachner converted an old milking barn into a lodge. Six rooms in the main building are small but cozy, and an upstairs common area has a fireplace; a wood stove in the dining room radiates welcome heat on chilly days. An additional six rooms have been added beside the lodge, each with its own tiny wood stove for heat. Electricity had just been connected when I was there, so the cappuccino machine was still a novelty. Food is delicious. In afternoons, *tortillas con queso* are a real treat. Homemade cheese served here.

A two-night stay including lodging, meals, three tours, and taxes is $175. Lodging and three meals is $57 each for a double, but take it from me, one night is not enough. Tours are offered to day visitors, with horseback tours starting at $20 and hiking tours $10 to $15. Transport arranged.

Details: 37 miles (60 km) from San José; cellular 506/383-6084, tel/fax 506/273-4335, info@volcanturrialbalodge.com, www.volcanturrialbalodge. com. From Cartago, one route is via Pacayas and Pastora, another through Santa Rosa and San Pedro. From Turriabla, head north to Santa Cruz and Pastora. Ask about road conditions—four-wheel-drive recommended.

GUIDES AND OUTFITTERS

Turrialba has fine small companies that specialize in river expeditions of all kinds, offering a greater variety of rivers than larger San

José tour operators; but white-water is not all. A full-range of adventure options includes hiking, biking, canyoning. See Chapter 3 for other outfitters.

Kayaks and canoes are the forte for **Costa Rica Ríos Aventuras,** 506/556-9617, in U.S. 888/434-0776, rmclain@racsa.co.cr, www.costaricarios.com, although custom tours encompass a full range of activities. Sign up for kayak and canoe instruction from beginner to advanced; ask about the Week of Rivers and Open Canoe Cruising trips. Nine-day trips are from $1,600; 13-day ones from $2,200. A Potpourri Tour takes travelers to Turrialba Volcano, Guayabo, the Caribbean, La Fortuna, Rincón de la Vieja and a Pacific beach, with rafting, hiking, estuary paddling, snorkeling, a boat trip, and horseback riding. Family discounts, shuttle service, and rental of kayaks and canoes are available. Find Ray McClain and his company 25 meters north of the evangelical church on Central Park.

Experience the area by hot-air balloon. **Costa Rica Serendipity Adventures,** 506/556-2592, fax 506/556-2593, 800/635-2325, costarica@serendipityadventures.com, www.serendipityadventures.com. Serendipity offers a trip that features the Turrialba Valley, with trees in touching distance of the basket and white water below; flight is $500 for a minimum of two. Pilots are U.S. FAA-licensed commercial pilots. Ask about charter flights elsewhere and adventure trips that include rafting, hiking, mountain biking, and canyoning.

Adventure unlimited awaits at **Jungla Expeditions,** 506/556-9525, tel/fax 506/556-6225, jungla@racsa.co.cr, www.jungla.net. Choose backpacking, rafting, river and sea kayaking, mountain biking, horseback riding (day or overnight), trekking, or canyoning. What is canyoning? The descent of waterfall-rich canyons using mountaineering techniques and equipment. Try it for $105. A specialty is white-water kayak trips, with 21 rivers on the list—from lowland jungle rivers to high-elevation mountain streams, from $70 to $110 per day. Kayak instruction offered: beginner levels to rodeo and slalom options for $90 per day. Jungla Store rents equipment and sells everything from kayaks and dry boxes to backpacks and clothes. Show this book and get 10 percent off of any activity. Look for Jungla in the yellow building 20 meters south of Palí Supermarket in Turrialba.

Loco's Tropical Tours, tel/fax 506/556-6035, 506/556-6071, riolocos@whiteh2o.com, www.whiteh2o.com, is about rafting, but Betty (born in Costa Rica) and Lee Poundstone can customize a trip to include bird-watching, hiking, camping, photography, swimming, and, of course, kayaking, including instruction and gear. Wild-water excursions run four sections on the Reventazón and two on the Pacuare. Half-day trips start at $55; full days at $85, including gourmet buffet-style lunches. Office is at home, but the boat house is behind the Hotel Wagelia downtown in Turrialba.

Ticos River Adventures, tel/fax 506/556-1231, cellular 506/394-4479, info@ticoriver.com, www.ticoriver.com, has five options for rafting trips—Pacuare, Reventazón, Chirripó, Pejibaye, and Sarapiquí. The one-day Class IV Pacuare from Turrialba is $80, from San José $90. The one-day Reventazón options are from $60 to $80 starting in Turrialba. Other trips include three days on the Chirripó, $350, and two days on the Pacuare, $200 from Turrialba, with campouts, happy hour, meals, and time for hiking. Kayak rentals and instruction are available.

CAMPING

Refer to "Nature and Adventure Sights" for fuller descriptions of Guayabo and Tapantí, and "Lodging" for Monte Sky and Turrialtico.

Guayabo National Monument has campsites with toilets and water across from the entrance to the archaeological site. Admission fee $6, camping fee $2 per person. Telephone hotline 506/192, 506/ 290-1927, fax 506/232-5324, in Turrialba tel/fax 506/556-9507.

Monte Sky is three miles (five km) from Orosi toward Tapantí, 506/231-3536, tel/fax 506/228-0010, montesky@intnet.co.cr. Reservations necessary.

Tapantí National Park has campsites. Admission $6, camping fee $2 per person. Telephone hotline 506/192, tel/fax 506/551-2970.

Turrialtico, just five miles (eight km) east of Turrialba, 506/556-1111, tel/fax 506/556-1575, turrialt@racsa.co.cr, has a small space for campers, with access to a bath. Bring your own gear.

LODGING

Casa Turire, just east of Turrialba, 506/531-1111, fax 506/531-1075, turire@racsa.co.cr, www.hotelcasaturire.com, is a splendid country house on the 2,000-acre (800-ha) Atirro Hacienda. Once on a bend above the Reventazón River, Casa Turire becomes lakeside with completion of the Angostura Hydroelectric Project that creates a 633-acre (256-ha) artificial lake. The hacienda belongs to the Rojas family, who extended their agricultural enterprises (sugarcane, coffee, and macadamia nuts) to include tourism in 1991. Turire's 494-acre (200-ha) forest offers visitors an opportunity to walk the trails, maybe to see a sloth, morpho and owl butterflies, motmots and toucans, or armadillos.

The 16-room, four-suite grand "plantation house" sits amid formal gardens whose tropical plants, flowers, and trees attract colorful birds. The attractive swimming pool and hot tub are spring fed. Rooms are elegant, furnished in soft tones. Each has satellite TV, ceiling fan, hair dryer, direct-dial telephone, and a stunning view of mountains from a private balcony. Floor-to-ceiling windows welcome light that shines on polished hardwood floors. Doubles are $126, suites from $147. No children under 12; no facilities for the handicapped.

Choose mountain biking, rain-forest tours, horseback riding, kayaking and white-water rafting, or tours to Guayabo, CATIE, and Turrialba Volcano. On the hacienda, visit processing plants for cane, coffee, and macadamia nuts; relax in the hot tub; play tennis, have a massage, or enjoy a driving range. The gourmet restaurant is open to the public for lunch and dinner, reservations required. Service is excellent, the staff friendly. Countrywide transfers are available, and there's a nearby airstrip for charter flights. The hotel is a member of the Small Distinctive Hotels of Costa Rica.

Hotel Geliwa, 0.9 miles (1.5 km) north of downtown Turrialba, 506/1721, fax 506/556-1029, is a 25-room inn on a quiet street backed by coffee fields. Doubles are $61, including breakfast and taxes. Large upstairs rooms, completely remodeled, would be my pick. There's a swimming pool, and the glassed-in restaurant has great views of the valley.

Hotel Wagelia in Turrialba, 506/556-1566, fax 506/556-1596, is an 18-room downtown hotel, its restaurant a favorite with locals and tourists. Simple, comfortable rooms with ceiling fans open onto terraces around a courtyard; some have air conditioning, a refrigerator, and TV. Tours are to Guayabo, Turrialba Volcano, and CATIE, as well as rafting trips. Doubles with air conditioning, refrigerator, and TV are $74, including breakfast and taxes, less with fans only.

Kirí Lodge is one-half mile (one km) from the entrance to Tapantí National Park, 506/284-2024, beeper phone 506/225-2500. A charming mountain hideaway, it is a natural reserve in its own right, where you're likely to see troops of white-faced monkeys along with coatis, deer, and armadillos. Blue morpho butterflies are abundant and hummingbirds visit feeders and a profusion of flowering plants in the garden. You'll see bay-headed and scarlet-rumped tanagers, blue-crowned motmots, and yellow-faced grassquits—260 bird species around here. Basic trails lead into misty mountains to rivers and waterfalls on some of the farm's 173 acres (70 ha).

Kirí's six cabins, terraced up the hillside, have memorable vistas. The rooms are simple but comfortable, and river rocks are featured in the decor. Owners Dagoberto Torres and family offer Costa Rican hospitality. Among the restaurant's tasty dishes are organically grown vegetables and fruits and trout fresh from the farm's own ponds. Guests can fish with the fishing equipment provided. Stop by for a meal if nothing else, but be advised: you will wish you were staying. Double is $35, breakfast and taxes included. Transfers and area tours arranged. Bring a jacket.

The turnoff for **Monte Sky** is three miles (five km) from Orosi toward Tapantí, 506/231-3536, tel/fax 506/228-0010, montesky @intnet.co.cr, www.intent.co.cr/montesky. Here is a rustic mountain retreat that is as much a philosophy as a place. Owner Rafael (Billy) Montero seems to have a sacred agreement with his mountain to keep impact low, to let the forest reveal its truths to visitors, and to share the history of the place. That history starts in the 1920 lodge with old photographs and memorabilia. Rooms are basic (shared baths), with a nearby cabin for up to six people; the rate is $55 per person including meals, lodging, and guide. Camping is permitted December to April, $35 per person.

One- to four-hour guided walks reveal a spectacular waterfall, 400-year-old oaks, and 260 species of birds. From the mountaintop setting on a clear day, four volcanoes are visible, with an inspirational mountains-and-sky panorama even on cloudy days. Entrance fee for a day tour is $10, $20 with lunch and guide; day tour from San José $69. From the turnoff to Monte Sky, continue almost two miles (three km) on an exciting dirt/mud road to the parking area. The lodge is up a well-marked trail; allow 30 minutes for the climb to enjoy vistas and read inspirational signs. Overnight and day visits are by reservation only.

Pochotel 2000 is a hilltop lodge seven miles (11 km) east of Turrialba, 506/556-0111, 506/284-7292, fax 506/556-6222. From its *mirador* on a clear day, see not only the Reventazón Valley but also Cerro de la Muerte, Chirripó, the Caribbean coast, and Irazú and Turrialba Volcanoes. Ten rooms are simply furnished, but the ones in more secluded bungalows along the edge of the forest have rustic charm. There is a pool, and the restaurant has a *cocina de leña* (wood-burning stove) in the dining room. Owner Oscar Garcia arranges rafting tours, horseback riding in the forest, helicopter rides, and visits to Lagunas de San Joaquín for fishing and hiking. Doubles $35, taxes included.

Sanchirí Mirador and Lodge is one mile (two km) from Paraíso toward Orosi, 506/533-3210, fax 506/533-3873, sanchiri@ racsa.co.cr, www.sanchiri.com. From the restaurant and six cabins gaze at an out-of-this-world vista of beautiful Orosi Valley. Expect personal service from nine brothers and sisters of the Mata family, who have lived and worked this land for five generations. Each wooden hillside cabin is simply furnished, with telephone and attractive local-stone bathroom walls and floors. Doubles are $40, breakfast included. A three-room house is available.

Across from the cabins is forest where quetzals reside year-round; the Matas continue to plant native trees that provide food for these resplendent birds and other wildlife. A butterfly garden is near the restaurant, admission $2. Tours are to Tapantí (25 minutes away), Guayabo, and Irazú (one hour away); local tours via jeep or horseback include a look at the hydroelectric plant and a coffee stop at a rustic campesino house. Rafting trips and transfers are arranged. The restaurant is open to the public.

Turrialtico is about five miles (eight km) east of Turrialba, 506/556-1111, fax 506/556-1575, turrialt@racsa.co.cr. Fourteen rooms with private baths are above the lodge's locally popular restaurant, which has a dynamite view of the valley. Pleasant rooms, brightened by Guatemalan bedspreads, open onto a common space with two appealing sitting areas—corner rooms have balconies. Bird-watching from the lodge is not bad; as many as 80 species in a day have been reported. Doubles with view are $40; without, $35, including tax.

It's a family affair. Started by Aracelly and Marcial Garcia in 1968, Turrialtico is now operated by their daughter Lucrecia, husband Hector, and their two children. Hector's orchids decorate the dining room, while some 3,000 plants, mostly from this area, hang in his orchid garden—open to hotel guests at no charge. Trips are arranged to nearby Viborana and to Guayabo and Turrialba Volcano; other options are rafting, horseback riding, and hiking. Camping is permitted, and there is a playground for children, a gift shop, and an international phone. Delicious *tico* food, specialties cooked over a wood fire, is served in the large open-air restaurant, which has an adjoining bar.

FOOD

As you travel throughout the zone, you will find many *sodas*. These are small cafes, usually serving inexpensive typical food. Join the local crowd in one of these. A sample of good restaurants follows.

Charming **La Casona del Cafetal** is on a coffee plantation run by the same family for four generations, seven miles (11 km) from Paraíso near Cachí in the Orosi Valley, 506/533-3280. Dine on specialties such as fresh trout, lasagna and spaghetti, pork ribs, or shrimp and tenderloin; try extraordinary rice entrees. Follow up with desserts that feature plantation coffee. Weekend buffet is $15; don't overlook the *taco suizo* or plantains. Open daily 11:30 A.M. to 6 P.M.

Fresh trout is on the menu daily at **Kirí Lodge,** just outside the entrance to Tapantí National Park, 506/284-2024. The Dagoberto Torres family are gracious hosts—daughter Laura will probably wait on you. Organically grown vegetables and fruits are served. Enjoy bird-watching through the windows while you dine. This is a great stop after a park tour.

In Cervantes, between Paraíso and Turrialba, watch for **La Posada de la Luna** restaurant. I cannot pass this place without stopping for a freshly made *tortilla de queso* (cheese tortilla) and a glass of hot *agua dulce con leche* (a hot drink made with boiling water, brown sugar, and, in this case, milk). Some people swear that the best *gallo pinto* (beans and rice) in the country is served here. Showcases hold bits of history, from indigenous artifacts to old telephones, radios, and flatirons. The Luna Solana family welcomes you. Open 8 A.M. to 8:30 P.M., closed Monday.

Restaurant 1910, between Cartago and Irazú Volcano, 506/536-6063, is a restaurant-museum, with a décor tied to the year 1910, when a devastating earthquake destroyed much of Cartago. Owner Olga Fernández combined her interest in history, antiques, and architecture to create this cultural tribute. Typical and international dishes are on the menu, even hamburgers. Try fried plantains with cheese to start; filet mignon and sea bass are delicious. Open daily 11 A.M. to 8 P.M., until 11 P.M. on Sunday.

Restaurante Wagelia in downtown Turrialba, 125 meters west of the Catholic church, 506/556-1566, has a long tradition of good food. Try the typical *casado, arroz a la marinera* (rice with sea specialties), shrimp, pastas, or grilled sea bass (*corvina*). Good breakfasts. Open daily 6 A.M. to 11 P.M.

Turrialtico, 10 minutes east of Turrialba, five miles (eight km), 506/556-1111, is a long-time favorite of visitors and locals. From the large open-air, hilltop dining room, drink in vistas of mountains, rivers, and valley. Meats are a specialty: the Yunta is pork, beef, and chicken grilled over a wood fire and served with *yuca* or *patacones* (fried plantains). Try the *tayuyas*, tortillas stuffed with cheese, tomato, onion, and beans. Open daily 7 A.M. to 10 P.M.

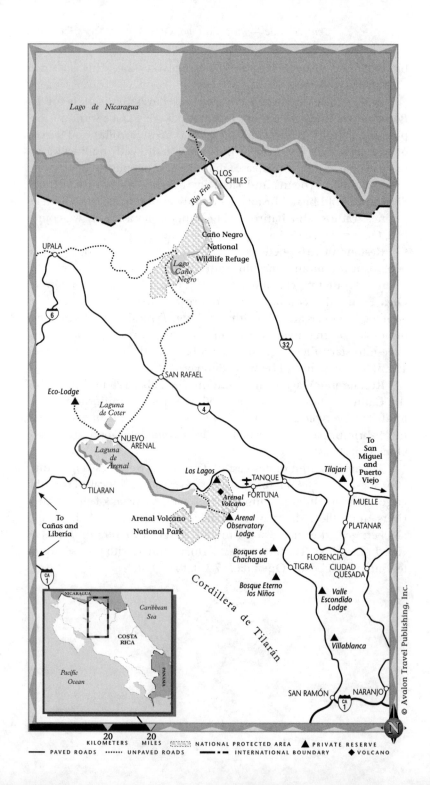

Lago de Nicaragua

LOS CHILES

Río Frío

Caño Negro National Wildlife Refuge

Lago Caño Negro

UPALA

6

SAN RAFAEL

4

Eco-Lodge

Laguna de Coter

NUEVO ARENAL

Laguna de Arenal

TILARAN

To Cañas and Libería

CA 1

Los Lagos

Arenal Volcano

TANQUE

FORTUNA

Arenal Volcano National Park

Arenal Observatory Lodge

Bosques de Chachagua

Bosque Eterno los Niños

Tilajari

To San Miguel and Puerto Viejo

MUELLE

PLATANAR

FLORENCIA

TIGRA

CIUDAD QUESADA

Valle Escondido Lodge

Villablanca

Cordillera de Tilarán

SAN RAMÓN

NARANJO

CA 1

NICARAGUA

Caribbean Sea

COSTA RICA

PANAMA

Pacific Ocean

© Avalon Travel Publishing, Inc.

20 KILOMETERS   20 MILES   NATIONAL PROTECTED AREA   ▲ PRIVATE RESERVE
— PAVED ROADS   ••••• UNPAVED ROADS   —•—• INTERNATIONAL BOUNDARY   ◆ VOLCANO

N

CHAPTER 7

North Central—West:
Fortuna, Arenal, Caño Negro

Mountains, plains, volcanoes, lakes, rivers, forests, fruit farms, agricultural lands, and cattle ranches form a colorful and diverse mosaic in this region. Some of the major natural history attractions include Arenal Volcano National Park, Lake Arenal, and Caño Negro National Wildlife Refuge, as well as notable private reserves that protect natural resources and offer a colorful palette of nature and adventure options.

Arenal Volcano and Lake Arenal are dominant forces in this region. Just as the volcano's activity makes its presence felt in the zone, so do the winds at Lake Arenal, especially at its northern end, creating conditions for world-class windsurfing as well as wind energy projects.

It is not a zone of large cities but of small towns and rural communities with big hearts set amid a natural wonderland.

LAY OF THE LAND

La Fortuna, located 93 miles (150 km) northwest of San José, is the center of this region as the eastern gateway to Arenal Volcano and Lake Arenal and a major player providing tours north to Caño

Negro National Wildlife Refuge, a top natural history destination. The active volcano, a presence in this small place (population 7,385), dominates the horizon. Hot springs are nearby; the 230-foot (70-meter) La Fortuna Waterfall is just south of town (very steep trail); and Venado Caves, a nearly two-mile (three-km) subterranean adventure not for the claustrophobic, are just north. The bank and gasoline stations here are the last you will see for a while if you're heading west; *sodas* (small cafes), restaurants, tour operators, and gift shops are strung along the main street.

From La Fortuna, the 10 miles (16 km) to the Arenal Volcano National Park turnoff skirt the volcano; forested slopes give way to ash and fumaroles as you approach its western face. If you continue around the lake toward Tilarán, watch after you pass Nuevo Arenal for wind energy projects and, on clear days, views of three other volcanoes to the north: Rincón de la Vieja, Miravalles, and Tenorio.

One of the principal routes to the area from San José is through Naranjo to Ciudad Quesada. This road goes through **Zarcero,** the friendly, picturesque mountain town of 3,831 people famous for its animals—that is, animals sculpted from plants: topiary art. The fantastic gardens in front of the church hold an evergreen elephant, bull, and rabbit, plus dozens of other forms. Zarcero is 15 miles (24 km) north of Naranjo and 43 miles (69 km) northwest of San José.

Muelle is a crossroads where the north-south route from Ciudad Quesada to Los Chiles and Caño Negro crosses an east-west route that links this region with the eastern part of the north central zone—Aguas Zarcas, Boca Tapada, and the Sarapiquí areas— as well as a route to the Caribbean without returning to San José.

Nuevo Arenal, a quiet little place on the shores of Lake Arenal 25 miles (41 km) northwest of La Fortuna, was built by the Costa Rican Electrical Institute to replace, house by house, the existing town of Arenal, which now lies beneath the waters of the lake, flooded as a result of the Arenal-Corobicí Hydroelectric Project, the country's largest. The dam is just east of the entrance to Arenal National Park.

Archaeological studies show that indigenous peoples had small settlements around **Lake Arenal,** near the volcano, as long ago as 2000 B.C. Today's lake is much larger because of the dam completed in 1979. Waters that feed the turbines flow into an irrigation project in the drier Guanacaste lowlands. On slopes above the lake, magnificent forests preserved by the national park and private reserves protect this all-important watershed.

The 24-mile-long (39-km) reservoir is a favorite for fishing, sailing, boating, and kayaking. Windsurfing, however, might be considered king. With its steady strong winds from December to March, Lake Arenal is one of the world's best windsurfing destinations. The lake covers about 87 square kilometers, elevation 1,791 feet (546 m).

If driving around the lake, be alert for one-lane bridges that seem to be mostly on curves. The scenery is magnificent. Spot howler monkeys in trees along the road and see colorful scarlet-rumped tanager flash by. Volcano views framed in forest are memorable; tree ferns, glorious.

DON QUIXOTE, ARE YOU HERE?

Modern-day windmills march like giants across the horizon above Lake Arenal's northwest shore between Tilarán and Nuevo Arenal. Giant turbines mounted on 130-foot (40-m) towers reap the wind and turn it into electricity. Private wind farms sell the electricity to the Costa Rican Electricity Institute (ICE), and ICE has its own project.

Wind energy projects qualify for joint implementation programs that allow industrialized countries to mitigate their carbon emissions by supporting alternative energy-generation projects in developing countries—projects that have lower or nonexistent greenhouse gas emissions (see "Carbon Credits" in Chapter 2). Why? International agreements bind industrialized nations to cut their greenhouse gas emissions. Several countries are interested. This does indeed put Costa Rica in a position to fence with giant powers.

NATURE AND ADVENTURE ACTIVITIES

Visitors can bathe in thermal waters, windsurf, fish, mountain bike, enjoy bird-watching, hike, climb into the canopy, kayak and raft, ride horses, and take river wildlife tours. Of course, most travelers come to see one of the most active volcanoes in the world, Arenal. Even when blanketed by clouds, especially in rainy season May through November, the giant's presence is felt—it is there, resting, breathing, rumbling—visible or not.

At its northern end, Lake Arenal is considered one of the top five windsurf spots in the world; average wind velocity from December to April is 25 mph—but those aren't the only months to windsurf. Actually the only unpredictable months for winds are September through November. Water temperature is 73°F. Another good surfing lake in the area is Coter Lake.

The Río Toro and Peñas Blancas have become white-water destinations in recent years, and the tropical forest preserved in parks and private reserves open up the natural world for exploration.

FLORA AND FAUNA

Birding is terrific here. Among species you may see are crimson-fronted and orange-chinned parakeets, keel-billed and chestnut-mandibled toucans, blue-gray tanagers, violaceous trogons, and white crowned parrots. Around Caño Negro, add roseate spoonbills, black-bellied whistling ducks, bare-throated tiger herons, purple gallinules, and ringed, Amazon, and green-and-rufous kingfishers.

Among mammals, you may find crocodiles, river otters, caimans, sloths, coatis, and agoutis. You are certain to hear howler monkeys as you traverse this region and likely to see white-faced capuchin monkeys (*Cebus capucinus*), *mono cara blanca*. In Costa Rica this black monkey with a white or yellowish face, head, upper chest, and shoulders is found from sea level to 4,900 feet (1,500 m). Capuchins spend up to 80 percent of their days traveling and eating from canopy level to lower trees and sometimes even on the ground. Their diet consists largely of fruits and green plant material, but they eat everything from insects to lizards to young birds or bird eggs.

Insect favorites include grasshoppers, ants, and butterfly larvae. The monkeys rarely swallow fleshy fruits but rather chew them and then spit them out. You might observe them knocking a hard fruit on a branch to soften it or split it open for the seeds. Because of their eating habits, these monkeys are important seed disseminators for some tree species. Research indicates that for some species the seeds that passed through the monkey had a higher germination rate than uneaten seeds.

White-faced capuchin monkey

When you spot one capuchin, look around for others: troops can include more than 24 individuals. Don't confuse the capuchin with the squirrel monkey. If you can't distinguish coloring, look at the tail. Capuchins coil theirs, while squirrel monkeys keep their tails straight. Like other monkey species in Costa Rica, white-faced capuchins produce one offspring at a time. If you see a young one clutching the fur of the adult as the troop moves, it is probably less than six months old. Main capuchin predators are humans, boas, cats, and large raptors.

VISITOR INFORMATION

Best sources of information are at the national park, the private reserves, area lodges, and the numerous tour agencies in and around La Fortuna.

GETTING THERE

From San José, the principal routes to the region are through Naranjo/Ciudad Quesada (often called San Carlos) or via San

Ramón; from the northern Pacific region, via Cañas and Tilarán. Several highway routes facilitate moving within the north central region and simplify combining destinations here with Caribbean or Northwest region attractions. For a link with Monteverde, travelers can choose Tilarán and a back road through Quebrada Grande; there are also boat and hiking or horseback options from La Fortuna (Think twice about the horseback ride, especially in rainy season: the impact on trails, horses, and riders seems to be negative.) Access from the Caribbean is via Puerto Viejo de Sarapiquí. Principal roads via San Ramón, Ciudad Quesada, Tilarán, and Puerto Viejo are paved.

Direct bus service to La Fortuna is available from San José, San Ramón, Tilarán, and Ciudad Quesada. Connections with Puerto Viejo de Sarapiquí and Los Chiles (access to Caño Negro) are via Ciudad Quesada; with Monteverde and Cañas (for Pacific beaches and the northwest), Tilarán. SANSA and Travelair, domestic airlines, have daily flights service to La Fortuna from San José. See Appendix A for bus and flight information, including a couple of private van/bus options with regular routes to the area.

NATURE AND ADVENTURE SIGHTS

Arenal Botanical Gardens and Butterfly Sanctuary

Heliconias, begonias, orchids, tree ferns, gingers, anthuriums, euphorbias: 2,500 varieties of plants from around the world thrive here, including many native to Costa Rica. In 1991 owner Michael LeMay began to convert degraded pastureland into a breathtaking garden; he opened it to the public in 1993. Easy trails weave through dazzling displays laid out to resemble natural forest but with groupings that permit the visitor to stand in one area and see varieties in the same genus or family. There are 200 kinds of bromeliads, 200 orchid varieties, and more than 300 types of palms and ferns. See cycads, dracaena, gingers, heliconias, passiflora, schefflera, spathifphyllum, and many more. An added attraction is the new Butterfly Sanctuary—you'll be glad you stopped for this.

These rich acres of plant life form a natural home for birds, including six species of hummingbirds. Take a walk on a trail through natural forest, where monkeys hang out. Booklets are available in English, Spanish, and German for self-guided walks.

Michael, who can tell you where he got each plant, set up the garden to preserve native species of plants, to create a habitat for birds, insects, and other wildlife, and to provide a living classroom for the study of plants, whether for amateurs or professionals. Special attention is given to forest degradation in the Lake Arenal area. Ask about volunteer opportunities.

Details: *2.5 miles (four km) east of the town of Nuevo Arenal; 506/694-4273, fax 506/694-4086, exoticseeds@hotmail.com, www.exoticseeds.com. Open daily 9 A.M. to 5 P.M., admission $8, including a packet of seeds; no children under 12 years.*

Arenal Observatory Lodge

At 4:30 A.M. a thunderous explosion brought us from our beds to the door in one swift leap. Outside, Arenal Volcano's cone, about a 1.1 miles (1.8 km) away, was sharp against the dark blue of the night sky; stars were brilliant. From the crater, red rocks and thin streams of lava began to make their way down the slopes.

Arenal Observatory Lodge is front-row center for viewing eruptions of one of the world's most active volcanoes. Built in 1987 as a laboratory and base for scientists doing long-term geological and biological research, the lodge and its private reserve is now a top destination for nature travelers, Smithsonian scientists, and Earthwatch groups.

I was in a small group that jumped up twice during dinner to pay homage. Later, two of us sat patiently on the elevated, covered observatory platform trying to elicit a command performance, but Arenal seemed unconcerned with our schedules—the real show began after everyone was in bed. I sprang up and ran outside for four explosions. That was in the old days before volcano-view rooms were added, rooms from which, theoretically, you can lie in bed and watch what some call "cosmic fireworks." The power of it, however, somehow demands getting to one's feet.

Guests have access to almost 860 acres (348 ha) of primary and secondary forest, a reforestation project, and the working farm (watch macadamia nuts being harvested and husked). Trails through lush forest lead to a lovely waterfall or to Cerro Chato (an extinct crater near Arenal) and its green lagoon. Incredibly beautiful forest entices you step after step up the steep crater trail, even when it's bathed in cloud or washed by rain. Guided Cerro Chato walk is $43 for four persons. Walking is easy around the farm and along roads.

Guests get a free daily guided hike to recent lava flows, paying only the $6 park fee. Other options include mountain biking, lake fishing, bird-watching and photography, and horseback riding. Arrangements are made for canopy tours, white-water rafting, kayaking, and visits to Tabacón hot springs, and Caño Negro.

Elevation at the observatory is 2,428 feet (740 m); annual rainfall is 197 inches (5,000 mm). Drier months are December through May. In the glassed-in dining room, guests view the volcano and sample local fruits and vegetables and enjoy such typical meals as *olla de carne* (a meat-and-vegetable soup) or *arroz con pollo* (chicken and rice). Breakfast buffet is $8, lunch $12, dinner $14, box lunches $8, plus taxes.

The 27 rooms offer different options: more rustic standard rooms were originally built for the researchers, some with volcano views, doubles $91. Observatory rooms with oversized window to Arenal are $129. The beautiful Smithsonian block, across a 134-foot (40-m) suspension bridge from the dining room, has walls of glass that bring the energy of the fiery colossus into each room, $119. There is a volcano-viewing deck upstairs and a volcano museum—check out the working seismograph that monitors volcanic and seismic activity. For budget-minded travelers, the original farmhouse (La Casona) is a short distance from the lodge; it has four rooms with two shared baths, double $63. Rates include breakfast buffet. Ask about packages, some including countrywide travel. A three-day, two-night tour at Arenal Volcano Lodge is $285 per person double occupancy, including San José round-trip transportation, lodging, most meals, and a guided walk to the waterfall and recent lava flow.

Details: *15.5 miles (25 km) west of La Fortuna; 506/290-7011, fax 506/290-8427, lodge tel/fax 506/695-5033, info@arenal-observatory.co.cr, www.arenal-observatory.co.cr— find daily update on volcanic activity and weather. The observatory is 5.6 miles (nine km) from the turnoff to Arenal Volcano National Park (road is quite tame now with bridges over rivers—no more standing at the edge of rushing water in rainy season with a thumping*

heart, wondering if you and the jeep would make it
Fortuna/Tilarán bus leaves you at the park turnoff, or yo
Fortuna.

Arenal Volcano National Park

Arenal Volcano, one of the world's most active volcanoes, dominates the landscape of this 5,436-acre (2,200-ha) park. It has been
thundering and blowing since 7:30 A.M., July 29, 1968. After a 400-
year dormancy, Arenal devastated more than four square miles (10
sq. km) in the last three days of July. It has been continuously active
ever since, sometimes quiet for a month at a time and at other times
erupting every few minutes. Eruptions send clouds of ash and fiery
materials into the sky. Lava flows, visible with binoculars in daytime,
are spectacular at night.

Continuously monitored today, the volcano draws tens of thousands of visitors simply to marvel at this natural force or to walk the
trails in its shadow. Las Coladas Trail, which begins at the first park
station from the highway, goes to a lava bed from a 1993 flow. Allow
about 90 minutes for the 1.7-mile (2.8-km), mostly level trail. Los
Tucanes Trail, named for the five species of toucans here, crosses
the lava flow and continues into forest from this same entrance
(allow about three hours)—you can enter it farther down the road.
Howler and white-faced monkeys also roam these parts. Las
Heliconias Trail, which can be walked in 30 minutes, shows visitors
some of the vegetation that has returned since the big eruption. It
crosses Las Coladas Trail for those who wish to continue to the lava
flow. Ask about the trail to La Fortuna Waterfall.

Though Arenal Volcano is the most popular attraction, the park
also includes habitat along Lake Arenal's shores and protects important watershed for Lake Arenal, whose waters feed the country's largest
hydroelectric project and an irrigation project that encompasses some
172,970 acres (70,000 ha) in Guanacaste. Take Sendero Los Miradores
Trail near the park's main entrance; less than a mile long (1.2 km), it
leads to a lookout point for the lake, volcano, and dam. Signs along the
dirt road alongside Arenal caution visitors to view the fiery colossus
from a safe distance. Climbing to the crater would be hazardous to
your health; in fact, it could be fatal. Respect warning signs.

Temperatures are between 55°F and 64°F (12.6°C and 17.5°C); average annual rainfall is 197 inches (5,000 mm). Maximum elevation is 5,538 feet (1,633 m).

Though Arenal became a national park only in 1994, it had previously been in a protected zone. Located in the Tilarán Mountains, it is part of the Arenal Conservation Area. The park station has a visitor center with exhibits, gift shop, cafeteria, and restrooms. For a daily update on volcanic activity and weather at Arenal Volcano, check out www.arenal-observatory.co.cr.

Details: *10 miles (16 km) west of La Fortuna, four hours northwest of San José; telephone hotline 506/192, 506/695-5180, fax 506/695-5082. Open 8 A.M. to 6 P.M.; admission $6. Turnoff to the park entrance is at the east end of the dam, which is about a mile (two km) from the visitor center. For bus travel, take the La Fortuna/Tilarán bus to the turnoff. Local and San José tour operators and lodges offer guided tours.*

Baldi Termae

The new kid on the block when it comes to hot springs, Baldi is getting rave reviews. Located at the base of Arenal Volcano and surrounded by lush gardens, the thermal mineral water is pumped from deep streams, free of bacteria and mineral concentration. Laboratory test results are available. Bathe in three pools with temperatures from 98.6°F to 145°F (37°C to 63°C), and then enjoy a meal in the restaurant. Though there are no therapeutic treatments yet, there may be by the time you arrive. This is an alternative to higher-priced hot springs in the area.

Details: *Five miles (eight km) west of La Fortuna; 506/479-9651, fax 506/290-6681, larevue@racsa.co.cr, www.larevuenet.com/baldi. Open 10 A.M. to 8 P.M.; admission $10; a $20 package includes entrance and a meal.*

Bosque Eterno de los Niños, Poco Sol Sector

This is the eastern access to the private reserve of Bosque Eterno de los Niños (Children's Eternal Rain Forest), a 56,800-acre (23,000-ha) reserve created by and protected with gifts from children and adults around the world. The Monteverde Conservation League, a private nonprofit organization, owns and manages this valuable resource, which reaches over the Tilarán Mountains to Monteverde on the Pacific slope.

Here on the Atlantic slope is Poco Sol Field Station, where natural history visitors can be a part of the special magic spun by nature, children's love, and dedication of countless individuals. Vistas lift the soul: forest across undulating hills; Poco Sol Lagoon, mysterious in the mists, shimmering in the sun; the San Carlos Valley below in the distance. From the covered porch off the dining room, watch toucans, hummingbirds, oropendolas, and other of the 330-plus species of birds identified in Poco Sol.

More than six miles (10 km) of well-maintained trails lead through a variety of habitats (regenerating pasture and primary and secondary forest) to the lake, small hot springs, and a waterfall that speaks of eternity. Vegetation is incredible: epiphytes, lianas, philodendrons. On the way to the waterfall, your first glimpse of a giant fig will stop you in your tracks.

You may see a white-fronted nunbird, white hawk, bare-necked umbrellabird, scarlet-rumped cacique, red-legged honeycreeper, rufous-tailed jacamar, ornate hawk-eagle, ocellated antbird, or some of the more than 20 species of tanagers here. Butterflies, including the morpho, waft by. More than one visitor has mistaken the large hawkmoth for a hummingbird. Keep your eyes open for snakes. A beautiful but venomous fer-de-lance, camouflaged beside the trail, was inches from my rubber boots—fortunately, he slept. Hear and see howler monkeys, along with white-faced monkeys, coatis, kinkajous, sloths, and agoutis. Station personnel can recommend local guides.

The rustic, two-level main building has a kitchen and dining area (buffet-style meals) and dormitory-style bedrooms (25 bunk beds in all), shared bathrooms and no hot water. Lodging and meals is $30 per person. A solar panel provides electricity.

Altitude ranges from 1,640 to 3,280 feet (500 to 1,000 m). Bring rain gear. Have your camera ready for the one-lane suspension bridge over the Peñas Blancas River on the way to Poco Sol. Because of the shelter's small size and isolation, reservations are necessary. Ask about the Children's Nature Center, two miles (three km) from La Tigra. See more about the children's forest in Chapter 10 and a Chapter 2 sidebar.

Details: Office at La Tigra, 31 miles (50 km) north of San Ramón. Poco Sol Field Station is 7.4 miles (12 km) by unpaved road into the mountains to the west; the turnoff is a little more than 100 yards (500 m) north of the La Tigra office; in La Tigra, 506/468-0148, fax 506/468-0260, acmtigra@racsa.co.cr; in Monteverde 506/645-5003, fax 506/645-5104; acmmcl@racsa.co.cr, www.monteverde.or.cr. The San Ramón/La Fortuna bus passes by the office. La Fortuna tour operators offer day trips to Poco Sol.

Bosques de Chachagua

Where else can you awaken to a morning greeting from two collared aracaris pecking at the window? Bosques de Chachagua in the Tilarán Mountains south of La Fortuna offers an unforgettable experience in a tropical paradise.

In the 10-minute dirt-road drive up from the paved highway, you move from the workaday world to a rain-forest hideaway, which, in some wondrous way, helps put that other world in better perspective. The 23 attractive individual bungalows of the Chachagua Rain Forest Hotel offer creature comforts: broad wooden-plank walls and polished hardwood floors harmonize with the soft colors of comforters and drapes; artwork, and flower arrangements of heliconia, anthurium, and varicolored tropical leaves. Wood and glass doors open onto a generous terrace with benches and chairs. The pièce de résistance, however, has to be the bathrooms, as large as some hotel rooms. Bilevel, each one has two small garden areas, mirrored windows providing privacy and a view of the outdoors at the same time, almost like having an outdoor shower.

Walkways lead from bungalows across a stream to the reception area, a natural swimming pool, covered outdoor bar, and the open-air dining room, a tablecloth place with excellent service by friendly staff. Meals are delicious. You may find owner Carlos Salazar in the kitchen adding his special touches, especially at breakfast. Try pineapple, papaya, *yuca*, squash, and black beans grown here. Beef, poultry (despite an ocelot's interest in the chicken population), eggs, milk, and cheese are also produced on the ranch. Breakfast was embellished one morning with a flight overhead of at least 60 red-lored parrots. An anteater appears more often than not at 8 A.M. The resident scarlet macaw, which hangs out at the dining room, may deign to speak to you.

Chachagua is an almost-250-acre (100-ha) ranch with glorious rain forest. The magic of the contiguous International Children's Rain Forest spills over into this rich reserve. Trails go to small waterfalls, along rivers, and through forest inhabited by sloths, white-faced and howler monkeys, keel-billed toucans, blue morpho butterflies, and poison-dart frogs. Have the guide show you the blood-of-Christ plant and monkey ladders, and watch for the large, beautiful golden orb-spiders that live here. Boots and walking sticks are provided. The reserve can be a base for trips to nearby Arenal, Tabacón Resort, and Caño Negro. Half-day horseback tours are available.

Guests at Chachagua are invited to donate to the neighboring community's school for books, supplies, and building improvements. A new classroom and bathrooms have already been added, the building painted, and students now have books and school supplies.

Doubles are $84. Breakfast is $8, lunch or dinner $12. A three-day package includes lodging; meals, visits to Sarchí, Tabacón, and Arenal, and a guided walk and natural history slide presentation: $304 per person, double occupancy. A four-day package adds a visit to Caño Negro.

Details: Eight miles (12 km) south of La Fortuna off of the road to San Ramón; reservations through San José office, 506/231-0356, fax 506/290-6506, chachagua@novanet.co.cr, www.novanet.co.cr/chachagua. There is no reliable phone service to the hotel yet, but there is radio contact.

Caño Negro National Wildlife Refuge

Centerpiece of this refuge for about 400 species of resident and migrant birds is Caño Negro Lake, which covers some 2,225 acres (900 ha) with up to 10 feet (three m) of water in the rainy season. As dry season progresses, it diminishes to a few pools, streams, and an arm of the river that feeds it. In drier months, January to April, visitors who wait patiently and discreetly in sight of remaining water holes can watch a variety of animals come to drink.

The country's largest colony of Neotropical olivaceous cormorants is found here, and it's a good place to see roseate spoonbills (the only pink bird in the country), wood storks, species of ducks you never imagined existed, snowy egrets, five species of kingfisher, and green-backed herons. Jabiru storks sometimes visit.

167

Other animals at Caño Negro include three species of monkeys, sloths, river otters, peccaries, white-tailed deer, silky anteaters, bats, and tayras. Endangered species include the tapir, jaguar, ocelot, cougar, and crocodile.

During a few magical hours on a boat, I saw some of these birds plus jacanas, two groups of spider monkeys, three of howlers, a red-lored parrot, a black-bellied whistling duck, anhingas with their wings spread to dry, caimans, iguanas, a great egret, and, for the thrill of the day, a common potoo looking for all the world like a part of the branch on which it was perched. How the boatman spotted it is a mystery.

From January to April, less than four inches (100 mm) of rain falls; but total average is 138 inches (3,500 mm). South and west of the lake, where the land rises abruptly from the plain to the Guanacaste Mountain Range, rainfall can reach 158 inches (4,000 mm) a year. Elevation of the lake is about 100 feet (30 m); its land area totals 25,132 acres (10,171 ha).

One aim of this refuge is to help improve the economic well-being of its neighbors by promoting sustainable ways to exploit natural resources. A tree nursery established with area families provides trees to reforest in the refuge and Río Frío basin, with some sold for profit. Freshwater turtles are raised; 30 percent are released and the rest sold. Families are allowed to fish in lagoons when they are drying up, and the refuge helps find a market for the catch. About 50 species of fish are found at Caño Negro, including an unusual gar. Under an agreement with the local development association, the wildlife department allows cattle to graze here in dry season when the lake recedes, a controversial issue with some who point to the erosion that cattle cause along riverbanks and the damage to wildlife, such as destruction of caiman eggs.

Protection of these wetlands and remaining forest has received a shot in the arm with creation of a Friends of the Earth biological research center at Caño Negro, near refuge headquarters, to facilitate the study of tropical wetlands, a fragile ecosystem. Equally important are sustainable development projects with the 200 families who live within the refuge, to provide economic alternatives and discourage poaching.

Camping is allowed at the ranger station on the Caño Negro side. A bunk at the ranger station there is sometimes available. In dry season, visitors explore on foot or rent horses; in rainy months, community members take visitors out in their boats for $12 an hour.

Details: 22 miles (36 km) east of Upala, 14 miles (23 km) southwest of Los Chiles; telephone hotline 506/192, 506/661-8464, fax 506/460-0644. Open 8 A.M. to 4 P.M.; admission $1, camping $2 per person per day. There are two main refuge entrances: the town of Caño Negro, site of headquarters, and on the Río Frío from Los Chiles. Many river tours do not go all the way to headquarters. Take a Ciudad Quesada/Los Chiles bus to get to the Río Frío side of the refuge. On the other side, take a Upala/Caño Negro bus. Tours include transfer, guide, and boat ride, but you can hire a local guide and boat at Los Chiles or Caño Negro.

Eco-Lodge, Lago Coter

Marvelous nature trails traverse the biologically rich forest of this private reserve. Learn about such things as flying sticks and why some tropical trees shed their bark (to keep epiphytes from taking hold). See a huge mound built by busy leaf-cutter ants and marvel at the free-form sculpture of a vine called "monkey ladder."

On 18 miles (29 km) of marked trails, hike on your own or go with well-trained bilingual naturalists who help guests appreciate that tropical forests are more than monkeys jumping from branch to branch or coatis darting across a trail, or the turquoise flash of a scarlet-thighed dacnis contrasting against the varied greens of trees and plants. Tropical forests are all of these things, but they're also the tiny flower almost hidden among fallen leaves, an insect disguised as a dried leaf, an animal track in the mud, an elegant tree fern, and thousands of plant and animal species intertwined in a web of life.

A half-day canopy tour for $45 views this web in the top of the forest, where so much of the life is found. After a hike, climb to the first platform via a ladder and then move between eight platforms along cables. Finally, rappel back to the forest floor. Platforms range from 92 to 115 feet (28 to 35 m) high. Be sure to explore the trail to a *palenque* built by Maleku people, visit with them about their culture, and see their crafts.

Guests are invited to record wildlife seen here; more than 350 birds have been sighted. Leafing through the sightings book, you find monkeys, brocket deer, keel-billed toucans, bare-necked umbrella birds, squirrel cuckoos, and coatis, among others. Eco-Lodge is a comfortable home base for horseback riding, lake fishing, windsurfing (on Coter and Arenal Lakes), canoeing, and kayaking; for trips to the volcano and hot springs, even to the Bebedero River, Palo Verde and Rincón de la Vieja National Parks, and Caño Negro. Rubber boots, flashlights, and rain ponchos provided.

The main building feels like a mountain lodge, with its spacious living/recreation area, welcoming fire in the fireplace, TV and video room, bar, and dining room. Ample, tasty meals are served buffet style. Interesting photographs, many of an earlier Costa Rica, adorn walls of the lodge; one of the most intriguing shows a flying saucer near Arenal volcano and mysterious, heart-shaped Coter Lake.

The 23 cozy, carpeted lodge rooms are of rock and wood, each with pretty comforters. Fourteen attractively furnished rooms in seven bungalows are within a five-minute walk of the lodge. Rooms have high ceilings and a glass wall that faces the porch and volcano, Arenal and Coter Lakes. Doubles $49 per person in lodge, $66 in bungalows. Breakfast $6, lunch or dinner $12. A two-night package includes lodging, meals, transfers, taxes, hiking, horseback riding, canoeing, kayaking, and visits to Arenal Volcano, hot springs, and Caño Negro, from $456.

Dry season is not as pronounced here: rainfall amounts to about 152 inches (3,857 mm) a year. Elevation at the lodge is 2,329 feet (710 m). Forested slopes have both rain-forest and cloud-forest characteristics.

Details: 29 miles (46 km) west of Arenal Volcano, 17 miles (28 km) northeast of Tilarán; 506/257-5075, lodge for non-office hours 506/382-3043, fax 506/257-7065, in U.S. 888/326-5634, information@eco-lodge.com, www.ecolodge.com. The turnoff is near kilometer 46 between Nuevo Arenal and Tilarán. Tilarán/Ciudad Quesada (San Carlos) buses pass by on the highway two miles (three km) below.

Los Lagos

Here under the volcano is a placid lake with reflections of forest around it, the quiet sound of the chestnut-mandibled toucan, and a sky dramatically dominated by Arenal Volcano. It is a special, silent place. The lake is a centerpiece of the 500-acre (202-ha) reserve and ranch owned and operated by the Cedeño Villegas family. In this other-world atmosphere, where no music and no motorcycles are allowed, you can hike forest trails, paddle the lake, or ride horseback. A 2,624-foot (800-m) trail leads to lava beds. The family plans to keep this secluded area nature oriented. Eight rustic lakeside cabins are constructed of river rock, wood, and bamboo, and have a cold-water shower and electricity, $30 for two, including taxes. Sheltered outdoor areas are available for relaxing and cooking.

A guided horseback tour, $13, takes guests through primary forest, over an old lava flow, to a *mirador* with impressive views of Arenal, Tenorio, and Miravalles Volcanoes. Fishing and swimming are permitted in this lake and another. Bring a camera and binoculars not only for the vistas but for the birds—lots here, both land and water birds. The lake is a 10-minute drive from the entrance to Los Lagos. At the entrance, there is an eye-catching multilevel swimming pool with a water slide. At the top, water flows out of a cone-shaped replica of the volcano, which rises like a giant behind it. A large hot tub is fed by hot water from the river. There is a small crocodile farm and butterfly farm.

Here are modern rooms that have fans, small refrigerators, and big showers with hot water; doubles from $87. A covered, open-air restaurant welcomes both guests and day visitors, and there is a gift shop. Los Lagos is open for day visits; admission is $5 for adults and $3 for children to swim in pools, visit the lake, and hike trails. A tractor-driven cart gets visitors without transport to the lakes.

Los Lagos is affiliated with Tri-Med, in which a group of small mountain lodges in the Arenal area belonging to individuals of the same extended family have joined forces to market their places and provide common tours. These are rural, local folks for the most part, who opted to invest in tourism on their lands. Ask about their tours, both around Arenal and combinations with other sites.

Details: *3.7 miles (six km) from La Fortuna on the main road to Arenal Volcano park, at Los Lagos; tel/fax 506/479-9126, in U.S. 800/648-2141, TheBest@CostaRicaHotels.cc, www.americas-paradise.com.*

Tabacón Resort

In the shadow of Arenal Volcano, Tabacón is a wonderland of gardens, paths, ponds, streams, and pools fed by hot springs: 12 natural mineral pools plus man-made ones. The rush of river water blends with the sound of the small waterfalls where bathers sit beneath naturally heated waters for an invigorating water massage. Rising steam lends mystery to this fairyland with a phenomenal view of the volcano. Don't miss this treat for body and spirit.

Guests may hike a half-mile (one-km) trail along the forest to a small volcanic lake. Bring binoculars—birding is good here. After-dark visits are also popular for a chance to relax after a day of sightseeing or to experience the glow of Arenal's fireworks.

Choose from the full-service Ave del Paraíso restaurant overlooking the gardens or Congo Café, for coffees, pastries, light snacks. Tabacón also has a gift shop and bars. Spa treatments such as massages, aromatherapy, and mud masks are available—reservations recommended.

Across the road Tabacón offers another attractive, less-expensive option: bathe in hot springs for $5. With a more natural ambience, set in the forest along the river, it lacks volcano views but offers such amenities as changing rooms, restrooms, and landscaped grounds.

Details: 7.5 miles (12 km) west of La Fortuna; 506/256-1500, fax 506/221-3075, at Tabacón tel/fax 506/479-9033, sales@tabacon.com, www.tabacon.com. Open daily 10 A.M. to 10 P.M.; admission $16 for adults, $9 for children. The La Fortuna/Tilarán bus passes in front.

Tilajari Resort Hotel and Private Reserve

Combine a 42-acre (17-ha) tropical garden and recreation area along the banks of the San Carlos River with a 1,000-acre (405-ha) humid tropical forest for a Tilajari experience with volcano views thrown in.

The resort's setting along the river on the Plains of San Carlos offers nature and adventure. Watch for crocodiles along the riverbank. Keel-billed and chestnut-mandibled toucans raised here have chosen to stay—they have unclipped wings—and seem to enjoy posing for photos. Owners Jaime Hamilton and Ricardo Araya hope that a great green macaw added to the menagerie will do the same. I saw a young sloth curled up in one of the many fruit trees, which are among more than 550 plants here. Look for the medicinal plant/spice garden, orchids, and other tropical superstars. A butterfly garden (so far, about 200 butterflies representing 10 species) has a pretty fountain and flowering plants, with educational displays in an adjoining open-air pavilion. On a guided hiking/horseback tour of the thousand-acre woods, see 400-year-old trees, including some spectacular strangler figs, monkeys, tropical frogs, and birds galore, $15 each for two persons. If horses are not your thing, go by tractor-driven trailer.

Gracious lodging quarters are quiet, located away from the sports areas, restaurant, and pools. Surrounded by manicured lawns and gardens, 76 spacious rooms have air conditioning, ceiling fans, satellite TV, hair dryers, and telephones. All open onto private covered terraces. Doubles are from $85; family suites, $110. Meals are excellent: enjoy homegrown tropical fruits. Breakfast is $9, lunch or dinner $15, and meal plans are available. Bring your camera to the dining room: at bird-feeding stations you are sure to see scarlet-rumped tanagers.

Resort facilities include pools, indoor and outdoor lighted tennis courts, racquetball courts, a sauna, and a hot tub. Offsite nature/adventure tours include Caño Negro, Venado Caves; La Fortuna Waterfall, Arenal Volcano and hot springs at Tabacón, a safari float on the Peñas Blancas River in two- and seven-person inflatable kayaks (stopping to visit a rural family), and white-water rafting on the Sarapiquí. Guides for Tilajari trips are bilingual, excellent at spotting species, and knowledgeable about local history and geography. A two-night package covers lodging, meals, tours to Arenal/Tabacón, rain forest reserve, butterfly garden, and Caño Negro or float trip, $407 each, double occupancy.

Details: Just west of Muelle intersection, 73 miles (117 km) from San José, 2.5 hours, 40 minutes from Arenal Volcano; 506/469-9091, fax 506/469-9095, info@tilajari.com, www.tilajari.com.

GUIDES AND OUTFITTERS

Aguas Bravas Arenal Outdoor Center is on the main street through La Fortuna, across from the plaza, 506/479-9025; fax 506/229-4837; info@aguas-bravas.co.cr, www.aguas-bravas.co.cr. It offers rafting on the Peñas Blancas River, class II-III rapids, for $37; and rafting and kayaking trips on the Sarapiquí, for beginners or experienced rafters. Half-day and full-day mountain-bike trips range from $45 to $65, guides and bicycles provided. Ask about horseback options. Custom packages encompass Sarapiquí and Arenal areas, Monteverde, and the Caribbean, including kayaking, rafting, biking, surfing, hiking, snorkeling, diving, and horseback riding.

Aventuras Arenal in La Fortuna, 506/479-9133, fax 506/479-9259, avarenal@racsa.co.cr, www.arenaladventures.com, offers a four-hour mountain-bike tour that takes in Lake Arenal and Arenal Volcano plus a forest trail, for $45; horseback riding to La Fortuna Waterfall is $20 per person (bilingual guide arranged for an added fee). A trip to Venado Caves is $35 and Caño Negro $47. Transfers are available from La Fortuna and area hotels to anywhere in the country. Ask about packages from San José that include Arenal Volcano, Tabacón Resort, and Caño Negro. The office is on the main road, one block east of the gas station; international telephone and fax service is available.

For a canopy experience in the Children's Rain Forest, reserve with **Canopy Tour La Fortuna,** tel/fax 506/479-9456, contactus @canopyfortuna.com, www.canopyfortuna.com, located across from the gas station in La Fortuna. The four-hour tour starts with a horseback ride, followed by a short guided hike, and then a climb to the first of three platforms—ranging from 69 feet (21 m) to 115 feet (35 m). Move between platforms harnessed to a transverse cable over distances up to of almost 200 feet (60 m). Finish with a rappel to the ground. From platforms, look out at canopy life. Part of each $45 tour goes to the Monteverde Conservation League, owner of the Children's Forest, Bosque Eterno de los Niños.

Contact Norman List at **Rock River Lodge,** 31 miles (50 km) west of La Fortuna, for windsurfing or biking, tel/fax 506/695-5644, rokriver@racsa.co.cr, www.rockriver.mastermind.net. Norman was one of the pioneer windsurfers at Arenal; he also does ocean wind-surfing in Bahia Salinas, but no wave sailing, however. Check out his unusual mountain biking tours: the three-day Volcano Trail for intermediate bikers goes to Orosi Volcano near Nicaragua, $100 a day. A Quipilapa tour goes to Miravalles, and two- to five-hour day tours visit Cañas for a swim in the Corobicí or go to a waterfall for a swim in the Tenorio River.

Sunset Tours, 506/479-9415, fax 506/479-9099, info@sunset-tours.com, www.sunset-tours.com, has a full tour menu: hiking at Arenal Volcano National Park, $25; boat trip to Caño Negro, $45; hiking and canoeing at Cerro Chato, $65; horseback and hike to La Fortuna Waterfall, $18; Peñas Blancas float safari, $40; guided walks at Poco Sol station in the children's rain forest, Bosque Eterno de los Niños, $45; and sportfishing. Transfers are available. Go to Monteverde from La Fortuna by boat and car, three hours, $45. Ask about one- and two-night packages from San José; Mainor Castro will do his best to fit your needs. The office, next to Rancho La Cascada Restaurant, offers fax and international telephone services, sells stamps, and has a gift shop.

Ree Strange Sheck

La Fortuna

CAMPING

Campers are welcome at **Caño Negro National Wildlife Refuge** at park headquarters in the town of Caño Negro on the western border (see under "Nature Adventure Sights" above).

Jungla y Senderos Los Lagos, 3.7 miles (six km) from La Fortuna on the main road to Arenal Volcano National Park, has campsites; tel/fax 506/479-9126, in U.S. 800/648-2141 (see under "Nature Adventure Sights").

LODGING

Albergue Ecoturistico La Catarata, turnoff about 1.2 miles (two km) from the center of La Fortuna on the road to the volcano, tel/fax 506/479-9168, is owned and operated by a community association. It has eight rustic cabins and a typical restaurant. Doubles are $48, including breakfast. A sustainable development project started with help from World Wildlife Fund Canada, Canadian International Development Agency, and Arenal Conservation Area, this ecolodge brings increased income to members of this farming and dairying village while helping protect the region's biological diversity. Community members do cooking, cleaning, and guiding, in addition to farm work. They have medicinal, butterfly, and orchid gardens and a *tepezcuintle* breeding program. *Tepezcuintles*— large, nocturnal rodents—have been hunted heavily in Costa Rica for their excellent meat.

Members lead trips to Arenal Volcano, La Fortuna Waterfall, and Lake Arenal for fishing or boating. The restaurant is open to the public, so stop by, meet the members and see community and conservation at work. This is one of three such ecolodge projects; the others are Las Heliconias in Bijagua near Upala, and Albergue EcoVerde in Monte Los Olivos near Monteverde. These are part of a consortium of ecotourism cooperatives (COOPRENA) through which you can also get information and make reservations: tel/fax 506/286-4203, cooprena@racsa.co.cr, www.agroecoturismo.net.

Arenal Lodge, 506/228-3189, fax 506/289-6798, in U.S. 800/948-3770, ArenaLodge@centralamerica.com, www.centralamerica.com, is just west of the dam at Lake Arenal and about a mile (two km) up a paving-stone road through a macadamia farm. Front rooms at the main lodge have impressive volcano views, while those in back are around a brick courtyard graced with orchids. The 12 view rooms are junior suites, with private balconies, double $107; standard doubles (without a balcony) are $65. Five spacious duplex chalets up from the lodge have kitchenettes, balconies, and spectacular volcano views, $117 for two persons. Rates include breakfast. Amenities include a big fireplace in the lounge, a small library, and a hot tub. Guests often see howler monkeys in forest at garden's edge and may even spot a tayra or anteater. Hummingbird feeders and platforms for fruit bring a variety of birds to the grounds. The specialty here is fishing, but an in-house tour operator also arranges mountain biking, horseback riding, hiking and area tours.

Hotel Arenal Paraíso is 4.3 miles (seven km) west of La Fortuna, cellular phone 506/383-5658, U.S. number 800/648-2141, tel/fax 506/479-9006, TheBest@CostaRicaHotels.cc, www.americas-paradise.com. The volcano looms practically in the front yard for 40

Glassed-in porch with views to Arenal Volcano, Hotel Arenal Paraíso

rooms set in pretty gardens. Each room is of beautiful tropical woods, with ceiling fan, small refrigerator, good mattress, and floral comforter. Every cabin has a front porch and windows that face the volcano; deluxe units have glassed-in porches for protected volcano viewing in windy weather. Doubles are $45 to $64. Enjoy the hot tub and pool, natural mineral waters, and forest trails to a hot spring and the Arenal River. This working 148-acre (60-ha) farm has 49 acres (20 ha) of primary forest. Wake up to the sounds of howler monkeys, toucans, parrots, and oropendolas; watch hummingbirds out your door and cows being moved on the highway to the milking barn—with Arenal as a backdrop. Pool and restaurant are open to the public, as is the gift shop, which offers T-shirts hand-painted by members of a local cooperative. Owners Oscar and Roxana and family are gracious hosts who offer tours to Los Lagos and La Fortuna Waterfall and arrange transfers.

Hotel San Bosco, 1.5 blocks north of the plaza on the main road through La Fortuna, 506/479-9050, fax 506/479-9109, fortuna@racsa.co.cr, www.arenal-volcano.com, is a pleasant place to stay created by owners Celso, Flor, and family. Not all 29 rooms have volcanic views, but not to worry. Watch to your heart's content from a third-floor covered open-air covered terrace. Swimming pool, hot tub, gym, porches, verandas, orthopedic mattresses, architectural accents of river stone, and reading lamps are among amenities. Tours arranged. Rancho La Cascada Restaurant, in the family, is handy for meals. Doubles in the 18 air-conditioned rooms are $50; in 11 original rooms, $40.

Hotel Tilawa, 13 miles (21 km) northeast of Cañas, 506/695-5050, fax 506/695-5766, tilawa@racsa.co.cr, www.hotel-tilawa.com, is an imposing two-story building above Lake Arenal, where color is key and the architecture recalls the Palace of Knossos. Every room has large windows looking out on the water or attractive gardens, two queen-size beds with orthopedic mattresses, writing desk, and both tub and shower. There are 28 rooms, some with kitchenettes, from $77, taxes included, for standard doubles. The restaurant is open to the public, and there is a poolside bar.

Trails take off into the forest next to the swimming pool; howler monkeys call, and guests will likely see keel-billed toucans. The hotel offers tennis, bass fishing, guided horseback tours, sailing tours, and mountain bikes. Tilawa's strong suit is windsurfing: the lakeside Marina and WindSurf Center (www.windsurfcostarica.com) offers rental equipment and lessons for adults and children. A half-day volcano and hot springs tour for $49 is by boat across the lake, and a Tilawa exclusive waterfall adventure with swimming at the base of the 90-foot cascade is $40. A weeklong surfing package is $500 each for two.

La Ceiba Tree Lodge Nature Resort is about one hour from La Fortuna and four miles (six km) before Nuevo Arenal, tel/fax 506/ 385-1540, 506/694-4297, ceibaldg@racsa.co.cr, www.charminghotels .net. The bed-and-breakfast has five bright, airy rooms that open off a tiled terrace with a panoramic view of Lake Arenal and spectacular sunsets, double $64, including breakfast and taxes. Owner Malte von Schlippenbach can provide evening meals on request, from simple dishes to exclusive dinners. In front of the lodge is its namesake: the 197-foot (60-m) ceiba tree, thought to be more than 500 years old. Ceibas (kapok trees in English) were revered by indigenous peoples; let its energy speak to you. Enjoy the orchid collection, and on paths in the forest around the lodge, see three kinds of toucans, howler monkeys, or sloths and enjoy two brooks with small cascades. Rent boats for sailing, rowing, and fishing; take sailing lessons; tour the lake on a Hobie Cat; rent a mountain bike; or go horseback riding. Malte suggests day tours to the hot springs or volcano, rafting, or jungle hikes.

Mystica Resort, cellular phone 506/382-1499, fax 506/695-5387, mystica@racsa.co.cr, www.members.aol.com/mysticacr, offers mist, hills, lake, and volcano. It's a mystical place, hence its name. One rainy night it was a haven for this traveler. I was welcomed by the warm fire in the fireplace, calmed by the soft music, and tempted by the smells of pizza and pasta from the Italian kitchen. Owners Barbara Moglia and Francesco Carullo serve 12 kinds of pizza and nine kinds of pasta, most from $4 to $7. Pizzas are cooked in a big brick oven. I recommend the gnocchi with Gorgonzola sauce—terrific. Homemade bread arrives at breakfast.

Each of six large, comfortable rooms, up a garden path from the restaurant, sleeps four in a double and bunk beds. Patchwork-quilt coverlets and wooden chairs and desk give a Shaker flavor. Animal cutouts on wooden lampshades create interesting effects. A common veranda with chairs affords lake viewing. Double $50, breakfast included. Windsurfing, mountain biking, fishing, Arenal visits, and horseback rides arranged. VISA only accepted.

Rock River Lodge, 31 miles (50 km) west of La Fortuna, tel/fax 506/695-5644, rokriver@racsa.co.cr, www.rockriver.mastermind.net, is delightfully casual. Most nights find a fire in the big fireplace near the main building's open-air lounge. There are views of the volcano and the lake, pretty at night with the lights on the far shore. Tropical woods warm the cozy bar, which has good music, and Arturo shakes a mean margarita. The restaurant and bar are open to the public. Owner Norman List's breakfasts are famous, and he may serve you himself. No lunch is served, but the $12 dinner with a variety of main dishes is excellent. Rooms are terraced on the hillside behind. Standard rooms are wood-paneled and inviting; windows onto a terrace face the lake, double room $53, including taxes. Eight newer bungalows have a definite Southwestern United States flair, $75. Norman engineered the unusual bathtubs. Sitting on the private terrace could be habit forming.

Guests windsurf—rentals $57 per day, lunch included—or bicycle (Rock River's two specialties), as well as raft the Corobicí River, ride horseback, take a Canopy Tour near Rincón de la Vieja, fish, or go birding. Norman has created unusual biking tours and was a pioneer in windsurfing at Arenal. The lodge is at kilometer 40, 11 miles (18 km) northeast of Tilarán.

Tabacón Lodge is 200 meters before Tabacón Resort on the road from La Fortuna, 506/256-1500, fax 506/221-3075, sales@tabacon .com, www.tabacon.com. The lodge has 42 lovely rooms featuring handcrafted Costa Rican furniture, individual terraces and balconies, volcano views, air conditioning, in-room telephones, and hot mineral-water showers. Many rooms are handicapped accessible and all have front-row seats for volcano watching, doubles $125, including breakfast buffet and entry to Tabacón Resort. Find ice machines and TV with satellite programming. There is an onsite restaurant and snack bar; guests may also eat at the restaurant at Tabacón Resort. Daily transport from San José and La Fortuna.

Five acres (two ha) of grounds include gardens (more than 300 plant species), forest, trails, artificial lake, swimming pool (half hot and half cold), and a natural hot tub. Bird-watching decks look at canopy level into the Tabacón River Canyon, and spider and howler monkeys move through this habitat. A new canopy operation gets visitors into upper forest levels.

Villa Decary is about one mile (two km) west of Arenal Botanical Gardens and one mile east of Nuevo Arenal, cellular 506/383-3012, tel/fax 506/694-4330, info@villadecary.com, www. villadecary.com. Here guests are more than just a name on the register. Owners Jeff Crandall and Bill Hemmer are innkeepers in the finest tradition. They tell guests about local fairs—even go with them—and advise on local restaurants and sightseeing. Take time to enjoy the orchids in the garden and the path around some of this seven-acre (2.8-ha) former fruit-and-coffee farm. Howler monkeys cross the yard to eat in the papaya trees. Jeff is a birder, and Bill's specialty is palms. The pretty dining room opens onto a deck through two sets of double doors. With notice, lunch or dinner can be served.

Each of the main building's five tastefully decorated rooms has orthopedic mattresses, reading lamp, ceiling fan, desk, private balcony set up for bird-watching, and great lake views. Beautiful tropical woods, woven Guatemalan bedspreads, hand-carved doors, and other decorator touches make this a real jewel, doubles $69. Three separate *casitas* with equipped kitchens and verandas with panoramic views are $79 to $129. Great breakfast is included. No credit cards are accepted.

FOOD

Many of the lodges and hotels in this section have good restaurants open to the public, so you can sample places other than where you are staying.

Swiss it is at **Los Héroes,** 18.6 miles (30 km) northwest of La Fortuna and 10.5 (17 km) from Arenal Volcano, 506/443-9505, tel/fax 506/284-6315, heroes@racsa.co.cr. Decor is straight from the Alps—big cowbells, red-and-white-checkered curtains. Choose from a menu that includes meat or cheese fondue, *rösti* (a great potato dish), spaghetti, and sausage and sauerkraut. The restaurant is in a chalet-style inn with lake and volcano views and a nice pool. A

Villa Decary—an inn above Lake Arenal

one-night tour from San José, including Arenal, Baldi Hot Springs, transfer, lodging, and Swiss fondue dinner is $87.

A must is **Pizzería e Ristorante Tramonti** in Nuevo Arenal, 506/694-4282. Gianni and Adriana make 16 types of pizza and homemade pasta—lasagna, fettuccine, and spaghetti—with Italian cheese and oil. Italian wine is available, too. Open 11:30 A.M. to 3 P.M. and 5 to 10 P.M., closed Monday in low season. Nuevo Arenal is 25 miles (41 km) northwest of La Fortuna, 20 miles (32 km) northeast of Tilarán.

Restaurante Rancho La Cascada on the main drag in La Fortuna has a complete menu and serves up good Costa Rican fare along with some international dishes. Watch the goings on in town from the open-air, rancho-style restaurant.

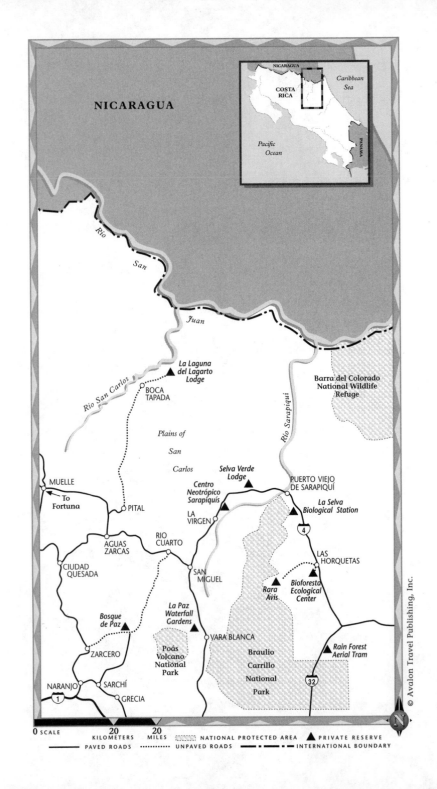

NICARAGUA

NICARAGUA

COSTA RICA

Caribbean Sea

Pacific Ocean

PANAMA

Rio San

Juan

Rio San Carlos

La Laguna del Lagarto Lodge

BOCA TAPADA

Barra del Colorado National Wildlife Refuge

Plains of

San

Carlos

Rio Sarapiquí

MUELLE

To Fortuna

PITAL

Selva Verde Lodge

Centro Neotrópico Sarapíquis

PUERTO VIEJO DE SARAPIQUÍ

La Selva Biological Station

LA VIRGEN

4

AGUAS ZARCAS

RIO CUARTO

LAS HORQUETAS

CIUDAD QUESADA

SAN MIGUEL

Bioforesta Ecological Center

Rara Avis

Bosque de Paz

La Paz Waterfall Gardens

ZARCERO

VARA BLANCA

Poás Volcano National Park

Braulio

Rain Forest Aerial Tram

Carrillo

National

32

NARANJO

SARCHÍ

Park

1

GRECIA

© Avalon Travel Publishing, Inc.

0 SCALE   20 KILOMETERS   20 MILES   ▒▒▒ NATIONAL PROTECTED AREA ▲ PRIVATE RESERVE
──── PAVED ROADS   ········· UNPAVED ROADS   ─·─·─ INTERNATIONAL BOUNDARY

N

CHAPTER 8

North Central—East: Puerto Viejo de Sarapiquí, Las Horquetas, Braulio Carrillo

This eastern part of the North Central region has rivers and forest to explore, top private reserves, an internationally known biological research station, and a high-tech canopy option. Known for great birding, it is also a wonderland of butterflies and brightly colored tropical frogs.

Because of its location, rivers, and highway system, it is easy to combine destinations here with Tortuguero, Braulio Carrillo and Poás, the southern Caribbean, and the Arenal area.

LAY OF THE LAND

On the banks of the Puerto Viejo River, 42 miles (67 km) north of San José, is **Puerto Viejo de Sarapiquí** (population 9,258), a center for river rafting, wildlife boat trips, kayaking, and rain forest exploration.

The Puerto Viejo River flows into the Sarapiquí on its way to the San Juan River, which forms the Costa Rica-Nicaragua boundary. These waters have history: indigenous peoples, Spanish explorers, and English pirates. Later some of California's forty-niners made their way from the U.S. east coast to San Francisco via the San Juan and through Lake Nicaragua to the Pacific. Today's travelers leave Puerto Viejo for Barra del Colorado National Wildlife Refuge or Tortuguero National Park in search of a different kind of treasure.

One route from San José to the north-central region is through Vara Blanca, passing through coffee plantations and dairy farms, with Barva Volcano and Cacho Negro on one side and Poás Volcano and Cerro Congo on the other. Huge expanses of black shade cloths shelter ornamental plants and flowers, important nontraditional exports. Strawberries are offered at roadside stands. The turnoff to Poás is just before Vara Blanca. The winding descent after Vara Blanca passes gorgeous waterfalls, the most photographed being **Catarata de la Paz (Peace Waterfall).** Stop in the small parking area at the picturesque

Ree Strange Sheck

Peace Waterfall between
Vara Blanca and Cariblanco

one-way bridge for picture taking. Another must-see is **Mirador San Fernando** at Cinchona, between La Paz and San Miguel. Have a cup of coffee for $1 while you view stunning San Fernando Waterfall across the river gorge and marvel at 21 species of dazzling hummingbirds at feeders.

Another route from San José is just as beautiful, through forest-covered mountains of Braulio Carrillo National Park, turning north through agricultural land and Las Horquetas, where fields of *pejibaye* palm, grown for its fruit, which Costa Ricans love, and the heart, *palmito.* Some travelers come from the northern Caribbean via the San Juan River. The only other town of size is **Ciudad Quesada** (population 34,161), most often referred to as San Carlos. This is the region's major north/south and east/west transportation hub, especially important for bus connections. Sixty miles (95 km) northwest of San José on the edge of the Plains of San Carlos, it is a commercial center. **Juan Castro Blanco National Park,** east of Ciudad Quesada, created in 1992, protects primary forest and is important watershed for the northern zone. Though it so far has no visitor facilities, some area lodges and tour operators are beginning to take people in. **La Marina Zoo,** 506/460-0946, is west of Aguas Zarcas, between Ciudad Quesada and San Miguel. Doña Alba María Alfaro has taken in sick, wounded, and abandoned animals to the tune of 65 species of birds and 30 of mammals and reptiles, including toucans, a crested eagle, a king vulture, an ocelot, four jaguars, white-tailed deer, and both collared and white-lipped peccaries (including one albino). Rescued tapirs are now reproducing. Open daily 8 A.M. to 4 P.M.; admission $2 adults, $1 children.

NATURE AND ADVENTURE ACTIVITIES

Rivers and forests take center stage for nature and adventure activities. The Sarapiquí River has up to class V rapids, excellent for white-water rafting and kayaking. At its lower elevations, it is popular for wildlife-viewing boat trips.

Boat trips on the San Juan River to Tortuguero and Barro Colorado are increasingly popular not only for the scenery and wildlife but for retracing a historical travel route and stepping into Nicaragua, at least long enough to pay for traversing the river, which Nicaragua claims.

The historical aspect of flora and fauna is touched upon at the new Centro Neotrópico Sarapiquís, while modern research underway is shared at La Selva Biological Station. Superb is the word for guided walks and hiking options in forests at Braulio Carrillo National Park and in reserves around Puerto Viejo. Visit butterfly, zoological, and botanical gardens, and take a tour of the canopy, bathe in thermal waters, and go mountain biking. Short distances and paved roads allow this area to be a base for travel to destinations such as Caño Negro and Arenal (see Chapter 7).

FLORA AND FAUNA

Wildlife most often seen here includes big iguanas, howler and white-faced monkeys, caimans and crocodiles, keel-billed and chestnut-mandibled toucans, agoutis, coatis, sloths, and a wealth of water birds. There is a chance to see groups of peccaries, not so easy elsewhere. Many of the colorful tropical birds regularly sighted here are mentioned in descriptions under "Nature and Adventure Sights."

Rare is the visitor who does not see the tiny, colorful strawberry poison-dart frog (*Dendrobates pumilio*), with its bright red body and dark blue hind legs. Species with conspicuous colors usually have strong toxins: their colors warn predators. This frog secretes toxin from skin glands, usually not harmful to humans unless it gets into open cuts. Toxins from some dendrobatid species were used by Colombian indigenous peoples on tips of blowgun darts—hence the name.

A TAYRA? NEVER HEARD OF IT.

So, what's a tayra? A member of the weasel family, it has a glossy chocolate-brown to black coat and a long, bushy tail, its long back slightly humped at the hindquarters. Although in some places the tayra's head and neck are tan, gray, or yellowish, in Costa Rica the entire animal is dark colored. Its den is in a tree hollow or a hole in the ground, and it searches during the day for food both on the ground and in trees—it's an agile climber. Tayras (Eira barbara) *eat bird eggs and nestlings, along with small mammals, lizards, insects, and fruit.*

Active in daytime, these frogs feed mostly on ants and termites. Coloration varies: frogs can be completely red or sport black spots on the back; limbs can be red or partly or entirely blue or black. Naturalist guides sometimes refer to them as the blue-jeans frog. Found from sea level to 3,150 feet (960 m) throughout the Caribbean lowlands, they are fairly easy to see in the Puerto Viejo de Sarapiquí area. Watch for them in leaf litter along trails or on tree trunks and exposed tree roots. Listen for their calls, which resemble some insect sounds.

When tadpoles hatch, the female (possibly the male, too) carries them off one or two at a time to sites such as a reservoir of water in a bromeliad high in a tree. Studies indicate that the female continues to visit her young, depositing an unfertilized egg in the water as food. Females have been observed returning at intervals of up to nine days to leave more eggs.

VISITOR INFORMATION

In general, lodges and tour companies are the sources for information, though if you pass through Ciudad Quesada, watch on the left as you come into town from the south for the CATUZON office, 506/460-1672, tourism chamber for the northern zone. Open weekdays 8:30 to 11:30 A.M. and 1:30 to 5 P.M.; Saturday 8 A.M. to 3 P.M. Staff is helpful. Pick up brochures, pamphlets, and maps.

GETTING THERE

From San José, travelers can come via Braulio Carrillo National Park/Las Horquetas or through Heredia/Vara Blanca/San Miguel. From the La Fortuna/Arenal area, access is via Ciudad Quesada or Muelle/Aguas Zarcas. Boats ply the Sarapiquí and San Juan Rivers to the northern Caribbean. Direct buses go from San José to Puerto Viejo de Sarapiquí, Braulio Carrillo National Park, Las Horquetas, and Ciudad Quesada, with connections to other destinations, such as Arenal and Boca Tapada. Nearest scheduled airline service is in La Fortuna. See Appendix A for airline and bus information, including some private van/bus options.

NATURE AND ADVENTURE SIGHTS

Bioforesta Ecological Center

Exuberance is what comes to mind—overflowing riches of rain forest, pristine rivers, and waterfalls. About 80 minutes from San José at Las Horquetas, beautiful trails go through beautiful forest, across streams, under towering trees up to 150 feet (45 m) high, including the endangered *caobilla* of the mahogany family and *jícaro,* or monkey pot. Why monkey pot? When a monkey puts its hand into the opening of the seed case to extract the seed, it cannot get its closed hand out. Perhaps the naturalist can show you one of the pots on a guided walk. Where the seeds fall is a good place to look for agoutis, pacas, or peccaries.

In Bioforesta's nearly 99-acre (400-ha) forest, you may also see the great green macaw and the almendro trees that attract it, white-faced and howler monkeys, agoutis, coatis, three-wattled bellbirds, morpho butterflies, or the bare-necked umbrella bird. Guided walks of up to four hours with a bilingual naturalist are $15.

Guests can go on horseback to see waterfalls and enjoy river pools, $20, or take a tour to butterfly and botanical gardens, stomping grounds of tropical frogs and hummingbirds. Visit the native trees reforestation project. Fish or canoe on four lagoons. River raft on the Sarapiquí or take a boat trip on the Puerto Viejo River.

Your adventure starts off with the walk across a long suspension bridge to the lodge, located above the junction of the Puerto Viejo and San Rafael Rivers. An open-air restaurant/bar looks down on this picture-perfect setting, with a swimming pool in the foreground. Rocking chairs on the veranda make this a great spot for bird-watching. Find out why there are three levels in the Bribri-style thatched rancho.

Comfortable rooms are in bungalows, each with covered terraces and designed for good cross-ventilation. Doubles are $68 per person, including meals and taxes. Delicious Costa Rican meals, prepared with a flair, are served buffet-style; the restaurant is open to the public.

Conservation and education are key words for owners Federico Gallegos and Pablo Sánchez, one of the country's foremost biologists. Research and education facilities for students are planned, and by the time you arrive, a wildlife rehabilitation center may be open.

Details: *80 minutes from San José, about one mile (two km) from the paved road at Las Horquetas; 506/253-2020, fax 506/224-3552, fegaso@yahoo.com, www.geocities.com/RainForest/vines/6365/biofor2.html. See Appendix A for bus schedules to Las Horquetas, including private van/bus options.*

Braulio Carrillo National Park

Braulio Carrillo is a symphony in green. Waterfalls, deep canyons, and raging rivers lend vibrant tones, and the great thing is that the concert begins only 30 minutes north of San José—and on a paved road. In fact, the road is the principal highway between the Central Valley and Limón. While roads cut through virgin forest usually spell ecological disaster, this particular highway spurred creation of this magnificent national park. Braulio Carrillo was established in 1977, and the road laid down through this rugged, largely untouched landscape opened in 1987.

The 117,867-acre (47,700-ha) park offers many levels of enjoyment—just driving the 14 miles (23 m) through is a thrill. This is a good place to see poor man's umbrella (*sombrilla del pobre*), a plant whose leaves grow up to seven feet (two m) across. People surprised by countryside rainstorms have used them for protection. If you're caught in the rain, which averages 177 inches (4,500 mm) a year, notice waterfalls that pour down the roadside; keep your eyes open for landslides. Lowland rainfall can be as much as 315 inches (8,000 mm). Elevation is from 9,534 to 112 feet (2,906 to 34 m). Because of topography and the elevation range within the park, temperatures can be 59°F (15°C) at Zurquí, 37°F (3°C) at Barva, or 86°F (30°C) in the Atlantic lowlands.

Among animals in the park are three species of monkey, sloths, kinkajous, deer, jaguarundi, two species of peccaries, and five of the six species of cats in Costa Rica. In all, there are 135 mammal species here, 73 of which are bats. The bare-necked umbrella bird knows these forests, as do eagles, trogons, hawks, curassows, and guans—515 bird species. Bromeliads and orchids adorn the trees: 6,000 species of plants.

The Zurquí ranger station, 30 minutes from San José, is small, but you can take the 10-minute Los Niños trail behind as a photo op and for good vistas. A good network of trails takes off from the

191

Quebrada González park station about a mile (two km) east of the Sucio River. You can't miss the Sucio (*sucio* means dirty) because of mineral content carried from its origins on Irazú. A long bridge is over its confluence with the Hondura River, and the interplay of blue and brown waters as they flow together is spectacular. Use pull-offs at either end of the bridge.

Or walk the Botarrama Trail from the station to a Río Sucio overlook, about two hours). The shorter Ceibo Trail is suitable for children and those who can't walk far, while Las Palmas takes about 1.5 hours. Remember to stay on trails and to check in at a ranger station before setting out. Vegetation is extremely dense in this rugged region. Even experienced hikers have gotten lost; as one Costa Rican put it, the forest has eaten several small planes and a few people.

The Quebrada González ranger station has a picnic area, restrooms, small gift shop, and water. See Chapter 5 for a description of the Barva sector at the upper reaches of the park, a very different habitat.

Details: *From San José, 7.5 miles (20 km) to the Zurquí entrance, open 8 A.M. to 4 P.M.; Quebrada González ranger station is east of the Sucio River, open 8 A.M. to 3:30 P.M. Telephone hotline 506/192, 506/290-1927, fax 506/290-4869, accvccr@racsa.co.cr, www.minae.go.cr/~accvc. Don't leave items in a car parked along the road and do not park in isolated areas. Check Appendix A for bus schedules. Tour operators offer guided nature walks.*

Centro Neotrópico Sarapiquís

One of a kind, this is a must-see. Built on the model of a 15th-century village of Botos people from this area, Sarapiquís blends the past with state-of-the-art technology in a rain forest setting. Opened in 2000, the center has a 24-room ecolodge, a multimedia, high-tech museum, botanical garden, archeological garden, and access to 865-acre (350-ha) Tirimbina Rainforest Reserve.

Visitors to Sarapiquís Museum are led on a tour via high-tech methods by 19th-century naturalists and explorers Anastasio Alfaro and José Cástulo Zeledón, beginning in the office of the two scientists. Hear stories of the world of plants, insects, birds, reptiles, and mammals, walking from daylight to twilight to a night tour of the forest, complete with a rain forest thunderstorm. Then experience pre-Columbian archaeological treasures of peoples who lived in these forests and learn the importance of conservation and research, ending with a documentary on the rain forest in the comfortable amphitheater.

Three *palenques* (round, thatched ranchos) each contain eight rooms, opening off of a common 59-foot (18-m) central area like "petals of an inverted flower," as described by Jean Pierre Knockaert, the Belgian architect who conceived the project and president of the nonprofit Landscape Foundation, which owns the project. Natural stone and handmade furniture highlight a décor of earth tones, and each room opens onto a terrace facing gardens or forest, $100 double room. The *palenques* are linked by walkways with a fourth that houses restaurant, bar, gift shop, and lobby. Have breakfast on the restaurant terrace overlooking the Sarapiquí River and forest. Meals, buffet style, are highlighted by spices and edible flowers used by early indigenous peoples. Breakfast is $5, lunch or dinner $10. Open to the public.

The archaeological garden sprung unexpected into the project when large pre-Columbian tombs were discovered during construction; some of the unearthed pottery and intricate stonework are among museum treasures. Visit a formal botanical garden of more than 500 native medicinal and edible plants of historical or economic value, tropical gardens around the buildings, an old orange orchard that demonstrates natural succession, and a reforested area. Guided walks in lush Tirimbina Rain Forest Reserve offer opportunities to observe wildlife and tropical biodiversity. Entrance is via a suspended walkway over the river and an island at canopy level.

Sarapiquís is designed to be an eco model, using ecological, sustainable technologies, solar energy, local natural materials, and a waste-water system that uses plants in the purification process.

Details: *About one mile (two km) east of La Virgen de Sarapiquí; 506/761-1004, fax 506/761-1415, magistra@racsa.co.cr, www.sarapiquis.org. Museum open 8 A.M. to 5 P.M.; admission, $25 for adults, $12.50 for children under 12, which also includes a tour of gardens, canopy bridge, and Tirimbina Biological Reserve—allow four to six hours. Lodge rooms are $100, double occupancy.*

Heliconia Island

Alongside the Puerto Viejo River Tim Ryan has created a wonderland of showy heliconias (70 species) plus prayer plants, gingers, palms, ornamental bananas, orchids, and fruit trees in a botanical garden arranged under native trees. See the traveler's palm from Madagascar, a three-sided palm, and heliconias that will knock your socks off. One is like a giant bouquet, another (Purple Throat) has an inflorescence that grows in a spiral, and you won't want to miss the Prince of Darkness, Lobster Claw, or the Sexy series. Entrance and a one-hour guided tour is $7.50 per person; stay as long as you want. On the tour hear about interactions of insects and birds with flowers as examples of the web of life. Bring binoculars for birding: commonly seen are oropendolas, scarlet-rumped and golden-hooded tanagers, hummingbirds, and trogons. Bring lunch and eat at picnic tables in the gardens and along the river. Camping is allowed, $15 per person per night, including admission; bring your own gear. Cook on barbecue grills or eat at the open-air restaurant, $8 per meal. Campers can swim, fish, and boat in the river.

On full-moon weeks, Tim gives a deluxe night tour, with the garden lit by torches, and a gourmet buffet dinner, $35, by reservation only. Check the website for dates.

Details: Between Horquetas and El Tigre, five miles (eight km) south of Puerto Viejo de Sarapiquí; fax 506/766-6247, heliconia@sarapiquirainforest.com, www.sarapiquirainforest.com/heliconia_island.

La Laguna del Lagarto Lodge and Private Reserve

Located 2.5 hours north of San José, La Laguna del Lagarto is a secluded watery world of lagoons, rivers, swamps—and a place of striking forest and incredible wildlife. Seated on a bench beside a small pond, I observed spider monkeys moving through tall treetops, sometimes with spectacular leaps—one seemed to slide down a long liana. Hanging by their tails, they fed on tall-forest fruits. Flock after flock of noisy parrots and parakeets flew in, stayed a bit, and moved on. Jesus Christ lizards skittered across the water. On the short walk from the lodge, I had observed white-fronted and brown-hooded parrots, a Montezuma oropendola, blue-gray tanagers, a

Dwarfed by forest giant at La Laguna del Lagarto Lodge

black-cheeked woodpecker, and squirrels eating pejibayes. This was all before breakfast.

Owner Vinzenz Schmack has almost 250 acres (100 ha), adjoining a neighboring forest of 1,000 acres (400 ha) that extends the habitat for such species as white-faced, howler, and spider monkeys, *tepezcuintle*, great curassow, aracaris, chestnut-mandibled and keel-billed toucans, and snowy cotingas. Some 368 bird species have been identified so far, among them the endangered great green macaw. The lodge supports a research project on these macaws, both financially and by protecting a forest rich in *almendro* trees, an important food source for these beautiful birds.

Ten miles (16 km) of marked trails open the forest for exploration. Tiny red frogs with blue legs, known as strawberry poison-dart frogs, and small green poison-dart frogs with black patterns are easily seen on the forest floor. Look for tapir tracks. Watch for battalions of army ants, accompanied by bicolored or ocellated antbirds feasting on insects that flee from the ants.

Ree Strange Sheck

Canoeing on a lagoon in late afternoon is sublime—moving silently, reflections of trees in the water. On my quiet trip, green-backed herons appeared, kingfishers flashed by, a lineated woodpecker perched on a lifeless trunk in the water, and small sleeping bats made a dark line down another trunk. Orchids and bromeliads were everywhere.

A nighttime walk with a good flashlight reveals bright eyes of caimans, or *lagartos*, which gave the place its name. Guests can ride horses along the edge of the forest, $15; or take a boat down the San Carlos River to the San Juan, which forms Costa Rica's border with Nicaragua, $30. There is no charge for canoes or for a walk in the butterfly garden, which focuses on area species, especially the remarkable morpho. Enjoy bird-watching from the lodge veranda, with the resident green macaw usually in the garden. Local guides are available.

Twenty comfortable rooms have simple furnishings, ceiling fans, and screened windows, but bring repellent for trail walks. Newer rooms are next to the forest. Doubles are $68, including tax, no credit cards. Ask about packages.

In the open-air dining room, food is an appetizing mix of Costa Rican and European. Pineapple, papaya, both black and white pepper, oranges, *yuca*, *tiquisque*, and pejibaye palms are grown near the lodge. The pejibaye supply heart of palm—watch it being cut fresh for your meal. Breakfast is $5.50, lunch $7.50, dinner $11, including taxes.

The lodge is about 330 feet (100 m) above sea level; temperatures range from 68°F to 95°F (20°C to 35°C). February to mid-May is driest, but for rainy times, boots and ponchos are available.

Details: 23 miles (37 km) north of Pital, four miles (seven km) from Boca Tapada; 506/289-8163, tel/fax 506/289-5295, lagarto@ racsa.co.cr www.adventure-costarica.com/laguna-del-lagarto. Take a Pital direct bus from San José, with connecting bus to Boca Tapada; pickup available with advance notice from. Lodge round-trip transfer from San José, $90.

La Paz Waterfall Gardens

A breathtaking land of waterfalls awaits just one hour north of San José. La Paz Waterfall has long been a stop on the road between Vara Blanca and San Miguel. Now the family that owns the land has created at nature park and private wildlife refuge that not only allows up-close observation of La Paz from a bridge suspended over it but of three other magnificent waterfalls: El Templo (feel the spray on the deck alongside), Magia Blanca, and Encantada. In all, six bridges span the La Paz River and the falls.

Interconnected trails takes visitors through the 100-acre (40-ha) refuge that borders on Poás Volcano National Park. The waterfall walk takes about 40 minutes; the stone Indian Trail, about two hours; others are longer. Along well-maintained trails in this rain and cloud forest are gazebos where you can sit and observe lush surroundings. Guides are available, or you may explore on a self-guided tour. Visit the hummingbird garden before or after hiking, and enjoy an orchid garden and amazing butterfly garden. A restaurant with breathtaking views serves typical food but, the Fallas family hastens to add, with international quality standards. Check out the gift shop.

Details: *Four miles (six km) north of Vara Blanca on the road to San Miguel and Puerto Viejo de Sarapiquí, 20 minutes from Poás Volcano; 506/482-2720, fax 506/482-2722, wgardens@racsa.co.cr, www. waterfallgardens.com. Open daily 8 A.M. to 4 P.M. Admission is $24; buffet lunch $8.*

La Selva Biological Station

One of the top two biological research stations in the Neotropics, this research center and forest reserve just south of Puerto Viejo de Sarapiquí offers a unique opportunity to experience and learn about tropical ecosystems. La Selva, owned and operated by the international research and education consortium, the Organization for Tropical Studies (OTS), attracts some 250 researchers from 26 countries each year and thousands of students and natural history visitors.

Situated at the confluence of the Puerto Viejo and Sarapiquí Rivers, La Selva's 3,954 acres (1,600 ha) is home to 120 species of mammals, including howler, spider, and white-faced monkeys, agoutis, jaguars, tapirs, and 60 species of bats. There are 1,900 species of plants in this tropical rain forest, 411 bird species, and 500 species of butterflies.

From the terrace in front of reception, the panorama can include flocks of parakeets, the red flash of scarlet-rumped tanagers, a sloth in the cecropia tree, and hummingbirds. At the start of the long suspension bridge over the Puerto Viejo River, look for the granddaddy of all iguanas in riverside trees, turtles sunning on partially submerged tree trunks, kingfishers, and morphos. Around laboratories and researcher cabins, depending on what's in fruit, families of coatis are at home, and agoutis and peccaries (yes, peccaries!) feed quietly. Because of the long history of protection and research here, forest mammals such as these no longer flee at the sight of human beings.

Half-day guided walks begin daily at 8 A.M. and 1:30 P.M. Groups are limited to 12 people per guide, so reserve beforehand, $25 per person. These are high-quality educational experiences led by excellent bilingual guides. The three-hour tour is a good introduction to lowland rain forest biology. Guides point out the *bala*, or giant tropical ant, infamous for its powerful sting and the largest ant in Costa Rica (up to one inch [33 mm] long); they spot the tiny blue and red poison-dart frog and tell you its life history. Learn about the ALAS project, an inventory of arthropods (insects, spiders, crustaceans) at La Selva that has already identified more than 420 species of ants alone. Check out the exhibit in the welcome center for other research underway. A day trip from San José including transport, lunch, and morning walk is $65 per person, minimum two.

On the easy, wheelchair-accessible Sendero Tres Ríos Trail, a 3.7-mile (six-km) paved path, you'll encounter staff and researchers traveling by bicycle to more distant research sites. Watch for toucans, agoutis, and peccaries as you gaze at flowering bromeliads in towering trees. There are 35 miles (57 km) of trails in all. Don't miss the arboretum, with labeled trees, where your may see a coati, monkeys, a keel-billed toucan, purple-throated fruitcrow, collared aracari, or a yellow-billed cacique. Ask about Bird-watching 101 and other classes.

Overnight stays are in 10 rustic dormitory-style rooms with shared baths; priority is given to researchers or students; $66 per person double occupancy, including room, meals and guided walk. Meals are served cafeteria style in the modern dining room, where you may find yourself rubbing elbows with leading tropical scientists, field assistants, or student researchers. Check the chalkboard for evening talks.

La Selva is contiguous with Braulio Carrillo National Park. Annual rainfall is about 152 inches, which is 13 feet or four meters! Rainiest months are July, November, and December; La Selva has some of its best weather in October, when rain falls in most of the rest of the country. Elevation ranges from 115 to 492 feet (35 to 150 m) and average temperature is 75°F (24°C)—it can get cool enough for a blanket toward morning.

Details: *Two miles (three km) south of Puerto Viejo de Sarapiquí, 90 minutes from San José via Braulio Carrillo Park. Office is open 7:30 A.M. to 5 P.M. For overnight visitors or day package from San José, call 506/240-6696, fax 506/240-6783, reservas@ots.ac.cr, www.ots.ac.cr/en/laselva; for guided walks only, 506/766-6565, fax 506/766-6535, laselva@sloth .ots.ac.cr. See Appendix A for bus options to Puerto Viejo, including private van/bus options. Call about direct La Selva-San José shuttle options. Entrance to La Selva is on the left side of the road, next to a covered bus stop.*

Rain Forest Aerial Tram

Located just east of Braulio Carrillo National Park, about an hour from San José, the aerial tram (*teleférico* in Spanish) brings ski-lift technology to the tropical forest. Riding in gondola-type cars, visitors pass through what founder Donald Perry calls "the hanging gardens of Central America," the forest canopy. It is estimated that two-thirds of the forest species live at this upper forest level.

As you move slowly along a 1.6-mile (2.6-km), 80-minute round trip, you have a chance to see the plants whose flowers you find when walking on trails. Perhaps you'll see monkeys or sloths and some of the area's more than 300 bird species—or, as I did, an anteater making its way through upper branches. The highest part of the ride is on the return trip, 100 feet (30 m) above the ground.

At each end of the tram are short loop trails where the guide points out the colorful rufous-winged woodpecker, a *canfín* tree that exudes a flammable liquid, sleeping bats, and other forest treasures. A beautiful *bocaracá* (eyelash viper) rested in foliage near the restaurant when I was there, and the lovely *flor de un día* shared its one-day flower. The private reserve totals 1,000 acres (400 ha), and has marked nature trails for hiking.

An open-air restaurant serves breakfast and lunch, and there is a snack bar. In the visitor center a video introduces canopy exploration and describes tram construction, which involved a Sandinista helicopter as well as banana-plantation technology.

Access is controlled: From the highway, Rain Forest Aerial Tram vehicles carry visitors almost a mile (1.5 km) to the tram and visitor center area. Some visitors make a day of it—allow at least three hours. Bring binoculars. Entry fee covers tram ride and guided walk.

Details: 32 miles (52 km) north of San José, 506/257-5961, fax 506/257-6053, info@rainforesttram.com, www.rainforesttram.com. Opens daily at 6 A.M., with first tram at 7 A.M. except 9 A.M. on Monday; the last tour leaves entrance at 3:30 P.M. Adults $49.50, students with I.D. and children 5 to 18 $24.50. Children under five enter free but are not permitted to ride the tram. See Appendix A for bus options (Guapiles bus). A six-hour aerial tram package from San José is $78.50 including transport, breakfast or lunch, tram ride, and optional 45-minute hike.

Rara Avis Rainforest Lodge and Reserve

Visiting the beautiful Waterfall Lodge out of Horquetas shortly after it opened, a local tour operator remarked to Amos Bien, founder of Rara Avis, "You know, Amos, most people would have put the road in first." But Amos Bien is not most people, and Rara Avis is not your ordinary tourist destination.

Now, a few years down the line, the road has progressed quite a lot: the famous three-hour ride in a tractor-driven cart is much tamer now—but for the final two miles (three km), guests still lurch in the cart or hike in on forest trails. Adventure is not dead.

Going is still slow enough that there is a chance to see the great green macaw as you bump along, to hear about a nearby achiote plantation (the plants are grown in Costa Rica as ornamentals and

Ree Strange Sheck

Famous transport between Las Horquetas and Rara Avis

as a source of red dye), to observe the pasture lands clear-cut from tropical rain forest, reforestation projects, and secondary forest. If Amos is along, he spins tales: one about a horse who died along the way and the budding biology student who later lugged the bones for miles thinking it was a giant tapir.

Amos came to Costa Rica in 1977 as a biology student and returned to found Rara Avis, not only for nature/adventure tourism but also as a biological research center and a conservation proving ground to show neighbors they can make more money by maintaining forest than by clearing it for ranches or farms.

Rara Avis protects 1,011 acres (409 ha) of primary forest. Miles of marked trails travel this rain forest. On guided walks see such exotic birds as the slaty-tailed trogon and keel-billed and chestnut-mandibled toucans (more than 362 bird species have been identified), and learn about tent-making bats, which cut the leaf of a wild plantain on either side of the midrib and bend it to form a tent for daytime sleeping. Howler, white-faced capuchin, and spider monkeys are common, as are pacas, coatis, vested anteaters, kinkajous, and brocket deer. Tapirs, jaguars, collared peccaries, agoutis, and three-toed sloths live here, but you probably will not see them.

Take a path to the spectacular 180-foot (55-m) double waterfall that gave nearby Waterfall Lodge its name, great swimming here on a hot afternoon. Nearby is Treetop Cabin, almost 100 feet (30 m) above the forest floor where, in high season, guests can climb by rope and harness to the canopy. A climb is $35. Want to spend the night in it? You can: $55 for one, $45 per person for two. A butterfly house and orchid garden are open to guests.

The impressive two-story lodge has eight spacious rooms, each a corner unit with a wraparound balcony, a double and bunk beds downstairs plus a sleeping loft, brightly colored blankets, screened windows, and kerosene-lantern lighting. River-Edge Cabin, up a forest trail about 10 minutes from the lodge, is in a secluded, spectacular setting on the edge of a mountain above the river. The cabin has two spacious rooms and a covered deck with a to-die-for view of forest above and below—phenomenal birding. Solar panels provide electricity. Rates per person, double occupancy, are $70 for the lodge and $80 for the cabin, including room, meals, guided walk, and transport from Las Horquetas. For budget travelers, a *casita* has two rooms and a shared cold-water bath, $45 per person.

Meals are served family style in a dining room steps away from the lodge: plenty of food, beautiful salads, a variety of meat dishes, and well-prepared local vegetables (fried *yuca* is superb). A reference corner has lots of good material. An extraordinary variety of hummingbirds feed on flowers alongside the porch rail.

There is virtually no dry season at Rara Avis; rubber boots are essential. A fellow visitor, after an hour on the wet slippery trail to Waterfall Lodge, commented, "This must be the only trail in the world with an undertow." In a four-day period, we explored Rara Avis in 4.5 inches (114 mm) of rain; annual rainfall is about 26 feet (eight m)!

People from 2 to 86 years of age have enjoyed this remote spot, but access and trails can be rough for those not in good physical condition. There are few mosquitoes. Elevation at Waterfall Lodge is 2,300 feet (700 m), and temperature year-round is about 76°F (24°C).

Rara Avis quietly extends its commitment to education. Local elementary-school students and their families are invited to visit, school supplies find their way to the Las Horquetas school, and two sixth-grade students each year are sponsored to continue studies at the high school in Río Frío. Ask about volunteer opportunities.

Details: *Starting point at Las Horquetas, 62 miles (100 km) from San José via Braulio Carrillo National Park, 120 miles (193 km) via Poás Volcano; 506/256-4993, fax 506/764-4187, at lodge 506/710-8032, at Horquetas 506/764-3214, raraavis@racsa.co.cr, www.rara-avis.com. The cart leaves the office daily at 9 A.M. Be on time—departure is. Ask Rara Avis which bus will get you to Las Horquetas in time. Ask about horseback options. Rara Avis arranges transfers anywhere in Costa Rica, using local taxis; an airstrip for charters is 30 minutes by taxi from Las Horquetas.*

Selva Verde Lodge and Private Reserve

At dusk along the Sarapiquí River, behind the lodge, the only sound is rushing water; the green forest that gives Selva Verde its name guards the river. Brilliant blue morpho butterflies flutter along the forest's edge above the water. Dusk becomes darkness, but the magic of the moment lives forever.

Selva Verde protects a reserve of 529 acres (214 ha), located across an impressive hanging bridge over the river from its comfortable lodge. Explore this lowland forest on well-marked trails that range from easy to sometimes steep. Go with a bilingual guide, $15 for three hours; or follow a map. Benches provide a place to rest or to wait and see what the forest reveals: a coati, sloth, raccoon, kinkajou, brocket deer, anteater, river otter, monkey, or maybe a tiny lizard. There are more than 2,000 plant species, 700 butterfly species, and 400 species of birds. Among most commonly seen birds are tanagers, honeycreepers, oropendolas, trogons, toucans, and chachalacas. Wander paths behind the lodge to the river and see abundant birds and butterflies. Take time to smell the heliotrope. Tiny red and blue poison-dart frogs call on every side; watch for them in leaf litter or at the base of a tree, be still, and watch them speak. Small green and black frogs may precede you down the path. Every day at 6 A.M. a guide leads a bird walk for guests, no charge.

Selva Verde Butterfly Garden (open from dawn to dusk) is tucked among trees, $5 per person. The enclosed portion of the garden is marvelous: colorful rattlesnake and hot-lips plants, dozens of butterflies representing more than 20 species, and benches to sit on. Medicinal plants and endangered local species are the focus in another section. Do a self-guided garden tour with a booklet that includes plant names and some medicinal uses; you'll see birds galore, free-flying butterflies, and a heliconia collection. Visit the information kiosk.

Off-site options include a Sarapiquí River boat ride—see river otters, crocodiles, a white-crowned parrot, kingfishers, keel-billed toucans, parakeets, blue herons, aracaris, a three-toed sloth, anhingas, egrets, flycatchers, a bananaquit, oropendolas, turtles, a scarlet-rumped tanager, trees full of vultures, and iguanas draped on limbs high above the water. Children play along the river, women do laundry, and men ride horseback along a high bank. Guests can also take horseback tours or go canoeing or river rafting.

The River Lodge consists of 40 rooms in 12 modules built off the ground and connected by thatched walkways through fantastic gardens. Constructed of beautiful tropical woods, each double room has a small desk, reading lights, convenient closet space, and lots of windows with louvered shutters. Five newly refurbished bungalows are in forest across the road. Doubles are $68 per person, including lodging, meals, and taxes. For lodging only, $44.

A large dining room shares a river view with an outdoor deck where birding is terrific; meals served buffet style. A new restaurant gives guests the option of ordering from a menu. It is adjacent to Trogones Reception Hall, which features an interactive rain forest exhibit. The gift shop offers a good selection of nature books, tropical-forest posters, basketry, belts, primitive carvings, jewelry, and lots more—even slide film.

Selva Verde's commitment to community involvement created the Sarapiquí Conservation Learning Center. Drop by. In its library, auditorium, and workrooms, local people study English, attend natural history classes, or work on handcrafts, sold in the hotel's shop. Scholarships help local children continue their education. Three-month volunteers are needed to teach English and work in community development and environmental education.

Details: *Five miles (eight km) west of Puerto Viejo de Sarapiquí, two hours from San José; 506/766-6800, fax 506/766-6011, 800/451-7111, selvaver@racsa.co.cr, www.selvaverde.com. See Appendix A for bus information; if you take a bus through Braulio Carrillo to Puerto Viejo, get a taxi to the lodge.*

GUIDES AND OUTFITTERS

For great birding, contact Aaron Sekerak, owner of **AveRica Bird Tours,** located three miles (4.8 km) south of San Miguel, 506/476-0315, fax 506/258-0303, averica@yellowweb.co.cr. Aaron, author of *A Travel and Site Guide to Birds of Costa Rica,* prefers no more than four persons per group and specializes in personal service and unique tours. From his small lodge in this bird-rich area, he leads morning tours for $30, afternoon tours for $20. He offers trips to Poás Volcano, La Virgin de Socorro (a top birding site and one of his favorites), La Selva, and fantastic Laguna Hule. He does custom tours anywhere in the country and in Panama and Nicaragua. Daily rates are $125 for one person, $25 for each additional person up to four, which covers guide service and transport; Aaron arranges lodging. Travelers can stay in his comfortable cabins at the edge of a canyon; a double cabin is $25; cabin for four with kitchenette is $40.

Aguas Bravas Whitewater Center between La Vírgen and Puerto Viejo, 506/292-2072, fax 506/229-4837, info@aguas-bravas.co.cr, www.aguas-bravas.co.cr, specializes in rafting on the Sarapiquí River. The class IV-V upper Sarapiquí is $50 from Sarapiquí; there are also beginners' trips on the Sarapiquí, some especially for bird-watching. One-day kayaking tours are both for beginners and experienced kayakers, $60 to $80, lessons available. Custom packages including other parts of the country encompass kayaking, rafting, biking, surfing, hiking, snorkeling or diving, and horseback riding. The company's Aguas Bravas Arenal Outdoor Center is in La Fortuna.

William Rojas, owner of **Oasis Nature Tours** in Puerto Viejo, tel/fax 506/766-6108, at home 506/766-6260, oasis@tourism.com, www.sarapiquirainforest.com/oasis, offers excellent two-hour wildlife boat tours on the Sarapiquí, $15 per person; tours leave daily at 8:30 A.M. and 1:30 P.M. A longer day tour all the way to the San Juan River and the border with Nicaragua is $65, including lunch at La Casa de Marta where you'll see passion fruit and orchids growing and can photograph the free-flying toucan. William does boat transfers between Puerto Viejo, Barra del Colorado, and Tortuguero, a terrific way to combine the north-central portion of the country with two top natural history destinations on the Caribbean. His two-night package from San José includes the boat trip from Puerto Viejo to Tortugero, either returning to Puerto Viejo or continuing south via the canals to Matina, $215 per person. A three-night tour includes Poás, Sarapiquí, Arenal Volcano, and Tortuguero, $1,000 for two persons. An eight-night tour takes in Poás, Puerto Viejo, Braulio Carrillo, Aerial Tram, Tortuguero, Arenal, and Monteverde, $1,250 per person double occupancy. William, a genuinely nice guy, knows the country and its history and puts himself at your service. Office is one block north of downtown plaza in Comercial Rojas Ugalde.

Ken Upcraft's kayak tours out of **Rancho Leona** in La Virgen de Sarapiquí, tel/fax 506/761-1019, kayak@rancholeona.com, www .rancholeona.com, are famous in these parts, and a bargain. A one-day kayak trip on the Sarapiquí is $75, including equipment, guide, picnic lunch, and lodging the night before and after at the Rancho Leona hostel in La Virgen. He offers a four-day camping/kayaking trip and other packages on the Sarapiquí, Toro, and Peñas Blancas Rivers.

CAMPING

Contact **Rancho Leona** in La Vírgen, tel/fax 506/761-1019, kayak@rancholeona.com, www.rancholeona.com, about camping near the Peje River in its private forest reserve, which borders Braulio Carrillo; camping pads are available Campsites are available at **Heliconia Island** just south of Puerto Viejo de Sarapiquí. See description under "Nature and Adventure Sights."

LODGING

El Gavilán Lodge just outside Puerto Viejo, 506/234-9507, fax 506/253-6556, at lodge 506/766-6743, gavilan@racsa.co.cr, www. gavilanlodge.com, lies between the Sucio and Sarapiquí Rivers. Twelve comfortable, simply furnished rooms look out on 25 acres (10 ha) of gardens, double $50. Wander among orchids, coconut palms, fruit trees, heliconias, and other flowering tropical plants. Walk river paths to tree decks terrific for bird-watching, soak in the hot tub, or read and relax in two thatched ranchos furnished with hammocks and chairs.

Choose from a variety of offsite activities: horseback riding, rafting, or boat tour. On my most recent El Gavilán boat trip, those of us aboard spotted crocodiles, sloths, turtles, iguanas, howler monkeys, long-nosed bats, kingfishers, parrots, a laughing falcon, an anhinga, mangrove swallows, and several species of heron. Try a Tortuguero Safari, $85, minimum four people; or a San Juan River trip, $95. A one-day tour from San José includes a boat trip or horseback ride, $75.

Meals are tasty: breakfast $7, lunch $9, dinner $12. Green coconuts, *pipas* in Spanish, are served as natural refreshment, along with drinks from other fruits that grow here: starfruit, oranges, guayabas, cas, passion fruit, mangos, and pineapples. From Puerto Viejo, turn south at the intersection into town, next to the rural guard checkpoint, and watch on the left for El Gavilan's sign.

A country inn set amid 500 wooded acres (182 ha), **El Tucano Resort and Thermal Spa** is five miles (eight km) northeast of Ciudad Quesada on the road to Aguas Zarcas, 506/460-3152, fax 506/460-1692, tucano@racsa.co.cr. Amenities include a fine Italian restaurant, tennis courts, swimming pools, miniature golf, health clinic, paths through a primary forest, a natural sauna whose steam comes from hot springs, and two hot tubs fed by thermal water. Fresh flowers grace the desks in the 90 spacious, carpeted, tastefully furnished rooms; doubles $83, suites from $110.

Guests can bathe at the base of a small waterfall in the cold river water and choose the temperature they like best by their distance from the hot springs. The small resort offers ample opportunity to enjoy nature by bird-watching, hiking on forest trails, horseback riding, or simply contemplating the forest from river or pools. An outdoor fitness area in the forest promotes exercise in harmony with nature. The spa has dry and humid saunas, hot tubs, and a gym, with separate areas for men and women. These thermal waters were long believed to be effective for treatment of arthritis, skin and kidney disorders, rheumatism, and sinus problems. A clinic offers treatments for healing, beauty, body care, and rejuvenation. Therapies include the thermal water, mud baths, massage, aromatherapy, and electrotherapy. Packages and transfers from San José.

Across from the downtown plaza in Puerto Viejo is **Hotel El Bambú,** 506/766-6005, fax 506/766-6132, info@elbambu.com, www.elbambu.co.cr, a pleasant, airy 14-room hotel with telephones, TV, and ceiling fans, double $45 including breakfast. Bamboo furniture decorates rooms and a tall stand of natural bamboo is a backdrop for the spacious restaurant and bar, which offer excellent food, including vegetarian dishes. The swimming pool is also a good bird-watching place, with tall trees around. Keep an eye on plaza life from a second-floor terrace. Boat rides and tours arranged.

La Quinta de Sarapiquí, three miles (five km) north of La Virgen and seven miles (12 km) west of Puerto Viejo, 506/761-1052, fax 506/761-1395, quinta@racsa.co.cr, www.quintasarapiqui.com, is a quintessential country inn set in a curve along the Sardinal River. The large, inviting 23 rooms in bungalows are surrounded by a tropical garden rich in heliconias, gingers, palms, and flowering trees, doubles $50. The brilliant flash of hummingbirds feeding along paths in the morning sun is dazzling. Sit on shaded porches to enjoy flowers and birds—115 species here. A bar and lounge next to the dining room has a lovely outdoor eating deck facing forest and river. The food is delicious and nicely served: breakfast is $5.50, lunch $8, dinner $9. Delicacies from the garden can include *yuca*, pineapple, plantains, papaya, and heart of palm. This is where I finally got to taste breadfruit.

Enjoy the swimming pool, butterfly garden, and a frog garden featuring tiny strawberry poison-dart frogs. Ride mountain bikes on rural roads; cross a picturesque hanging bridge to a forest patch for bird-watching (toucans, brown-hooded parrots, maybe even a great green macaw). By your arrival, Richard Whitten's fabulous entomology collection, Jewels of the Rainforest, will have a home at La Quinta—a must-see, and free for overnight guests who come with this book. A short trail on the farm goes to a pond where you can fish for tilapia and a reforestation project where you can plant a tree. Owners Leonardo and Beatriz Jenkins like to share their Costa Rican heritage and the region's attractions. They arrange rafting or wildlife boating and visits to La Selva Biological Station, Tortuguero, and the Rain Forest Aerial Tram. The inn helps a local school—visits arranged—and plants almendro trees along a river. La Quinta is one-half mile (one km) from the highway across an unforgettable bridge.

The unexpected lives at **Rancho Leona,** La Virgen de Sarapiquí, tel/fax 506/761-1019, kayak@rancholeona.com, www.rancholeona. com. Find a workshop where Tiffany-style stained glass and rain-forest jewelry are created—watch artisans at work—along with kayak jungle tours, an open-air restaurant with vegetarian and typical fare (homemade brown bread, eggplant Parmesan, French onion soup, banana splits), a sauna, computer service, and rustic rooms, but with stained-glass windows. The two creative people who keep all of this going are Ken Upcraft and Leona Wellington. Leona is now offering two-week art retreats that travel from Rancho Leona to other parts of the country. The hostel's rooms have double and bunk beds, $9 per person, shared baths, often occupied as part of a kayak package. Ken and Leona use proceeds from stained-glass work and kayak tours to help purchase and protect forest bordering Braulio Carrillo National Park. Ask about volunteer and camping opportunities.

Twelve families operate **San Juan Agro-Ecoturism Lodge** near Muelle and Aguas Zarcas, tel/fax 506/286-4203, cooprena@racsa .co.cr, www.agroecoturismo.net. Of its 1,028 acres (416 ha), the cooperative has more than half in a protected area and the rest in pineapple, basic grains, medicinal plants, reforestation, and dairy pastures. The lodge has six rooms, a restaurant, and a family cabin; doubles $45 including breakfast. Guests can participate in farm activities from milking to sowing or harvesting crops, and they can enjoy river and lagoons, hike, ride horses, and go birding: among species are toucans and great green macaws. It is affiliated with COOPRENA, an initiative that promotes rural tourism.

FOOD

The hotels, lodges, and destination sites listed serve excellent food, many open to the public as well as to guests. Here are a few others:

Bar Restaurante El Muelle at the Puerto Viejo dock, 506/766-6019, serves up typical food and local flavor. Watch boats on the river and boatmen and travelers as they come and go at this open-air riverside spot and try a chicken *gallo*, roasted chicken, *gallo pinto*, or a *casado* with meat, rice, beans, and plantain. Owner Gerardo Rojas provides quick service and good prices.

Bar Restaurant Los Portones in Chilamate, 506/766-6643, is open from 10 A.M. to 11 P.M. Owner Elizabeth Peralta offers a range of bocas you can make a dinner from, at good prices. Her family helped settle this area. She also has some very clean rooms off the road, $20 per room.

La Abuelita Típica, 506/766-6775, has, according to some locals, the best typical food in Puerto Viejo. You can even get *olla de carne* here, a hearty meat and vegetable soup that *ticos* love. Locals can point it out to you.

Mi Lindo Sarapiquí, tel/fax 506/766-6281, in downtown Puerto Viejo next to the plaza is a large open-air restaurant popular with locals and tourists. The menu is mostly typical food. There are six simple, clean rooms with ceiling fans upstairs.

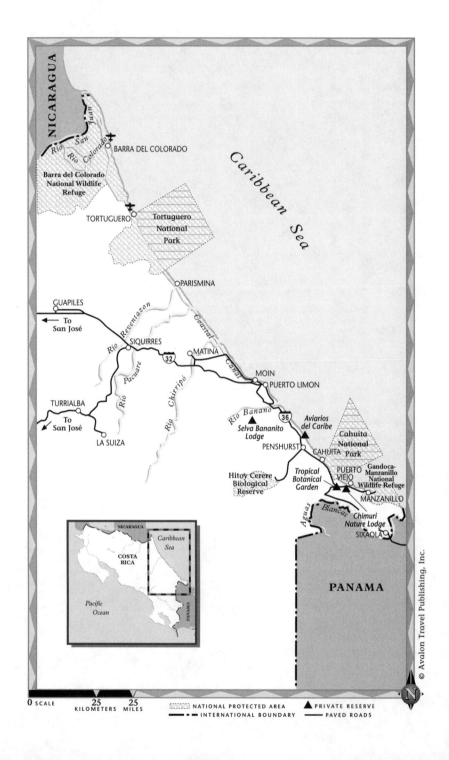

NICARAGUA

Rio San Juan

Rio Colorado

BARRA DEL COLORADO

Barra del Colorado
National Wildlife
Refuge

TORTUGUERO

Tortuguero
National
Park

Caribbean Sea

PARISMINA

GUAPILES

← To
San José

Rio Reventazon

SIQUIRRES

Rio Pacuare

Rio Chiripó

Canal

Coavar

MATINA

32

MOIN

PUERTO LIMON

TURRIALBA

← To
San José

LA SUIZA

Rio Banano

Selva Bananito
Lodge

36

PENSHURST

Aviarios
del Caribe

Cahuita
National
Park

CAHUITA

Hitoy Cerere
Biological
Reserve

Tropical
Botanical
Garden

PUERTO
VIEJO

Gandoca-
Manzanillo
National
Wildlife Refuge

MANZANILLO

Aguas

Blancas

Chimuri
Nature Lodge

SIXAOLA

PANAMA

NICARAGUA

Caribbean
Sea

COSTA
RICA

Pacific
Ocean

PANAMA

© Avalon Travel Publishing, Inc.

0 SCALE

25
KILOMETERS

25
MILES

NATIONAL PROTECTED AREA

PRIVATE RESERVE

INTERNATIONAL BOUNDARY

PAVED ROADS

N

CHAPTER 9

Caribbean Coast

The Atlantic Coast offers long, uncluttered beaches, high forested mountains, coconut palms, plantations of cacao and bananas, national parks and wildlife refuges, sleepy villages, and a commercial port. Mountains, coastal plains, and marine areas contain a rich mixture of species and habitats to explore.

The cultural landscape is unique—nowhere else in Costa Rica do black and indigenous influences leave such an imprint. While African Americans countrywide make up about three percent of the country's total population, the percentage in Limón Province is about one-third. This culture adds to the flavor of the Caribbean zone and because many speak English, broadens communications for monolingual English-speaking tourists. It is, however, a Creole English with unique expressions. The influence of indigenous peoples in the Caribbean is more heavily felt as you go farther south to the Talamanca area, with three main reserves: Kekoldi, Talamanca-Bribrí, and Talamanca-Cabecar.

Lodges and hotels tend to be small, and reserves both public and private are fertile grounds for nature and adventure experiences.

LAY OF THE LAND

Two distinct areas are described here: the first is the land of canals, rivers, turtle beaches, and rich protected areas to the north, bordering Nicaragua, and the second is from Limón south to Gandoca/Manzanillo near Panama, a land of cultural diversity, forests, terrific public and private reserves, and palm-fringed beaches.

Part of the journey from San José is the same for either region, traveling through Braulio Carrillo National Park, dropping to the coastal lowlands. If driving through Braulio, be careful of heavy fog and landslides, and also of drivers who use climbing lanes to go down. Even after leaving the park, keep your eyes peeled for wildlife, especially for sloths in roadside trees. Plantation lands begin; you'll see ornamental plants, cacao, plantains, bananas.

The highway crosses two mighty rivers famous for white-water rafting: the Reventazón just before Siquirres, and the Pacuare after Siquirres. Remote refuges along the Pacuare are overnight bases for

Turtles nest on Costa Rica's beaches.

Ree Strange Sheck

river trips that begin in this area. The town of Siquirres is also where the older, alternate highland route from Turrialba joins the main road.

Notice the deep imprint of steel rails on this area. It took from 1871 to 1890 to build the main line to San José, with Chinese and West Indians brought in as workers. To help finance the project (and to feed workers), bananas were grown for export, and that brought more African Americans from British colonies, many from Jamaica. That's how the United Fruit Company got its start in Costa Rica. Some short-line freight service still exists within the region, though the passenger rail link to the Central Valley was cut in 1991. A tourist "jungle train" runs from Limón to Siquirres; call 506/758-5852 for details.

Some travelers reach this zone via the San Juan River, most leaving from Puerto Viejo de Sarapiquí (see Chapter 8).

Northern Caribbean

Overland travelers to the northern Caribbean leave the main road before Limón to journey by boat. Roads have yet to link some of this area with the rest of the country. Canals built in the 1970s run parallel to the sea, connecting existing rivers and lagoons to provide an 80-mile (129-km) inland waterway from Moín, just north of Limón, to Tortuguero National Park and Barra del Colorado National Wildlife Refuge, top destinations for nature and adventure travelers. Famous for the wildlife in and along the waters, this lifeline of canals and rivers is a highway for canoes loaded with bananas and coconuts, logs that are floated south, and barges carrying supplies north. Families travel in tiny dugouts to small farms and small settlements. Sportfishing is another draw here.

The principal town for travelers is **Tortuguero,** a base for visits to Tortuguero National Park. Isolated for so long—the first public telephone arrived in 1972—it still feels like an out-of-the-way place despite thousands of tourists who arrive every year. The village is small, with fewer than 500 residents, who work mainly in farming (rice, coconuts, fruits, and vegetables) and tourism. Some visitors never get to the village, but I hope you do. Tortuguero is turtles and forest and rivers, but it's also a special kind of people who live on the edge of land and sea. Stop by the **Joshua B. Powers Information Kiosk** to learn about area history: from settlement by peoples related to the Maya, to its fame in the 1700s among merchants and seamen for the thousands of turtles nesting here, to the impact of the Atlantic railroad and the canals. There is information on green turtles and the protected areas. Sign up here for nighttime turtle walks led by local guides July 1 through October 15: the ticket office is open 4 to 6 P.M.; $5 per person plus about $1 that goes to the local development association. *Sodas,* hotels, and gift shops are tucked away on the few paths that meander through the village. Don't miss the Caribbean Conservation Corporation's visitor center just a five-minute walk from the village (see "Nature and Adventure Sights" below). Even those staying further north in the biologically rich Barra del Colorado area generally make the boat trip to Tortuguero.

Central and Southern Caribbean

Towns that travelers usually visit are along the main road that runs mostly parallel to the ocean: Limón, or more correctly Puerto Limón, Cahuita, Puerto Viejo de Limón, and tiny Manzanillo. Towns south of Limón were also relatively isolated until recently. Roads were not connected until a crucial bridge was finished in 1976, the same year Cahuita got electricity. Puerto Viejo got electricity in 1987 and had only three phone lines until 1996. As you travel, you will see farms of cacao and bananas, nets of fishermen, lots of coconut palms, cleared land and rich forest, and shimmering sea in a land that has marched to its own beat for a long time.

Limón, 81 miles (131 km) east of San José, is the capital of Limón Province and the principal port on the Caribbean. Christopher Columbus dropped anchor offshore near La Uvita Island, in front of Limón, on September 18, 1502. Though he stayed about 20 days, he apparently never set foot on the mainland. Today it is a port of call for cruise ships as well as freighters. Limón is a center of commerce (docking facilities at nearby Moín) for fishing, shipping, agriculture, and tourism. A downtown beautification project is scrubbing down the old city, which is both multicultured and multicolored. Walk a new pedestrian mall downtown. If sloths have so far eluded you, visit **Vargas Park** near the seawall, where several live. If you can't spot the well-camouflaged mammals, a passerby will usually help. At the **Municipal Market,** stop by one of the food stands to try rice and beans, a fried cake, or *agua de sapo*—literally, "toad water," but actually a kind of cold *agua dulce* with lemon. *Pan bon* is glazed bread with dried fruits.

In Limón and heading south, scars of a 1991 earthquake that walloped the region are still evident, though reconstruction of damaged buildings, roads, and bridges has whittled away at the evidence. The quake, 7.4 on the Richter scale, raised the Atlantic coast about five feet (1.5 m) at Limón and about a foot (30 cm) at Gandoca. Scientists predict no major earthquake here for another 100 years.

At **Penhurst,** a road west goes through cacao plantations. Platforms are covered with seeds spread out to dry. You may see *guanábana* fruit covered with the same blue plastic, insecticide-impregnated bags that cover banana bunches. Follow this dirt road through banana and plantain plantations to Hitoy-Cerere Biological Reserve. Little visited, it holds treasures for those who reach its forests. Top private reserves are also near Penhurst.

Still a small town (population 4,141) with unpaved streets, **Cahuita** hosts people from around the world, drawn to the beauty of its natural surroundings, a combination of forest and beach showcased in Cahuita National Park. The laid-back lifestyle and rich mix of cultures that form the Caribbean character of this place are evident in language, food, dress, and music. And music is a given— stroll downtown streets until you find the beat you like: salsa, reggae. Lodges and hotels tend to be small. Cahuita is 27 miles (44 km) south of Limón by paved road.

Puerto Viejo de Limón is to the Caribbean what Montezuma is to the Pacific. Laid back, it has its own slow and sultry beat. The village is a mecca for surfers—home of the biggest wave in the country. It is also home to ATEC, the Talamanca Association for Ecotourism and Conservation, an organization that works from Cahuita south to Gandoca. Puerto Viejo is about five hours from San José, 40 miles (65 km) southeast of Limón. Coral forms large tide pools for swimming along the beach. The town is off the main paved road that goes on to Sixaola and the Panamanian border. Not

Ree Strange Sheck

Basketry at Iguana Farm on Kekoldi Indian Reserve

long after pavement gives way to gravel, watch on the right for an **Iguana Farm** sign and a road beside a little store called El Cruce. Entrance to the farm on the Kekoldi Indian Reserve is about 700 feet (200 m) down that road, open daily 8 A.M. to 4 P.M.; admission $1. Kekoldi people are raising green iguanas, traditionally important to this group for meat and skins; even the fat is used for medicinal purposes. At a small thatched hut are artistically carved gourds, baskets, drums, and other items made by children and adults. Hikes into the Kekoldi reserve are led by certified local guides. A tour of the iguana project and/or walks in the Kekoldi Reserve can also be arranged at ATEC (see "Guides and Outfitters"). If no one is in the hut, go up the hill to a private house. Someone will show you around.

Continuing south from Puerto Viejo on a gravel road, pass **Punta Uva** and don't miss sheltered Uva Beach, thought by many to be the prettiest on this coast; here you're already in the Gandoca-Manzanillo National Wildlife Refuge, which has mixed private and government ownership and is administered by La

Amistad-Caribbean Conservation Area, with an office in the tiny village of **Manzanillo.** This is a shorts and T-shirt place with life attuned to the sea. Dolphins are sometimes visible even from the long beach, and it is headquarters for an admirable foundation to do with research and protection of dolphins (see sidebar). Though the road peters out after Manzanillo, walking trails continue through forest and along beach. Stand on a rocky point near Punta Manzanillo and see all the way north along the coast to Puerto Vargas and Cahuita National Park—spectacular scenery.

NATURE AND ADVENTURE ACTIVITIES

Hiking, horseback riding, birding, snorkeling or diving at coral reefs at Cahuita or Manzanillo, observing dolphins or nesting turtles, tree climbing, bicycling, and sportfishing (tarpon, snook, Atlantic blue marlin, wahoo)—these are all options. Some of best wildlife boat trips in the country are on the canals and rivers of the northern Caribbean. Travelers can visit reserves in the Talamancas, the highest mountain range in Costa Rica. White-water rafting and kayaking on the Pacuare River are big time, and kayaking quieter waters in the coastal area is popular. Surfers are drawn to breaks at Playa Bonita and Playa Portete north of downtown Limón and at Uvita Island. Farther south, Black Beach at Cahuita has a good break, and Puerto Viejo has the biggest and most powerful wave in the country: Salsa Brava. Hiking tours and boat trips go to Gandoca Lagoon.

Keep in mind that September and October, traditionally very wet months in the rest of Costa Rica, are generally drier in the south Caribbean, with clear water for snorkeling and diving—some flat spells, however, for surfers. July and December are months of heaviest rainfall.

FLORA AND FAUNA

The northern Caribbean is a famous site for turtle nesting (see sidebar). Several species of colorful tropical frogs are relatively easy to

SEA TURTLES

Six of the world's eight species of sea turtles nest on Costa Rica's coasts—English, scientific, and Spanish names are
- *green turtle* (Chelonia mydas), tortuga verde
- *leatherback turtle* (Dermochelys coriacea) baula or canal
- *hawksbill turtle* (Eretmochelys imbricata), carey
- *olive ridley turtle* (Lepidochelys olivacea), lora or carpintera
- *Pacific green turtle* (Chelonia agassizii), negra
- *loggerhead turtle* (Caretta caretta), cabezona

The Pacific green, hawksbill, and leatherback are found on both coasts, while the ridleys are only on the Pacific. The loggerhead is mainly in the Caribbean. Hawksbills, loggerheads, and leatherbacks are usually solitary nesters; the greens come ashore to lay eggs in concentrated colonies; and the olive ridleys come singly, in small colonies, or in massive arribadas (large numbers of turtles). Though it's possible to see a turtle laying eggs on a beach almost any night of the year, there are times when turtles arrive in arribadas at particular sites. The most important nesting beaches are listed here.

- **Tortuguero:** *Green turtles nest from June to September; hawksbills, from April to November. Leatherbacks nest from March to May, as do loggerheads.*
- **Playa Grande** *in Las Baulas National Marine Park: Peak*

see, as are white-faced and howler monkeys and sloths. Among birds, expect keel-billed toucans, Amazon kingfishers, collared aracaris, mealy parrots, scarlet-rumped tanagers, brown pelicans, green-backed herons, and hundreds more. Dolphins are regularly seen not far offshore. The Manzanillo area has bottlenose, Atlantic spotted, and tucuxi dolphins.

nesting for leatherbacks, the largest sea turtles, is from October to March.

- **Ostional Wildlife** Refuge: July to December are peak months for olive ridley turtles, though there are nesting turtles or hatchlings almost all year.
- **Santa Rosa National Park:** July to December brings olive ridley turtles, especially on Nancite Beach. Leatherbacks and Pacific greens also nest at Nancite and Playa Naranjo.
- **Barra de Matina Beach,** north of Limón: Leatherbacks come ashore from February to July, with peaks in April and May; green turtle nesting peaks from July to September; hawksbills also come ashore.

Green turtles are prized as meat, especially in the Caribbean area. Hawksbills are hunted for their shells (source of tortoiseshell jewelry) along both coasts. While eating turtle meat is not a tradition on the Pacific, the eggs are prized as aphrodisiacs. Turtle protection and conservation programs range from beach patrols and public education to egg hatcheries, controlled harvesting of eggs, and setting of legal catches of turtles to sell for meat.

Practice proper turtle-watching etiquette. Stay still when a turtle comes onto the beach—movement may scare it back into the water. Light disturbs the turtles, so restrict use of flashlights; no flash cameras. Wear dark clothing. Wait until turtles are laying their eggs before drawing near. Be quiet!

If you are lucky, you may see the remarkable Jesus Christ lizard, so named because it seems to "walk" on water: actually, it runs. The secret to this phenomenon is quick movement and large hind feet with flaps of skin along each toe that allow it to skip over the surface of streams and ponds. Found on both Atlantic and Pacific slopes, species vary by size, form, and color.

VISITOR INFORMATION

Good sources of information are national parks, private refuges, and other destinations described under "Nature and Adventure Sights," as well as tour agencies. In Tortuguero area, visit the Joshua B. Powers Information Kiosk. In Puerto Viejo de Limón, ATEC, has loads of information: open daily but hours vary, 506/750-0191.

GETTING THERE

Two land routes bring travelers to this area: the highway through Braulio Carrillo National Park and the older road from San José through Cartago and Turrialba (described in Chapter 6). The two highways join at Siquirres for the final lap into Limón.

Boat travel to the northern Caribbean is either via the canals off the Braulio Carrillo highway or via the San Juan River from the north central region (3.5-hour boat ride to Caribbean), principally Puerto Viejo de Sarapiquí. Area lodges offer package tours including transport, food, guided tours, and lodging. You can do it on your own, hiring a boat in Puerto Viejo or at Moín, outside Limón, and booking your own lodge and tours.

Two domestic airlines offer scheduled service to the northern Caribbean. As for bus travel, direct buses go from San José to Limón, Cahuita, Puerto Viejo, and Manzanillo. Buses from Limón south are also available. See Appendix A for air and bus information, including private van/bus options.

If you're driving, fill up at gas stations between Siquirres and Limón; they are harder to find south of Limón—there is one at Penhurst or filling by hand from a barrel in Puerto Viejo. Landslides can delay travel through Braulio Carrillo National Park to San José. You can wait or consider two alternate routes: one through Puerto Viejo de Sarapiquí, at least 3.5 hours; another back to Siquirres to return through Turrialba, at least 2.5 hours. Both routes involve narrow, mountainous roads. If it's late in the day, the safer option is to get a room nearby (see "Lodging") and wait until morning.

NATURE AND ADVENTURE SIGHTS

Aviarios del Caribe

At night a flashlight revealed yellow caiman eyes along the bank of the river. At midmorning, from the same spot, I saw a river otter playing in the water, a purple gallinule strutting his stuff, and a little blue heron foraging at river's edge—all of this from the upstairs veranda of the lodge.

Aviarios del Caribe, a private wildlife refuge and rescue center just north of Penhurst, is a labor of love for owners Luis and Judy Arroyo. Gracious hosts, they warmly share with guests their lives and their vision of humanity as caretaker of habitat and creatures. They have succeeded in having the island at the mouth of the Estrella River and the river delta declared a private wildlife refuge. Here are freshwater canals and lagoons, humid tropical forest, sandy beaches, and marshland, along with the forest and waterways. Its creatures are monkeys, sloths, river turtles, sea turtles, frogs, lizards, butterflies, and aquatic, arboreal, migratory, and marine birds, plus birds of prey. According to Luis, all six species of kingfishers found in Costa Rica are found at Aviarios, as well as white-collared manakins, migrating orioles and warblers, collared aracaris, toucans, and even the black-crowned night-heron, which nests here but is uncommon in the Caribbean lowlands—314 bird species so far.

On a quiet canoe trip with Cali, a local guide who takes guests through canals to the river's mouth and the Caribbean, we watched a boat-billed heron 15 feet (4.5 m) away as he watched us. I was almost within touching distance of a northern jacana, a pretty black-and-chestnut-colored bird with a striking yellow patch above its bill, before it took flight, revealing the yellow underside of its wing. When we left the canoe to walk on an island, Cali deftly whacked off the top of a coconut with his machete; the liquid tasted marvelous in the morning heat. The three-hour trip, $30 per person, is open to day visitors and overnight guests.

On short, self-guided trails through forest next to the lodge, you'll probably see a sloth. You're sure to see Buttercup, the three-toed sloth Judy took in when its mother was killed on the highway. She has become a star of documentary films and research projects. Her rescue was a beginning that has led to creation of a rescue center that takes in not only other sloths but also fauna such as agoutis, ocelots, and kinkajous. There's no telling what you'll find when you arrive. The Buttercup Foundation set up by the Arroyos has built rescue and rehabilitation facilities and supports environmental education programs for schoolchildren, a scholarship for a Costa Rican veterinarian to study exotic wildlife medicine, purchase of adjacent land to expand the sanctuary, and a sloth research center. It's ambitious; donations are welcome. Overnight guests as well as day visitors may tour the rescue center.

The inviting lodge has six large, attractive bedrooms with queen or king beds from $75 up to $95 for a delightful junior suite, full breakfast included. Fresh flowers say welcome. Upstairs are indoor and outdoor dining areas and a comfortable lounge area with a library and TV/VCR. On the outdoor deck bird-watching is excellent, a resident iguana drops by, and poison dart frogs are bred in an aquarium for release. In a two-hour period, 51 species of birds were spotted from here, not counting river birds.

Details: 19 miles (30 km) south of Limón, four miles (seven km) north of Cahuita; cellular tel/fax 506/382-1335, aviarios@costarica.net, www.members.xoom.com/aviarios. Direct buses from San José to Cahuita, Puerto Viejo de Limón, or Sixaola pass the entrance, as well as buses heading south from Limón.

Barra del Colorado National Wildlife Refuge

Access within this refuge, located near Costa Rica's northern border with Nicaragua, is largely by its waterways. Virtually no land trails exist, and part of the western region of this 242,158-acre (98,000-ha) area has yet to be explored. But there's plenty to see from the network of rivers, channels, and lakes, and there are fewer visitors than at Tortuguero. Among endangered species are the West Indian manatee, tapir, cougar, jaguar, ocelot, and jaguarundi. Species most often seen are caimans and crocodiles, white-faced and howler monkeys, red brocket deer, and sloths. Birds include the great green macaw, great curassow, red-lored parrot, great tinamou, cormorant, keel-billed toucan, and various species of herons.

See swamp forests, swamp palm forests, and mixed forests growing above the swamps. Caña brava, a wild cane, grows mainly along the rivers. Its stiff, solid stems are used to make decorative ceilings and prop up banana plants. Another forest species with commercial value is cativo, used in plywood. If you come via canals, you may see lumber being floated down to Moín, supposedly all having been cut outside parklands. The area along the San Juan River is remarkable. Some local lodges offer a canoe trip to Laguna Nueve, an outstanding site for wildlife observation.

Resident fish in the lakes, rivers, and estuaries include snook, tarpon, mackerel, snapper, gar, and guapote (a tropical rainbow bass). The area draws many sportfishers. You can easily combine a trip to Tortuguero and Barra del Colorado, either on a tour or by hiring a boat to go from one to the other.

A very wet rain forest, the area averages from 158 inches (4,000 mm) on the western edge to 221 inches (5,600 mm) at the village of Barra del Colorado. The sun can shine, however, even in rainiest months. Go prepared for rain, but take your sunscreen.

Details: Across the San Juan River from Nicaragua in the northern Caribbean region; telephone hotline 506/192, 506/710-2929, fax 506/710-7673. Technically there is a small admission fee, but so far nobody collects it. Access by boat is via the San Juan River or the canals north from Tortuguero; scheduled air service is from San José (see Appendix A). Tour companies offer one-day or multiday trips.

Cahuita National Park

Take white sands, coconut palms, a coral reef, the wreck of an 18th-century slave ship just offshore, and clear Caribbean waters; add at least 123 species of fish, abundant birdlife, and an assortment of other animals from monkeys to caimans. This winning combination is known as Cahuita National Park. Park offices are at Puerto Vargas, just north of Cahuita, and another entrance is in the town of Cahuita itself. A four-mile (seven-km) nature trail links the two entrances; allow at least 2.5 hours to enjoy this experience in the exuberance of tropical moist forest vegetation. Abundance of land and sea birds makes it a bird-watcher's delight. Troops of howler monkeys roam the area; look for coatis and raccoons. You may encounter a three-toed anteater, an otter, a four-toed armadillo, or a three-toed sloth.

A 1,483-acre (600-ha) reef encircles Cahuita Point, forming a rich undersea garden of 35 species of varicolored coral some 1,640 feet (500 m) from shore. Brightly colored fish such as rock beauty, blue parrot fish, and angelfish swim among the formations, with sea urchins, barracudas, moray eels, sharks, lobsters, sea cucumbers, and green turtles, which feed on the expanse of turtle grass. There is, however, trouble in paradise. Increased erosion from deforestation in the Talamanca Mountains is affecting the reef, a vivid reminder of the distance damage can travel from a mismanaged forest, and runoff from banana plantations is having an effect.

Sea colors on a sunny day run from almost transparent near the white sand to bright green, turquoise, and aquamarine. At some points, water is knee-deep at quite a distance from shore. Certain areas, however, have strong currents where swimming is not safe; two are in the first 1,312 feet (400 m) past the park entrance in Cahuita, and another is at Puerto Vargas. Heed warning signs and ask if in doubt. The park receives about 118 inches (3,000 mm) of rain a year; distinction between wet and dry seasons is not as clear as in the Central Valley..

Stop by the information center at the town entrance, administered by a community group that also helps maintain trails and organizes beach cleanups. Park headquarters are at Puerto Vargas, where camping is allowed; there are beachside picnic sites, restrooms, and showers. The park, which contains 2,639 acres (1,068 ha) of land and 55,350 acres (22,400 ha) of sea, is administered as part of the Amistad-Caribe Conservation Area.

Details: *At Cahuita, 27 miles (44 km) south of Limón; telephone hotline 506/192, 506/755-0302, tel/fax 506/755-0060. Open daily: Puerto Vargas entrance 8 A.M. to 4 P.M., town entrance 6 A.M. to 5 P.M. Admission at Puerto Vargas $6, camping $2; at the town entrance, donations solicited. The Puerto Vargas entrance is south of town; watch for the sign on the east side of the road. Tour companies, lodges, and hotels offer day trips; local guides trained by Talamanca Association for Ecotourism and Conservation (ATEC) are available.*

Caribbean Conservation Corporation

The CCC's H. Clay Frick Natural History Visitor Center in Tortuguero is a must. Beautiful, colorful, informative exhibits focus on ecological relationships, highlighting turtles and the area's other diverse wildlife as well as CCC projects. Founded in 1959 to support the work of the late Dr. Archie Carr, CCC is the oldest sea-turtle conservation organization in the world. It strives to preserve sea turtles and other marine and coastal life through research, training, education, and protection of natural areas. You can purchase some of Dr. Carr's books, T-shirts, and information packets on turtles and other gift items. An 18-minute video (English or Spanish) describes Tortuguero's unique relationship with sea turtles. A biologist is on hand to answer questions.

Volunteers are needed for both the CCC turtle-tagging program and a Neotropical bird study on resident and migratory species, one-week minimum stay. Contact the U.S. office for information: P.O. Box 2866, Gainesville, FL 32602, 800/678-7853, www.cccturtle.org. In Costa Rica, contact CCC at Apartado 246-2050, San Pedro.

Details: *In Tortuguero, a five-minute walk north of the village center; San José office tel/fax 506/224-9215, telephone in Tortuguero 506/710-0547. Open daily 10 A.M. to noon and 2 to 5:30 P.M. Admission $1 adults, children up to 12 free.*

Chimuri Nature Lodge

Seeking adventure in a rustic jungle setting? The nature lodge bordering the Kekoldi Indian reserve offers hikes, natural massages under a waterfall, bathing in a transparent river pool, excellent bird-watching, and guided experiences that share Talamanca cultural traditions. This 49-acre (20-ha) natural reserve offers an out-of-the-ordinary experience.

Four traditional Bribrí structures house guests. Built off the ground, each is of tropical wood and bamboo, with cane-thatched roofs; shared baths and flush toilets are steps away. Simply furnished, the rustic rooms have a certain charm; terraces overlook the forest, double $25. Breakfast is $4 per person, dinner $6 to $8. A new dorm used principally for student groups is also open for low-budget travel-

Chimuri Nature Lodge on the outskirts of Puerto Viejo de Limón

ers, bedding furnished, $11 per person. The complex, in a clearing surrounded by forest, is reached by a five-minute foot trail from the road below, and the Caribbean is only 600 yards (500 m) away.

Animals seen on the property include sloths, porcupines, agoutis, armadillos, tayras, coatis, anteaters, kinkajous, bats, poison-dart frogs, boa constrictors, opossums, and iguanas. There are birds of prey, parrots, hummingbirds, trogons, motmots, jacamars, toucans, manakins, orioles, and tanagers. On the short trail in, you'll probably spot oropendolas, keel-billed toucans, black and green frogs, and hummingbirds. Multitudes of butterflies live in the forest.

A three-hour interpretive nature walk or guided bird-watching at Chimuri is $15 per person. Go on your own to explore a marked 1.2-mile (two-km) trail or sign up for a night walk. Visit the green iguana farm and have a typical dinner with a local Black family. Explore farther on a one-day walking tour through abandoned cacao plantations to traditional Bribrí stomping grounds in the Kekoldi reserve: learn about plants used for medicine, food, and construction. Along trails, see sloths, raccoons, toucans, iguanas, and perhaps a snake. The group, limited to five, stops by a private home to eat a picnic lunch and glimpse life on the reserve. Good physical condition is required. It's a good idea to bring insect repellent.

Chimuri means "ripe bananas" in Bribrí, and a stalk is always hanging where any hungry hand may take one. Try tropical fruits grown here. Indigenous handcrafts are for sale. Chimuri is owned by Mauricio Salazar, of the Bribrí people, and his Austrian wife, Colocha, both of whom have been leaders in conservation and responsible tourism in the zone.

Details: *Near the entrance to Puerto Viejo; tel/fax 506/750-0119, atecmail@racsa.co.cr (this is an address used for public e-mail, so put Chimuri as intended recipient), www.greencoast.com/chimuri. If driving, turn right at Chimuri's sign; short trail leads up to lodge from parking area. For bus travel, ask to be let off at Chimuri's sign.*

Gandoca-Manzanillo National Wildlife Refuge

Nature has spread a visual feast in this refuge at the southern end of the Costa Rican coastline. Beaches here appear on postcards: white sand, graceful palms, jungle-looking vegetation, just the right amount of logs and coconuts washed up on shore. Coral reefs create a snorkeler's and diver's paradise: blue parrot fish, green angelfish, white shrimp, red sea urchins and long-spined black ones, anemones, sea cucumbers, sea fans, lobsters, sponges. Turtle grass sometimes attracts Pacific green turtles. Three species of dolphins live in these waters.

Explore the refuge's land portion by foot from Manzanillo. Gandoca Lagoon is about a six-hour hike from Manzanillo, but even a short walk on a trail that meanders from forest to beach to forest rewards with unexpected beauty. From the *mirador,* watch tropical fish through dazzlingly clear water or view coastline north to Puerto Vargas. Go by boat with a local captain to the lagoon, a remote, mysterious place.

Terrain in the refuge ranges from flat to rolling country with small, forest-covered hills. You might discover a freshwater marsh, the only natural banks of mangrove oysters in the country, or the place where tarpon fish larvae grow to adulthood. Endangered species protected here include the manatee, crocodile, and tapir. There are also tepezcuintles, caimans, opossums, five species of parrots, sloths, ocelots, margays, otters, bats, falcons, hawks, frigate birds, pelicans, chestnut-mandibled toucans, and collared aracaris— some 400 bird species.

As for weather, forget the Costa Rican rule of thumb for wet and dry seasons. Rain falls year-round, though driest months are

March through May and September October. Expect cooler temperatures with wind and rain in December and January. Temperatures average 82°F (28°C).

Gandoca-Manzanillo, 23,348 acres (9,449 ha), is a mixed-management reserve. That means its goal is not only to conserve the rich biological resources but also to work with the community in sustainable use of resources to promote economic development: tourism is one component. Several hotels and lodges exist on private land within the refuge. The Amistad-Caribe Conservation Area office is at the village of Manzanillo, where you can get help finding a local guide, $15 for a half day, $25 for a whole day.

Details: *44 miles (71 km) south of Limón, beyond Puerto Viejo; telephone hotline 506/192, 506/798-3170, tel/fax 506/758-3996, 506/754-2133. No admission charge at press time. There is one San José/Manzanillo direct bus daily and several buses from Limón.*

Hitoy-Cerere Biological Reserve

Off the beaten path, Hitoy-Cerere is not a stopping-off point on the way to somewhere else but a destination in itself. Your map may not even show a road in, but it's there and passable even in wettest months.

Parts of this rugged portion of the Talamanca Mountains have yet to be explored. Fauna that live in its forested habitat include tapirs, jaguars, peccaries, pacas, porcupines, weasels, white-faced and howler monkeys, agoutis, anteaters, armadillos, kinkajous, sloths, squirrels, otters, and deer. Among the 276 bird species identified are the blue-headed parrot, keel-billed toucan, squirrel cuckoo, spectacled owl, green kingfisher, and slaty-tailed trogon. Numbers aren't in on frogs, toads, insects, and snakes.

The forest canopy hovers at about 100 feet (30 m), but some tree species protrude through the top, reaching more than 160 feet (50 m). Buttresses from these giants' trunks widen their base of support, some with a horizontal reach of almost 50 feet (15 m). There are black palms with spiny stilt roots, tree ferns, orchids, and bromeliads. Mosses and lichens cushion trunks and branches.

Trails in this perpendicular place can be difficult: three are the Tepezcuintle, Espavel, and Bobocara. You can hike in the rivers, though moss-covered rocks make streambeds slippery. *Hitoy* in Bribrí refers to moss- and algae-covered rocks in the river of that name; *Cerere* to another river's clear waters. Pools surrounded by exuberant vegetation invite a solitary dip, while waterfalls almost 100 feet (30 m) high inspire awe. Bring rain gear; there is no defined dry season. Yearly amounts average 138 inches (3,500 mm). Humidity is high year-round; temperatures average 77°F (25°C). Elevation ranges from 328 to 3,363 feet (100 to 1,025 m). The 22,622-acre (9,155-ha) reserve is surrounded by legally protected indigenous lands.

Check about the possibility of bunking overnight at reserve headquarters.

Details: 42 miles (67 km) southwest of Limón, 90 minutes from Cahuita; telephone hotline 506/192, 506/798-3170, tel/fax 506/758-3996. Open daily 8 A.M. to 4 P.M. Admission $6. If driving, turn west at Penhurst and follow the road through plantations and settlements of Pandora and Concepción. Day tours are offered by agencies and lodges from Limón south.

Selva Bananito Lodge

At the foot of Cerro Muchilla, Selva Bananito feels like frontier country. Perhaps the adventure-filled ride in on backcountry roads has something to do with it, fording two streams and one river and crossing a few sturdy but daunting bridges. Don't miss it.

At the lodge, 11 individual cabins built off the ground in the Caribbean style have forest out the back door—out the front, too, for that matter: 2,100 acres (850 ha) of the private Selva Bananito Reserve is a 10-minute walk away. A neighbor to La Amistad Biosphere Reserve and the largest park in the country, Selva Bananito protects primary forest, waterfalls, wildlife, rivers and streams, while offering the chance to experience incredible rain-forest diversity.

The lodge and reserve are on the Stein family farm, which also has land in organic bananas and cattle. Brother and sister Sofia and Jurgen, who moved with their parents to Costa Rica in 1974 from Colombia, run the tourism operation. Conservation was paramount in lodge design and construction; those gleaming floors are of salvaged hardwoods. Hot water is supplied by solar energy, and wastewater is treated via a series of marshes and lily ponds. No electricity: candles with pretty chimneys give off a soft light, or gas lanterns can be lit. Each spacious bungalow, rustic but charming, has a queen and double bed and a wraparound balcony with a hammock, a superb bird-watching spot. The shower in the pretty tiled bath is big enough to walk around in. Meals are served in an attractive open-air restaurant, breakfast and lunch accompanied by panoramas and a parade of birds flashing by, dinners by candlelight.

Guides accompany guests on a range of optional tours. A three-hour Jungle at Dawn tour for bird-watchers and photographers is $30. More than 300 species of birds have been counted on the preserve and environs. A natural history tour is $15. Some trails can be steep in places, and muddy. Cross small creeks and walk along streambeds, where it feels like the beginning of time. See red frogs, black and green frogs, the track of a cat, scratching marks of an anteater, termites, *guarumo* trees and Azteca ants; see where palm fruit drops and learn to watch for snakes that lay in wait for small mammals that eat the fruit. Go on an all-day waterfall hike up the Bananito River; add rappelling for extra thrills.

Learn to tree climb using ropes, harnesses, and ascenders. Overnight forest camping is another option, and guests can ride horseback and rent a mountain bike. Bicycle down to the beach in the morning and be picked up in the late afternoon. Selva Bananito's tour company has several multiday packages that combine this site with others around the country.

Doubles are $100 per person, including lodging, meals, and taxes. A two-night package includes San José transfers, lodging, meals, taxes, and tree climbing, waterfall tour, and horseback ride, for $300 per person, double occupancy.

Ten percent of the income from Selva Bananito activities goes to the Limón Watershed Foundation, established by the Steins; foundation goals include protection of rain-forest vegetation along watersheds of rivers such as the Bananito, which is the primary water source for Puerto Limón. Ask about volunteer programs.

Details: *12 miles (20 km) south of Limón and nine miles (15 km) inland; tel/fax 506/253-8118, U.S. tel/fax 515/236-3894, conselva*

▲ Oxcarts still add color to the Costa Rican landscape. (Ree Strange Sheck)

▼ Miles of beaches near La Leona entrance to Corcovado National Park (Ree Strange Sheck)

▲ Bridal veil mushroom at La Selva Biological Station (Ree Strange Sheck)

▲ Orchids at oxcart parade (Ree Strange Sheck)

▼ Hotel Ocotal in Pacific northwest region (Ree Strange Sheck)

▲ Impressive orange-kneed tarantula
(Ree Strange Sheck)

▲ Resplendent quetzal
(Ree Strange Sheck)

▼ Owl butterfly
(Ree Strange Sheck)

▼ Scarlet macaw
(Ree Strange Sheck)

▲ Arrival at enchanting Rainbow Adventures on the Golfo Dulce
   (Ree Strange Sheck)

▼ Corcovado Lodge Tent Camp for the adventurous spirit
   (Ree Strange Sheck)

▲ A symphony in green—Braulio Carrillo National Park
(Ree Strange Sheck)

▲ Eyelash viper or palm viper (Ree Strange Sheck)

▼ Arenal Volcano and Lake Arenal (Ree Strange Sheck)

▲ On the trails at Volcán Turrialba Lodge (Ree Strange Sheck)

▲ Jaguarundi (Ree Strange Sheck)

▼ Exploring tide pools at Nosara (Ron Sheck)

▲ Waterfall and pool on beach at Casa Corcovado Jungle Lodge
   (Ree Strange Sheck)

@racsa.co.cr, www.selvabananito.com. Four-wheel-drive is necessary for the drive inland to the lodge. The lodge recommends taxi from Limón to the village of Bananito, where staff will pick you up. Transport is included in San José packages; Bananito transfer is $20 per person roundtrip.

Tortuguero National Park

Visions of Hepburn and Bogart on the *African Queen* come to mind as you wind through the rivers and canals of Tortuguero National Park in the northern Caribbean region. Flora, fauna, and the boat's condition may differ, but the feeling is here—you, the water, vegetation, and wildlife in an intimate encounter. By boat the dramatic contrast of settled with protected lands along the water vividly portrays the difference a park can make. From the air Tortuguero is a mass of greens from the coastal plain to the Sierpe Hills, broken only by narrow ribbons of water.

However you get here, to explore Tortuguero is to discover a crocodile along the bank, a small turtle sunning on a trunk in the water, a monkey or sloth asleep in a tree, vultures peering down from a lofty perch. Perhaps a river otter will slip into the water as the boat approaches. Water and land birds keep binoculars busy: more than 400 species live here. Watch for green macaws, herons, egrets, parrots, kingfishers, oropendolas (notice their large, hanging nests), tanagers, toucans, and bananaquits.

Tortuguero is tall forest and palm groves, lianas trailing into the water, and floating gardens of water hyacinths. The endangered West Indian manatee feeds on these and other aquatic plants. This large sea cow can be 13 feet (four m) long and weigh about 1,300 pounds (600 kg). But Tortuguero is also beaches, important nesting sites for the sea turtles *(tortugas)* that gave the place its name. Green, leatherback, hawksbill, and occasionally loggerhead turtles return to these beaches every year to lay eggs. Some come in massive *arribadas*, others singly. Though you could see a turtle any night, there are peaks (see sidebar). Rangers from other parks and volunteers help patrol beaches during busiest months to thwart egg poachers. Researchers with the Caribbean Conservation Corporation have been tagging nesting turtles since 1955. Each female green turtle comes ashore to lay eggs an average of two or three times during her season here, staying not far offshore in between. It may be up to four years before she returns to Tortuguero.

There are many crustaceans (prawns feed under the water hyacinths), eels, 52 species of freshwater fish (including the gar, considered a living fossil because species of that genus lived 90 million years ago), and sharks.

Self-guided forest nature trails take off from ranger stations at either end of the park: one at the southern Jalova station, and three trails at the Cuatro Esquinas station near Tortuguero Village. On foot in this wet tropical forest, you may spot small, brightly colored frogs that live here. Mammals include peccaries, raccoons, kinkajous, ocelots, pacas, cougars, and skunks. The park protects more than 15 endangered mammal species, including the tapir, jaguar, giant anteater, and three species of monkeys. All six species of kingfishers are here, along with three species of toucans.

Rainfall averages about 197 inches (5,000 mm), but can reach 236 inches (6,000 mm) in parts. It is hot and humid, with an average temperature of 79°F (26°C). Elevation is from sea level to 1,020 feet (311 m). The park has 46,816 acres (18,946 ha) of land and 129,147 acres (52,265 ha) of marine habitat. It is possible to visit Tortuguero in a day trip, but overnight is better: Camping is allowed near the stations.

Details: Northern Caribbean; telephone hotline 506/192, 506/710-2929, fax 506/710-7673. Open daily 8 A.M. to 4 P.M.; admission $6, camping $2 per person per day. Access by boat is via the canals north of Limón or south from the San Juan River (see Chapter 8). Daily air service from San José (see Appendix A).

Tropical Botanical Garden

This 10-acre (four-ha) garden between Hone Creek and Puerto Viejo combines natural settings with landscaped grounds, showcasing bromeliads, heliconias, palms, orchids, gingers, and a variety of other native and exotic plants. The bromeliads, grown commercially as well, are fascinating not only in themselves but also as habitat for three varieties of small poison-dart frogs: the strawberry, green, and the one called lovely, a black frog with yellow stripes down its back. It's worth the price of admission just to see them. Learn about the

THAT'S CHOCOLATE?

The cacao tree, whose seeds are used for cocoa, chocolate, and cocoa butter, is native to tropical America. Cacao is a short tree, about 26 feet (eight m) high with interesting biological peculiarities. Leaves are both green (mature) and red (young). They go from a horizontal to a vertical position depending on the amount of sunlight—the more intense the sun, the more they droop. The fruits, or pods (called **mazorcas***), grow directly from trunk or branches, hanging like ornaments. As pods ripen, they change from green to yellow or red. As many as 60 seeds—the commercial cocoa beans— can be in one oval-shaped fruit. One opened for me had 43, all covered in a slippery, soft, tasty pulp. Watch for seeds drying on platforms in the Caribbean countryside.*

chicle tree, the cola nut tree (of Coca-Cola fame), cacao, and the breadfruit tree. Owners Peter and Lindy Kring are extremely knowledgeable, with fascinating natural history stories to share.

Cultivated crops include black pepper, cinnamon, vanilla, and ginger; 60 varieties of tropical fruits bring birds and butterflies. Visit the medicinal plant section. An up-and-down loop trail opens access to 22 acres (nine ha) of private forest reserve, which borders reserves set aside for indigenous peoples. At the end of the tour, visitors get to sample intriguing tropical fruits, perhaps a sweet *abui*, the sour *araza*, or starfruit.

Details: *506/750-0046, jardbot@racsa.co.cr, www.greencoast/garden. Open Friday through Monday, 10 A.M. to 4 P.M.; entrance fee $2.50, with a two-hour guided tour $8; self-guiding booklets available. Rain forest loop is $2.50.*

GUIDES AND OUTFITTERS

Aquamor in Manzanillo is the oldest diving shop on the coast, steps away from the reef, cellular 506/391-3417, beeper 506/225-4049, aquamor@racsa.co.cr, www.greencoast.com/aquamor. Diving, kayaking, and snorkeling are specialties. The Rainforest and Reef Expedition is $45 for scuba and $25 for snorkeling. A one-tank beach dive is $30, a one-tank kayak dive is $35, as are night dives. Do yourself a favor and drop by to meet owner Shawn Larkin, who helped established the Talamanca Dolphin Foundation (see sidebar) and knows the region like the back of his hand. Kayak with dolphins in the Gandoca Lagoon ($55), or rent a kayak for $5 an hour to explore rainforest creeks, rivers, streams, swamps, and caves. Do kayak surfing. Explore secret places where only kayaks can go. Aquamor offers PADI certifications. Kayaks and snorkeling gear for rent. Telephones here at road's end are sometimes unreliable, but Shawn says to come: "We're always ready."

Cahuita Tours, 506/755-0232, fax 506/755-0082, is a full-service operation where you can send a fax, exchange money, make reservations, and find a public telephone. Owners Antonio Mora and Rudolfo Henriquez offer area information. Snorkeling and scuba gear is available. For $20 enjoy a glass-bottomed-boat tour, viewing the marvels of the offshore coral reefs. Take a morning guided nature walk, $20; visit the Bribrí reserve, $25; go fishing or horseback riding; or take tours to Manzanillo and the Gandoca-Manzanillo Wildlife Refuge, to Tortuguero National Park, or to Hitoy-Cerere Biological Reserve. Ask about the Telire River boat trip, which offers the option on the return trip of abandoning the boat and floating, letting the current carry you back. Open daily 7 A.M. to noon and 1:30 to 7 P.M. Office in downtown Cahuita.

Horseback Riding Expeditions, 506/750-0497, just south of Puerto Viejo specializes in custom trips, from beach and jungle rides to wildlife tours, $30 per person per hour. For more experienced rides, owner Ivan Mejía offers two- or three-day expeditions to Gandoca, $100 per day including food, lodging, guide, and horse. Choose your saddle: English or western, and there are children's saddles for family outings. Riding lessons are available. Reservations are required.

Reef Runner Divers in Puerto Viejo along the beach, 506/750-0480, reefrun@racsa.co.cr, does PADI certifications, boat and dolphin tours, and both day and night dives.

Based in Puerto Viejo, the **Talamanca Association for Ecotourism and Conservation (ATEC),** 506/750-0398, tel/fax 506/750-0191, atecmail@racsa.co.cr, www.greencoast.com/atec, promotes ecologically sound tourism along with cultural interchange and ethnic pride among indigenous and African Caribbean people of Talamanca. Personalized naturalist/cultural trips go to Gandoca-Manzanillo for hiking and/or snorkeling, to Gandoca Beach from March to July to watch leatherback turtles and gather data on turtle populations, to a family farm in Punta Uva for hiking and snorkeling, to the Kekoldi Indian Reserve for a hike and visit to a green iguana project, and to an Afro-Caribbean farm to learn about traditional farming methods within the forest. Tours are led by trained local guides. Guided walks are $15 half-day, $25 full day. A one-day trip from Limón to Tortuguero is $50 per person. Hiking and boat trips through reserves are an option (two weeks' notice), but a 10-day trek over the Talamanca Mountains is only for the fit. ATEC guides lead birding trips to Cahuita, Puerto Viejo, Punta Uva, and Gandoca-Manzanillo. The ATEC office, on the main road through town, is open daily from early to late; hours vary.

For tours on the **Pacuare River** see Chapters 3 and 6. Some of these operators offer multiday trips with overnights in tents or rustic lodges on the riverbank.

For tours to **Tortuguero and Barra del Colorado** refer to "Lodges" below as well as to Chapters 3 and 8. Another recommended Tortuguero tour is with **Fran and Modesto Watson,** either on the *Riverboat Francesca* or pontoon boat *Fiesta.* A two-day tour from San José includes the canal boat trip, lodging, meals, a visit to CCC, boat tour in the park, and a turtle nesting or hatchling tour (seasonal), from $170 per person. Go fishing with Modesto: river fishing at $40 per hour or salt water fishing at $50 per hour, including boat, captain, and gear—four-hour minimum. Tel/fax 506/226-0986, fvwatson@racsa.co.cr, www.tortugerocanals.com.

CAMPING

Cahuita and **Tortuguero** National Parks have camping facilities, $2 per person per night. **Selva Bananito Lodge** offers overnight camping as part of a stay there, equipment provided. See descriptions under "Nature and Adventure Sights." Look under "Lodging" for **Almonds and Corals,** an upscale tent camp.

LODGING

A delightful place to stay between the Caribbean and the Central Valley and north central regions is **Río Palmas Hotel and Restaurant** near Pocora, 506/760-0330, fax 506/760-0296. Remember it, also, if landslides close Braulio Carrillo. Twenty-three pleasant rooms open onto a lushly landscaped courtyard with a swimming pool and towering traditional thatched rancho backed by forest and surrounded by a virtual botanical garden of heliconias, flowering gingers, palms, and fruit trees—great birding. Owner Erick Berlin, in the tropical plant business, showcases 500 varieties of tropical plants here. A delightful nature trail winds through riparian habitat. Walk it early in the morning when the light just begins to play on the waters. Kingfishers, herons, toucans, and poison-dart frogs (red with blue limbs) reward you. Near the first long cement walkway along the water's edge, notice a woody vine that tied itself in a knot. Tour neighboring EARTH, visit Erick's ornamental plant farm, walk trails here, go horseback riding, or, for the truly fit, trek to Pocora Waterfalls. Tortuguero tours are easy from here. Public buses to Limón and southern Caribbean pass by.

Northern Caribbean

All of the lodges listed offer packages from San José, guided canal and/or river trips, and turtle nesting tours in season. Some offer land/water routes from Puerto Viejo de Sarapiquí as well as the one north from the Limón area, and the alternative of one-way or round-trip air is available. Fortunately, many lodges are going to electric motors for canal tours, which are quieter and reduce pollution.

Jungle Lodge Hotel, 506/233-0133, fax 506/233-0778, cotour @racsa.co.cr, www.tortuguero.com, nestles beneath palm trees between the Tortuguero River and the forest. Fifty comfortable rooms with ceiling fans are in wooden buildings set in a tropical

Ree Strange Sheck

Jungle Lodge on the Tortuguero River

garden, many connected by covered walkways. The swimming pool has a river view. Happy hour is in a thatched bar, and tasty buffet-style meals are served in a separate dining room. New is the Butterfly Jungle, with 60 species of butterflies and colorful tropical plants, as well as the Frog Garden with 12 species. A short loop trail goes to Penitencia Lagoon and into a forest corridor. Remember repellent. On a morning canal tour the naturalist guide may tell about mating habits of the northern jacana—the male cares for the nest and young—and about buttress roots of the gavilán and other large trees. Seeing the ringed kingfisher in early morning light and observing howler monkey behavior is a thrill. A one-day tour from San José is $79, a two-day is $185 each, double occupancy; three days $230. Night and turtle nesting tours are offered. Ask about one- to four-day sportfishing packages.

Red-eyed tree frogs are the symbol of **Laguna Lodge,** 506/225-3740, at Tortuguero 506/710-0355, fax 506/283-8031, laguna @racsa.co.cr, www.lagunalodgetortuguero.com. If you haven't yet seen this green amphibian decked out with large red eyes, orange hands and feet, blue or purple on sides and thigh, see it here. Also called a red-eyed leaf frog, it lives on plants in the 15 acres (six ha) of gardens and has a protected breeding area inside the butterfly garden. Mosaics of the frog accent a pretty pool and welcome guests in reception—mosaics created by family members. This is a family operation, with Rodolfo and family attentive hosts. Situated on the narrow strip of land between Tortuguero Lagoon and the Caribbean, the lodge has 34 comfortable rooms (some handicapped accessible) in wood cabins, with louvered windows and ceiling fans. Showers in tiled baths have eye-level screens opening into the garden—watch birds while you bathe. Food in the lagoon-side restaurant is excellent. Amenities include a popular bar and an outdoor hot tub. A turtle-nesting beach is steps away and Tortuguero Village an easy walk. A two-day package from San José is $187, a three-day is $234. Add $45 for one-way air. Included are visits to the CCC visitor center, a guided canal boat tour, lodging, and meals.

Río Colorado Lodge, 506/232-4063, fax 506/231-5987, at lodge 506/710-6879, 800/243-9777, tarpon@racsa.co.cr, www.sportsmansweb.com/riocolorado, is like something out of a Hemingway novel. Sprawled along the banks of the Colorado River, the complex is built on stilts—18 large rooms (10 air conditioned), a dining room, bar, recreation room, video room, all joined by covered walkways. Even the dock is covered. A tropical menagerie thrives in ground-level courtyards surrounded by elevated walkways: a tapir named Baby, some tepezcuintle, a pregnant monkey. The aviary includes breeding scarlet macaws (in cooperation with a breeding program in the Central Valley), and inherited caged parakeets: 20 other parakeets were successfully released last year. Great green macaws can be seen on the nearby lagoon, and guests are invited to visit a butterfly farm that belongs to the local school, with proceeds from export of pupa financing books, fans, lights, and other school necessities—a project that receives lodge support. Located within the wildlife refuge, the lodge has forest out the back door and a long Caribbean beach steps away. Stroll in the laid-back village of Barra del Colorado. Breakfast is on the front terrace, buffet lunch in the bar, and a hearty dinner in the upstairs dining room—fishing stories for sure (free rum drinks and sodas at happy hour). This is a prime sportfishing site—ask about packages. Río Colorado pioneered the boat tour from Puerto Viejo de Sarapiquí to the San Juan and the Colorado River. A two-day trip follows this route in and returns via Tortuguero to San José, $196 per person, including a turtle tour in nesting season.

Samay Lagoon Lodge, 506/384-7047, fax 506/383-6370, U.S. fax 707/202-3644, info@samay.com, www.samay.com, is on a peninsula between Samay Lagoon and the Caribbean. Explore lagoons, rivers and forests of Barra del Colorado Wildlife Refuge and the northern part of the Tortuguero canals on hiking and canoe trips. Don't miss Laguna Nueve—an out-of-this-world experience for wildlife and scenic beauty. The lodge has 22 simply furnished rooms cooled by ceiling fans and hammocks on terraces. Meals are served family style, with garden vegetables and fruit. A three-day, two-night Samay Jungle Safari begins in San José and takes to the river from Puerto Viejo to the lodge. Day two includes a canoe trip and jungle hike in the refuge and on canals, plus Laguna Nueve and a night tour. In turtle season, the itinerary adjusts to observe nesting at Tortuguero. Return is also through Puerto Viejo, $278 per person. Options include flying in and out with more time for area tours, $375 per person. A budget package starts and ends at Puerto Viejo de Sarapiquí, $199. Sportfishing packages begin at $255 per person, double occupancy, which includes one day of fishing, one night's lodging, and meals, excluding air fare and transfers.

Silver King Lodge, 506/381-1403, fax 506/381-0849, 800/847-3474, slvrkng@racsa.co.cr, www.silverkinglodge.com, has spacious, attractive rooms with tongue-and-groove floors and walls, bamboo ceilings, queen-size beds with orthopedic mattresses, and coffeemakers in each room. Gourmet meals are served buffet style with complimentary wine. Enjoy the enclosed 10-person hot tub and a swimming pool with an eight-foot (2.4-m) waterfall. Explore backwater lagoons and rivers in aluminum canoes at no charge. Fiberglass kayaks are available for estuary trips into the rain forest at Barra del Colorado. Private paths also lead into the jungle. Take guided tours to the wildlife refuge, to Tortuguero, and to see turtle-nesting (July through September) or crocodiles at night. Get a guided tour to Laguna Nueve. Sportfishing is a specialty, as the name indicates: the silver king is the tarpon. A three-day fishing option is $1,810, double occupancy, including round-trip airfare from San José, lodging, food, and boat tours of Barra del Colorado and Tortuguero canals. Another package includes a guided canoe trip. The daily rate for nonfishermen is $130 per person.

Tortuga Lodge, 506/222-0333, fax 506/257-1665, ecotur@expeditions.co.cr, www.expeditions.co.cr, has a sense of place The openness integrates river, forest, and gardens into inside spaces. Set in a botanical garden of palms, orchids, and heliconias with the forest as a backdrop, 25 rooms are in two-story modules. Polished floors gleam in large rooms, which have as much window as wall; tasteful, bright colors in furnishings are in tune with tropical colors outside. Each has ceiling fan, ample closet, and water-conserving features. Shady verandas invite relaxation while you observe river life in front or birdlife in the garden. Watch the moon rise across the river, looking seaward. The restaurant, with good food and lots of it, begins at water's edge. A swimming pool with a waterfall is next to a terrace and the river.

Be generous with repellent and venture into the forest behind the lodge on a short loop trail. Optional activities include a dawn boat trip, turtle walks, and transportation to Tortuguero Village, $8 one-way for up to three. Whether you take the turtle walk or not, attend the excellent natural history slide presentation about Tortuguero, turtles, other wildlife, and the park—it's free. Canal/river trips with a local guide are included in some packages. One I took was magical—a flock of collared aracaris, the beautiful chestnut-colored woodpecker, a days-old howler clinging to his mother, bare-throated tiger herons, crocodiles, three-toed sloths, kingfishers, crocodiles, and Jesus Christ lizards. Two-day trips start at $379 per person, double occupancy, including transportation (one-way by air), lodging, meals, and taxes. For lodging alone, $115 per person double occupancy, taxes included. Breakfast is $13, lunch $18, dinner $21, taxes included. Meal plans are available. Ask about fishing packages. Tortuga Lodge is operated by Costa Rica Expeditions, which has established the Tortuguero Foundation to help in health, education, and protection of the wilderness area, working with the Tortuguero Community Development Association.

Central and Southern Caribbean

Realize your fantasy of camping in the rain forest at **Almonds and Corals Lodge Tent Camp,** just north Manzanillo, 506/272-2024, at lodge 506/752-0232, fax 506/272-2220, almonds@racsa.co.cr, www.geoexpeditions.com. Twenty-three covered platforms on stilts, each complete with tent, bathroom, corner sitting area, and hammock, are tucked among forest flora. In the cozy tent are a double or two single beds with pretty quilted spreads, floor fan, nightstand, and lamps. The bath, set off by a partition, has a flush toilet, built-in sink, and shower—water at ambient temperature. There's even an electric plug. Doubles are $61 per person including breakfast and dinner. Meals in the open-air dining room are tasty, with a set menu each day; it's open to the public. Staff is friendly and helpful, including delightful owners Aurora and Marcos.

Raised wooden walkways connect the clusters of cabins with the dining room/bar and, through the forest, with the beach. On the walk through forest you may see toucans, parrots, howler monkeys, or a slaty-tailed trogon. Located within the Gandoca-Manzanillo Wildlife Refuge, the lodge offers guided tours. Hike, kayak or snorkel at Punta Uva, go horseback riding, or visit Cahuita or the Kekoldi Indian Reserve. The tent camp has a leadership role in an area recycling project. Aurora owns Geo Expediciones, a travel agency that specializes in the Caribbean area. One package combines Almonds and Corals with charming La Quinta de Sarapiquí Lodge, owned by Aurora's sister and brother-in-law. A three-day package includes a guided walk in Gandoca-Manzanillo, snorkeling, and round-trip transfer from San José: $250 per person, double occupancy. The Manzanillo bus passes by, leaving a short walk on the road through the forest to the lodge.

Directly across from Playa Negra in Cahuita is **Atlántida Lodge,** 506/755-0115, fax 506/755-0213, atlantis@racsa.co.cr; www.Atlantida .co.cr. Each of 30 high-ceilinged, simply furnished rooms has a porch fringed with a thatched-roof overhang. Cane motifs are throughout, in ceilings and furniture. Screened windows have wooden shutters and cooling is by ceiling fan; doubles $55. New deluxe double rooms in a separate building are $100. Look for red-eyed tree frogs in gardens ablaze with color, especially near the pool, gym, and bar. The open-air restaurant has everything from sandwiches to filet mignon. At check-in, don't miss the antique crank cash register. Atlántida offers 15 tours, including jungle walks, snorkeling at Cahuita reef, sea kayaking, tree climbing, horseback riding to a waterfall, bird-watching at Aviarios del Caribe, or a visit to an orchid farm or a Bribri village. Therapeutic massage available.

Bungalow Malú, 506/755-0006, has four rooms in charming bungalows of river stone and wood, nestled among colorful tropical vegetation in expansive gardens across the road from the beach in Cahuita. Decorator touches abound. Wood washed ashore after storms has been polished and used as door handles and light fixtures—natural sculptures. Bathrooms have river stone floors. Rooms have built-in desks, reading lamps, and small refrigerators; some have queen-size beds. Closets and headboards are wood and bamboo, doubles $30. Stone paths lead to a rancho-style restaurant where owner Alessandra Bucci features Italian dishes and fresh fish along with typical Caribbean dishes, sometimes breadfruit; open to public.

In Puerto Viejo just steps from the Caribbean Sea and the famous Salsa Brava surfing site is appealing **Cabinas Casa Verde,** 506/750-0015, fax 506/750-0047, atecmail@racsa.co.cr, www. greencoast.com/casaverd.htm. Surrounded by pretty gardens enhanced by orchids, bromeliads, heliconias, birds, and butterflies, the friendly hotel is a complex of six cabins, seven rooms, and a spic-and-span bathhouse for the rooms; doubles with shared bath are $22. Each room has a fan, mosquito net, garden view, original watercolor paintings, and hammock. Six have balconies and private baths, doubles $34. A tiny, charming bungalow with kitchenette (shared bath) is $25 for two. Large open sitting areas add to the feeling of spaciousness. The small hotel is in a residential neighborhood just blocks from downtown restaurants. Owners René and Carolina have added a frog garden.

About a mile (1.5 km) south of Puerto Viejo is a paradise called **Cariblue,** tel/fax 506/750-0057, Cariblue@racsa.co.cr, www. cariblue.com. Nine secluded bungalows are ensconced in heliconia-studded gardens surrounded by forest. Four are of tropical hardwoods, and five newer ones of cement. All are spacious with terraces and private views, doubles $45 to $65, including full breakfast served in the rancho-style restaurant. Attentive owners Sandra and

Leonardo specialize in Italian dishes for dinner. The small souvenir shop has unusual local handcrafts—jewelry made from *tagua* nuts, Bribri baskets. Cocles Beach is just across the road, with 12 miles (20 km) of white-sand beach to explore. Tours arranged throughout the area.

In Cahuita, **Hotel Jaguar,** 506/226-3775, fax 506/226-4693, at hotel 506/755-0238, jaguar@racsa.co.cr, www.centralamerica.com/cr/hotel/jaguar, has 45 rooms across the road from the beach at the north end of town. Building design incorporates cross-ventilation and thermo-siphoning, resulting in passively cooled rooms that have queen-size beds with orthopedic mattresses and louvered shutters over screened windows. Just outside the front door are lounge chairs on long porches facing the beach. Varied fruit trees draw birds to hotel grounds. Watch for the flash of the scarlet-rumped tanager, and listen to parrots. Doubles are $70 for superior rooms, $55 for standards, breakfast included. Paul and Melba Vigneault, hotel owners, have created a menu fit for a gourmet, true elegance by the sea, with such delicacies as avocado omelets for breakfast and French Caribbean cooking that uses fresh herbs and spices in 10 sauces served with fish, beef, or chicken. Sea bass with heart of palm sauce is memorable, or try chicken with cashew fruit sauce. The restaurant, in the garden near the swimming pool, is open to the public. Nature trails on 18 acres (seven ha) offer possible sightings of crocodiles, armadillos, sloths, kinkajous, agoutis, or colorful frogs. Trips arranged to area attractions. A rental shop has mountain bikes, boogie boards, beach mats, fins, and snorkeling equipment, as well as books and souvenirs.

La Costa de Papito, about a mile (two km) south of Puerto Viejo facing Cocles Beach, is a jewel, 506/221-3925, in Puerto Viejo, tel/fax 506/798-1844, 506/798-4244, www.greencoast.com/papito. Five cabins of spectacular tropical woods, spaced for secluded privacy, have wraparound verandas with bamboo rails. Each is large, built off the ground in Caribbean style, with wood and bamboo tables, ceiling fans, pitched ceilings, shutters on ample windows, and two double beds: doubles are $50 including taxes. Breakfast can be served at your bungalow upon request, while tropical drinks and bocas are served among the tall palms or in a thatched rancho, with the sound of waves as background music. Gardens are glorious: heliconias, palms, bananas, papayas, *guanábana*, plantains, passion fruit.

Owner Eddie Ryan is pleased to help guests arrange area tours such as nature walks in the reserve, visits to the green iguana farm, dolphin tours, kayaking, horseback riding, or jungle treks in Gandoca-Manzanillo Wildlife Refuge. The lodge rents bicycles and has a beautician and massage therapist.

Pangea at Manzanillo, 506/750-0191, atec@racsa.co.cr, is one of the few places to stay right in Manzanillo, and the best. With Swiss-Italian owners, it has four extremely neat rooms with some nice touches—fresh flowers, painted floors, night tables suspended by ropes; a double is $35 including breakfast served on the porch: coffee, fruit, crepes, eggs. Pangea is one block west of Aquamor.

A refurbished **Park Hotel** in Limón by the esplanade along the

TALAMANCA DOLPHIN FOUNDATION

In Manzanillo, a tiny place at the edge of the sea, a big project is underway: to increase knowledge, awareness, and protection of the area's dolphins and promote responsible marine ecotourism. Ever hear of "dolphin etiquette"? Well, local boat captains, schoolchildren, and now national and international tourists are learning it as a result of the Talamanca Dolphin Foundation, begun in 1998. Respect is the bottom line, but for specifics, check out the website or send for a brochure. Three dolphin species live in waters in and around Gandoca-Manzanillo National Wildlife Refuge: Atlantic spotted dolphin, bottlenose, and tucuxi, the smallest member of the Cetacea group, which includes whales, dolphins, and porpoises. Through a nonintrusive style of research tied to respectful observation, more than 30 individual dolphins have been identified based on body and fin markings, and researchers are learning about their personalities, daily life, and habitat. Local knowledge formed the base for scientific studies. Shawn Larkin, a prime mover in the foundation, says, "Many of the locals speak of the dolphins as friends."

Captains, all members of the foundation, and volunteer

seawall is clean and bright, downtown but away from heavily trafficked streets, 506/798-0555, fax 506/758-4364. Thirty-two rooms have air conditioning, TV, telephones. Doubles from $39, with sea view rooms with balconies $45. A pleasant restaurant with big windows to the sea is on the ground floor.

As exotic as its name, **Shawandha Lodge** is sensational, 506/750-0018, fax 506/750-0037, shawandha@racsa.co.cr. Created by artist/designer Maho Diaz, each of 10 raised bungalows is unique, featuring furniture she designed. Spacious rooms with polished hardwood floors and walls open onto private verandas that shelter a small sofa, table, and hammock. Bathrooms are enchanting: sinks with designs in mosaic tiles, showers down spiral steps—no two alike. Choose

observers and interns log sightings and behavior on every boat trip with tourists, where dolphins are spotted about 90 percent of the time. Boats wait at a distance—it's up to the dolphins to approach. The foundation certifies the captains, and they in turn give a donation from every dolphin tour. Fascinating data are being collected: interspecies mating has been observed between tucuxi and bottlenose, with probable offspring. The behavior of the more reclusive tucuxi actually becomes more social and aerial when in association with the bottlenose, known for its interaction with humans. On dolphin trips, learn about the four dolphin behaviors—traveling, feeding, socializing, resting—and which are conducive for interaction with humans. Information is shared with dolphin groups in Manuel Antonio, Drake Bay, Golfo Dulce, and Flamingo. At least 30 of the 80 known species in the world ply Costa Rica's waters. Book the Dolphin Interaction and Observation Boat Trip, $25, through the foundation or Aquamor (see "Guides and Outfitters"). Learn more about the foundation, dolphin research, tours, and intern and volunteer opportunities: P.O. Box 1336, Bozeman, MT 59771, 800/231-7422, info@dolphinlink.org, www.dolphinlink.org. In Costa Rica, 506/750-0431, or show up in Manzanillo.

from among single, queen- and king-size beds. Doubles are $80, including a tropical breakfast. Partner Nicolas Buffile brought to the project his creative experience with restaurants. The open-air restaurant and bar, with carved stone motifs, is striking with its towering thatched roof. Sofa, chairs, and tables offer places to relax with a drink and enjoy tropical garden colors. Dinner is an event: subtle lighting in the garden, perfume of heliotrope from nearby plants, nice music, spectacular floral arrangements, special entrees every night. Chef Françoise creates food fit for the gods. Guests can enjoy the five acres (two ha) of gardens—good birding—or take a short walk on a private arborlike trail to beautiful Playa Chiquita, an interesting beach with tide pools to explore. The friendly, attentive staff arranges tours. Shawandha is three miles (five km) south of Puerto Viejo.

FOOD

Amimodo at the east end of Puerto Viejo, 506/750-0257, has homemade Italian food like gnocchi, ravioli, and carpaccio as well as lobster and grilled shrimp. Open from noon to 3:30 P.M. and 6 to 10:30 P.M. in high season, it has reduced hours in low season.

Canadian chef Bert and wife Julie have charming **Cha Cha Cha** in downtown Cahuita 506/755-0232. For food with a flair try the tenderloin specialty, lobster in white wine served on a sizzling plate, nutty salad with cashew and orange dressing, or Tex-Mex fare like fajitas or nachos. For dessert, choose banana flambé or Black Magic Woman. Open 5 to 11 P.M., closed Monday.

The **Garden Restaurant** in Puerto Viejo, 506/750-0069, is known for good food. Owner Vera Khan serves chicken tandoori, three or four curries, shrimp, fish grilled with different sauces, and vegetarian fare. Try the Chocolate Decadence for dessert. Vera also has the adjoining Jacaranda, where simple, clean rooms are from $16.

100% Natural in downtown Cahuita, 506/755-0055, is open 7 A.M. to midnight. Breakfast can be eggs any style, French toast, or a fruit plate. Menu includes vegetarian dishes, sandwiches, and specialties cooked on the outdoor grill: lobster and sirloin. Try the chicken breast in curry, onions, and olive oil. Grilled banana split for dessert?

Owners Mario, Denis, and Silvana offer e-mail and fax service. Closed Sunday. Be sure to look at the mural map of Cahuita next door.

Miss Junie in Tortuguero, 506/710-0523, has more than 50 years of history. Try the typical Caribbean rice and beans (cooked in coconut milk), *rondón* (a soup of fish, coconut milk, and vegetables), *yuca*, or a punch served in a coconut. Breakfast is 7 to 9 A.M., lunch noon to 1:30 P.M., dinner 7 to 8 P.M. Small but clean rooms are available for $15 per person.

Upstairs **Restaurant Maxi** in Manzanillo is open daily 11 A.M. to 10 P.M. All dishes are served with rice and beans, *patacones* (fried plantains), and salad, Caribbean style. There are also lobster, shrimp. red snapper, steak, chicken, and vegetarian plates.

Restaurante La Selva at the entrance to Manzanillo is not only an open-air restaurant, it has trees inside that go right through the roof—trees with fruits that attract howler monkeys. Diners also see birds, butterflies, and other animals that move through the forest alongside. Specialties are lobster with garlic, sea bass, *arroz con camarones* (shrimp and rice). Try natural fruit drinks. Open daily 11 A.M. to 9 P.M. in high season, closed Tuesday April to October. Owners are Pablo and Sandra. Brother Abel does guided jungle tours. Contact him here.

A local favorite is **Restaurante Tamara** on the main street in Puerto Viejo, 506/750-0148. Owner Edwin Patterson promises typical Caribbean-style food, served from 7:30 A.M. to 10 P.M. except Tuesday, when the place opens at noon. Try the rice and beans and *pan bon*. Or there's lobster, chicken, and fresh fish. Talk to Edwin, a community leader, about local politics.

Dinner at **Shawandha Lodge,** three miles (five km) south of Puerto Viejo, 506/750-0018, is not to be missed. Chef Françoise combines French cuisine with Caribbean flavors for nightly specials. Try salmon, mango and spinach salad, melted goat cheese on bread over a bed of lettuce, or sea shrimp in sweet cream. The *pescado de chef* (chef's fish specialty) is remarkable. Open 6 to 9 P.M.

Santa Elena

To Tilarán via Cañitas

To SkyWalk and SkyTrek, Santa Elena Forest Reserve, Tilarán via Las Nubes,
San Gerardo sector of Bosque Eterno de los Niños

Cloud Forest Lodge

Cerro Plano

Sapo Dorado
Hotel and Restaurant

Monteverde Orchids

La Pizzería de Johnny

Hotel Heliconia

Arco
Iris
Lodge

Hotel Finca
Valverde's

Serpentario
Santa Elena

Banco Nacional
Bus Stop

Post Office

Restaurant
de Lucía

Pensión
Manakin

Hotel de
Montaña Monteverde

Monteverde
Lodge

Toll
Booth

Monteverde
Butterfly Garden

Monteverde
Conservation League

Aventuras
Aéreas

Gasoline Station

Meg's Riding
Stables

Hotel/Restaurant
El Bosque

Stella's
Bakery

CASEM

Bajo del Tigre Trail

Dairy Plant (Cheese Factory)

Monteverde

Friends' Meeting House

Hotel Fonda Vela

Trapp Family
Lodge

Entrance to
Monteverde
Cloud Forest Preserve

To Inter-American Highway
and San Luis

PRIMARY ROAD   SECONDARY ROAD   ■ SITE OF INTEREST   ▲ PRIVATE RESERVE

MAP NOT TO SCALE

© Avalon Travel Publishing, Inc.

CHAPTER 10

Monteverde Region

Monteverde, in the Tilarán Mountains south of Lake Arenal, is the best-known destination in Costa Rica. Travelers are drawn to this other-worldly place in search of its most famous denizen, the quetzal; to experience the magical cloud forest; and frankly, to see what all the hullabaloo is about.

Even before Costa Rica was a top tourism destination, natural history travelers made their way up the mountain, lured by articles, television specials, and word of mouth about golden toads and resplendent quetzals, about scientific research in a remote mountaintop setting, about community efforts to save tropical forest, and about friendly, peace-loving Quakers who settled here. Today private reserves and nature/adventure tourism operators offer a rich mix of ways to experience and learn about this biologically rich place.

LAY OF THE LAND

Monteverde is not only the name of a village but the name that describes the zone. Three communities form the core of an "urban area" of perhaps 3,000 persons: the largest is Santa Elena, with bank,

251

shops, and the local high school; next along the road is Cerro Plano; and finally, Monteverde, where even the gas station has a view.

T-shirts and postcards brag "I survived the road to Monteverde," but take it from someone who has traveled Costa Rica's highways and byways, roads to Monteverde no longer rank among the worst. Paving stones make getting around in Santa Elena easier now in rainy season, perhaps a portent of improvement at the end of the bumpy road.

The tiny, progressive community of Monteverde is worth a visit. Quakers came here in 1951 from the United States, drawn by Costa Rica's demilitarized environment. They put down roots and set up a business that now makes some of the finest cheeses in the country. The Quakers bought milk from neighboring farmers and invited them to become shareholders in Productores de Monteverde, still the largest single area employer. Visit the **Monteverde Cheese Factory,** known as La Lechería, Monday through Saturday 7:30 A.M. to 4 P.M., Sunday till 12:30 P.M. Watch cheesemakers through a glass partition and buy cheeses or ice cream. The Quaker way of consensus, participatory decision making, and working together for common good has strongly influenced the way things are done in the area.

The sound of birds and wind in the trees is not the only music heard here. The **Monteverde Music Festival,** January-March, brings some of the country's finest musicians for nighttime performances. Proceeds support music in schools and community. Contact Monteverde Institute for details, 506/645-5053, fax 506/645-5219, mviimv@racsa.co.cr.

The arts get strong billing, right along with nature/adventure activities. For galleries, see Meg and Stella Wallace's work at Stella's Bakery, across from CASEM—paintings, jewelry, pottery, and stained glass—or at studios at Meg's Stables. Don't miss Marco Tulio Brenes's beautiful creations in wood at Galeria Extasis, tucked in the forest south of La Cascada Restaurant. Monteverde Studios of the Arts, 800/370-3331, www.mvstudios.com., offers weeklong workshops in pottery, basketry, painting, stained glass, woodcarving, sculpture, and photography.

CASEM, a women's craft cooperative, sells locally handcrafted items, many with designs from the area's rich biological diversity:

Ree Strange Sheck

Gray fox at Monteverde

quetzals, bellbirds, golden toads. Find hand-painted cards and stationery, embroidery and weaving—open Monday through Saturday 8 A.M. to 6 P.M., Sunday 10 A.M. to 4 P.M. Next door is Coope Santa Elena's coffee-roasting operation; stop in and try Café Monteverde. **Hummingbird Gallery,** 506/645-5030, near the entrance to Monteverde Cloud Forest Preserve, displays spectacular natural history photographs and art in wood. A gift shop has jewelry, textiles, original T-shirts, and loads of natural history books. Hummers put on a show-stopping performance as they zoom around garden feeders—open daily 8:30 A.M. to 4:30 P.M.

For a preview or review, go to a rain-forest slide show. Images captured by internationally known photographers Patricia and Michael Fogden are presented daily next to the Hummingbird Gallery, $3; proceeds help support an environmental education program for 16 schools. Check for times, 506/645-5010. A multimedia show is presented nightly at 6:15 at El Sapo Dorado, 506/645-5057, with excellent photos by biologist Richard Laval, $5. Visit the **Serpentario Santa Elena,** 506/645-5238, at the entrance to Hotel Finca Valverdes, to observe more than 40 species of frogs, lizards, and snakes, including fer-de-lance, tropical rat snake, false coral, and boa—open daily 8 A.M. to 5 P.M.; admission $5.

To help spot orchids in the wild, go by **Monteverde Orchids,** tel/fax 506/645-5510, next to La Pizzería de Johnny in Cerro Plano, which showcases 450 of the 500 orchid species in the region. A terraced garden includes miniature orchids so tiny that owner Gabriel Barbosa hands out magnifying glasses. At least 40 species are in bloom at any time. The display, also part of a research project, is organized into 22 family groups with signs describing group characteristics. Gabriel, who has a species of orchid named after him, investigates orchid pollinators and is working on an inventory of Monteverde's orchid species. Open 8 A.M. to 5 P.M.; admission $5.

For small trails, try **Valle Escondido Trail,** past the Butterfly Garden, a good place to photograph mammals; open daily 7 A.M. to 5 P.M., 506/645-5156, or **Sendero Tranquilo** for highly personalized guided walks in glorious forest open only to small groups, 506/645-5010.

A minibus runs between Santa Elena and the Monteverde Cloud Forest Preserve, facilitating access to attractions along this 3.5-mile (six-km) stretch. It leaves Santa Elena at 6:15 A.M. and 1 P.M.; from the preserve at noon and 4 P.M., a 45-minute ride.

NATURE AND ADVENTURE ACTIVITIES

Most areas this size are pleased to have one protected area; the Monteverde region has five large private reserves and several smaller ones for nature hikes and bird-watching as well as top adventure attractions such as canopy experiences and horseback riding. The opportunity to see wildlife is good. Take a guided walk to learn more about cloud-forest habitat and species. Guides here are usually superb. Don't pack your schedule too full here—take a walk along the roads, have some quiet time in the forest. And don't leave your room without binoculars.

FLORA AND FAUNA

It is not uncommon to see a coati or agouti cross the road in front of you or a sloth resting in a roadside tree. Howler, white-faced, and spider monkeys are here, as are kinkajous and big marine toads. Birding is excellent, more than 400 species. You are likely to see emerald toucanets, blue-crowned motmots, euphonias, brown jays, and a world of hummingbirds, including the violet sabrewing and purple-throated mountain gem. From March to August, hear the booming call of the three-wattled bellbird. Monteverde is the only known home of the golden toad (*Bufo periglenes*), a brilliantly colored two-inch amphibian: orange males, yellow and black females with patches of scarlet. Last seen in 1989, only time will tell if this species has disappeared.

The resplendent quetzal (*Pharomachrus mocinno*), however, is alive and well here though considered an endangered species in Central America, primarily because of habitat destruction. In the trogon family, this bird was a symbol of freedom to Aztec and Mayan peoples; for some it is practically the symbol of Monteverde, though it is also lives in forests in and around Braulio Carrillo, Poás, and Chirripó parks and year-round in the Cerro de la Muerte zone.

This fantastic iridescent bird has a shimmering green head, neck, and body and a crimson belly. The male has graceful tail streamers more than two feet (0.6 m) long. While the female's barred black-and-white tail and duller crimson belly cannot match the male's magnificence, she is regal. Depending on the light, quetzal feathers can shine in shades of blue. Like other members of the trogon family, quetzals tend to sit still for long periods. Go with a guide who knows how to spot them.

Quetzals are partial to fruit from wild relatives of the avocado; look for them around fig trees as well. At Monteverde they are altitudinal migrants, leaving cloud forest about July for lower Pacific slopes (sometimes only a few miles away), where they feed until October when they move to the Caribbean side of the mountains; they usually return to Monteverde in January. As they follow fruiting patterns and move away from protected lands, they can face peril.

As reserves become isolated by deforested land, survival of migrating species such as this is jeopardized.

Breeding is March to June, the easiest time to see quetzals because they come down lower in the trees to nest, using a hole in rotting limbs or dead tree trunks. The female generally lays two blue eggs, which hatch in 18 to 22 days. Both male and female build the nest, incubate eggs (parts of the male's longer tail streamers often protrude from the hole when he is on the nest), and feed young. After August the male sheds his by-now-tattered streamers and grows new ones. Main predators of eggs and chicks are short-tailed weasels, toucanets, tayras, and perhaps snakes.

VISITOR INFORMATION

Visitor centers at reserves are good sources of information about the zone, as well as area lodges. **Cloud Forest Tours,** 506/645-6110, at the front of Stella's Bakery is a good source—Glenda Wallace is happy to help.

GETTING THERE

Monteverde is 113 miles (182 km) northwest of San José. Two principal routes are off the Inter-American Highway: one near km 134 goes through Sardinal (paved for a short distance); the other, near km 149, is immediately south of the Río Lagarto bridge. These two join near Guacimal. Count on 90 minutes from the highway to Monteverde by either route. A bumpy road gives breathtaking views of lowlands. As you wind through thin clouds, cows across deep valleys look like brown or white dots scattered on the steep pastures. Roads seem to hang by grace along mountain's edge. Cars with high clearance make driving easier.

From La Fortuna, go to Tilarán and then on mostly unpaved road through Quebrada Grande to Santa Elena, or choose tours that offer a boat/horseback or boat/car options. Hotels have details.

When coming from Liberia or northwest Pacific beaches, routes off the Inter-American are at Cañas to Tilarán or at Las Juntas de

Abangares. Public buses run from Puntarenas, San José, and Tilarán; check Appendix A for schedules, including private vans/buses; some hotels have shuttles. Taxis are available in Santa Elena, where the bus stops first. It proceeds along the main road to Monteverde; have a flashlight handy to walk from the main road to your hotel after dark.

NATURE AND ADVENTURE SIGHTS

Aventuras Aereas
See various levels of the forest in two-person cars suspended from overhead lines and moved by electricity. The route also passes over some open areas excellent for birds and other wildlife. The aerial cars move slowly, allowing plenty of time to observe flora and fauna, and passengers have the option of stopping to take photos or to get a great look when that coati or toucanet or monkey appears. The route is about one mile (1.5 km) and usually takes 1.5 hours. This is an option for all ages. Night tours are an option.

   Details: *Southwest of the Cerro Plano School; 506/645-5960, tel/fax 506/645-5315, wmvargas@racsa.co.cr. Open 6 A.M. to 6 P.M.; admission $12.*

Bajo del Tigre Trail
The two-mile (3.3-km) system of trails has sections named for manakins, monkeys, bellbirds, and bats, all of which are found here along with emerald toucanets, blue-crowned motmots, coatis, swallow-tailed kites, sloths, agoutis, and vegetation different from the nearby cloud forest. This type of lower-elevation forest and its wildlife has become rare in Costa Rica as a result of deforestation and agriculture.

   A part of Bosque Eterno de los Niños (Children's Eternal Forest), Bajo del Tigre has a Children's Nature Center and a Children's Information Trail, where kids of all ages can learn about rain-forest wonders. A short loop trail and extensions from it go through forest and around an emerging arboretum (60 tagged native species) to viewpoints with fantastic vistas of river canyon, forest, and the Gulf of Nicoya.

Buy a copy of the artistic, informative self-guiding trail booklet. Bajo del Tigre is owned and operated by the Monteverde Conservation League, a nonprofit organization founded in 1986. Its activities include research, education, protection of flora and fauna, and habitat rehabilitation. Volunteers are often needed.

Details: *Look for sign on the main road in Monteverde, about a half mile (one km) west of the cheese factory; 506/645-5003, fax 506/645-5104, acmmcl@racsa.co.cr, www.monteverde.or.cr. Open daily 8 A.M. to 4:30 P.M.; admission $5 for adults, children under 12 free.*

Bosque Eterno de los Niños, San Gerardo Sector

The adventure of staying at San Gerardo begins with getting there. Where vehicles leave off, guests start a two-mile (3.5-km) trek to the San Gerardo Field Station. It's a terrific walk. Lush vegetation, fantastic views, and birdlife along the way make up for the often-muddy track. Then you round a bend, and Arenal Volcano is on the horizon and Lake Arenal's waters glisten. As you come off a forest trail into a clearing, the two-story wooden station appears.

It's somehow a surprise to find such a facility in this remote place. Rustic, yes; but comfortable. Six upstairs rooms, each with four beds (two bunks) and private bath, open onto a wonderful veranda great for bird-watching and volcano viewing. When Arenal rumbles, all eyes look for the thin molten-red lines flowing down the sides: a natural sound-and-light show. This field station, built primarily for researchers and student groups, has laboratory and lecture space on the first floor, along with the dining area, where local staff serve up delicious food.

About four miles (two km) of hiking trails wind through primary, secondary, and regenerating forest. Epiphyte-laden trees, ferns, vines, heliconias, and other tropical vegetation abound. Among 200-plus species of birds are black guans, hummingbirds, toucans, tanagers, and swallow-tailed kites. Howler monkeys announce the day, and you can also find white-faced monkeys, agoutis, coatis, and armadillos. The margay is here, but you probably won't see it.

The San Gerardo sector is in the 56,800-acre (23,000-ha) Children's Rain Forest, the largest private reserve in the country. It is operated by the Monteverde Conservation League, a private nonprofit organization with offices in Monteverde and La Tigra de San Carlos. Donations from children and adults preserve this rich resource for tomorrow's children. At San Gerardo, one of the many reasons for protecting these forests is crystal clear. Sources for Lake Arenal's water are here, waters that feed a hydroelectric plant that produces almost half of the electricity in Costa Rica and then flow into lowlands to be used for irrigation. Ask about volunteer opportunities.

Details: *Five miles (8.5 km) north of Santa Elena; 506/645-5003, fax 506/645-5104, acmmcl@racsa.co.cr, www.monteverde.or.cr. Lodging and meals $30 per person, student discount available. From Santa Elena, follow signs to the Santa Elena Forest Reserve (this part by vehicle—taxis available). From here, take a 1.6-mile (2.5-km) walk down an old forest road and another half mile on a forest trail.*

Ecolodge San Luis & Biological Station

Ever dream of what it would be like to be a researcher in the tropical rain forest? Well, here's your chance to have a hands-on experience that mixes activities of a biological research station with nature and adventure tourism and a working farm.

Located in the San Luis Valley only 30 minutes from Monteverde, Ecolodge San Luis, a private reserve, was designed by tropical researchers Diane and Milton Lieberman to foster interaction among guests, scientists, students, staff, and members of the San Luis community. In the rustic dining room, researchers and visitors sit elbow-to-elbow at long tables for meals served family style. Neighbors drop by for coffee or to use the corner reference library.

Guests can participate in studies on the seasonal migration of birds or seed dispersal by birds and mammals, help with research on living fence posts, plant trees, take daily weather data, and sit in on lectures or slide shows when student groups are present. There are orchid, medicinal plant, and organic gardens, plus coffee fields and a small dairy.

Hike in a stupendous forest, either alone or accompanied by guides who are active researchers. The ecolodge property, 175 acres (70 ha), borders Monteverde Cloud Forest Preserve and Bosque

Ree Strange Sheck

*Balconies onto the forest at Ecolodge
San Luis & Biological Station*

Eterno de los Niños. More than 225 species of birds have been seen here, along with mammals such as howler and white-faced monkeys, coatis, kinkajous, sloths, tayras, pumas, and agoutis.

Night walks, bird-watching (see 60 species before breakfast), horseback riding, swimming in the San Luis River, hiking to a waterfall—many options are available. You really can pick coffee and even help take it by horseback to the local processing plant. Harvest bananas. Join cooks in the kitchen to learn how to make tamales and *gallo pinto* or, as I did, learn how to cook eggs on a banana leaf. Cooking is in the traditional way, on a woodstove. Take part in local fiestas, soccer games, and dances. Go on a day trip to Monteverde. Sign up for a seven-day tropical biology experience with field lectures, hikes, lab work, and small-group activities.

Accommodations come in three types. The four-room research bunkhouse (formerly a milking barn) has bunk beds, shared baths, and varnished mahogany walls. A four-room bungalow of varnished hardwoods offers wide verandas with hammocks; one room is wheelchair accessible. Spacious, lovely cabins a short walk up the hill are in two six-room wings joined by a large covered deck. High-ceilinged rooms open onto a balcony with panoramic views. Cabins are $95 per person, bungalow rooms $75, bunkhouse $60, including meals, lodging, guides, and activities.

Details: *In the San Luis Valley, 506/282-4160, fax 506/282-4162; at Ecolodge tel/fax 506/380-3255; in U.S. 888/388-2582, info@altatravelplanners.com, www.altatravelplanners.com. Same directions as to Monteverde, but turn off for San Luis at the orange bus stop and continue* *to the blue San Luis school; turn right to Ecolodge. For bus travel, take the Monteverde bus and a taxi to San Luis.*

EcoVerde Lodge and Private Reserve

Monte los Olivos, northwest of Monteverde, is a small mountain village that could serve as a case study for how communities in areas around national parks and reserves can be involved in local conservation projects. This group of families who struggled together to form a community, build a one-room school for their children, find a teacher, and buy textbooks, have gone on to build EcoVerde Lodge to supplement income from dairy farming and secure alternatives for their children.

It is operated by the town's Ecological Association; members do construction, cook, clean cabins, maintain trails, and guide visitors, in addition to dairy farming. The idea is to share not only the biological richness of the place but also a way of life. Guests can participate in dairy farming, walk on three miles (five km) of cloud-forest trails in the private reserve, climb to a lookout with expansive views of Arenal Volcano and Lake Arenal, ride horses, and get to know the community, many of whom share the last name of Barquero. Villagers accompany guests to Arenal Lake or the volcano and to the waterfall at Río Chiquito; tours are arranged to Sky Walk and Monteverde. Expect hummingbirds here, and quetzals, monkeys, and other cloud-forest flora and fauna.

Nine cabins, four with private baths, were built largely with wood from fallen or diseased trees. Facilities are rustic but comfortable; doubles $45, breakfast included; packages are available. Typical food, country style, is served in the small restaurant. The project incorporates recycling, organic gardening, and forest management. Support has come from Arenal Conservation Area, World Wildlife Fund-Canada, and Canadian International Development Fund. EcoVerde is a member of Cooprena R.L., a national consortium of ecotourism cooperatives.

Details: *Four miles (six km) northwest of Santa Elena in Monte los Olivos, on the road to Tilarán via Las Nubes; tel/fax 506/286-4203, at EcoVerde tel/fax 506/661-8126, cooprena@racsa.co.cr, www.agroecoturismo.net. Take a bus to Santa Elena and taxi to the lodge.*

Monteverde Butterfly Garden

The garden is nothing short of glorious. Experience a butterfly world set amid rich forest, sometimes with the sounds of howler monkeys reverberating through the air, always with fluttering colors of *mariposas* both inside enclosures and along garden paths.

The hour-long guided walk with well-trained bilingual guides goes through four enclosed gardens that represent different habitats. Afterward you can have as much time as you like to walk along the paths or sit alone to watch or photograph the free-flying butterflies. It is a magical place.

Biologist Jim Wolfe and Marta Iris Salazar, his wife, started the garden in 1991, from the beginning with a strong environmental education bent. Jim, a teacher by nature, shares fascinating tidbits about insects, plants, and their relationships. Tours start out from the Nature Center full of fascinating displays: live butterfly eggs, caterpillars, and chrysalids, and other live local insects such as scarab beetles or katydids. You may get to see a butterfly emerge from its pupal case. Look at butterfly wings under a microscope. A small reference library and a video are available to visitors, along with a colorful pamphlet chock-full of butterfly ecology: feeding, defense, migration, and life cycle. Ask for the plant guide, which gives scientific and family names of labeled plants in the gardens and on the trail, along with brief information about them.

Fifty local species are raised to keep the gardens "blooming;" some 550 butterfly species are found in Monteverde, among them the heavenly blue morpho, owl butterflies, clearwings, and zebra longwings. Mornings are best for butterfly activity.

An added feature of the garden is the inside view of an active leaf-cutter ant nest. You must see how Jim and the ants created this marvel. Visitors can also walk a self-guided trail to see medicinal plants. Visit the small gift shop, with its melodious fountain, stained glass window, and mural. Shirts with elegant butterfly designs are the work of Marta Iris. Ask about volunteer opportunities.

Details: *Turn at Cerro Plano School and follow butterfly signs down the hill; tel/fax 506/645-5512, wolfej@racsa.co.cr, www.best.com/~mariposa. Open daily 9:30 A.M. to 4 P.M.; $7 for adults, $3 for children.*

Monteverde Cloud Forest Preserve

The flash of a quetzal above a waterfall made every bump on the road to the Monteverde Cloud Forest worthwhile. It was a rainy day, and the guide's search for the bird at familiar haunts had turned up nothing. Then suddenly, appearing almost turquoise against the rich, dark green of the forest, the red and emerald bird with its magnificent tail swooped across a picture-postcard setting.

Though thousands of people come to see what many consider the most beautiful bird in the New World, the Monteverde reserve is more than quetzals: 400 species of birds, 490 butterfly species, 100 mammal species, 120 species of reptiles and amphibians, and 2,500 plant species live here. The preserve also protects habitat for the tapir (with a greater chance of seeing tracks than the wary, once-common, now-endangered animal itself), ocelot, olingo, and three species of monkeys. A fantastic variety of epiphytes cover cloud-forest trees: more than 400 species of orchids and 200 of ferns—walk the Orchid Trail. The preserve has checklists of birds and mammals, an informative nature trail guide, and a trails map.

Monteverde Cloud Forest Preserve is a private reserve, not a national park. It is managed by the Tropical Science Center (TSC), a nonprofit scientific research and education organization based in San José. Founded in 1972, the reserve encompasses some 27,181 acres (11,000 ha) on the Continental Divide in the Tilarán Mountain Range, protecting both Atlantic and Pacific watersheds, containing eight ecological life zones.

Temperature ranges between 56°F and 64°F (16°C and 18°C); average annual rainfall at the *casona* is about 118 inches (3,000 mm), but the reserve can get up to 236 inches (6,000 mm). Bring rain gear. Though little rain falls December through March, mist rolls in on strong trade winds from the Atlantic and moisture forms on the abundant forest vegetation, dripping from the canopy to the ground. This "indirect rain" is a striking demonstration of the importance of forest conservation. Without trees and forest plants to collect and disseminate this water, the mist would vaporize in hot dry air to the west, and rivers that flow to the lowlands would carry less water. Watershed protection was why the small group of dairy-farming Quakers who settled here put aside 1,369 acres (554 ha) of forest. That parcel is now part of the reserve, leased to TSC for management.

Limits are placed on the number of people allowed on eight miles (12.4 km) of trails—seven trails, in all. Priority is given to those taking the natural history walks, led by bilingual naturalist guides. Make reservations, especially December through April. In addition to marked trails, there are longer ones for backpackers, with an opportunity to stay in a refuge in the Peñas Blancas Valley.

Overnight accommodations at the preserve's field station are dorm-style rooms for 40 people, sometimes filled by researchers and students. Baths are shared. A snack bar and gift shop are at the entrance, rubber boots for rent. Volunteers accepted: two-week minimum.

Details: *Less than four miles (six km) from Santa Elena, open daily 7 A.M. to 4 P.M. Admission is $8.50 for adults, $4.50 for students with I.D., children under 12 free. Walks led by bilingual guides are $23.50, including admission. Night walks are $13, and special birding walks are $25. Use of shelters on backpacking trips, $3 per night. Lodging and meals in the rustic field station* (casona), *$21 per person. For guided natural history walks, call 506/645-5112 or arrange through a hotel; for lodging 506/645-5564; for overnight in shelters 506/645-5122, fax 506/645-5034, montever@cct.or.cr, www.cct.or.cr. From Santa Elena, taxis and a twice-daily bus go to the reserve; some hotels provide shuttle service. Walking at least one way, about one mile (two km) from the cheese plant or three miles (six km) from Santa Elena, allows terrific bird-watching.*

Santa Elena Forest Reserve

This private reserve protects cloud-forest habitat. It has about eight miles (12 km) of trails at an elevation of 5,600 feet (1,700 m). Arenal Volcano, some seven miles (14 km) away, can be seen from Bajo and Youth Challenge Trails when weather cooperates. Observation platforms are ideal spots to take in the verdant landscape and watch the ever-changing patterns of sunlight and mist. Flocks of mixed species of birds move through the forest, howler monkeys sound off, small streams gurgle softly, and epiphytes and dangling roots and vines help weave a magical spell.

Some trails have self-guiding booklets ($1), and most involve loops ranging from less than a mile (1.4 km) to almost three miles (4.8 km) long. Guided walks are available: rubber boots and ponchos are for rent. Visitation is limited to 80 persons at a time, so make reservations, especially January through March.

The visitor center has a gift shop and exhibits made by students of the local high school, which manages the reserve. Visit a small café at the entrance. The center and trails were built with assistance of many volunteers. Proceeds from entrance fees help provide courses in environmental education, biology, language, and tourism.

Ree Strange Sheck

Young anteater found on a farm and released in Monteverde forest

Volunteers are always needed—minimum age 16, minimum time three days. Housing is provided. Contact Santa Elena High School Cloud Forest Reserve, Apartado 90-5655, Santa Elena, Monteverde, Puntarenas, or call or fax.

Details: *Three miles (five km) northeast of Santa Elena; 506/645-5390, fax 506/645-5014. Open daily 7 A.M. to 4 P.M.; admission $5, free for children under 12. Guided walks are $19, including entrance fee. From Santa Elena, taxis and horses available. Hotels offer tours.*

Sky Walk and Sky Trek

Spectacular is the word for these companion adventures in the cloud forest. Don't miss them! Created by the Valverde family, longtime local folks, the two allow visitors to experience the forest from floor to ceiling in a system of paths, suspended bridges, and ziplines. Choose either or both, depending on your interest and nerve.

Sky Walk is ideal for naturalists. A loop through mostly primary forest is along well-maintained trails and across six hanging bridges: the highest and longest is 121 feet (37 m) and 400 feet (120 m)

265

long. From these suspended walkways, look into the middle and upper reaches of an epiphyte-laden forest and down at rivers and canyons. A black guan, a treetop bird with glossy black feathers, red legs, and bright blue face, stayed perched beside one bridge as we quietly observed him. Monkeys and toucans called in the distance. Feeding flocks passed through. You can go on your own or with a guide. Small groups and spaced tours means unhurried time at good vantage points without crowds.

Sky Trek combines nature observations with guaranteed adrenaline rushes. Gather up your gear and your nerve to zoom from platform to platform at what seems like dizzying heights. You are harnessed to cables up to 700 feet (214 m) long, some of which pass between canopy trees (I tucked my elbows in). Staff carefully coach each step of the way, and "catchers" are on each platform to help fliers land safely. In all, Sky Trek allows nine passes via cables, plus walks along forest paths and suspended bridges with breathtaking vistas of this 563-acre (228-ha) reserve and beyond.

Climb to an observation platform above the canopy, which has a clear-day panorama of Arenal Volcano, the Nicoya Peninsula, and Guanacaste. Each tour lasts up to three hours. At the reception center find a snack bar, gifts, and exhibits on flora and fauna in Monteverde.

Details: *Two miles (3.5 km) north of Santa Elena; 506/645-5238, 506/645-5796, info@skywalk.co.cr, www.skywalk.co.cr. Open daily 7 A.M. to 4 P.M., reservations recommended. Sky Walk admission is $12 for adults, $6 for children; add $12 for a guided walk offered at 8 A.M. and 1 P.M. Sky Trek admission is $35, with tours between 7:30 A.M. and 2 P.M. The Zip Package includes both, $40. Student discounts. Sky Trek is not for small children.*

GUIDES AND OUTFITTERS

Ask at your hotel if you would like a private naturalist guide: some local biologists guide, specialists in trees, birds, orchids, butterflies.

For a specialized experience with bats, go out with biologist/researcher **Richard Laval,** 506/645-5052, rlaval@racsa.co.cr, with a chance to mist net these fascinating, often-misunderstood mammals and even hold one in your hand, $75 per group. Or ask for a private slide lecture on bats, mammals, reptiles, or birds, also $75.

The Canopy Tour, 506/645-5243, in San José, tel/fax 506/257-5149, canopy@racsa.co.cr, www.canopytour.co.cr, offers a two-hour adventure in upper layers of the cloud forest. Start with a guided hike, climb on a rope ladder up the center of a strangler fig, then slide from platform to platform, assisted by expert guides, with time on platforms for canopy observation. Platforms are 66 to 98 feet (20 and 30 m) above the ground. Finish up with a rappel to the forest floor. The tour is $45, students with I.D. $35, children $30. Canopy Tour contributes to a community fund that purchased an ambulance, and it assists with paramedic/rescue services.

Meg's Stables, 506/645-5419, rlaval@racsa.co.cr, has a popular two-hour horseback tour on a private forest trail in Monteverde, $23. For the hardy and adventurous, there is the four-hour ride/hike to San Luis Waterfall, $45. One-hour rides to an overlook with an Arenal Volcano view are $10, with guide. Meg has small saddles for children.

THE TOURIST TREE

The gumbo limbo tree (Bursera simaruba) *has reddish-brown bark, which inspired the popular name in Spanish—* indio desnudo, *meaning naked Indian. Since the light reddish skin has a tendency to peel, ticos sometimes irreverently refer to it as the tourist tree. The bark peels off in thin layers, showing green underneath. Perhaps this peeling helps protect the tree from parasites and epiphytes—note that the trunk is almost always clear of these plants. The gumbo limbo is often used in living fences; it grows easily from a cutting stuck in the ground.*

CAMPING

Inquire at Monteverde Cloud Forest Preserve about camping.

LODGING

Arco Iris Lodge, 506/645-5067, fax 506/645-5022, arcoiris @racsa.co.cr, www.bbb.or.cr/Lodges/ArcosIris, with its hillside setting has a first-class view of spectacular rainbows that grace this high land (*arco iris* means "rainbow"). Seven cabins are of wood or concrete and wood; a favorite is Honeymooners' cabin next to forest and a small stream. It's intimate—windows on three sides and a porch facing forest. Doubles are $30 to $45, including taxes, no credit cards. Owners Haymo Heyder and Susanna Stoiber arrange tours with local naturalist guides or accompany guests on scenic horseback rides. The lodge is a two-minute walk from downtown Santa Elena. Homemade bread, marmalade, granola, and kefir are on the menu, along with harvests from an organic garden; both breakfast and dinner are available with advance notice. International phone, fax, and e-mail service are available.

    El Bosque Hotel and Restaurant, 506/645-5158, fax 506/645-5129, elbosque@racsa.co.cr, is near CASEM gift shop. The 23 rooms are in buildings curved around a clearing off the main road, surrounded by trees. Each opens onto a covered porch and has tile floors, rough white-plaster walls, and a high wooden ceiling. Bright bedspreads add color, double $35. The hotel has a short nature trail plus the Bosque Restaurant, a Monteverde favorite. Reception is in the restaurant on the main road.

    El Sapo Dorado, 506/645-5010, fax 506/645-5180, elsapo @racsa.co.cr, www.cool.co.cr/usr/sapodorado, features 20 charming mountain suites in 10 bungalows tucked among fruit trees and gardens in a clearing surrounded by forest. Each room has a quiet, spacious feel to it, with a pretty table and chairs and two queen-size beds. Classic suites have corner fireplaces; wood supplied. Sunset Terrace suites have dynamite views of the Gulf of Nicoya, stained-glass window panels, terrace, and small refrigerator. Doubles are $70 for Classic suites, from $80 for Sunset Terrace, VISA only. The restaurant, open to the public, offers gourmet dining. Private cloud-forest walks arranged at Sendero Tranquilo; three miles (five km) of trails are adjacent to the hotel, exclusively for guests. There is a nightly rain-forest slide show. Microbus service is available to any-where in the country. El Sapo Dorado is just past Santa Elena.

Hotel de Montaña Monteverde in Cerro Plano, 506/645-5046, fax 506/645-5320, monteverde@ticonet.co.cr, www.ticonet.co.cr/monteverde, has its own 37-acre (15-ha) private forest with trails and a small lagoon, an indoor hot tub with a great view of forested mountains and the Gulf of Nicoya, a sauna, and bar and restaurant that offers Costa Rican cuisine. The 32 spacious rooms open onto terraces and pretty gardens. Junior suites have fireplaces. Doubles are $76, suites from $94. A honeymoon suite has its own hot tub and balcony. The hotel rents horses, has guided tours to the Monteverde Cloud Forest Preserve, and offers transfers elsewhere in the country and in the zone.

Hotel Finca Valverde's, 506/645-5157, fax 506/645-5216, info @monteverde.co.cr, www.monteverde.co.cr, is nestled in a hillside forest minutes from downtown. Paths through flowered grounds lead to five duplex cabins of tropical woods—porches good for bird-watching. Each pleasant room also has a sleeping loft. Eight stan-dard rooms across a bridge from the restaurant are next to an embankment where blue-crowned motmots tend to nest. Doubles are $75 for cabins, $65 standards, breakfast included. The open-air restaurant/bar, open to the public and serving traditional food from family recipes, is surrounded by greenery. On a short forest trail, one naturalist saw 90 species of birds in two days; wildlife includes toucans, trogons, agoutis, sloths, gray foxes, and kinkajous. Guests can help pick coffee here at harvest time. Ask manager Victor Valverde about this farm where he and his brothers and sis-ters were raised. The next-door serpentarium is also in the family.

Hotel Fonda Vela, San José 506/257-1413, fax 506/257-1416, at hotel 506/645-5125, fax 506/645-5119, fondavel@racsa.co.cr, www.centralamerica.com/cr/hotel/fondavel, is a 15-minute walk from Monteverde Cloud Forest Preserve. Set on hills of the 35-acre (14-ha) Smith farm, the 40 rooms and suites are in seven buildings situated to give guests maximum privacy, surrounded by forest and flowers on landscaped grounds. Spacious, with gleaming wood floors, area rugs, big windows, and rich-colored comforters, rooms are pleasant—and wheelchair accessible. Suites have refrigerators, sitting areas, and a sleeping loft. Doubles are $85, suites from $94. Trails offer wildlife viewing opportunities, but balconies are also vantage points—morpho butterflies, agoutis, and turquoise-browed motmots. Enjoy guided horseback rides. Through the dining room's enormous glass windows, watch hummingbirds feed, mists roll in, and sunlight sparkle. A small stage hosts evening musical performances by local or visiting artists. An impressive wood-railed ramp leads to the second-level bar area. Artwork by Paul Smith (father of Stephen and Pablo, who manage the hotel) adorns walls.

Hotel Heliconia, 506/645-5109, fax 506/645-5007, 800/948-3770, Heliconia@centralamerica.com, www.centralamerica.com/cr/hotel/heliconia, is backed by forest and has loads of tropical plants around the complex of 32 rooms, a garden room with floor-to-ceiling glass and a hot tub, and a restaurant/bar. Suites in the hillside addition have spectacular views of forest and the Gulf of Nicoya. Doubles are $75, suites from $85. The hotel has its own 600-acre (243-ha) reserve with a nature center, land that serves as a bird sanctuary for species such as the three-wattled bellbird and long-tailed manakin; guests are admitted free. Take a sunset horseback ride and guided natural history tours. Transfers are available to reserves and throughout the country.

Monteverde Lodge, 506/257-0766, fax 506/257-1665, ecotur @expeditions.co.cr, www.expeditions.co.cr, a short walk from down-town Santa Elena, has the feel of an upscale mountain lodge. The gardens were designed to attract hummingbirds and other wildlife, complete with small stream and waterfall. Here in the tranquility of its forest setting, the lodge offers guests distinctive architecture and some out-of-the-ordinary features: a 15-person solar-heated indoor hot tub in a glassed-in alcove, an impressive freestanding fireplace in the spacious, open bar/restaurant area, chandeliers, and wonder-ful vistas of surrounding forest. The 27 forest-view rooms are bright and comfortably furnished, with sitting areas next to high windows and baths with both tubs and showers: doubles are $115, taxes included. Breakfast is $13, lunch $19, dinner $21; meal plans are available. Ask about packages. The lodge integrates solar water heat-ing, recycling, and water-saving features. Transfers are available to

San José and shuttle to reserves. The lodge belongs to Costa Rica Expeditions.

Pensión Manakin, 506/645-5080, fax 506/645-5516, manakin@racsa.co.cr, has 11 rooms, three with private tiled baths. Windows make rooms bright, and they are very clean. Mario and Yolanda and their four children are caring hosts. Good typical food is served in the dining room. Doubles are $12 with shared bath; with private bath $20. VISA only accepted.

Trapp Family Lodge, 506/645-5858, fax 506/645-5990, trappfam @racsa.co.cr, www.ticoweb.com/trappfam, is less than a mile (one km) from the Monteverde Cloud Forest Preserve, a two-story lodge of warm tropical hardwoods, with forest in back and gardens in front. Large rooms have big glass doors out to balconies and terraces, upstairs with treetop views. Doubles are $65. The Trapps aim to please. Food in the pleasant dining room is excellent, with good Chilean wines: breakfast is $6, lunch and dinner $10. Andreas will arrange tours to area attractions, but leave time to enjoy the cloud forest flora and fauna right here—good birding, and coatis wander by.

FOOD

Chunches, 506/645-5147, in Santa Elena just south of the bank, is a coffeehouse, bookstore, and laundry all rolled into one. Owners Wendy Rockwell and Jim Standley serve homemade desserts and light meals along with espresso or other coffees. Find here a good selection of natural history publications, books in English and Spanish, newspapers, and magazines. Closed Sunday.

El Bosque Restaurant, 506/645-5158, described in the hotel listing, is a tradition with visitors and residents alike. The food is good and prices reasonable. Great milk shakes. Watch wildlife from outdoor dining areas.

El Sapo Dorado's intimate restaurant, 506/645-5010, is known for its excellent food and quality service. Daily specials may include sailfish Niçoise, beef in peppercorn sauce, or chicken in olive sauce. A vegetarian dish is always available. Desserts are scrumptious.

La Pizzería de Johnny, 506/645-5066, serves good pizza plus a full range of delicious Italian food, friendly service and nice *ambiente.* Eat inside or on a covered outdoor terrace or call for delivery service. It is in Cerro Plano next to the Monteverde Orchids.

Restaurante de Lucia, 506/645-5337, in Cerro Plano on the road to the Butterfly Garden, offers good atmosphere, superb food nicely served, candlelight at dinner, wines. José and Lucía are attentive hosts. Open daily 11:00 A.M. to 9:30 P.M.; reserve in high season.

Stella's Bakery and Coffee Shop, 506/645-5560 has breakfast fare from *gallo pinto* to French toast to ham and eggs or sticky buns. Try a lunch of homemade soups, organic green salads, and sandwiches with homemade bread. There are frozen fruit shakes and yogurt and yummy sweets. Enjoy art and crafts by Stella and Meg and, when Stella's around, interesting conversation. Open 6 A.M. to 6 P.M. high season, 7 A.M. to 5 P.M. other months. Located across from CASEM.

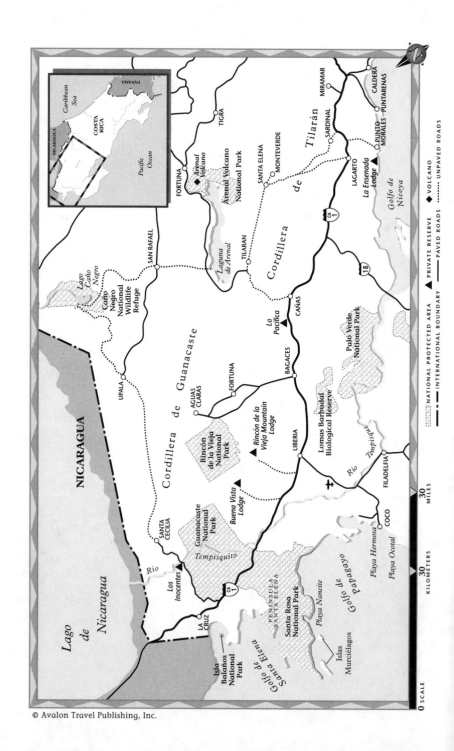

© Avalon Travel Publishing, Inc.

CHAPTER 11

Northwest

Rain forests, deciduous dry forests, rivers, marshes, boiling mud pots, volcanoes, national parks, private reserves, cattle ranches, and rice farms. This northwest part of the country has a varied landscape: Guanacaste highlands maintain a moist temperate climate year round while the lowlands have a marked dry season from December into May. Varied habitat means diverse flora and fauna and nature/adventure activities. This chapter describes principally the destinations off the Inter-American highway from the mainland side of the Gulf of Nicoya almost to Nicaragua. The port of Puntarenas is included in Chapter 12 with the Nicoya Peninsula and northwest beach areas.

LAY OF THE LAND

Excellent private nature reserves and national parks are here as are rivers popular for both rafting and wildlife boat trips. The Cañas/Bagaces area, Liberia, and La Cruz are principal transportation centers from which many of these activities are accessed. Note the vegetation changes as the Inter-American Highway winds between the coastal zone and the mountains to the east. In dry sea-

*Visit Las Plumas to see margays and the
five other species of cats found in Costa Rica.*

Ree Strange Sheck

son, flowering red, white, pink, and yellow trees decorate a brown landscape. Travelers to Monteverde (Chapter 10) and to the Nicoya Peninsula via both the Tempisque ferry and the overland route through Liberia pass along part of this route, making it easy to combine destinations in those areas with visits to this northwest region.

Cañas (population 17,763), 107 miles (172 km) northwest of San José, is a junction for bus and car travel to Tilarán and access to Arenal and other north central destinations. About four miles (six km) northwest of Cañas is a paved road to Upala, a gateway to the western side of Caño Negro National Wildlife Refuge (see Chapter 7). Cañas offers gas stations, banks, a clinic, pharmacies, and restaurants. Though not a tourist destination per se, it is near Lomas Barbudal Biological Reserve and Palo Verde National Park. Worth a stop is **Las Pumas,** 506/669-0444, off the Inter-American just north of Cañas. Werner and Lily Hagenauer have operated this small animal sanctuary for many years. The six species of cats found in Costa Rica are here: jaguar, puma, margay, jaguarundi, ocelot, and *oncilla* (little spotted cat), along with scarlet macaws and other animals brought by individuals or wildlife agencies. Open daily 8 A.M. to 5 P.M.; no charge, but donations needed and gladly accepted.

Big ditches in this area are part of the government's ambitious Arenal-Tempisque irrigation project (SENARA) to supply Guanacaste farms with water. By the time the water gets to the lowlands, it has already generated electricity three times: at Arenal, Corobicí, and Sandillal hydroelectric plants. The project benefits more than 1,000 farm families, providing water to land that would otherwise be dry for half the year. Main agricultural crops are rice, sugarcane, sorghum, and cotton; cattle ranching is also important.

Bagaces (population 8,386), 120 miles (194 km) northwest of San José, is another crossroads for nature/adventure destinations Here roads take off the Inter-American Highway for Palo Verde National Park, about 45 minutes away. For park information stop by the Tempisque Conservation Area office, a white house next to the gas station, just across from the road to Palo Verde. A bit north of Bagaces is the road to **Lomas Barbudal Biological Reserve,** a great place to see howler monkeys, birds, and bees. Unfortunately it is frequently unstaffed, but there is a small trail to walk, and the beautiful Cabuya River, with natural, sandy-bottomed pools, is ideal for a swim under big trees. Deciduous forests make up 70 percent of the 5,631-acre (2,279-ha) reserve, one being *cortesa amarilla* (yellow cortez), which flowers profusely in dry season when branches are bare of leaves. A curious tree is the cannonball. You'll know it when you see it: the fruit looks like big balls hanging on strings down the trunk and lower branches. The reserve is only four miles (six km) west of the Inter-American. Contact the Bagaces office of the Tempisque Conservation Area for information or to arrange for a local guide: tel/fax 506/671-1290, 506/671-1062:

By far the most important hub for this region is **Liberia** (population 34,099), capital of Guanacaste Province. Located 154 miles (248 km) northwest of San José and 48 miles (77 km) south of the border with Nicaragua, it is a commercial and transportation center. Scheduled national and international flights and charters land at Daniel Oduber Quirós International Airport about 11 miles (17 km) west of town and principal bus routes converge here. The main road west is a gateway to the Nicoya Peninsula, beach resorts, and the northern Pacific coast. Wherever you are headed, it's a good idea to fill up with gasoline here.

Liberia is sometimes referred to as the White City because early adobe houses got a coating of the area's abundant lime. Some old houses have the unusual architectural feature of two doors on their northeast corners, offering views of the rising sun and twilight and giving long hours of natural daylight inside. Stop by **El Sabanero Museum: Casa de la Cultura,** tel/fax 506/666-1606, in a house with these *puertas del sol* (the corner doors that let the sun in), to learn about area history and places to visit. Signs direct you to the 150-year-old building three blocks from the park; open 8 A.M. to noon and 1:30 to 4 P.M., closed Sunday. Liberia can be a base for day trips to Rincón de la Vieja, Santa Rosa, Palo Verde, and Lomas Barbudal, as well as beaches such as Ocotal, Hermosa, Coco, and Tamarindo.

La Cruz (population 9,190), near the border with Nicaragua, overlooks Salinas Bay and Bolaños Island. It is not far from the

*El Sabanero Museum in Liberia, a traditional house
with two doors on northeast corner*

Murciélagos sector of Santa Rosa National Park, and from here travelers can reach the western entrance of Caño Negro National Wildlife Refuge via the road east to Upala.

NATURE AND ADVENTURE ACTIVITIES

The volcano park of Rincón de la Vieja and surrounding areas open up the world of geysers, mud pots, and hot springs for exploration. Bird-watching is terrific from high mountains to the bird sanctuary at Palo Verde, and the Bebedero, Tempisque, and Corobicí Rivers are watery avenues to wildlife observation. White-water rafting, kayaking, horseback riding, hiking, turtle watching, and tree climbing into the canopy are possibilities in this area.

FLORA AND FAUNA

Because of the diversity of habitats and dry forest and rain forest in proximity, a variety of flora and fauna is represented. In the dry forest of Santa Rosa, take a close look at the acacia tree (*Acacia collinsii* or *Acacia cornigera*) for a lesson in plant and animal relationships. The tree provides food for acacia ants (*Pseudomyrmex ferruginea*), and the ants protect it from animal predators and foreign vegetation. Find the small hole near the base of one of the thorns and watch what happens when the tree is disturbed. Keep your fingers out of the way as ants rush out; stings are painful. When hiking, be careful not to brush against an acacia branch.

Birdlife encompasses roseate spoonbills, black-headed trogons, white-throated magpie jays, black-necked stilts, orange-chinned parakeets, laughing falcons, wood storks, great curassows, motmots, toucans, and loads of doves, including the Inca dove. See caimans and ctenosaurs (black iguanas), deer, peccaries, coatis, boas, and three species of monkeys.

Watch for the Central American agouti (*Dasyprocta punctata*), a member of the rodent family. It has no tail but does have telltale rodent-like whiskers. Generally its coat is reddish-brown, a distinctive pink inside its ears. The agouti eats seedlings, flowers, insects, and fungi. You may see it at any hour of the day. In times of plenty, the agouti buries single large, hard-husked nuts so that when pickings get slim, it can return for them. Seeds it doesn't dig up may sprout, so this small mammal is a kind of Johnny Appleseed.

Care of the offspring is unique. Born in a nighttime den, the single offspring (occasionally twins) is transferred the next day by its mother to a burrow where it lives for about eight weeks. The burrow's entrance is small to discourage predators, too small even for the mother to enter. She calls her offspring out every morning and evening to nurse and care for it. As a further precaution against predators, before nursing, the mother stimulates the offspring to urinate and defecate by licking its perineum; she then eats the wastes. The mother may give birth two or three times a year, but more than half of the offspring don't survive beyond the first few months of life. Adults can live three to five years. Predators include cats, large snakes (the boa and fer-de-lance), coyotes, coatis, tayras, owls, and eagles, some preying only on the young. Humans have been major predators—hunting agoutis for meat and destroying habitat.

VISITOR INFORMATION

Staff at parks and private reserves are information sources as are hotels and tour operators. In Liberia, **El Sabanero Museum: Casa de la Cultura,** three blocks from the park, has friendly, helpful staff and written descriptions and photos of most area lodging, tel/fax 506/666-1606. Open 8 A.M. to 4 P.M., closed Sunday and lunchtime.

The **Tempisque Conservation Area** office in Bagaces, tel/fax 506/671-1290, 506/671-1062, a white house on the highway next to the gas station, just across from the road to Palo Verde, has general information as well as specifics on Lomas Barbudal, Palo Verde, and Barra Honda.

GETTING THERE

Destinations in the northwest region are accessed from the Inter-American Highway. Direct buses go from San José to Cañas, Liberia, and La Cruz, and the direct Tilarán/San José passes through Cañas. Connections go to beaches and the Nicoya Peninsula. Scheduled domestic airline flights are between San José and the Daniel Oduber Quiros Airport west of Liberia. Some international flights (LACSA and charters) land in Liberia. See Appendix A for airline and bus schedules, including private van/bus options. A local tour company **Edi-Tur,** 506/666-5055, fax 506/666-5115, editur@adven-tour.com, www.adven-tour.com, has reasonable transfer services from San José to Liberia, from Liberia throughout the area, and to and from Monteverde and Arenal regions. Liberia is about a four-hour drive from San José. Highway connections to the north central region through Cañas and Tilarán are good, as are routes to the Nicoya Peninsula and Pacific beaches, either via Liberia or the Tempisque ferry.

NATURE AND ADVENTURE SIGHTS

Buena Vista Lodge

On the slopes of Rincón de la Vieja Volcano, next to the national park, Gerardo Ocampo, his wife, Amalia, and their children share and conserve nature's bounty. Buena Vista is both a private nature reserve and a working farm. Visitors are invited to hike forest trails, bird-watch, help ranch hands with cattle, bathe in thermal waters or mountain streams, explore the canopy, and walk or ride horseback to waterfalls—six large ones to choose from. Day visitors are welcome to come for a horseback ride to the spring, trail walk, and lunch ($35), with other options such as the canopy tour or a new 1,378-foot (420-m) natural waterslide at additional cost..

All of this is on the 3,950-acre, (1,600-ha) farm, but there's also the option of a tour to Rincón de la Vieja National Park less than two miles (three km) away. Gerardo suggests March to May and July or August as best months to climb the crater.

At an intriguing spa about 30 minutes by horseback from the lodge, a cold mountain stream rushes, mud pots bubble, and steam escapes from open fissures in the earth and drifts up from pools of hot water to play hide-and-seek with the tall trees of primary forest. Enjoy a natural sauna in a simple wooden house built over one of the *pailas* (mud pots). A concrete and stone hot tub is fed by a mix of hot mineral waters and a cold mountain stream. Guided spa tours are $20 by horseback, $10 on foot.

Well-maintained forest trails take off just behind the lodge. Five trails wind through the almost 100 acres (40 ha) of primary forest. A troop of white-faced capuchin monkeys fussed at me as I explored at dusk. You might see a paca, peccary, deer, river otter, macaw (either the scarlet or the rarer green), toucan, oropendola, or agouti. Perhaps you'll hear a coyote concert or sounds of the howler monkey. A half-day hiking tour is $10. Move through the canopy among 10 platforms, $30. Check out the water slide.

On one Buena Vista visit, a pregnant peccary named Gerardina helped my sister hurry across the garden. That night, a friendly skunk nosed around my Jeep and waddled off. The resident scarlet macaw is always around, and now a toucan and two parrots have joined the menagerie. I must report that Gerardina is no longer around—my sister is glad.

Buena Vista has 47 rooms, all but four with private baths. Rooms in the rustic main lodge are around a tropical patio; others are grouped in bungalows near the forest, in landscaped gardens, and near a small lake. A creative mix of wood and river stone decorates some rooms; all have shared or private porches.

On weekends, cowboys present customs of the Guanacaste *sabanero* (cowboy); nighttime marimba music during dinner in an outdoor rancho/bar is a possibility, large frogs are a definite. Breakfast is served in the main house, where cooking is on a wood stove. Meals are ample, varied, delicious. Drinking water comes from a spring; electrical energy, from a hydroelectric plant.

Buena Vista means "good view." There is an almost-touchable one of Rincón Volcano, a more-distant look at Orosi Volcano and the Pacific, and on a clear night, lights of Bagaces and Liberia shine below. Rainy season, May 15 to November 30, brings some 6.5 feet (two m) of rainfall. Lodge elevation is 2,592 feet (790 m). Temperatures average 82°F to 86°F (28°C to 30°C), but early on December mornings it can be 64°F (18°C).

Doubles are $40 to $45; bunk-bed rooms with private bath $15 per person—10 percent discount if you have this book and reserve directly with Buena Vista. Breakfast is $6, lunch and dinner $8 each. Day visit $35. On the drive up to the lodge, pause just past a wooden bridge in magnificent forest: there's always something there—a spider monkey, golden red hair shining on its back, or a motmot, quail, cuckoos, or morpho butterflies. **Details:** *About 19 miles (31 km) northeast of Liberia; tel/fax 506/661-8158, 506/666-2069. From the sign at km 247 on the Inter-American Highway north of Liberia, go east 12 miles (19 km); the road is paved to Cañas Dulces, mainly gravel afterward. Transfers available from Liberia.*

Guanacaste National Park

Established in 1989, Guanacaste encompasses dry tropical forest and rain forest stretching from lowlands to mountains of the Guanacaste range. Preservation and restoration of one of the last remaining tropical dry forests was an impetus for forming Guanacaste National Park, now 80,337 acres (32,512 ha). Tropical dry forests once stretched along the Pacific from central Mexico to Panama, but most have fallen to agricultural and residential use. Another impetus was to protect habitats used by seasonal migrants from adjoining Santa Rosa National Park.

Biological stations offer accommodations for tourists when not in use by researchers and student groups, prior reservation. Only overnight visitors have access to trails—no day visits. **Cacao Biological Station** sits in cloud forest at 3,609 feet (1,100 m). Cacao Volcano, at 5,443 feet (1,659 m), looms above. Dormitory-style sleeping quarters for 30 persons are in rustic wooden buildings with no electricity, cold-water showers, and blankets provided. A panorama of forest and distant coastline unfolds from a long, covered porch. The kitchen is alongside; bring your own food. Virgin forest holds tapirs, cats, bellbirds, orchids, and bromeliads. Howler monkeys announce daybreak. On an afternoon hike, we saw howler, spider, and white-faced monkeys within 300 feet (90 m) of each other. Habitats here include transitional dry-humid forest and some of the lowest cloud forest in the country. Trails go to Maritza Biological Station (a three-hour hike) and to Cacao's summit. A local guide is recommended for getting to the station—when the last 11 miles (18 km) of bad, unpaved road ends, continue on a not-well-marked trail by foot or horseback.

Maritza is accessible by four-wheel-drive vehicles. I can attest to that, having slid the entire 11 miles (18 km) of unpaved road after a serious downpour, and in a four-wheel-drive. Maritza lies on the skirts of Orosi Volcano in a windier, cooler area. A more modern facility, the station houses 32; shared baths, bring your own food. Wildlife is abundant: toucans, bellbirds, peccaries, sun bitterns, monkeys. Jaguars have been known to kill cattle in the area. Coatis frequently visit the station. Hike two hours to petroglyphs carved in volcanic stone, more than 80 pieces of 1,500-year-old rock art. Situated near the Continental Divide with river headwaters nearby, the station is a center for research on aquatic organisms.

In the Atlantic watershed, **Pitilla Biological Station** houses 20 persons, shared cold-water baths; bring your own food. Both facilities and the road leading to it are rustic: no electricity and four-wheel-drive essential. Entrance is via Santa Cecilia. The station is at 1,968 feet (600 m) in mostly primary forest—very good birding and trails to explore. Views from Pitilla include the Lake Nicaragua and Orosi Volcano.

Details: North of Liberia on the east side of the Inter-American Highway; telephone hotline 506/192, tel/fax 506/695-5598, 506/666-0630, acg@acguanacaste.ac.cr, www.acguanacaste.ac.cr. Access only to overnight visitors at biological stations. Lodging at biological stations is $15 per person.

La Ensenada Lodge

A private wildlife refuge on the eastern shores of the Gulf of Nicoya, La Ensenada is a delightful surprise at the end of a dirt road through rural landscapes. Guests can enjoy water- and land-based birds—more than 140 species, including white ibis, tricolored heron, purple gallinule, double-striped thick-knee, parrots, parakeets, bellbirds, trogons, and kingfishers. With luck you might see a jabiru. Crocodiles, coyotes, howler and white-faced monkeys, sloths, agoutis, and iguanas are about. A freshwater and saltwater lagoon add to mangrove, river, and forest habitats.

Also a working farm, Ensenada offers a chance to participate in Costa Rican farm life: cattle, horses, and various fruit crops, including watermelon. Ride native criollo horses, $15, to explore refuge trails, visit a salt flat (January to April see salt produced much the way indigenous peoples did it), and go to a freshwater lagoon and through forest to a hilltop view of the gulf at sundown. The property covers 865-acres (350-ha).

On a two-hour island and mangrove boat tour, see roseate spoonbills, hawks, black-bellied whistling ducks, and egrets, along with crocodiles and howler monkeys, $29 each for two. A three-hour boat trip to Palo Verde National Park is $58 each. Marked hiking trails go through dry forest, mangroves, and wetlands. Tennis, swimming in the pool, waterskiing, and windsurfing are other options, but be sure to leave time to relax in the front-porch hammock.

Lodging is in wooden bungalows facing gulf waters (*ensenada* means cove or small bay). Eight cabins have two rooms, each with its own bath, while four larger cabins are ideal for families; one has a ramp for wheelchairs. Doubles are $25 per person; no credit cards. Meals are in a large thatched rancho with checkered tablecloths: breakfast is $3.50, lunch $8.50, dinner $10.

Details: 87 miles (140 km) northwest of San José, 56 miles (90 km) southeast of Liberia, on Gulf of Nicoya north of Punta Morales; 506/289-6655, 506/289-7443, fax 506/289-5281. From San José turn off the Inter-American for Punta Morales and continue for 12 miles (19 km) on gravel road (watch out for the chickens). From Liberia take Inter-American to Costa de Pájaros turnoff and continue nine miles (15 km). Ask about bus connections.

Los Inocentes

There's something special about waking at dawn's early light to the bass-toned barks of howler monkeys. When you open the big windows of a south-facing room at Los Inocentes, Orosi Volcano looms big enough to touch. Teak floors, polished wood, wide L-shaped verandas both upstairs and down—the hacienda is so inviting that nothing less than those intriguing barks from the forest down by the river spur you to get dressed and leave it for an early morning horseback ride.

Los Inocentes, east of La Cruz near the border with Nicaragua, is a working ranch as well as a naturalist lodge. Perhaps that accounts for horses that are a pleasure to ride. Don't worry if you're not an expert; Dennis Ortiz, your nature-tour guide, will have you

Los Inocentes

Ree Strange Sheck

riding like a pro. We found the howlers and white-faced monkeys. Dennis patiently tracked the shyer spider monkeys three times so I could get a perfect camera angle. He and the horses tried not to laugh when a tree and I tangled while I juggled cameras, lenses, reins, and binoculars. We saw deer and coatis; others to watch for are raccoons, sloths, and peccaries. Birding is excellent, with more than 120 species recorded on ranch property. Among those commonly seen in this premontane moist forest, elevation 1,000 feet (280 m), are laughing falcons, white-fronted and yellow-naped parrots, orange-fronted and orange-chinned parakeets, hummingbirds, Montezuma oropendolas, black-headed trogons, and *pauraques* (nightjars). You could spot the elusive king vulture.

The three-hour guided horseback tour is $18, or if horses are not your thing, manager Jaime Víquez has a tractor-driven trailer to get you to the forest, which generally is along *quebradas* (ravines) and riverbeds. Day visitors are welcome for the guided nature tour. The Viquez family has owned the ranch since 1956; previous owners were a father and son named Inocente, hence the ranch's name.

Enjoy a small pool at the lodge or swim in natural river pools. Turn your eyes to the heavens for a bit of stargazing; there may be constellations that you've never seen before visible in Guanacaste's vast sky. Lodge meals are something to look forward to, including fresh fish, fruit from trees near the house—limes, mangoes, guavas, *nances,* star fruit— and fresh milk from the dairy.

The hacienda, built in 1890, was remodeled with an eye to maintaining its architectural integrity. Stone corrals, like those at Santa Rosa, testify to the age of the property. The main house has 11 nicely decorated rooms with large closets: some baths do not adjoin the rooms, a necessary adjustment to preserve original architecture. All baths have solar hot water. Five small worker houses have been redone as cottages for visitors. Lodging and meals is $62 per person. The day trip $30, including lunch and tour.

Nearby is Guanacaste National Park. Maybe you do want to touch 4,879-foot (1,487-m) Orosi Volcano; sign up for a trip that explores its slopes. Transportation is arranged for day trips to beaches on the bays of Salinas and Santa Elena (Jaime says La Rajada is the second-best beach in the word—the first is his secret), to Murciélago in Santa Rosa Park, to Las Pailas and its bubbling mud at Rincón de la Vieja, and to Santa Rosa.

Details: *South of La Cruz, turn right toward Santa Cecilia; continue nine miles (14 km) on paved road. From Upala, head east toward La Cruz; 506/265-5484, fax 506/265-4385, tel/fax 888/613-2532, orosina @racsa.co.cr, www.arweb.com/orosi. A direct San José/Santa Cecilia bus passes in front; for the San José/Peñas Blancas bus, get off in La Cruz, and take a taxi.*

La Pacífica

Scientific researchers have been coming to "Finca La Pacífica" since the 1960s. The rich diversity of habitats that draws scientists—tropical dry forest, river habitat, swampland, pastures—makes a rich destination for nature/adventure visitors. La Pacífica, just north of Cañas, is modeled for economic self-sufficiency and protection of natural resources, combining agricultural activities, tourism, and research.

About 40 percent of Hacienda La Pacífica's almost 5,000 acres (2,000 ha) is covered with natural forest, windbreaks, and reforested areas, including tree species such as the increasingly rare *cocobolo* (rosewood), *caoba* (mahogany), and spiny pochote. Birdlife is abundant, with more than 220 species. Lagoon and rivers lure water birds. Bird and tree lists are available. Forest animals include armadillos, squirrels, *tamandus* (anteaters), deer, and monkeys. Studies on the howler monkey at Pacífica go back more than 20 years.

Follow roads and trails on your own or with a bilingual naturalist guide, go by horseback with a local guide ($10 per hour), or bicycle. Las Garzas is a short forest trail along the Corobicí, good for catching a glimpse of water birds and turquoise-browed motmots, black-headed trogons, yellow-naped parrots, and orange-chinned parakeets. The two-mile (3.5-km) Chocuaco Trail, named for the boat-billed heron, has both riparian and deciduous forest. Learn about the monkey ladder vine, the chewing-gum tree, the water vine, and the *bejuco* (vine) used locally as sandpaper. Seen here are long-tailed manakins, howler monkeys, Jesus Christ lizards, great egrets, and iguanas.

The beautiful Corobicí River, popular with rafters, forms part of the ranch's boundary. Rafting trips and river trips on the Bebedero to Palo Verde Park are arranged. The namesake of the ranch and lodge was Doña Pacífica Fernandez, who with her husband Bernardo Soto, a former president of Costa Rica, once lived here. You can visit Doña Pacífica's house, now a museum. Tour agricultural operations, including a modern dairy and organic garden. The ranch produces beef, milk products, mangoes, pepper, sugar, rice, and heart of palm.

Grouped in buildings on spacious grounds are 33 pleasant rooms, ceiling fans. Interiors reflect cool earth tones, from tile floor to striped, woven bedspreads. Sliding wood and glass doors of some rooms open onto small terraces. Older cabins are completely remodeled, with lots of light and modern baths. Doubles are $70. What a treat the swimming pool is on a hot Guanacaste day. Average high temperature is 91°F (33°C) and average low 73°F (23°C); rainfall is 66 inches (1,674 mm).

Food in the attractive dining room (one wall is "art in pottery" from Nicoya) is excellent. Dining is a la carte or buffet: breakfast buffet is $6; lunch and dinner $12. Open to the public 6:15 A.M. to 10 P.M.

Details: From Cañas, three miles (five km) north on the Inter-American; 30 miles (48 km) southwest of Liberia; 506/669-0050, fax 506/669-0555, pacifica@nicoya.com, www.nicoya.com/pacifica. Take a San José/Liberia bus and ask driver to let you off at La Pacífica, or get off in Cañas and take a taxi.

Palo Verde National Park

This is one of the most important sanctuaries for migrating water-fowl in Central America and is habitat for many resident species. About 280 bird species have been counted. Situated along the east bank of the Tempisque River above where it flows into the Gulf of Nicoya, this 48,936-acre (19,804-ha) park, a Ramsar site (an international program to conserve wetlands), encompasses deciduous dry forest and wetlands, both salt and fresh, probably 15 habitats in all.

Herons, ibis, ducks, storks, and jacanas are among those that descend on the lowlands to feed and mate. The rare, endangered jabiru nests here, most commonly seen from November to January. The largest stork in the world, the jabiru has a white body, gray neck and head, and a rose-red necklace. The only scarlet macaws left in the tropical dry forest of the Pacific live in this area.

In rainy season, flooding of the plains is widespread. In the dry months of November through April some waterholes disappear; those that remain attract birds and other wildlife, allowing the patient visitor a good chance to see them. An observation tower open to visitors is near the large marsh. A trail system takes visitors into the forest past flowing springs that attract wildlife, past a natural cactus garden, to a superb lookout over the Tempisque floodplain, through a marsh and second-growth forest that is reclaiming pastureland, and to virgin tropical dry forest.

From the park entrance, it is 7.5 miles (12 km) to Puerto Chamorro on the banks of the Tempisque, where huge iguanas forage. On the way, pass trailhead signs: one is Sendero La Venada (Deer Trail), a 2.5-km (1.5-mile) loop. Near the station operated by the Organization for Tropical Studies (OTS) are mango trees; approach quietly for a chance to see some of the 145 mammal species that make their home in the park. Peccaries, iguanas, deer, monkeys, and coatis feed on the fruits. The white-tailed deer that watched me while I watched him did not seem the least frightened. Camping is allowed. In dry season the Catalina sector can be reached by car (about 7.5 miles or 12 km), but rainy season is another story. The Manigordo Trail takes off from the station there, as does a trail to a viewpoint on Cerro Pelón, the highest place in the park, 774 feet (236 m). Annual rainfall is 59 to 79 inches (1,500 to 2,000 mm); average temperature is 81°F (27°C), though it can reach 98.6°F (37°C) in dry season. While it is windy in the dry season and insects are scarce, the rainy season brings humidity, little breeze, mosquitoes, and gnats. In dry season most trees lose their leaves to conserve water, but many wear bright flowers. The *palo verde* tree, which gave the park its name, has pretty yellow flowers that adorn its green, thorn-clad branches.

The Tempisque River has a 13-foot (four-m) rise and fall with the tide. Sometimes it flows backward. River trips are a popular way to see some of the park's wildlife. Crocodiles and caimans can often be seen on its banks, along with howler monkeys and a multitude of birds. Tours pass by Isla de los Pájaros in the Tempisque, part of Palo Verde. An important nesting site, the small island seems covered with birds. See the lovely color of the roseate spoonbills as fly overhead. There are wood storks, glossy ibis, anhingas, and great egrets. Many boas inhabit the island, feeding on bird eggs and nestlings.

Cattle grazing inside the park is part of a controversial management plan to keep marshes open for waterfowl, free of invasive cattails, as well as to control jaragua grass as a fire-prevention measure. Forest fires are a threat in this dry forest. Park relations with neighbors are important; nearby rice farmers lose more of their crops than they'd like to birds. Some farmers have automatic cannons whose sounds help keep birds away. When fields are flooded, they can be terrific sites for bird-watching.

Details: One hour southwest of Bagaces on a 17-miles (28-km) unpaved road, and 1.5 hours south of Liberia; telephone hotline 506/192, 506/671-1290, tel/fax 506/671-1062. Tempisque Conservation Area staff can arrange for a local guide to accompany you (some bilingual). Open daily 8 A.M. to 4 P.M.; admission $6, camping $2 per person per night. Take a bus to Bagaces and taxi from there. Tour companies and lodges offer both land and water trips. Boat trips often include Isla de los Pájaros.

Rincón de la Vieja National Park

A doe and fawn walked without fear at the edge of the clearing near the century-old ranch house that is headquarters for the Santa María sector of this park. On the way up the mountain, a blue morpho fluttered across the road; four species of this brilliant butterfly are here, as are howler, capuchin, and spider monkeys. The armadillo is so abundant it could practically be the symbol of the park. Peccaries are common, and there's evidence that jaguar and puma stalk this preserve. The white-fronted Amazon parrot and spectacled owl are among 257 species of birds. Doves are everywhere; at lower elevations is the curassow. There are kites, toucans and toucanets, redstarts, and motmots. A small cicada with the voice of a frog lives underground.

The 34,801-acre (14,084-ha) park in the Guanacaste Mountain Range is the source of 32 rivers. As much as 197 inches (5,000 mm) of rain falls at higher elevations. Park forests are important not only in maintaining water in rivers in the lowlands in dry season but also in flood prevention in rainy months.

Two volcanoes crown this mountain mass: active Rincón de la Vieja, and dormant Santa María. In fact, Rincón de la Vieja has two craters; the dormant one has a crystal-clear cold-water lake, while the lake in the other crater steams. Rincón erupted again in 1995, spewing ash and sending hot mud into area rivers. The best time to climb to the craters is in the driest months, February through April—subject, of course, to volcanic activity.

Visitors have access to the park's scenic beauty and geologic attractions through two entrances. The ranch house, or *casona*, is the administrative center for the Santa María sector. The Enchanted Forest Trail begins here—a walk through a fairyland of tall trees, ferns, mosses, and delicate orchids. The national flower, the guaria morada orchid, thrives here. A small waterfall makes it picture-perfect. A shorter Sendero Colibrí (Hummingbird Trail) or a walk to a *mirador* with a view of Liberia and Miravalles Volcano are other possibilities. Less than two miles (three km) away bathe in sulfur waters that many say are medicinal. A 5.6-mile (eight-km), three-hour trek takes you to the other park entrance, at Las Pailas, a magic land of bubbling mud pots, hot-water pools, and steam and gas vents.

At Las Pailas sector, also accessible by road, various trails exist, including the climb to the craters, nine miles (15 km), and to hidden waterfalls. Las Pailas Loop Trail, 3.4 miles (5.4 km), leads to fumaroles and mud pots bordered by verdant forest and a pretty waterfall. Hanging bridges now cross the river, so no more wading through knee-deep water. A pool in the Río Blanco is only a short walk from the ranger station.

Camping is permitted at both sectors in designated areas. Average temperature is 59°F to 79°F (15°C to 26°C), and it can get cold at night. Elevation is from 2,133 to 6,286 feet (650 to 1,916 m).

Details: *Northeast of Liberia: to reach the Santa María entrance, take unpaved road toward Colonia Blanca and follow park signs. For the Las Pailas entrance, turn east about three miles (five km) north of Liberia and continue 12 unpaved miles (20 km) through Curubandé to the park; telephone hotline 506/192, 506/666-5051, fax 506/666-5020, acg@ acguanacaste.ac.cr, www.acguanacaste.ac.cr. Entrance stations are attended 7 A.M. to 5 P.M.; hikes to crater must begin before noon. Admission is $6, camping $2. Take a bus to Liberia, then go by jeep taxi to either entrance. Hotels, lodges, private reserves, and tour companies offer day trips.*

Rincón de la Vieja Mountain Lodge

Enchantment is a good word to describe what awaits in this private reserve on the slopes of Rincón de la Vieja Volcano. Guests can visit bubbling mud pots and geysers, hike to hidden waterfalls, bathe in mountain streams or thermal sulphur springs, ride horseback through pristine forest, and visit a mountain lake. Besides visiting the nearby national park, lodge guests may explore 30 miles (48 km) of trails in the ranch's 740-acre (300-ha) reserve, at elevations from 2,100 to 6,000 feet (640 to 2,520 m), visit a hot spring, or a Chorotega archaeological site. A full day of horseback riding and hiking takes in gurgling mud pots as well as a lake and 90-foot (27-m) waterfall, colored a spectacular blue from copper in the water.

Traverse an exhilarating trail through the treetops, moving among 17 platforms via strong steel cables and a 180-foot (55 m) hanging bridge. Tree Top Trails offers a four-hour forest canopy experience for $50, including horseback ride to platforms and lunch, or a full-day naturalist tour that adds bathing in thermal sulfur springs, $77. Nighttime on a platform in the canopy is another option.

Among the showier of 257 species of birds on the ranch are violaceous, elegant, and orange-bellied trogons; crested caracaras; red-lored, mealy, yellow-naped, and white-fronted parrots; toucans; motmots; and the three-wattled bellbird. Mammals include howler and white-faced monkeys, deer, coatis, peccaries, and pacas. Hikes can be with people who have grown up here or with bilingual naturalist guides.

Owner Alvaro Wiessel's family has a history of more than 100 years in the area; the lodge began in the family home. Alvaro has brought the number of rooms to 50 by adding guest cottages; front porches have hammocks and chairs. Furnishings are simple but comfortable. The newest group of rooms is built in rich forest beside a small stream. Doubles are $67. A small swimming pool and rancho/bar are in front of the original house, where the dining room is. Typical meals are served: breakfast is $9, lunch or dinner $11. A three-day package is $170 per person, double occupancy, for lodging, meals, horse tour to mud pots, and full canopy tour. Other packages are available

Details: *16 miles (26 km) northeast of Liberia; 506/661-8156, fax 506/666-1887, rincon@racsa.co.cr, www.guanacaste.co.cr/rincon. From Liberia, go north three miles (five km) on the Inter-American Highway (past Colorado River), turn east through Curubandé, and follow lodge signs; the last seven miles (11 km) are unpaved. Transfers to and from Liberia and other sites are available.*

Santa Rosa National Park

In times past, indigenous peoples have walked this land; hunters, woodcutters, cowboys, and soldiers, too. Footprints today belong mainly to researchers, park rangers, and nature lovers. What had been virgin tropical dry forest, cleared pastures, and a battlefield now is Santa Rosa National Park, a piece of property north of Liberia where history is still being written.

Santa Rosa's historical significance was a primary reason it was protected, first as a national monument and then a national park. Soon, however, the ecological importance of its flora and fauna and of the habitats that exist in this dry Pacific region was recognized. It is the ecological battle that's making history now, an effort not only to protect but also to restore some of these habitats. Research at Santa Rosa's 122,352 acres (49,515 ha) of land and 193,000 acres (78,000 ha) of marine habitat sheds light on plant and animal inter-relationships and how forests regenerate themselves.

The historical drawing card is the Battle of Santa Rosa (March 20, 1856), which pitted a well-trained, well-armed invading army against a ragtag band of Costa Rican peasants who had become soldiers overnight. The patriots won, routing adventurer William Walker's forces in 14 minutes. The battle took place around La Casona, the house at Hacienda Santa Rosa; it is four miles (seven km) from the park entrance. Visitors today can walk through the big house and see historical displays and stand on the wide wooden veranda and look toward 300-year-old stone corrals.

A stately guanacaste, Costa Rica's national tree, stands nearby. Its wood is good for construction; its ear-shaped fruit, which gives the tree its English name of ear fruit, has been used to wash clothes and is food for horses, cows, and small forest mammals.

Rangers at the park entrance can help you decide what to see in the time you have; maps are for sale. Among options are a climb on the short trail behind La Casona to see a monument to battles and heroes and a panoramic view of volcanoes and Guanacaste country-side. Take the short, well-marked Indio Desnudo Nature Trail, iden-tifiable by its reddish-brown trees. Keep your eyes open: I was within spitting distance of a handsome 5-foot (1.5-m) boa constrictor before I noticed it draped over a tree root by the path. Look also for petroglyphs carved by indigenous peoples at Quebrada Duende on the delightful, well-maintained trail. Trails to Los Patos and Playa Naranjo Mirador offer other hiking options.

Two of Santa Rosa's beaches are sea-turtle nesting sites: Naranjo, about eight miles (12 km) from park headquarters, and Nancite, 11 miles (17 km) away. Three species come ashore to lay eggs: olive ridley, green, and leatherback. Camping is permitted at Naranjo. A permit from the research center is required to visit Nancite.

Santa Rosa National Park has capuchin, howler, and spider monkeys, deer, armadillos, coyotes, coatis, raccoons, and cats—115 species of mammals, about half of them bats. Studies have identified more than 3,000 species of moths and butterflies among more than 30,000 insect species. Magpie jays and parrots make lots of noise, while some of the 253 species of birds get attention with their coloring: look for orange-fronted parakeets, elegant trogons, and crested caracaras.

The **Murciélago** section of Santa Rosa is four miles (seven km) west of Cuajiniquil. Ask about road conditions and rivers that must be forded to reach the ranger station. Murciélago ("bat" in English) belonged to Anastasio Somoza when he was president of Nicaragua. Go to the coast at Playa Blanca, 11 miles (17 km) away, or at Santa Elena or El Hachal Bays, or take a dip in Pozo del General, which has water year-round and is important for animals in dry season, which is November to May. Rainfall is about 63 inches (1,600 mm). Average temperature is 79°F (26°C).

Bolaños Island in Salinas Bay west of La Cruz is also part of this park. Rising 266 feet (81 m) from the Pacific, this rocky mound protects seabirds. Magnificent frigatebirds and American oystercatchers nest here, and this is one of the country's four nesting sites for brown pelicans. No visitor facilities exist, but watching through binoculars at a tactful distance is not against the rules. The island is three miles (five km) from Puerto Soley.

Camping is possible near the administrative center at Santa Rosa, at Naranjo Beach, and at Pozo del General. Beds are sometimes available at the Tropical Dry Forest Research Center in Santa Rosa's administrative area, though priority goes to researchers and students: dorm-style rooms and shared baths. Soft drinks and snacks are available at the cafeteria; meals only with advance notice.

Details: Main entrance 22 miles (35 km) north of Liberia; Murciélago entrance six miles farther (10 km) via Cuajiniquil; telephone hotline 506/192, 506/666-5051, fax 506/666-5020, acg@acguanacaste, www.acguanacaste.ac.cr. Enter anytime, but booth at main entrance is open 7:30 A.M. to 4:30 P.M. Admission $6, lodging in Tropical Research Station $15 per person, camping $2 per person. Buses to Peñas Blancas or La Cruz get you to the main park entrance, leaving a four-mile (seven-km) walk to La Casona and headquarters. For Murciélagos, take a bus to Cuajiniquil and walk to the station. Tourist operators, hotels, and lodges offer day trips. Taxis are available in Liberia.

WIND AND THE FRIGATEBIRD

Winds seem to be an important factor in determining where frigatebirds build nests. They need help landing and becoming airborne because of their small bodies, short feet, long wings, and deeply forked long tails. A nesting site for the magnificent frigatebirds (Fregata magnificens) *is on Bolaños Island in Salinas Bay near La Cruz, administered as part of Santa Rosa National Park. Wind during dry season—nesting time—is consistent and strong there. The only other nesting site in Costa Rica is on a small island in the Gulf of Nicoya. During mating season, the male blows out his bright red throat pouch to attract a female, who lays a single egg. The birds are called* tijeretas *(pronounced tea-hay-RAY-tahs) in Spanish because of their scissorlike tails (*tijeras *is Spanish for scissors).*

GUIDES AND OUTFITTERS

For a canopy experience with quite a different twist, try the **Canopy Tour's Kazm Cannon,** tel/fax 506/257-5149, canopy @racsa.co.cr, www.canopytour.com. Your canopy experience begins with a jump off a diving board—it's true. Platforms are suspended along spectacular cliff faces in a forested canyon on the skirts of Rincón de la Vieja Volcano—two are actually rock ledges of canyon wall itself. In all, there are 10 platforms, three wall climbs, and a Tarzan swing.

　　Tree Top Trails, 506/666-0473, fax 506/666-1887, canopy@guanacaste.co.cr, www.guanacaste.co.cr/rincon, at Rincón de la Vieja Mountain Lodge affords canopy views via a 180-foot (55-m) hanging bridge and 17 platforms connected by steel cables; the highest platform is 170 feet (52 m). The longest pass via harnesses and pulleys is 270 feet (82 m). A four-hour tour, including lunch and horseback ride, is $50, and a full-day adds bathing in thermal sulfur springs and hike, $77.

Edi-Tur, 506/666-5055, fax 506/666-5115, editur@adven-tour.com, www.adven-tour.com, takes travelers on one-day trips to Palo Verde and the Bebedero River, Rincón de la Vieja Volcano, and Buena Vista Lodge. Go by horseback or oxcart to Santa Clara's waterfall and thermal spring, or visit Santa Rosa and Barra Honda National Parks, most $85 or $95. Multiday trips are available and reasonable transfer services are available from San José to Liberia, from Liberia throughout the area, and to and from Monteverde and Arenal.

Watch for **Safaris Corobicí,** tel/fax 506/669-1091, safaris @nicoya.com, www.nicoya.com, at km 193, about 2.5 miles (1.5 km) north of Cañas. Specializing in scenic river trips for bird-watchers and naturalists, Safaris' tours are from two to five hours, $35 to $60 per person. Options include the two-hour bird-watchers float trip, three-hour trip to the Catalina entrance of Palo Verde, five-hour family float trip; half-day saltwater estuary trip to the border of Palo Verde, into the Tempisque River. Children under 14 accompanied by an adult are half price. Observe wildlife: monkeys, otters, caiman, coatis, iguanas, aracaris, parrots, motmots, cuckoos, trogons, seven heron species. People with special needs are welcomed: seniors, handicapped, children.

Check out "Rafting/Kayaking" in Chapter 3 for other operators with day trips on the Corobicí River." Horseback riding is offered at Buena Vista Lodge, La Ensenada, Los Inocentes, La Pacífica, and Rincón de la Vieja—refer to "Nature and Adventure Sights." Local hotels and private reserves also offer tours to parks and other area attractions.

CAMPING

Camping is available at Palo Verde, Rincón de la Vieja, Santa Rosa, and Palo Verde National Parks; see details under "Nature and Adventure Sights." Campers are also welcome at a small camping ground next to Rincón Corobicí Restaurant, 2.5 miles (four km) north of Cañas, 506/669-1234, fax 506/669-2121, rincon@nicoya.com and at Capazuri Bed and Breakfast, see under "Lodging."

LODGING

Albergue Hotel and Restaurant Bagaces, tel/fax 506/671-1267, wwnicoya@racsa.co.cr, has 13 simple, clean rooms (water at ambient temperature), each with desk, reading lamps, high wood ceilings, and fans, doubles $18 to $20, no credit cards at this modest, friendly place. Rooms open onto a large lounge and TV room (cable). Owners Cliff and Becky steer visitors to off-the-beaten-path attractions, and the location is ideal for visits to Palo Verde and Miravalles Volcano (only 45 minutes away). The restaurant opens for guests at 7 A.M. and to the public at 8 A.M. Join locals Friday for *ranchero* night with Mexican-style music and singers and Saturday night for dancing. It can be a noisy place these nights until 2 A.M.

Capazuri Bed and Breakfast, tel/fax 506/669-0580, is one mile (two km) north of Cañas; the Gamboas give a warm greeting. They have nine bright, pleasant rooms with bamboo furniture—water in baths at ambient temperature; doubles are $30, breakfast included. Campers are welcome, $2 per person, and camping facilities include

Vista Golfo de Nicoya Lodge

Ree Strange Sheck

a bath and access to the large rancho, furnished with a refrigerator and hammocks. Breakfast for campers from $1.50. Surrounding gardens showcase flowers and tropical fruit trees and lots of birds and even monkeys. The Gamboas keep lots of information on hand for guests and offer helpful travel tips. Capazuri is affiliated with Hostelling International.

Two-story **Hostal de Julia,** tel/fax 506/679-9084, is about a block (125 m) east of the Red Cross in La Cruz. It has 12 rooms with private baths. Brick floors and nice use of wood in wardrobes, desks, fans, and bathroom accessories make rooms inviting, doubles are $30. Julia arranges kayak, surfing, and boat trips; the beach is 20 minutes away.

Hotel El Sitio, 506/666-1211, fax 506/666-2059, in Liberia, has 52 large, attractive rooms opening onto landscaped grounds and courtyard, and an open-air restaurant, pool, gift shop, exercise room, parking, children's playground, and thatched bar. Rooms have air conditioning and ceiling fans (windows that open), satellite TV, and direct-dial telephones, doubles $65. A car-rental agency is on-site. Explore the hotel's 12 acres (five ha) on foot or horseback with a real Guanacaste *sabanero.* Transfers are available to nearby beaches and Liberia airport.

Hotel Las Espuelas, Las Espuelas 506/666-0144, fax 506/666-2441, 800/245-8420, cosol@aol.com, www.magni.com/costasol, has 44 bright air-conditioned rooms with satellite TV and telephones; double $68. Polished floor tiles gleam along covered walkways leading from the lobby and restaurant/bar areas through landscaped grounds to wings of rooms named for nearby parks and reserves. There is a large pool in the garden, a poolside bar, and a tour company on-site. The hotel is on the Inter-American Highway about one mile (two km) south of Liberia.

Inside Palo Verde National Park is **Palo Verde Biological Station,** 506/240-6696; fax 506/240-6783, reservas@ots.ac.cr; www.ots.ac.cr. The station, operated by the Organization for Tropical Studies (OTS) and designed primarily for researchers and student groups, is also open to natural history visitors. A screened dining room, where guests are served tasty, family-style meals, and a four-room, two-bath building with a small sitting area are backed by tropical vegetation. Next to the main road are dormitory rooms with shared baths, and a small gift shop. Solar energy is an important source of electricity at this remote spot. Overnight visitors may have a chance to talk to researchers or student groups at mealtimes. Lodging, meals, and a half-day guided walk are $40 per person, taxes included. A half-day visit includes a guided walk or talk by station personnel, $20; with prior reservation. Guests must also pay park entrance.

Vista Golfo de Nicoya Lodge, 506/639-8303, fax 506/639-8130, vistago@racsa.co.cr, www.vista-golf.com, is perched on a hillside three miles (five km) beyond the town of Miramar. As its name implies, there's a commanding view of the gulf as well as of Chira and San Lucas Islands and Isla de los Pájaros. Enjoy a cold glass of perhaps the best tropical fruit punch in existence as you relax in the shade of an enormous fig tree on the deck next to the restaurant/bar. Nearby is an aviary, a butterfly garden, a pool filled with natural spring water, hot tub, and a nature trail or two. In addition to a wealth of birds, you're likely to see coatis, white-faced monkeys, morpho butterflies, and agoutis. Plantations on this 66-acre (27-ha) former cattle ranch include pineapples, tomatoes, sugarcane, coffee, 400 tropical fruit trees, and some 3,000 coconut palms. See the forest canopy via a zipline operation, $28. Go by horseback to a gold mine, a waterfall, or a cloud forest. Staff arrange Tortuga Island tours and transfers around the country. For $65 a day, a car and driver will take you wherever. Fee for a day visit is $4. The 14 rooms look down on pool and garden. Each is a bit different; most have private baths; one is two stories with a living area, $50 for up to six. Furnishings are simple but comfortable (decorator touches) with fans; generally smallish rooms have a big view from the balcony. Doubles with private bath $50, with shared bath $20 to $30. The hotel is about two hours from San José or Liberia. Turn off the Inter-American to Miramar, four miles (six km) past the Puntarenas exit. From Miramar follow hotel signs.

FOOD

Hotels and nature lodges described serve good typical food. Here are a few more at key spots along the northwest route.

Garabito Restaurant is at km 125 on the Inter-American Highway, a good stopping place between San José and the northwest region. Some specialties are ceviche, fried *yuca*, shrimp, fresh fish, and beef. Restrooms are clean, and the open-air restaurant gives a view of comings and goings along this busy route. Cold bottled water is available.

Don't miss **Restaurant Rincón Coribicí,** 506/669-1234, fax 506/669-2121, rincon@nicoya.com, on the banks of the Corobicí River just 2.5 miles (four km) north of Cañas. It provides a delightful pause in the journey. Whether dining indoors or on the open terrace, views of the river and Tenorio Volcano are fabulous. Take binoculars and appreciate why birders like this area. Food is good— get a side order of fried *yuca* if you haven't yet tried it; order sea bass (*corvina*), rice dishes, even hamburgers. It has pleasant restrooms and a public phone outside. The gift shop is loaded with handcrafted items, natural history books, cards, and jewelry. Book river float trips here or stroll along a river trail. Open 8 A.M. to 10 P.M. It may be closed briefly in September or October. A campsite is alongside.

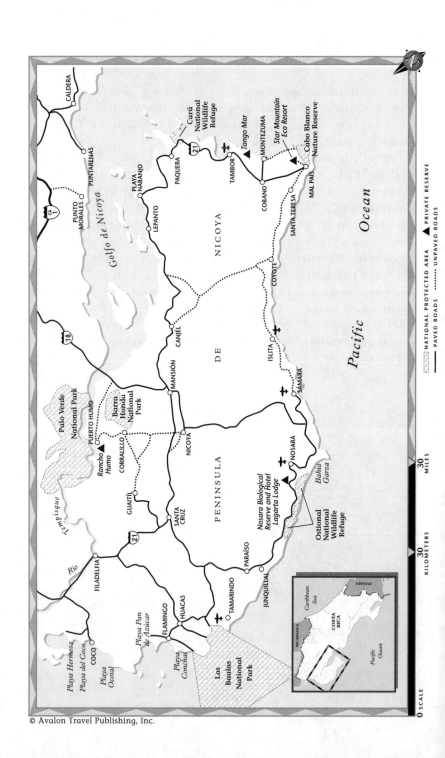

© Avalon Travel Publishing, Inc.

CHAPTER 12

Nicoya Peninsula and Pacific Northwest Beaches

Sun and sand, cattle ranches, forests green in rainy season and full of flowers in dry season, gulfs and ocean and rivers—this part of Costa Rica is a land of big skies, splendid sunsets, and surprising destinations.

LAY OF THE LAND

Depending on vacation time, travelers to this area will do best to focus on one or two clusters of nature/adventure destinations. Distances can be misleading because roads to some beach areas are unpaved and slow going. An increasing number of road signs now make travel here less by-guess-and-by-golly. Air travel allows jumps between some clusters.

The region is described in two parts: the Pacific northwest beaches from the Gulf of Papagayo to Punta Islita, and the southern Nicoya Peninsula, which encompasses Playa Naranjo, Tambor, Montezuma, and Mal Pais. Puntarenas is described briefly with the southern peninsula since it is the mainland departure point for many travelers to that area.

Pacific Northwest Beaches
to Central Nicoya Peninsula

Popular beach and natural history destinations are here. Swim, surf, watch turtles nest, hike, descend into caves, take an estuary tour, or visit national parks and reserves, including Las Baulas, Barra Honda, and Ostional. Some of the best scuba diving in Costa Rica is around Santa Catalina and Murciélagos Islands. Clusters of nature and adventure destinations to consider are Playa Hermosa/Playas del Coco/Playa Ocotal, Sugar Beach/Flamingo/Conchal, Tamarindo/Playa Grande, Junquillal/Ostional, Nosara/Sámara/Carrillo/Islita. Refer to the map as we go north to south.

In the works since 1974, the ambitious, government-directed Gulf of **Papagayo** project encompasses 17 beaches—mainly on Culebra Bay—and almost 5,000 acres (2,000 ha). Though small hotels have long been in the area, the plan calls for thousands of new hotel rooms, a marina, golf course, vacation homes, and shopping centers on land leased to developers. The project is a king-size measuring stick for the government's commitment to environmentally responsible tourism. So far only a few of the large hotels are open.

Mile-long (1.5-km) **Hermosa Beach** (beach is *playa* in Spanish) is on a bay with hills at both ends. It's not uncommon to see dolphins in the bay or howler monkeys moving through trees along the shore, especially in dry season. *Hermosa* means beautiful, and indeed it is. Another popular area is **Playas del Coco.** On a horseshoe-shaped bay that opens into the Gulf of Papagayo, the town of Playas del Coco is small, eclectic, and tied to the sea. It's easily reached by bus from San José and Liberia, and is about 30 minutes from the Liberia airport. Just two miles (three km) from Playas del Coco is **Ocotal Beach,** small and beautiful, a personal favorite. Tide pools are fascinating. At the north end of the beach, caves shoot the water from incoming tide back out with tremendous force. Big iguanas crawl at the edge of the sandy beach, parrots squawk.

Flamingo, Sugar Beach, and **Playa Conchal** are three curved beaches lovely to look at. Flamingo is a fishing and yachting center with its own marina and upscale summer homes. Conchal's shell-strewn beach draws olive ridley turtles from February to April and only recently has been developed for upscale tourism. For a more secluded, natural setting, I recommend special Sugar Beach (Playa Pan de Azúcar). All are accessible off the main road between Liberia and Santa Cruz. Buses run daily to Flamingo; the nearest airport is in Tamarindo.

Playa Grande is the site of Las Baulas National Park, famous turtle-nesting site. Though it is across an estuary from the tourism-dominated town of Tamarindo, with boats that quickly take travelers between them, the connecting road goes inland and takes at least 20 minutes. At Playa Grande is **El Mundo de la Tortuga (Turtle World),** tel/fax 506/653-0471, which offers self-guided 30-minute tours The audiovisual experience covers nesting, emergence of baby turtles and dangers they face, impact of humans on turtle survival, and turtle protection. Open from October 1 to March 15 from 4 P.M. until two hours after high tide; admission $5. Transfers are available from key area locations.

Tamarindo (population 3,030) is a long, narrow strip along Las Baulas Estuary and Tamarindo and Langosta Beaches, with fingers of development into the low-lying coastal hills. Some 43 miles (69

Making Chorotega traditional pottery at Guaitil

km) southwest of Liberia, it draws beach lovers, nature lovers, fisher-folk, and surfers. Estuary tours to see birds, crocodiles, and mangroves are attractions. Turtle tours are October to March. Night lighting is designed with turtles in mind—too much light and they would stay at sea.

If you are heading for Junquillal Beach or Ostional National Wildife Refuge, where massive numbers of olive ridley turtles come ashore to nest between July and December, head for **Santa Cruz** (population 17,508), a picturesque town 35 miles (56 km) southwest of Liberia, and fill up with gas. Visit nearby pottery-making villages of **Guaitil** and **San Vicente** to see artisans at work. Chorotega traditional pottery is sold in front of potters' houses and in shops. Cerámica Chorotega in San Vicente has a bilingual brochure on the history of this pottery-making, with many pieces styled after pre-Columbian pottery excavated nearby.

Long stretches of open beaches east of Santa Cruz to **Junquillal** are rarely crowded, with only a few small hotels. Most offer tours to Ostional—there is an unbridged river to contend with—and nesting coincides with rainy season. **Nicoya,** south of Santa Cruz, is a pretty town (population 24.054) that most tourists pass through on their way to somewhere else: either west to caves at Barra Honda National Park or south to Sámara, Carrillo, and Nosara. Take time to see the picturesque colonial church, a national monument, begun in the 1500s.

Sámara (population 2,842) is 22 miles (35 km) from Nicoya via paved road. It is a popular beach destination both for national and international visitors. On streets and in restaurants, you'll hear languages from around the world. On the highway into town is a modern gas station, and there are growing numbers of lodging, restaurant, and tourism-related businesses.

Nosara is a quiet, rural village (population 3,585) that has a substantial foreign community. There are several small grocery stores now, but if you need gas, you still get it funneled from a barrel. The many byways make it difficult to give directions to particular hotels; just follow signs and ask. Estuaries, tide pools, and forest make for a terrific, laid-back vacation.

Puntarenas and Southern Nicoya Peninsula

Though the southern part of the Nicoya Peninsula is accessible by road from Liberia or from the Tempisque Ferry, taking a ferry from Puntarenas is by far the shorter route from San José. As the principal port of embarkation to the peninsula, **Puntarenas** is included here although it is on the mainland. The city itself has a new pier where cruise ships dock, an Artisans' Plaza, and it's getting a general facelift thanks to Puntarenas Forever, a project funded by the government of Taiwan. On a narrow piece of land almost 10 miles (16 km) long, Puntarenas (population 21,659) has estuary on one side and Gulf of Nicoya on the other. It is 71 miles (115 km) from San José. Walk along the 1.4-mile (2.3-km) palm-lined oceanfront promenade called Paseo de los Turistas, swim under a warm blue sky, and watch people, ships anchored offshore, and sunsets.

Car/passenger ferries from Puntarenas to the Nicoya Peninsula dock at Playa Naranjo, directly across the gulf from Puntarenas, and near Paquera, on the southeastern end of the peninsula. **Playa Naranjo** is a tiny place, but you can fill up with gas and find restaurants and a couple of hotels. Both a car/passenger ferry and the passenger launch from Puntarenas arrive near **Paquera.** The terminal building has a snack bar and clean rest rooms, a small fee for use. A bus waits to meet the ferry, taking passengers as far as Montezuma. Nearby Curú Wildlife Refuge is worth a stop.

Bahía Ballena (Whale Bay) is down the road a piece. Waters lap on a long, curved beach with a very gentle slope. At sunset one July evening several years ago, two dogs and I were the only ones on the beach at the town of **Tambor,** 14 miles (23 km) southwest of Paquera. A roseate spoonbill perched in a tree at the mouth of the river, kingfishers darted back and forth, and howler monkeys sounded just out of sight. Now that tourism has increased, the chance of you, the dogs, and the wildlife having the beach to yourselves is somewhat reduced, but it remains a tranquil setting.

Just 23 miles (37 km) farther is the interesting little beach town of **Montezuma.** In the past, it could not seem to decide whether to dress up and go for big-time tourism or just hang out and take what came. New small hotels have sprung up, but it is still a laid-back place. Beaches are spectacular; some to the north have loads of gorgeous shells. Go horseback riding, hike to the waterfall east of downtown for a swim, snorkel, visit the Cabo Blanco reserve farther down the road, go bird-watching, or surf.

On the southwestern corner of the Nicoya Peninsula is the even more remote **Mal País** region, which has excellent possibilities for nature and adventure travelers: little-visited beaches, rural hospitality, and some beautiful forest. Year-round access is from Cóbano, 7.5 pleasant miles (12 km) via gravel road. At the coast, go right to Santa Teresa Beach or left to Mal País. Small hotels, lodges, and restaurants cater to those who like to be off the beaten path. Surfers, nature lovers, and fisherfolk find hosts here who love being where they are, doing what they do. Sunset is an event.

NATURE AND ADVENTURE ACTIVITIES

Diving, snorkeling, kayaking, surfing, horseback riding, beach combing, hiking, and birding are terrific throughout the region. Observe the phenomenon of marine turtles that come ashore to lay eggs and of tiny hatchlings making a run for the ocean and explore estuaries populated with living mangrove sculptures. See whales and dolphins, not strangers to these waters. Descend into caves at Barra Honda. Learn about the biodiversity of terrestrial and marine habitats. Marvel at sunsets and sunrises.

FLORA AND FAUNA

Sea turtles are a big draw at Playa Grande and Ostional, but actually turtles nest on beaches large and small all along the Pacific. Remember to use turtle etiquette if you come upon this natural phenomenon. Among birds seen here are magpie jays, black-headed trogons, turquoise-browed motmots, rufous-naped wrens, crested caracaras, boobies, pelicans, magnificent frigatebirds, roseate spoonbills, herons, parrots, parakeets, kingfishers, woodpeckers. Underwater life is rich, and crocodiles, boas, and basilisks are here. Mammals include agoutis, armadillos, kinkajous, and white-faced, spider, and howler monkeys.

You will definitely hear the loud bass vocalizations of adult male howler monkeys (*Alouatta palliata*) throughout the region. It is thought that these roars or barks, which carry about a mile, not only allow communication within the troop but also are territorial. Watch a dominant male through binoculars: see his threatening stance, mouth wide open as he roars. Daybreak and sunset are vocal times, but howlers also respond to thunder, loud noises, airplanes, other howlers, and even guides who imitate their call. Don't stand under the monkeys—they have been known to defecate on people.

Since howlers do not need large areas of forest, you may see them in the forest ribbons along streams, river, or roads. Strictly vegetarians, they feed on fruit, leaves, flowers, and leaf stems. They are the only monkeys in Costa Rica to eat significant amounts of leaves: specialized bacteria in their digestive tracts help break down cellulose, and they produce enzymes to counteract toxins in leaves, which many plants have developed to ward off herbivores. Research shows that when presented with a variety of leaves, howlers choose those with highest nutrients and lowest toxicity.

Because of their low-energy diet, howlers are more sedentary than other monkey species. They spend hours in the same tree resting, scratching, grooming, adults draped over a tree branch while babies play. Predators for adult monkeys are harpy and crested eagles and cats. Tayras, ocelots, and boas prey on the young. This monkey, *mono congo* in Spanish, is all black except for a saddle-like mantle of long, brown or golden hairs on its sides and back.

VISITOR INFORMATION

Parks, private reserves, and tour operators are good sources of area information.

In **Tamarindo,** the Tourist Information Center is on the right side as you enter town, open daily 8 A.M to 4 P.M. Get a handy town map and information on lodging, restaurants, tour agencies, attractions; make reservations and buy cold drinks. Proceeds from this private effort by local tourism businesses go toward road repair; tel/fax 506/653-0337.

In the **Montezuma** area, Aventuras en Montezuma serves as an information center, 506/642-0050, avenzuma@racsa.co.cr.

GETTING THERE

Major transportation hubs for the region are Liberia, Santa Cruz, Nicoya, Puntarenas, Playa Naranjo, and Paquera. Three main overland access routes are via Liberia, across the Tempisque River by ferry, or across the Gulf of Nicoya from Puntarenas to Playa Naranjo or Paquera. Scheduled airline service from San José quickly moves travelers to Liberia or Tamarindo, Nosara, Sámara (Carrillo), Punta Islita, and Tambor. See Appendix A for airline, ferry, and bus schedules, including some private van/bus options. Hotels and tour operators also offer transfer services from other areas and within the area, often cheaper than renting a car. Some coastal hotels offer beach-hopping boat tours to secluded hideaways.

Though signage on major roads is improving, signs on back roads anywhere in the Nicoya Peninsula are far too sparse for strangers. If you drive these roads at night, not recommended, have a flashlight handy: the voice of experience. When you finally spot a sign hung on a fence or attached to a tree in what feels like the middle of nowhere, you may have to get out of the car and use the flashlight to read it.

NATURE AND ADVENTURE SIGHTS

Barra Honda National Park

The main attraction is a network of caves through a peak that once was a coral reef beneath the sea. This 5,671-acre (2,295-ha) park, still holds many secrets. Of 42 caves discovered, only 19 have been explored. Human remains and pre-Columbian artifacts have yet to yield their stories, but exploration has revealed several large caverns adorned with stalactites, stalagmites, pearls, soda straws, columns, popcorn, and other intriguing formations. Nature's underground artistry is most profuse in the Terciopelo (fer-de-lance) Cave, so named because early speleologists found a snake of this species smashed on its floor. Terciopelo contains the Organ, a columnar formation that resounds with different tones when gently tapped. This is the only cave open to the public.

Shafts into these caves are mostly vertical; no elevators to carry you down or caverns lit with colored lights. Descent is down a metal ladder almost 90 feet (27 m) and back up the same way, not for the fainthearted or infirm. Cave visits are permitted only with trained guides from communities around Barra Honda. Allow a minimum of three hours, including the walk to and from the cave entrance. Below-ground wildlife includes bats, insects, blind salamanders, fish, and snails.

For noncavers, trails lead to a view point overlooking the Gulf of Nicoya, a tall evergreen forest, and waterfalls over natural travertine dams. The summit of Barra Honda Peak, pocked with large and small holes and decorated with sculptured rock, hints of the artistry in the caves below. Los Laureles Trail is 3.5 miles (5.5 km) long. Fauna include white-faced and howler monkey, Amazonian skunk, long-nosed armadillo, white-nosed coati, coyote, magpie jay, and orange-fronted parakeet. The vegetation is mostly deciduous. Bring water, and if you choose to go without a guide, buy the map and stay on the trail. Two tourists became lost and died here in 1992. Average annual rainfall is 78 inches (1,970 mm); average temperature, 81°F (27°C). Highest elevation is 1,385 feet (423 m). Camping is allowed: showers and toilets are here.

Community guides also work as park volunteers in trail maintenance, patrols, and fire-fighting. This is an example of how people who live in a buffer zone around the park benefit financially while the park receives needed help.

Details: 14 miles (22 km) northeast of Nicoya; telephone hotline 506/192, tel/fax 506/685-5667, fax 506/685-5276. Open daily 8 A.M to 4 P.M. for cave tours from 7 A.M; the last cave tour leaves at 1 P.M. Admission is $6; camping $2 per person per day. Access either via the Tempisque ferry, continuing 10 miles (16 km) to the sign for Barra Honda (unpaved from the village of Barra Honda) or Liberia. Take a Santa Ana bus from Nicoya, and walk the remaining mile (two km)—no Sunday bus. Cave tours (by reservation only) are $5 per person for equipment and $21 for up to four persons for the guide. Guided nature walks are $9 per person.

Cabo Blanco Strict Nature Reserve

Set aside as a protected area in 1963 before Costa Rica had a park service, the reserve was created largely through efforts of Olof Wessberg and Karen Mogensen, both now deceased, who came to live on the peninsula in 1955. This forest and sanctuary for seabirds exists today because of their love of nature and concern about forest destruction—plus personal commitment and persistence.

At the southernmost tip of the peninsula, Cabo Blanco is a treasure. Take your time on the path between the parking area and visitor center and walk quietly. A white-tailed deer, framed against the greens of the forest, studied our arrival. Further along the path, howler monkeys fed on the yellow fruit of the *jobo* tree. Howlers, white-faced monkeys, and coatis eat this fruit whole, defecating the large nuts in a day or two. An agouti moved through underbrush. Visitors often see monkeys and an admirable assortment of birds and butterflies in the picnic area next to the visitor center.

Birds are abundant, more than 130 species; one birder counted 74 species in four hours. Land species include thicket tinamou, great curassow, red-lored parrot, cinnamon hummingbird, masked tityra, scissor-tailed flycatcher, red-crowned ant-tanager, black-headed trogon, orange-chinned parakeet, blue-crowned motmot, and long-tailed manakin. Among water birds are olivaceous cormorants, bare-throated tiger-herons, American oystercatchers, and whimbrels.

The reserve claims 140 kinds of trees; predominant species are gumbo limbo, lemonwood, frangipani, dogwood, trumpet tree, and cedar. You'll pass the gumbo limbo, with its peeling bark, and the spiny pochote trees on the walk in. Rainfall is 118 inches (3,000 mm); average temperature, 81°F (27°C). The reserve encompasses 2,896 acres (1,172 ha) of land; 4,423 acres (1,790 ha) of marine habitat. Cabo Blanco (White Cape) got its name from the small island a short distance off the point. Pelicans, frigatebirds, and brown boobies hang out there. The area is rich in marine life: octopus, starfish, sea cucumber, lobster, giant conch, and fish such as snapper and snook.

The small visitor center has attractive exhibits on Cabo Blanco wildlife as well as a snack stand, drinking water, and restrooms. You can purchase various small publications on Cabo Blanco natural history.

A loop trail that takes about 90 minutes goes through secondary and some primary forest, hilly but not difficult. A two-hour trek through low mountains, steep in places, leads to Cabo Blanco Beach, a sandy spot on a mostly rocky shoreline. You may still have the beach practically to yourself, except for colored crabs and seabirds. Remember as you walk through this small fragile reserve that until the 1960s, 85 percent of it was pasture and agricultural land; now it's secondary forest. Primary forest still standing when the Swedish couple mounted their conservation campaign provided the gene bank for regeneration. Seeds dispersed by wind and by animals took root and grew. Some marine species on the point of disappearing are now thriving.

Details: *Seven miles (11 km) southwest of Montezuma; telephone hotline 506/192, tel/fax 506/642-0093. Open 8 A.M to 4 P.M., closed Monday and Tuesday; admission $6. From Montezuma, go by bus (runs four times a day), taxi, bike, or horse. Unpaved road from Montezuma; if the bridge is not finished, ford the usually shallow river.*

Curú National Wildlife Refuge

The Curú refuge, on the southern Nicoya Peninsula has a deserted-island kind of feeling—maybe from the coconut-strewn beach, or the mangrove swamp, or the jungled hills rising at the end of the bay. Walking through tall forest behind the palm-fringed beach, you sense the wildness of the place. Small islands jut up in front of Curú Beach, one of three sand beaches in the refuge. On the distant horizon is the mainland.

Boa constrictors are at home here, as are pacas, agoutis, ocelots, white-faced and howler monkeys, rattlesnakes, iguanas, white-tailed deer, herds of peccaries, mountain lions, and margays. Waters along the beach host giant conch, lobsters, and oysters—good snorkeling. Hawksbill and olive ridley turtles come ashore to nest. The magnificent frigatebird soars overhead. Parrots squawk. Hummingbirds, trogons, hawks, swallows, egrets, motmots, tanagers, roseate spoonbills, and fish eagles are among 223 species of birds. There are 78 mammal species, 87 of reptiles (two big crocodiles live in the river), 26 of amphibians, and more than 500 plant species. You'll see pochote trees and guanacaste trees, which indigenous peoples

Rustic bridge to trail at Curú Wildlife Refuge

Ree Strange Sheck

called *curú*, hence the name.

Creation of the Curú refuge was the doing of Federico and Julieta Schutt, who established Curú Hacienda in 1933. When squatters took over a chunk of the farm in 1974, the Schutts looked for ways to protect habitat and wildlife. Now forest and mangroves have protected forest status and fragile marine and beach habitat have national wildlife refuge status, covering 208 acres (84 ha). The rest of the farm is in agriculture and cattle production.

Visitors can explore 17 trails with names like Mango, Killer, Laguna, and Río, rated from easy to difficult. On some, the plants' scientific names are marked. One-hour Finca de los Monos (Monkey Farm) Trail gets off to a picturesque start across a rustic hanging bridge over the Curú River.

Walking with Doña Julieta or her children is walking with the best guides around. Doña Julieta took me to the corral to see baby white-tailed deer, brought from private property to be relocated on protected land. A spider monkey reintroduction program is off and running; this species has disappeared in many areas due to hunting and habitat loss. Daughter Adelina spearheads environmental education programs, leading more than 800 students from 16 area schools on walks and giving talks. Other conservation efforts include an artificial reef, built of old tires; rearing of sea turtles for release into the Pacific; reforestation with native tree species; and use of insect traps and natural pest predators to decrease pesticides in agricultural operations.

Though very rustic cabins along the beach at Curú are primarily for researchers and student groups, space may be available for an overnight stay—36 beds in all. Typical meals, served family-style, are ample and tasty. Lodging and meals are $25 per day. Most come for a day visit, $6, $15 for guided walk; advance reservations.

Details: *Four miles (seven km) south of Paquera; tel/fax 389-2957. Entrance is four miles (seven km) south of Paquera on main road to Cóbano. The sign is hard to see; watch on the left for a tall, gated entrance next to a house. From Paquera, take Cóbano or Montezuma bus and get off at Curú entrance, 1.5-mile (2.5-km) walk to refuge. Accessible by boat or kayak; area lodges offer tours.*

Las Baulas National Marine Park

Established to protect mangroves and big leatherback turtles (*baulas*), the park encompasses beaches that attract one of the largest leatherback turtle populations in the world. Peak nesting months are October through January, when as many as 200 females may come ashore per night. Smaller but noticeable numbers arrive until March, but there are actually turtles here year-round. Each nest contains from 70 to 100 eggs, and the babies hatch in about 70 days. Warmer temperatures in the nest produce females; cooler temperatures, males.

The *baula* is the largest sea turtle living today. Females can be six feet (1.8 m) long and weigh more than 1,300 pounds (590 kg). The species has a tough skin or hide instead of a true shell—hence its English name—leatherback. Major threats for these sea creatures are not only loss of habitat, egg poaching, and accidentally being caught by fishermen but also plastic pollution. Plastic in the water resembles jellyfish and may be ingested by the turtles, which love the Portuguese man-of-war. Olive ridley turtles also sometimes come ashore to lay eggs, though not in the masses experienced at Ostional.

To see the protected mangrove, take a boat along one of the estuaries. All five species that live in Costa Rica thrive here: black, white, buttonwood, tea, and the red, with its stilt or prop roots. Orchids, bromeliads, and termite nests decorate these woody plants. The American crocodile lives here.

Las Baulas is a good bird-watching area. Lowlands attract the wood stork, white ibis, jacana, roseate spoonbill, and American

Ree Strange Sheck

Touring the mangroves in Tamarindo estuary

egret—at least 174 species have been identified. There's also a fragment of tropical dry forest. Crabs abound: ghosts, hermits, and garish crabs with black bodies, orange legs, and purple pincers.

Boats can be rented in Tamarindo or Playa Grande for estuary trips: local tour operators and hotels arrange guided estuary tours. Park personnel oversee nighttime turtle-nesting tours. A small office of the Tempisque Conservation Area is located just before the beach. Stop by for information.

Details: Located at Playa Grande, across the estuary from Tamarindo; telephone hotline 506/192, tel/fax 506/653-0470. Open 24 hours; from October 1 to March 15, register at 6 P.M. at park huts near Hotel Las Tortugas or Hotel Villa Baula; a limited number of observers is permitted on the beach. To reach Playa Grande from the south, go through Villarreal to Matapalo; from Liberia continue to Belén and go east to Huacas and Matapalo. Then follow signs to Playa Grande. Bus and plane service is available to Tamarindo.

Ostional National Wildlife Refuge

The night was very dark. A young man led the small group across the beach of the refuge to high-tide line, where a Pacific or olive ridley turtle was patiently digging a hole in the sand with her back flippers. She dug as far as the flippers would reach, flinging sand out behind her shell. As soon as the flying sand had settled, soft eggs began to drop into the hole—one, two, or three at a time, plopping on top of each other until there were about 100. Once the egg laying began, the guide could use his flashlight briefly without disturbing the creative process. The whishing of sand off to the left signaled another turtle and another hole begun.

Within 25 minutes, the digging and laying were finished, and the turtle began methodically pushing sand back in, using both front and back flippers. Then she pounded her body against the surface to pack it down and moved around in a circle, scattering sand, leaves, and beach debris over the spot to obliterate any evidence of her buried treasure. Within an hour of emerging from the sea, she was back in it.

Nesting turtles can be found here practically any night of the year, though massive arrivals, called *arribadas,* peak from July to December, when as many as 120,000 ridleys nest over four- to eight-day periods. *Arribadas* are usually two weeks apart, but the interval can stretch to a month. Rule of thumb is that arrivals are related to the moon—the third quarter and first quarter. To observe nesting, join a guide from the local development association at the rancho at the upper edge of the beach.

Harvesting of turtle eggs for food (there's a popular notion that they are aphrodisiacs), along with the killing of adults for meat or leather, threaten these and other sea turtle species around the world. This refuge protects nesting sites of ridleys, leatherbacks, and the green turtles that occasionally come ashore. In an innovative program, local residents who once plundered the nests and now live mainly off subsistence agriculture harvest eggs from the first arrivals on the beach and then patrol it to prevent illegal egg taking. About 30 percent of the eggs deposited during an *arribada* are lost anyway when turtles dig up eggs laid earlier. In the first 36 hours of each *arribada,* about a million eggs are collected to sell nationally. This has come to be a major income source for villagers.

If you're here during the day, you may see the egg collection or horses with sacks of turtle eggs slung over them tied up at the local cantina.

Ridley eggs hatch in about 50 days, with many hatchlings picked off on their way to the water by vultures, crabs, or frigatebirds, while others become food for predators in the water, including other turtles. Survival rates are extremely low, about two percent, making protection of eggs all the more important. Ostional is the major nesting site for olive ridleys in Costa Rica.

A few patches of forest contain howler monkeys, kinkajous, coatis, and basilisks. The Ostional River estuary offers good bird-watching—190 species have been identified. Rainfall averages almost 67 inches (1,700 mm) a year; temperature averages 82°F (28°C). Ostional encompasses 790 acres (320 ha) of land; the marine portion is 19,768 acres (8,000 ha).

Details: North of Nosara, 40 miles (65 km) southeast of Santa Cruz; telephone hotline 506/192, tel/fax 506/680-0241(Tempisque Conservation Area office in Santa Cruz). Open daily 24 hours, admission $1. Ostional is accessible by car from Nosara, Nicoya, Santa Cruz, and Junquillal; by bus, forget it. The best deal is an organized tour; leave the night driving to others.

Rancho Humo

Located on the Nicoya Peninsula across the Tempisque River from Palo Verde National Park, Rancho Humo offers a marvelous opportunity to enjoy the rich birdlife that lives in or migrates to this habitat. Birds such as the roseate spoonbill, anhinga, jabiru, northern jacana, wood stork, and egret are among 279 species. Sounds of howler monkeys reverberate here; iguanas are guaranteed. Other wildlife includes crocodiles, boas, coatis, raccoons, and collared peccaries. Some 148 species of trees are known to exist on this 2,470-acre (1,000-ha) property.

Don't miss early morning and late afternoon flights of birds along the river. With the sun still low in the eastern sky and parrots moving noisily from tree to tree, an iguana and I once watched rays of light travel over the green of Palo Verde to shimmer on the waters of the Tempisque. Guests don't have to go outside and sit

WHAT IS THAT YELLOW TREE?

In this area it may well be a yellow cortez, corteza amarilla (Tabebuia ochracea). *In dry season, many trees, shrubs, and vines lose their leaves to conserve moisture. This tree is ornamented with a profusion of yellow blossoms. From a distance it resembles a giant bouquet. All trees in this species tend to flower on the same day, so the countryside can be studded with bouquets. Flowers in a single tree last only about four days, but the tree may bloom two or three times during the dry season. Its wood is hard and durable, favored by farmers for fence posts, and the bark has been used medicinally for malaria and chronic anemia.*

with an iguana for this early morning treat; it can be savored from one of 24 attractive air-conditioned rooms on a bluff above the river. Sliding glass doors open from each onto a terrace with treetop views of forest and the river below; doubles $80. Large picture windows in the spectacular restaurant give an almost 360-degree view. Meals are served buffet style: breakfast is $6.50, lunch or dinner $10; a meal plan is available.

Rancho Humo has covered boats equipped with life jackets for tours on the Tempisque and to Pájaros Island. A short trail from the hotel goes through forest to the dock at Puerto Lapas. *Lapas?* It's Spanish for "macaws"—scarlet macaws are found here, along with magpie jays, parrots, orioles, flycatchers, and parakeets. Mountain bike rental, $5 an hour, offers another option for seeing Palo Verde National Park and for exploring Rancho Humo's forests and floodplains. Rent horses for $5 per hour. Join in daily chores of the cattle ranch. Visit pottery makers at Gauitil and San Vicente, $57; a Barra Honda park tour includes transport, descent into the caverns, guides, and lunch, $100.

Details: *Near town of Puerto Humo on Tempisque River; 506/255-2463, fax 506/255-3573; at lodge 506/385-038; ecologic@racsa.co.cr, www.arweb.com/birds. From the Inter-American Highway, cross the*

Tempisque by ferry, turn at Quebrada Honda for Corralito and Puerto Humo; access also from Nicoya or Guatil. Boat transfers are available from Tempisque ferry, Palo Verde, or the Bebedero; San José land transfer $150 for up to four. Ask about air transfers.

Reserva Biologica Nosara and Hotel Lagarta Lodge

A terrific option for natural history visitors is Hotel Lagarta Lodge, set on a hill 130 feet (40 m) above the Pacific with views of the coast to Ostional and of the Nosara River twisting and turning its way to the sea. Nature trails lead through a 125-acre (50 ha) private wildlife reserve of mangroves and forest established by the hotel's Swiss owners, the Roths. So far the bird list includes 170 species, including toucans, motmots, manakins, and a wealth of seabirds. You may see a jaguarundi, monkeys, coatis, frogs, colorful crabs, and perhaps even snakes. Five main trails offer short and longer options to the river's mouth and across a tributary to the rich world of mangroves and humid tropical forest. Take a two-hour tour with an ornithologist to the Nosara/Montaña River delta in a quiet electric-powered boat, $20.

Some of the eight attractive rooms are in the main lodge; others are through landscaped grounds up a flight of stairs. Meals are served in an open-air restaurant. Explore the reserve, swim in the pool, go horseback riding or biking (bike rental $10 per day), or take excursions to Guaitil, Ostional, or San Juanillo for diving or snorkeling. The hotel is a 10-minute walk from a white-sand beach and five minutes from the mouth of the Nosara River. Day visitors are welcome.

Details: *At Nosara; 506/682-0035, fax 506/682-0135, lagarta @racsa.co.cr, www.nosara.com/lagarta. Doubles from $60. Lodge offers pickup from town for a fee.*

Star Mountain Eco Resort

Tucked away in the mountains above Mal País, this secluded retreat has all the charm of a country inn set amid 216 acres (87 ha) of forest that feels primeval. A jaguar had eaten a calf not long before I arrived; staff list anteater, margay, puma, jaguarundi, white-tailed deer, *tepezcuintle*, coati, armadillo, kinkajou, coyote, raccoon, skunk, and howler and white-faced monkeys among mammals they have seen. The growing bird list has 120 species, such as long-tailed and red-capped manakins, both fiery-billed and collared aracaris, squirrel cuckoos, laughing falcons, black-headed and violaceous trogons, and several species of hummingbirds, herons, and woodpeckers.

You want trails? You've got 'em, from short and easy (with arrows for self-guiding) to a six-hour adventure trek though the forest where, depending on time of year, you encounter several waterfalls. A steep two-hour walk affords an expansive view of both the Gulf of Nicoya and the Pacific. Walk back down the road you came on to watch birdlife along the stream and blue morpho butterflies. Go snorkeling, fishing, surfing, horseback riding, and sea kayaking. Star Mountain offers a boat tour to Cabo Blanco Island to see mantas, turtles, and birds. A day trip to Tortuga Island in a local *panga* (small boat but equipped with life jackets) is $150 for up to four.

The colorful open-air dining room with its rustic tree-trunk tables offers homemade bread, fresh fruits, beef, poultry, and seafood.

Charming Tiki Suites at Tango Mar

Ree Strange Sheck

Imagine crepe flambé in the forest. Expect light lunches and dinner menus that include a vegetarian choice. Four rooms open through double doors onto a long porch (with great Costa Rican leather rocking chairs) looking out on the landscaped grounds and down to a sun deck, pool, and hot tub. All have big showers, ceiling fans, and original Costa Rican artwork. Choose your room by color: the pink room has two double beds, a watermelon painting, and a big dressing area off the bathroom; doubles $65, including breakfast and taxes. For a group or family, a two-room bunkhouse accommodates up to nine for $25 per person. No credit cards are accepted.

Details: Nine miles (14 km) south of Cóbano, 1.5 miles (2.5 km) from Mal País, At lodge, tel/fax 506/640-0101, in U.S. tel/fax 786/242-4996, info@starmountaineco.com, www.starmountaineco.com, Transfers provided. In rainy season, four-wheel-drive may be necessary.

Tango Mar

A deluxe destination, Tango Mar on the southern Nicoya Peninsula combines a beach resort atmosphere with protection of habitat and wildlife. Sure, there's sportfishing, golf on a nine-hole course, tennis, first-rate rooms, restaurant, and service, but interesting conservation activities and the setting of this 150-acre (60-ha) property create a splendid nature/adventure retreat.

Reforestation with native species—8,000 trees so far—creates wildlife habitat, in some cases forming corridors between existing forest patches. A small artificial lake from surplus resort water is a sanctuary for aquatic birds. Troops of howler monkeys live here, and white-tailed deer. A project to increase populations of scarlet macaws and toucans is underway, along with a reintroduction program for domesticated birds. Green iguanas are reproducing in their natural habitat, and not only are the leatherback and olive ridley turtles that nest on Tango Mar's beach protected but Tango Mar collects data on hatchlings. The bird list numbers about 100, with species such as the white-fronted and yellow-naped parrot, black-headed trogon, long-tailed manakin, and turquoise-browed motmot. Water birds include the roseate spoonbill, black-crowned night-heron, northern jacana, black-bellied whistling duck, and brown pelican. Watch for white-faced monkeys, armadillos, sloths, anteaters, agoutis, coatis, porcupines, and kinkajous.

Almost two miles (three km) of nature trails exist. Take one to a nearby cove and swim in the pool at the base of a 40-foot (12-m) waterfall. Tango Mar offers horseback rides in jungle, across rivers and along the coast, and to local communities. Snorkel or dive among reefs off nearby Tortuga Island, go deep sea fishing, or surfing—boards are available. Visit Curú, see wildlife on the Pochote mangrove estuary, and take a jeep safari to Cabo Blanco. Try the sunset champagne cruise for two, have a massage.

In a jungle setting, two pools are fed by natural mineral water, a thatched bar and grill alongside. The open-air restaurant is surrounded by lush tropical plants; food and service are excellent, the evening ambiance romantic.

All accommodations have ocean views, satellite TV, air conditioning, ceiling fans, fresh flowers, and big towels. Sixteen large, elegantly simple oceanfront rooms have step-down whirlpool baths and balconies that face the sea. Twelve hillside Tropical Suites feature in-room hot tubs and etched glass windows, shared sun decks secluded in tropical foliage—monkeys pass by. The five deluxe Polynesian-style Tiki Suites are raised off the ground, each with in-room hot tub, sitting area, stained glass dome window, and its own minibus. Doubles are Oceanfront, $138, Tropical Suites $150, and Tiki Suites $190, breakfast included. Substantial reductions are offered mid-April to mid-December. Ask about villas and packages.

Details: *Two miles (three km) southwest of Tambor; 506/289-9328, fax 506/288-1257, at hotel 506/683-0001, fax 506/683-0003, in U.S. 888/259-2965, tangomar@racsa.co.cr, www.tangomar.com.*

GUIDES AND OUTFITTERS

At Playa Naranjo on the Gulf of Nicoya, **Seascape del Sur**, tel/fax 506/661-1555, in the U.S. and Canada dial 506/529-4866, fax 506/529-4012, specializes in sea kayaking trips from half- and full-day to multiday trips. A five-day trip explores the islands and sheltered waters of the gulf, maximum eight persons; from $800 including kayaking and camping equipment, meals, guides, and San José transfers. Seascape del Sur is based at Oasis del Pacífico.

Aventuras en Montezuma, tel/fax 506/642-0050, avenzuma
@racsa.co.cr, is a tour and information center in the town of Montezuma that has a helpful, friendly staff. Day tours include Curú,
Tortuga Island and snorkeling ($40 including lunch), rafting, and
horseback riding. Transfers by boat/land to such sites as Sámara,
Puntarenas, Tamarindo, Arenal, and Ostional (in September/
October for the turtles). Here you can rent motorcycles or cars,
make air arrangements and international phone calls, send faxes,
and find out where to get a massage. Internet and e-mail service is
$10 per hour. Open 8 A.M to noon and 2 to 7 P.M.

Bill Beard's Diving Safaris, 506/672-0012, fax 506/672-0231, in U.S.
877/853-0538, costarica@diveres.com, www.billbeardcostarica.com, is
based at Playa Hermosa. Two-tank dive trips are $65; 8:30 A.M and 1
P.M. daily departures. A night dive is $50, and dive trips to Catalina
Island are $90, $125 to Bat Island, available year-round. Stop by the
dive center at Hotel Sol Playa Hermosa, which hums with activity. Ask
about certification courses, including PADI and NITROX. Bill has
been diving off of Costa Rica's shores for more than 27 years. Some of
his tips: the best months for manta rays at Catalina Island are
December to May; whale sharks are seen year-round. Hotels, transfers,
car rentals, park tours, and other adventure activities can be arranged.

Hotel Ocotal Dive Shop, 506/670-0321, fax 506/670-0083, elo-
cotal@racsa.co.cr, www.ocotalresort.com, has equipment rental,
instruction, and specialty dive courses. Dive trips depart daily with
qualified dive masters and PADI instruction. A two-tank boat dive is
$59, a one-tank night dive $48, five to eight divers per boat. Special
tours are to Bat or Catalina Islands. A $373 per person dive package
includes five days and four nights (double occupancy) at the hotel,
two diving days, tanks, weights, guide, and breakfasts. Full-and half-
day sportfishing is available for novice or experienced anglers.
Crews are specially trained for saltwater fly fishing.

Iguana Surf in Tamarindo, tel/fax 506/653-0148, iguanasurf
@aol.com, www.tamarindo.com/iguana, is an experience: big gift
shop, restaurant, rent shop (surfboards, boogie boards, snorkeling
equipment, kayaks, bicycles, beach umbrellas, VCRs, videos), and
tour office. Take a boat or kayak snorkeling tour; get kayak instruction, too. Paddle up a mangrove estuary. In rainy season when roads
are bad, get around via a surf taxi, beach transfers anytime. Find

Iguana Surf on the road to Langosta Beach. A smaller tour center is on the main road.

Mary P. Ruth's **Papagayo Excursions** in Tamarindo, 506/653-0254, fax 506/653-0227, papagayo@racsa.co.cr, was a pioneer tour company in the area. Professionally trained, bilingual guides lead nature and estuary safaris. Sign up for sportfishing, coastal cruises, scuba diving, canopy experiences, horseback riding, and land trips to national parks. A two-hour jungle boat safari to Las Baulas is $31, a leatherback turtle nesting safari, $41, a safari to Ostional for turtle nesting, $60. Day trips go to Palo Verde and Guaitil, Arenal Volcano, Santa Rosa, and Rincón de la Vieja. There are two offices: one as you enter town at the estuary, the other at the Papagayo Boutique in Tamarindo Commercial Center.

In Tamarindo, a local cooperative offers a two-hour tour of the mangroves with guides who have good eyes but not much English, $12 per person, 506/653-0201. The boats are tied up at a small dock on the way into town. They also offer transfers across the estuary.

Ocotal Beach from Hotel Ocotal

Ree Strange Sheck

CAMPING

Camping is allowed at **Barra Honda National Park**, see "Nature and Adventure Sights." Beachfront **Mar Azul** in Mal País, also welcomes campers, tel/fax 506/640-0098. Owners Otto and Jeannette also have some rustic lodging and a restaurant that serves seafood and typical meals. Camping is allowed at specified spots in **Montezuma**, with latrines and water. Bring your own equipment for any of these.

LODGING

Gulf of Papagayo Area

Hotel Ocotal, 506/670-0321, fax 506/670-0083, elocotal@ racsa.co.cr, www.ocotalresort.com, has a spectacular view of coastline and sea from rooms and restaurant on a cliff above the beach. Sunset from here is an unfolding piece of art. Each of 50 standard cliffside and beachfront rooms and nine suites have a terrace, air conditioning, ceiling fans, telephones, satellite TV, small refrigerators, and coffeemakers. Pools and hot tub have sea views. Standard doubles are $92, bungalow rooms $114, suites $163. The restaurant serves buffet or a la carte meals either inside or on a covered terrace. Notice the great timbers in the dining room's remarkable roof structure. Father Rooster Bar on the beach has a barefoot atmosphere for informal dining and drinks. Beach and restaurant shuttle is available. There's an in-house dive shop and sportfishing fleet. Adventure tours are arranged at lobby desk.

    Hotel Sugar Beach, 506/654-4242, fax 506/654-4239, 800/458-4735, sugarb@racsa.co.cr, www.sugar-beach.com, is the only hotel on Playa Pan de Azúcar. The curve of the small bay, the rocky headlands, the forest, and the peace provide an unforgettable setting. Find an uncrowded white sand beach, seaside pool, beach ranchos. Hear monkeys and see iguanas, raccoons, coatis, and armadillos. Birding is good, beginning with the resident green macaw. Beach and mountain trails explore this 24-acre (9.7-ha) property. Go by boat to picnic on a secluded beach or surfing at Witches Rock. Use snorkeling equipment or boogie boards free. Fishing, scuba diving (Catalina Island is right out front), turtle tours, horseback riding, and estuary tours are arranged. A large open-air restaurant (Costa Rican and international menu) invites leisurely dining to the sound of gentle surf; breakfast is $10, lunch $14, dinner $18. All 29 rooms have air conditioning and fans. Spacious rooms in six duplexes have a garden setting, with windows on three sides and high native-hardwood tongue-and-groove ceilings. Six superior rooms have pool/sea views, and four charming rooms with wraparound balcony are oceanfront. Doubles begin at $110. A honeymoon suite, apartment, and beach house are available, as are transfers.

Hotel Villa Casa Blanca, telephone 506/670-0518, tel/fax 506/670-0448, vcblanca@racsa.co.cr; www.ticonet.co.cr/casablanca, at Ocotal, is a charming 15-room inn. Owners Janey and James Seip often join guests for breakfast on a large covered terrace in a tropical garden setting. Both company and breakfast are delightful. Besides typical *gallo pinto*, find Belgian waffles, cinnamon rolls, fruit, breads, and some of the best pancakes around. The Spanish-style villa, practically hidden in a tropical garden, is a short walk from the beach and has its own intimate pool and hot tub. Splashes of color abound in unique rooms: comforters, drapes, cushions, artwork, and plants. Staying here is like being a guest in a nice home. Each room has air conditioning and ceiling fans; doubles are $69, including breakfast. A second-floor blue-and-white honeymoon suite has a canopy bed, high wood ceilings, a sea view, and a raised tub on a tile platform, $95. A condo with garden views is $105 for two. No smoking is permitted. Though lunch and dinner are not served, restaurants are within walking distance, or have a meal delivered from restaurants in Playas del Coco. Tours to area attractions can be arranged, along with snorkeling, diving, fishing, bird-watching, canopy tour, dolphin trips. Rent horses and kayaks. The Seips handle villa rentals.

At Coco Beach, **Hotel Vista Mar**, tel/fax 506/670-0753, jplamar@racsa.co.cr, www.larevuenet.com/vistamar, is a hacienda-style inn with nine pleasant air-conditioned rooms that look out on a tropical garden studded with graceful palms and eye-catching orchids around an inviting swimming pool. Double rooms are $50, with breakfast included—a breakfast served on the long terrace facing the ocean. Attentive hosts Caroline and Jean Pierre grow their own herbs and enjoy using them in tasty dishes, from salads and fresh seafood to vegetarian fare.

Rancho Armadillo, 506/670-0108, fax 506/670-0441, info@ ronchoarmadillo.com, www.ranchoarmadillo.com, is a 10-acre (four-ha) retreat in the mountains only a mile (two km) from the blue Pacific, shuttle provided. Five spacious air-conditioned rooms with mini-fridges and cable tv start at $75; a two-bedroom suite is $119. The ocean-view restaurant attracts locals as well as visitors, with a menu not found elsewhere in these parts: Cajun shrimp or blackened chicken, Texas hamburger, chili without beans, foot-long subs, and more. Relax in the pool, go bird-watching, observe coatis, iguanas, armadillos (but of course), and deer. Off-site tours include canopy tours, sportfishing, diving, sailing, turtle-nesting trips, and visits to rain forests, volcanic parks, and hot springs. Go by boat to pre-Columbian sites. Look for the hotel sign near the boatyard coming into Playas del Coco.

Villa del Sueño, tel/fax 506/672-0026, delsueno@racsa.co.cr, www.villadelsueno.com, is near the first entrance to Playa Hermosa, 200 meters from the beach. Twenty large rooms in the villa, next to a sparkling pool, have decorator touches, rocking chairs, ceiling fans, shuttered windows, and pretty bedspreads; doubles from $59. Ask about condo rental next door. No small children. Meals are a highlight, from breakfast that can be crepes, French toast, fresh fruit, or eggs to lunch with something Italian included. Dinner is a four-course affair. The restaurant is open to the public—reservations recommended. The friendly owners, all from Montreal, set up area excursions with English-speaking guides. Visit Rincón de la Vieja, Las Baulas, Palo Verde, or Santa Rosa Parks, take a horseback nature tour at Los Inocentes, raft the Corobicí, or snorkel or kayak.

Playa Grande/Tamarindo Area

Friendly **Bella Vista Village Resort,** tel/fax 506/653-0036, belvista@racsa.co.cr, www.tamarindo.com/bella, has six thatched octagonal bungalows with million-dollar views of turquoise Tamarindo Bay. Under each high conical roof is a kitchen, comfortable living area, and sleeping loft. Fanciful murals outside and tasteful fabrics, hand-painted kitchen tiles, and artifacts inside give each a theme: choose Butterfly Room, Jungle Room, Fanta-Sea Room, or Indian Room; doubles $65. Terraced around a pretty pool, the bungalows do look like a tiny village, with light-colored walls brilliant against rock walls and greens of the garden. A short walk down a gentle slope goes to town and beach. Owners and hosts Gabe and Judy Bettinsoli aim for an air of serenity and service; they arrange nature trips, horseback riding, scuba, snorkeling, boating and canoeing, or sportfishing—even dinner reservations.

El Milagro, 506/653-0042, fax 506/653-0050, elmilagro@elmilagro.com, www.elmilagro.com, is across the road from Tamarindo Beach on the road into town. The 32 pleasant rooms have high wooden ceilings, tile floors, and wooden, louvered double doors that open onto small porches; doubles are $70 with fan, $80 with air conditioning, buffet breakfast included. The restaurant, with European kitchen, is open to pool and gardens, and there is a open-air bar. Staff arranges turtle-watching tours, estuary trips, horseback riding, surfing.

Hotel Capitán Suizo in Tamarindo, 506/653-0075, fax 506/653-0292, capsuizo@racsa.co.cr, www.hotelcapitansuizo.com, exudes quiet excellence and good service. Rooms with balconies or private terraces look onto a lush tropical garden and sea views. Paths lead to a large, open-air restaurant (with tablecloths) that has a glassed-in kitchen (watch the European chef at work). The free-form pool has one end banked like a beach—on a rope hanging from a tree, swing like Tarzan over the water. Eight tile-roofed bungalows feature two walls of sliding wood-and-glass doors, original works of art, fresh flowers, sitting area, raised bedroom alcove, and a huge bathroom with sunken tub and private outdoor shower; doubles $155. The 22 standard split-level rooms are equally attractive; from $110, breakfast included. All rooms have telephones, ceiling fans, screened windows and doors, and pretty Italian tile floors. Capitán Suizo has easy access to both Tamarindo and Langosta beaches. Activities include snorkeling diving, kayaking, guided estuary tours, horseback riding, and sportfishing. After all that, relax with a massage. Owners are Ruedi and Ursula Schmid of Switzerland. Capitán Suizo is affiliated with Small Distinctive Hotels of Costa Rica.

Hotel Las Tortugas, tel/fax 506/653-0458, nela@cool.co.cr; www.cool.co.cr/usr/turtles, at Playa Grande, is a few steps from the beach where giant leatherbacks nest from October to March.

Owners Louis Wilson and Marianela Pastor work to protect this important wildlife area and educate guests about turtle watching. Because turtles are sensitive to light, none of the 11 rooms or suites has views to the south where the nesting beach is. Each comfortable room is different in size and decor, all with air conditioning; doubles from $50 to $70, larger suites $100, taxes included. A covered deck for outdoor dining surrounds the main restaurant, which serves typical and international dishes. Next to the small, turtle-shaped pool is a thatched rancho with hammocks, and the hot tub is heated. Choose deep-sea fishing, estuary excursions by canoe or boat, and horseback riding. Tide pools are great for snorkeling, bathing, or exploring; there's a beach trail to the north, and a surf break is in front. Owners do not recommend ocean swimming here, however. Masks and snorkels, boogie boards, and surfboards can be rented. Trips around the country arranged with a local employee-turned-entrepreneur who now has his own tour-transport business. Ask about apartment and house rentals.

Beachside **Villa Baula,** 506/653-0650, fax 506/653-0459, hotelvb@racsa.co.cr, www.hotelvillabaula.com, is a rustic place with a good location at Playa Grande, just a five-minute beach walk from the estuary. Twenty five simple rooms are in thatched wooden structures, with ceiling fans, and screened windows; doubles are $60. Poolside, open-air Jaguarundi Restaurant has a varied menu. Tour the estuary with a local guide or ride a horse on forest trails, $25 for either. Kayak to Paradise Island or in the estuary, $25 half day, or mountain bike on two-mile (three-km) trail, $12 half day. Sportfishing is offered. Turtle-nesting tours at Las Baulas leave from the park station steps away $25. Hear and see howler monkeys and observe birds of the tropical dry forest on hotel grounds and in forest along estuary. Take the road from Huacas to Matapalo and follow Villa Baula signs. Don't try to find it in the dark. Transfers are available.

Junquillal Area

Secluded **Hotel Antumalal,** tel/fax 506/680-0506, antumal @racsa.co.cr, www.westnet.com/costarica/lodging/antumalal, on Junquillal Beach west of Santa Cruz, is beautifully situated in lush tropical gardens. The open-air restaurant has an international menu, and lovely, palm-fringed pools are steps away from a long, uncrowded beach. Restful rooms are in bungalows on a gentle slope down to the sea. The 23-high-ceilinged standard rooms are large, with red brick floors and rough-plastered white walls. Windows on two sides provide good ventilation, and there are ceiling fans. Each room has a porch with hammock for dozing, reading, or watching birds; doubles are $85. Seven suites, each with small refrigerator, private balcony, and living area, are $100. Hike to an estuary for good birding either around a rocky headland at low tide or on a road through dry forest. Tide pools invite exploration. Hear howler monkeys; look for them in trees near the dining area. Excursions are arranged, including to Ostional and Las Baulas. There's tennis and horse rental. The San José-Junquillal bus stops at the entrance.

Hotel Iguanazul, 506/653-0124, fax 506/653-0123, in Canada 604/608-3399, reservations@iguanazul.com, www.iguanazul.com, is a friendly place on Playa Blanca, 19 miles (30 km) west of Santa Cruz. The hotel sits on a bluff above the beach like an oasis; impressions are of sky and sea. The hub of activity is the dining room/bar/pool area. The setting sun is spectacular—view it from ranchos on the path to the ocean. On a clear night see the Milky Way and constellations galore, a natural planetarium. The 24 rooms have a white plaster walls, red brick floors, and exposed beams in high ceilings, decorated with folk-art rugs and wall hangings; doubles are from $70 to $90, including continental breakfast. Visiting French Canadian chefs have passed along recipes to local staff—excellent sauces, great pasta. Ask for a picnic and enjoy it on a secluded beach. Snorkel in a clear, low-tide lagoon; kayak on a nearby estuary. Surfing is the big thing: the hotel is minutes from Playa Negra, filming site of *Endless Summer II*. See turtles nesting at Ostional or Las Baulas, go panga fishing with a local fisherman, ride horses, or visit a nearby private nature reserve, $15. Beach walks may bring you face to face with coatis, armadillos, iguanas (yes, there are blue ones), or monkeys. Marvel at the fantastic multihued rocks along the shore—geologists are intrigued by them. Transfers are available.

Ree Strange Sheck

Iguanas galore

Sámara/Nosara/Carrillo/Islita

Guanamar, 506/656-0054, fax 506/656-0001, 800/245-8420, sales@guanamar.com, www.guanamar.com, is four miles (seven km) south of Sámara on Playa Carrillo. The 39 rooms and two suites are set in villas on a bluff above the blue Pacific and a white-sand, mile-long (1.5-km) beach. Broad, shaded wooden walkways with white railings connect the pool and other areas of the resort. White wicker furniture with bright cushions stands out against the rich wooden floors and ceiling of the restaurant/bar, open to the public, which also looks out on sea views and forest-covered hills. Spacious, airy rooms are carpeted, with balconies or terraces, satellite TV, tele-phone, room service, air conditioning, fan, and fresh flowers. Doubles are $94, including breakfast. Two-bedroom, two-bath suites are $160. Some balconies are at treetop level for close-up views of canopy wildlife. Monkeys drop by. The resort, which has more than 1,000 acres (470 ha) of land, offers trail walks with local guides, horseback riding, mountain biking, kayaking, snorkeling, waterskiing, boat rental, and sportfishing. Free beach shuttle. Packages and boat or air transfers are available. **Hotel Isla Chora** in Sámara, 506/656-0174, fax 506-656-0173, hechombo@racsa.co.cr, www.tourism.com.cr/hotels/chora, has style, from the rooms to the Italian restaurant to an outdoor theater and gardens. Ten rooms have interesting angles, colorful spreads, ceiling fans, and air conditioning; doubles are $75. Four two-room apartments, with kitchenettes and balconies, are $126 for up to five. Thick security windows keep out 75 percent of exterior noise. Dining is a treat: scallopini, gnocchi in Gorgonzola sauce, pizzas, etc. Italian ice cream is made on the premises—no need to look any further for cappuccino or espresso. Music groups perform in high season in the amphitheater. Tours go to secluded beaches, Ostional, Palo Verde, Barra Honda, Rincón de la Vieja, and Las Baulas. Sign up for dolphin tours, snorkeling, fishing, horseback riding. Car rental is available.

Hotel Playas de Nosara, 506/682-0121, fax 506/682-0123, uscontact@nosarabeachhotel.com, www.nosarabeachhotel.com, is unique. From a spectacular domed observation lounge, 360° views take in coastline, ocean, forest, and mountains. A free form pool has to be one of the most dramatic around. Expansive vistas from arched openings in the dining room bring balance to even the most restless mind. Sixteen rooms are terraced on this hillside setting above Playa Guiones, with walkways through flowered gardens. Each is large, with brick floors, ceiling fan, louvered doors to a romantic balcony, decorative wall hangings, double $80. Hammocks swing under thatched ranchos at cliff's edge. This is a favorite. Rock outcroppings on the beach create wonderful low-tide pools for exploring, swimming, and snorkeling. The hotel arranges turtle-nesting tours, river trips for birding, and horse rentals. There are nature trails on the property and birding is good. Don't miss sunset on the beach.

Extraordinary is the word for **Hotel Punta Islita,** 506/231-6122, fax 506/231-0715, 800/525-4800, ventas@hotelpuntaislita.com, www.puntaislita.com. Here in this remote place, discover unforgettable ocean views, secluded beaches, fine dining, rooms with Santa Fe-style elegance. A tall, impressive thatched roof covers a huge, circular, open dining room made intimate by good service, the right music, and decorator touches. Food is excellent and attractively served—a French chef presides. The infinity pool, which appears to flow off into the ocean below, is connected to a sun-warmed hot tub. Twelve thatch- and red-tile-roofed bungalows contain 20 rooms and four suites. Rich earth tones and marvelous blues predominate. All have air conditioning, ceiling fans, teak bed frames, cushioned bamboo chairs, mini-refrigerators, and a private patio with hammock and chairs. Doubles are $165, suites (sun-heated patio hot tub, wet bar, sunken living area, and cane ceilings) are from $220 to $325. Classy separate villas start at $350, breakfast included.

The beach is a 10-minute walk away, where the rancho-style Beach Club offers hammocks, beach chairs, and a bar. Take a guided walk or horseback ride in forest or along the coast. Fish with local folk, hunt oysters, or, at low tide, pass through a tunnel in rocks of Punta Islita to yet another secluded beach. Move through the treetops on a six-platform canopy tour. Snorkel, play tennis, kayak, go sportfishing, take a boat tour, and listen to howler monkeys. In season, join a turtle-nesting tour to adjacent Camaronal Wildlife Refuge. Rent Kawasaki golf-cart type vehicles to explore roads on the 75-acre (30-ha) property, 70 percent of which is forested. Travelair and charters land at a local airstrip. When the river is down and the road dries up, the adventurous can come overland in four-wheel-drive vehicles via Carrillo and Coyote; inquire first. Hotel Punta Islita is a member of Small Luxury Hotels of the World.

Rancho Suizo Lodge in Nosara, 506/682-0057, fax 506/682-0055, rsuizo@infoweb.co.cr, www.nosara.ch, is steps away from Pelada Beach, close enough to hear the surf. Ten bright, high-ceilinged rooms are in thatched bungalows, and there is a double-deluxe bungalow, double $35–68, breakfast and taxes included. Swiss owners René and Ruth are gracious hosts. The restaurant, open to the public, includes dishes from their homeland; flags of Swiss cantons hang in the pleasant, thatch-roofed dining room. A garden whirlpool and the bar near the beach, which has a beer garden and barbecue, are gathering places. Turtle watch at Ostional, observe crocodiles at Palo Verde, go horseback riding. Free use of boogie boards, snorkeling equipment, and mountain bikes.

Southern Nicoya Peninsula and Puntarenas

Amor de Mar, tel/fax 506/642-0262; shoebox@racsa.co.cr, www.costaricanet.net/amordemar, in Montezuma, is family-oriented; owners Ori and Richard Stocker welcome children. Eleven rooms range from $35 to $75 for doubles. The two-story hotel has sea in front and the river on one side. Hammocks are strategically placed under palms in a pretty, grassy garden. Swim in the tide pool in front; it's a tropical aquarium. The restaurant serves full breakfasts all day—marvelous homemade bread, banana pancakes, yogurt, and natural fruit juices.

In Montezuma **Cabinas El Sano Banano,** 506/642-0638, fax 506/642-0068, elbanano@racsa.co.cr, www.elbanano.com, is tucked into the forest near the beach, a 10-minute walk from town along the beach. Owned by Sano Banano restaurant owners Lenny and Patricia Iacona, it is as distinctive as the restaurant. Eight romantic geodesic-dome bungalows are tucked into the forest near the beach. Each has a refrigerator and coffeemaker, ceiling fan, and bathroom with private outdoor shower. A beautiful Mexican-style bungalow has a kitchen, king and queen bed in upstairs loft, and a private outdoor shower. Bungalows are from $89 to $120 for two. Rooms of a two-story unit are $65. Lighted paths through attractively landscaped grounds connect bungalows and rooms. New is a fabulous swimming pool and waterfall in a jungle setting. Upstairs suites with full kitchen are $75 per couple. Walking to this secluded complex is part of the treat; luggage can be delivered.

Hotel Celaje, tel/fax 506/642-0374, celaje@racsa.co.cr, is about a half mile (one km) before the entrance to Cabo Blanco in Cabuya. This charming hideaway features seven private bungalows; a thatched, open-air restaurant (open to public) that specializes in Italian food; and a graceful free-form pool separated from the sea by tall, picturesque palms. Candles in coconut shells glow at night along paths. Hosts Angelo and Erica take guests to Cabo Blanco, and arrange boat or horseback excursions. Transfers are provided. Each A-frame thatched bungalow has a fan-cooled upstairs oceanview bedroom for up to four persons. Downstairs is a living area with table, chairs, and hammock; louvered doors open up to sand and palms or close off for privacy; double $40, including tax. Meal plans are available.

Hotel Dos Lagartos, tel/fax 506/683-0236, aulwes@costarica
.net, is on the beach in Tambor. The 23 rooms are neat and simple
with ceiling fans—downstairs rooms seem cooler. Doubles are $25
for rooms with private baths, $17 for rooms with shared baths, no
hot water. The small dining room serves breakfast; several restaurants are nearby. Dos Lagartos arranges horseback rides and boat
tours. Nothing luxurious about this place, but guests consistently
give it high marks.

In Puntarenas, friendly **Hotel Tioga,** 506/661-0271, fax
506/661-0127, tiogacr@racsa.co.cr, www.hoteltioga.com, is downtown across from the beach. The 46 air-conditioned rooms range
from $45 around the pool to $60 behind a second-floor terrace that
looks out to the sea, and $75 for beachfront with balconies.
Hallways have a great selection of historical photos. Good food is in
the restaurant; a casino has been added. Take a Tortuga Island tour,
city tour, or visit nearby biological reserves.

In Playa Naranjo near the car ferry dock is **Oasis del Pacífico,**
tel/fax 506/661-1555. Its 36 rooms have louvered glass windows, large
desks/bureaus, and ceiling fans; doubles $45, taxes included. Owners
Lucky and Aggie, two of the world's truly nice people, won't charge
you for the room if the sun doesn't shine. The restaurant offers
indoor or outdoor dining, with a menu enhanced by dishes from
Aggie's native Singapore; homemade bread gets rave reviews. Palms
tower around two large pools. Relax under shaded ranchos to sounds
of howler monkeys, parakeets, squirrels, and family macaws and parrots. Views are of the sea, islands, and mainland. Fish off the end of
the hotel's 260-foot (80-m) pier. Walk along the beach or swim in the
generally clear, calm waters. There's an on-site sea-kayak tour operator. Day visitors are welcome. Hotel transportation meets each ferry.

Nature Lodge Finca Los Caballos, tel/fax 506/642-0124,
naturelc@racsa.co.cr, www.naturelodge.net, is a charming natural
history destination between Cóbano and Montezuma. Owner
Barbara MacGregor, designed and built the lodge in 1994. Eight
rooms in two Spanish ranch-style buildings have double beds with
Mexican serape bedcovers, orthopedic mattresses, and fans; double
are $55 to $65. Hammocks and chairs on terraces extend the living
space through double doors from each room. An outdoor patio dining room looks out to a small swimming pool on the edge of forever. Make a date with yourself to watch moonrise from here. The day-

time vista across the mountaintops to the coast is a keeper. Hear the sound of the ocean from the hilltop, watch for laughing falcons, gray hawks, toucans, hummingbirds, howler and white-faced monkeys. A two-bedroom house with full kitchen is also available; minimum of three nights. Barbara serves three healthy meals a day, featuring homemade bread, jams, and sauces. Horseback tours are a specialty, with excellent horses for riders from beginner to expert, $15 per hour. Ride through the countryside and along forest trails and beaches to secluded waterfalls and river pools. Take a two-hour river walk to the beach. Barbara arranges tours to Cabo Blanco or Tortuga Island. Rent bicycles, go diving, have a massage. Montezuma and its beach are a five-minute drive away, or a 20-minute walk, less than two miles (three km).

Sunset Reef Marine Lodge, 506/640-0012, fax (605) 640-0036, in U.S. 888/388-2582, sunreef@racsa.co.cr, www.altatravelplanners.com, faces the long curve of Mal País Bay, within view of Cabo Blanco. Surrounded by lush gardens, 14 air-conditioned rooms of tropical hardwoods are enhanced by original artwork, hand-crafted furniture, ceiling fans, tropical flower arrangements, and big-view windows; doubles start at $90 per person. Pretty plant-lined paths lead to a beachside lounge area and to an intimate pool and hot tub above the bay. Kayak, bicycle, dive, hike, fish, bird-watch, ride horses, and go on guided nature walks. In a buffer zone for the reserve, Sunset Reef is no stranger to wildlife: parrots, trogons, herons, hawks, kingfishers, motmots, woodpeckers, manakins, euphonias, brown boobies, and storks are on the bird list. You may see brocket deer, kinkajous, coatis, and monkeys. Marine life in tidal pools is rich: starfish, oysters, octopus, colorful fishes. The restaurant menu always includes fresh fish and seafood. Turn left at the Mal País-Santa Teresa junction and continue two miles (three km). Transfers arranged anywhere on the peninsula.

Tambor Tropical, 506/683-0011, fax 506/683-0013, in U.S. 503/365-2872, TamborT@aol.com, www.tambortropical.com, is a delightful one-of-a-kind destination on Tambor Beach. Ten outstanding rooms are in five two-story hexagonal bungalows fashioned with 15 varieties of wood. The handcrafting continues inside in the breakfast bar, chairs, stools, lamps, and beautiful cabinets in a blue-tiled bathroom. Doors and polished peg-and-groove floors are of purpleheart wood. These 1,000-square-foot open rooms have a well-equipped kitchen set off by a breakfast bar, a living area, and a raised sleeping area with queen-size bed. Leave screened, louvered windows open enough to see rich hues of sunrise. Attention to detail is everywhere. Doubles are $125 to $150, including continental breakfast, adults only. Grounds landscaped with tropical shrubs and flowers bring hummingbirds to the bungalow's wraparound terrace. Coconut palms reflect in waters of the graceful pool and hot tub. The small restaurant, open to the public, serves tasty, reasonably priced light meals: cheeseburgers, chicken nuggets, and burritos, as well as local lobster. Evening dining under the stars at poolside tables is private and romantic. Choose a boat tour to Curú Wildlife Refuge or Tortuga Island. Take a horseback tour to waterfalls and a small lagoon. Staff arranges fishing and visits to Mal País, Montezuma, or Cabo Blanco.

At Mal País, **Trópico Latino Lodge,** tel/fax 506/640-0062, tropico@ centralamerica.com, www.centralamerica.com/cr/hotel/tropico, has six miles (10 km) of white-sand beach at its front door. Go to sleep to the sound of the surf and wake up to calls of parrots and howler monkeys. Six spacious rooms have roll-up shades, screened windows, ceiling fans, and a porch with hammocks and chairs. Centerpiece of the room has to be the bed, with mosquito netting draped gracefully around a big bamboo frame; doubles $60, including taxes, no credit cards. Food is excellent, with fresh fish and dishes from northern Italy a specialty; the restaurant is open to the public. Marvel at the moon while relaxing in whirlpool or swimming pool; fireflies signal in the garden. Surf, hike along the beach (good tide pools and rock formations to poke around in), ride horses, or fish. On Santa Teresa Beach, just three miles (five km) north of Cabo Blanco, Trópico Latino has aracaris, blue jays, parakeets, coatis, iguanas, big frogs, and many seabirds. Transfers are arranged from ferry, airport, or Cóbano.

FOOD

Northwest Pacific Beaches and Upper Nicoya Peninsula

If you are in Flamingo, stop by **Marie's Restaurant,** 506/654-4136, meet Marie, and sample everything from Mexican food, lobster, and fresh fish to milkshakes, open 6:30 A.M to 9:30 P.M. **Amberes,** 506/ 654-4001, is another local dinner favorite, especially for fresh seafood—also a casino and disco.

It would take you days to eat your way through Tamarindo. Don't miss **Sunrise Cafe** on the town circle. The waffles (Belgian-style) with strawberries and cream for breakfast are to die for; cappuccino here, too. For fine Italian dining— traditional Italian dishes and sea specialties in a beautiful setting—try **La Meridiana,** 506/653-0230, and its handmade pasta, fresh-baked bread, spices and cheeses from Italy, and hospitality of the Ondei family; open for lunch and dinner. Stop by **Johann's Bakery** on the way into town for goodies galore.

In Nosara, don't miss **Café de Paris,** 506/682-0087, info @cafedeparis.net, a charming French bakery (open 7 A.M to 5 P.M.) and open-air French restaurant (7 A.M to 11 P.M.). Fresh daily are baguettes, croissants, éclairs, and coconut macaroons to die for. Try oven-baked pizza, fondue, paella. Bunglows in a tropical garden are also available.

Sueño Tropical, 506/656-0151, suetrop@racsa.co.cr, near Playa Carrillo, is a favorite with locals and travelers: Italian food is the specialty served in an open-air restaurant up a bougainvillea-lined stairway. The three brothers who run this place also have a charming hotel beside the restaurant

Southern Nicoya Peninsula and Puntarenas

In Puntarenas restaurants humble and fine are found downtown along the boulevard next to the beach. Try **La Caravelle** for good French food; **Steak House La Yunta,** specializing in meats; **La Casa de los Mariscos,** known for its fresh seafood; and **Restaurante Aloha,** with a long-standing reputation for good lobster.

Around Bahía Ballena try **Restaurant Perla Tambor** at the southern edge of Tambor. The **Cristobal Restaurant** at Tango Mar, 506/683-0001, has terrific atmosphere and good food (refer to "Nature and Adventure Sights").

One of Montezuma's claims to fame is **Sano Banano,** a macrobiotic restaurant that serves delicious food with a flair. It has frozen yogurt and slush machines and serves fresh popcorn. Frozen Yogurt Mocha chillers are highly recommended. No meat here—veggie burgers, avocado sandwiches, and fresh fish. Sitting in the outdoor eating area, shaded by trees, sipping a terrific tropical fruit shake gives you another perspective on Montezuma. Open 7 A.M to 9:30 P.M., nightly movies on a large screen; 506/683-0001.

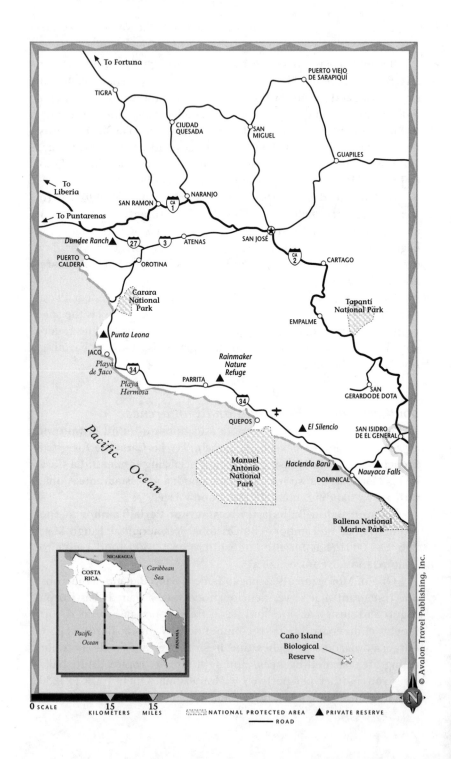

To Fortuna

PUERTO VIEJO
DE SARAPIQUÍ

TIGRA

CIUDAD
QUESADA

SAN
MIGUEL

GUAPILES

To
Liberia

To Puntarenas

SAN RAMON

NARANJO

CA 1

DUNDEE RANCH

27

3

ATENAS

SAN JOSÉ

CA 2

CARTAGO

PUERTO
CALDERA

OROTINA

Carara
National
Park

Tapantí
National Park

EMPALME

Punta Leona

JACO

Playa
de Jaco

34

Rainmaker
Nature
Refuge

PARRITA

34

SAN
GERARDO DE DOTA

Playa
Hermosa

QUEPOS

El Silencio

SAN ISIDRO
DE EL GENERAL

Pacific Ocean

Manuel
Antonio
National
Park

Hacienda Barú

Nauyaca Falls

DOMINICAL

Ballena National
Marine Park

NICARAGUA

COSTA
RICA

Caribbean
Sea

Pacific
Ocean

PANAMA

Caño Island
Biological
Reserve

© Avalon Travel Publishing, Inc.

0 SCALE   15   15
KILOMETERS   MILES   NATIONAL PROTECTED AREA   ▲ PRIVATE RESERVE
ROAD

N

CHAPTER 13

Central Pacific: Carara, Manuel Antonio, Dominical

Two of the most visited national parks in the country—Manuel Antonio and Carara—are here, along with a marine park, beautiful beaches, ranch retreats that combine beach with mountains, and private forest and marine reserves. Canopy experiences, water adventures, forest exploration, and superb options for wildlife observation, both ocean and land creatures, await travelers. The region is easily reached from the Central Valley and is often combined with trips to the south and northwest part of Costa Rica. Delightful destinations encourage adventure and relaxation surrounded by tropical nature.

LAY OF THE LAND

To explore this Central Pacific area of coastal mountains, pretty beaches, mangroves, and rivers big and small, travelers choose towns like Quepos/Manuel Antonio or Dominical as a base or any number of attractive hotels and lodges tucked along the way, as well as a few private reserves that are destinations in themselves. Some come overland from San José via Atenas and Orotina, tracing some of the old Spanish trail from San José to the Pacific. The narrow,

341

winding, mountain road passes through picturesque villages, farms, coffee fields, and patches of forest. Notice the "living fences."

Others opt for the high passes of Cerro de la Muerte before heading for the coast from San Isidro de El General, arriving at Dominical—passing through gorgeous landscapes all along the way. Flying in to the Quepos airport, human impact on the land is dramatic: forested slopes with clearings give way to cleared land with forest patches, cattle ranches, great expanses of African palms, and rice.

Get out binoculars for a stop near the bridge over the **Tarcoles River** at the northern boundary of Carara National Park. Crocodiles bask along its banks; birds enjoy the waters. See scarlet macaws overhead, especially between 5 and 6:30 A.M. and 4 and 5:30 P.M. Dozens of these gorgeous red, blue, and gold members of the parrot family fly between the reserve and roosts in mangroves—a spectacular sight.

Jacó (population 3,393) is the only town of any size near Carara—if you want to stay here, I recommend the less-crowded southern end of town. Jacó Beach is a lively place, popular with surfers and weekenders from the Central Valley. *Please read the tips on water safety; riptides are not uncommon here.* Actually, with the paved road, Carara is an easy drive from lodging all the way to Quepos.

On the other side of the town of Parrita between Jacó and Quepos, pass through miles of African palm plantations. In 1945, the Bananera Company started its first commercial palm plantation here, replacing banana plantations that had been badly affected by Panama disease. By 1965, plantations reached as far south as Golfito. Palm oil is used not only for fat, margarine, and cooking oil but also in soaps and perfumes.

Quepos (population 14,405) was named for the Quepo people whose artifacts often turn up in pastures and fields. Mogote Island, a sheer-sided land with a crown of thick vegetation visible from Cathedral Point in Manuel Antonio National Park, was Quepo ceremonial ground. Today Quepos is the center of an agricultural area of cattle, rice, beans, sorghum, African palm, papayas, and mangoes. A bustling town, 110 miles (177 km) southwest of San José, it has lots of small shops that serve area residents as well as tourists. Hotels are here, but I recommend staying somewhere along the hilly five miles (seven km) between Quepos and Manuel Antonio.

Why not be in a forest setting with fantastic sea views? Frequent inexpensive local buses ply the road between Quepos and Manuel Antonio.

Visit **Jardín Gaia,** a wildlife rescue center between Quepos and Manuel Antonio that receives animals confiscated by wildlife officials as well as injured animals. Those that can be rehabilitated are released into the wild. Begun by Dario Castelfranco in 1991, the center has taken in more than 500 birds and 150 other animals, many on the endangered list. Get a guided tour with explanations of ongoing research and education projects and see the fauna in residence at the time: perhaps a crocodile, howler or white-faced monkey, sloth, macaw, opossum, coati, or scarlet macaw. The center is largely supported by donations (both funds and volunteers who come from around the world; ask about volunteering). Open 2 to 5 P.M., closed Wednesday; $5 for adults, children up to 12 free; 506/777-0535, tel/fax (506)777-1004, wildlife@cariari.ucr.ac.cr, www.skynet.ul.ie/~gwh/jg/index.

As the road nears the park, a proliferation of small *sodas* detracts from the beauty of place and raises questions about pollution, but Manuel Antonio National Park itself continues to be a small jewel. Visitors must wade across an estuary to reach the entrance, an adventurous introduction to a special experience.

Dominical is 28 slow miles (45 km) south of Quepos via unpaved road with lots of one-lane bridges: allow 90 minutes and enjoy the birds along the road. This tiny place has the air of a frontier town where everybody knows everybody else. There is a filling station, small shopping center, and even an Internet Cafe. Lodging options from rustic to resort and restaurants with an international flavor are sprinkled from Dominical south along approximately 30 miles (50 km) of sandy beaches with names like Matapalo, Playa Hermosa, and Uvita. Phone service still has not reached all the way down the coastal road (*costanera*) from Dominical, so radio communication—the order of the day for most not so long ago—is still a lifeline for some. Ballena National Marine Park is nearby and Caño Island Biological Reserve (see Chapter 15) is easily reached from here. San Isidro de El General and the Inter-American are 42 miles (68 km) to the northeast, paved road: by this route, San José is three hours away.

NATURE AND ADVENTURE ACTIVITIES

In addition to experiencing the world of natural marvels in Carara, Manuel Antonio, and Ballena National Parks, travelers to this area can mountain bike, go horseback riding, take off on jungle jaunts or estuary tours, water-ski, parasail, fly in an ultralight, snorkel, scuba dive, or sea kayak. Take to the canopy or go sportfishing. From a base here, you can also visit Caño Island or Corcovado National Park (described in Chapter 15) on day trips. However don't let activities crowd out peaceful time for one-on-one conversations with nature.

FLORA AND FAUNA

Wildlife viewing is excellent. Though larger mammal species are not evident, monkeys (including the small squirrel monkey), coatis, and agoutis are fairly easy to see. Crocodiles, iguanas, and basilisks are here. Birds commonly seen include pale-billed and lineated woodpeckers, magnificent frigate birds, white-crowned parrots, brown pelicans, laughing falcons, caracaras, kingfishers, and, near Carara, scarlet macaws.

You may see a three-toed sloth *(Bradypus variegatus)*, called *perezoso* in Spanish, which means lazy. Yes, sloths do move slowly, but no, they do not spend their lives in a single tree. Yes, they are often seen in cecropia trees, but no, they don't feed exclusively in these trees, they are just spotted there more often because of the tree's open growth and because cecropias grow along roads, trails, and clearings. Arboreal animals that feed, live, and reproduce high above the forest floor, the Costa Rican brown-throated three-toed sloth has pale brown shaggy fur; a small, round head; long limbs; and three long, curved, hook-like claws on each foot. The face is light-colored, with dark stripes slanting down over the eyes and what looks like a perpetual slight smile. Males have a patch of shorter yellow hair on their backs with a black stripe down the center. The fur may take on a greenish cast from algae—not the only thing that lives in it: more than 900 beetles may make their home in the fur of a single sloth.

Since the diet of leaves and fruit is relatively energy-poor, sloths have an energy-conserving lifestyle: slow movement, heavy fur for insulation, and heat-conserving body postures. To get body temperatures up, they bask in the sunlight, preferring tree crowns exposed to early morning sun. A solitary creature, the sloth descends to the ground about once a week to defecate at the base of a tree it feeds in. Though no one knows for sure why it does this, one theory is that it is the sloth's way of returning nutrients to a tree it feeds from. Since sloths tend to return to favorite trees, it's a kind of investment in the tree's health.

An adult female produces one offspring a year. The mother carries the baby for about six months, showing it trees and lianas she feeds on. Abruptly, mother leaves the baby on its own to live in a home range where it has learned which species it may eat. Though mortality of young sloths is high, survivors can live to be 30 years old. Predators are large forest eagles and jaguars; habitat destruction and hunting also affect them. Hoffman's two-toed sloth (*Choleopus hoffmani*) is also found in this area, harder to see because it is nocturnal. Its face is different, with a longer snout and brown eye rings.

VISITOR INFORMATION

Staff at national parks, private reserves, tour companies, and hotels are good sources of information.

GETTING THERE

From the Central Valley, follow the Inter-American Highway west of the international airport to the turnoff for Atenas, Orotina, and Jacó. From Puntarenas and Liberia, head south for Puerto Caldera, Orotina, and Jacó. From San Isidro de El General, head west for Dominical. The coast road, though unpaved, is now open north from Ciudad Cortés, which gives a connection to the Osa and points in the far south of Costa Rica. Express buses go from San José to Jacó and Quepos, with buses also from Puntarenas and San Isidro de El General to the region. Several flights per day make the San José/Quepos run, about 30-minutes. Car rental available. For the southernmost part of the region, access can be via Palmar Sur, either by road or air.

NATURE AND ADVENTURE SIGHTS

Albergue El Silencio

About half way between Quepos and Dominical is a 2,471-acre (1,000-ha) agroecoturism project that offers hiking, fishing, horseback riding, rafting/kayaking, and divine forest and waterfall experiences, along with opportunity to learn about ecologically sensitive agriculture and the culture of a rural community. Operated by CoopeSilencio, a cooperative that combines production of grains, cattle, and African palm with reforestation and tourism, the project protects primary forest and Savegre River watershed. A rustic but attractive six-room inn, bamboo construction with thatched roof, has a capacity for 36 guests, double $48 including breakfast; La Cocina de Leña restaurant features national cuisine prepared on a wood-fired stove.

A tour to waterfalls starts out on horseback, climbing to a splendid view of the Pacific and the Savegre River Valley. Then a well-maintained hiking trail leads to two waterfalls, both with pools surrounded by the silence of pristine forest. For the adventurous and fit, the second waterfall has a natural hot tub half way up. For fishing or kayaking, make advance reservations. Beaches are nearby. Visit the butterfly project, find out how the coop is trying organically grown nontraditional crops, and watch cutting and collection of the palm fruit, which is used in vegetable oil. The project is affiliated with COOPRENA, an umbrella for 10 community projects around the country. All accept volunteers.

Details: 18.5 miles (30 km) south of Manuel Antonio and 15.5 miles (25 km) northeast of Dominical; 506/777-1938, fax 506/779-9545, cooprena@racsa.co.cr, www.agrotourism.net.

Ballena National Marine Park

Created in 1990, Ballena was established to protect marine resources. The six-mile-long (10-km) coast between Punta Uvita and Punta Piñuela is rich in well-preserved mangroves. Ballena Island and smaller rocky protrusions called Las Tres Hermanas are nesting sites for frigatebirds, pelicans, and boobies. The park is named for the humpbacked whales that visit from December to March. Dolphins are common here. It encompasses 13,282 acres (5,375 ha) of ocean and 272 acres (110 ha) of land.

This is the first marine park in Costa Rica to involve a fishing community, which has formed an association to assist in park development. There are no facilities for tourists yet, but you can snorkel around the coral reefs, dive, or do a boat tour. Visits can be arranged from Dominical and Uvita.

Details: *South of Punta Uvita on the Pacific; telephone hotline 506/192, tel/fax 506/786-7161. Open 8 A.M. to 4 P.M., admission $6.*

Carara National Park

The green forest of the Carara reserve stands tall against eroded hillsides—land whose soil, once the trees were cut, tired out quickly when turned into fields for crops or pastures for cattle. In a transition zone between the dry north Pacific and the more humid south, Carara averages rainfall as high as 126 inches (3,200 mm) in the interior and as low as 79 inches (2,000 mm) near the coast. A large lagoon, rivers, and streams supply life-giving moisture. A biological reserve since 1978, Carara became a national park in 1999.

Most of the park's 12,953 acres (5,242 ha) is primary forest, with regal giants that spread their branches in a tall canopy. Plants that live in the trees send roots to the ground; vines wind up trunks toward the light, epiphytes, ferns, and palms soften the setting.

Carara can be an excellent choice for a traveler's first tropical-forest experience—especially in company of a naturalist guide. Guides know animal territories, which trees are in fruit, and what to look for. They point out orchids that a novice would miss. In a three-hour guided tour, we saw a fiery-billed aracari, blue-gray tanager, spectacled owl, boat-billed heron, crested guan, anhinga, brown jay, white-tailed kite, wood stork, blue heron, orange-bellied trogon, roseate spoonbill, yellow-headed caracara, chestnut-mandibled toucan, dotted-winged antwren, blue-crowned motmot, great kiskadee, scarlet macaws, crocodiles, white-faced monkeys, iguanas, squirrels, leaf-cutting ants, and lizards. We didn't see the resident snakes, or the morpho butterfly, sloth, coati, agouti, peccary, porcupine, anteater, coyote, or howler or spider monkey. Perhaps you will.

In early morning and late afternoon, flocks of scarlet macaws fly overhead between the reserve and roosting sites in the mangroves. You may see them feeding in the reserve. At least 320 macaws live around here.

Las Aráceas Trail is through transitional evergreen forest, less than a mile (1.2 km) long. Laguna Meándrica Trail starts between the Tarcoles River and Quebrada Bonita; allow two to four hours for exploration. Quebrada Bonito Trail takes about 1.5 hours. Stay on trails; do not go down to the Tarcoles River or to the lagoon on the Meándrica Trail—large crocodiles live in both. Terrain is hilly and humidity is a factor—you may find yourself huffing and sweating. Average temperature is 82°F (27.8°C), elevation: 2,087 feet (636 m). Driest months are March and April.

No camping, but there are picnic areas, latrines, and water. The new ranger station has a cafeteria, a shop with local handcrafts, and area information. Inquire here about a guided walk.

Details: *56 miles (90 km) southwest of San José, bordering the Tarcoles River; telephone hotline 506/192, 506/383-9953, fax 506/416-7402. Open 7 A.M. to 5 P.M. November to April, 8 A.M. to 4 P.M. May to October; admission $6. Carara is 16 miles (25 km) southwest of Orotina and 11 miles (17 km) north of Jacó: Buses to Jacó and Quepos pass by. Guided tours are available from San José and within the region.*

Dundee Ranch Hotel and Reserve

Here horses are in, cattle are out, pastures are regenerating, forest is protected in a wildlife refuge, and guests have some unusual activities to choose from. A working horse ranch and resort, Dundee offers horseback riding tours. On one ride through the farm (acres of mangos) to the river in the forested Valley of the Monkeys, you have a chance to see groups of howler and spider monkeys, coatis, anteaters, and scarlet macaws during the three-hour ride.

On a shorter ride, go to lush Machuca River Canyon, watch for kingfishers as they swoop over the water and butterflies, including the blue morpho. Tall trees, vines, big rocks at the river—it's a place to linger. Birding at Rancho Dundee is terrific in forest and at lagoons, as well as back at the hotel where a boardwalk crosses a small lagoon to a covered pavilion, hangout for black-bellied whistling ducks, northern jacanas, boat-billed herons, motmots, egrets, parrots, crested caracaras, hummingbirds, trogons, hawks, and cuckoos. Guests can also visit the refuge in Cricket (a tractor-pulled tram). Guides are local people, but with advance notice, a bilingual naturalist can accompany you, $75 for the day.

Sign up for a workshop on pre-Columbian pottery, led by Rigo, an artisan from Guaitil, famous for its pottery making. Off-site tours go to Carara, Palo Verde, Manuel Antonio, and the Rainmaker canopy walk experience. Take a tour to nearby Orotina to visit a local handcraft association that receives support from Rancho Dundee, and watch these artisans at work. A local school also receives help.

Back at the ranch, swim in a sparkling pool with a small water-fall, and relax in a hot tub. next to the large restaurant bar. At night frogs big and small present a raucous serenade, and a walk on paths through the tropical gardens may reveal some, maybe even the red-eyed tree frog. Meals are delicious, with lots to choose from: pasta, fajitas, barbecued ribs, fresh fish, hamburgers, fried *yuca, patacones.* Good breakfasts. The 23 bright, comfortable rooms have red clay tile floors, colorful bedspreads, big closets, table and chairs, air conditioning and ceiling fans, and local TV, double $85.

Rancho Dundee is an hour from Juan Santamaría Airport. It belongs to the Batalla family, who also operate Hotel Chalet Tirol in the Central Valley. Tours mentioned can also be done as day trips from San José with transportation, lunch, and pool time.

Details: Near Orotina, easiest access is via the turnoff to Cascajal— follow the signs; 506/428-8776, fax 506/428-8096, info@dundee-ranch.com, www.chalet-tirol.com.

Hacienda Barú

Four young coatis had dashed across the trail and scampered up a tree, quickly disappearing in a leafy world hidden from our eyes. A blue-black grassquit did rapid little song-jumps, seeming to somer-sault in the air as it fluttered up and down from a low branch. What sounded like a giant crashing through the forest turned out to be

monkeys feeding noisily, knocking down fruit and throwing branches to the ground.

A hard act to follow? Doesn't seem to be at Hacienda Barú, an
830-acre (336-ha) private national wildlife refuge. Guests can ascend
into the canopy, watch birds in mangroves on the way to the beach,
hike to a jungle tent camp, marvel at a giant ceiba, and go by horse
to see pre-Columbian petroglyphs—discovering more about the natural world from a master teacher who still calls himself a student:
Jack Ewing. Jack and his wife, Diane, came to Costa Rica in the
1970s, expecting to stay four months. Come see what has kept them
here. Steve Stroud and Mayra Bonilla joined the partnership in
1993, equally committed to conservation and responsible tourism.

Some visitors to the tropical forest expect boas to hang from
trees and jaguars to appear on trails. Boas are on Barú's reptile list,
though you're not likely to see one. And no jaguars have been spotted here, though there are pumas, jaguarundis, and ocelots. But
there's plenty to see: more than 318 species of birds, 62 species of
mammals (including bats), and reptiles and amphibians that run
the gamut from caimans to red-eyed tree frogs and tiny, colorful,
poison-dart frogs. Humpbacked whales pass by offshore from
December to April, and olive ridley and hawksbill sea turtles nest on
the beach from May through November. The hacienda helps with a
nursery where about 2,500 baby turtles are hatched and released
every year. Dolphins inhabit these warm waters.

About half of the hacienda is forested, both primary and secondary forest; the rest is mangrove, river, and beach habitats.
Patches of lowland forest are being connected by a 100-acre (40-ha)
biological corridor to protect biodiversity.

Day visitors may choose from a variety of hikes with naturalists
or native guides: a three-hour Mangrove and Beach Walk takes in
seashore, mangrove, riverbank, and pasture ($15); the popular
Rainforest Experience explores tropical wet forest ($35); and horse-
back rides take in tropical waterfalls, beach, jungle trails, and pastures ($25). Kayak through mangroves, $40. Self-guiding trails traverse forest and beach, free to overnighters, $3 for day visitors

An incredible experience awaits in the canopy. Harnessed and
helmeted, the visitor is gently lifted more than 100 feet (30 meters)
to an observation platform—fantastic views of canopy vegetation

and surrounding forest guaranteed. Possibilities of wildlife to be seen are countless, $35. For more adventure, choose tree climbing, with a naturalist guide beside you all the way, $45. Spend a night in the jungle, camping in tents next to a shelter with flush toilets and shower: observe nocturnal animals; take a night hike bird-watch in the morning in the small clearing, $60.

Six cabins near both forest and beach have kitchenettes, fans, screened windows with shutters, and bamboo, cushioned sofas, double $60, including complimentary continental breakfast. Typical fare is served in an open-air dining room, special breakfasts $3, lunch $6, dinner $7. On a small hill nearby is a two-story observation tower, terrific for bird-watchers. Be sure to see the butterfly garden and Diane's orchid collection: 250 species and growing.

Details: One mile (two km) north of Dominical, 29 miles (47 km) south of Quepos (unpaved road), 24 miles (38 km) southwest of San Isidro de El General; 506/787-0003, fax 506/787-0004, sstroud@racsa.co.cr, www.haciendabaru.com. Quepos/San Isidro de El General buses pass by the office, or take a bus from San Isidro to Dominical and taxi to Barú.

Manuel Antonio National Park

White-faced monkeys leap from tree to tree along the beach in dazzling displays of aerial skill. Shyer squirrel monkeys, an endemic subspecies found only in this area, peek from behind leaves along trails. Slow-moving sloths give a lazy look at visitors from high vantage points. Coatis and agoutis frequent forest trails in Manuel Antonio. Large iguanas rustle through leaves on the forest floor or sun themselves on beach logs. Warm Pacific waters are home to a variety of marine life; snorkelers, divers, and even watchers at tide pools see brightly colored fish. Don't miss tiny bright-blue ones in pools among rocks at the western end of Manuel Antonio Beach. Whales pass by, and dolphins swim offshore. There are 10 species of sponge, 17 of algae, 78 of fish, 19 of coral, and 24 of crustaceans.

Researchers have identified 200 species of birds and 109 species of mammals, half of which are bats rarely seen by visitors. Among marine birds are brown pelicans, magnificent frigate birds, and brown boobies. Land birds include parrots, Baird's trogons, fiery-billed aracaris, green kingfishers, gray-headed chachalacas, and pale-billed woodpeckers.

The fun begins by wading across an estuary to the park entrance; water can be hip-high at high tide, or barely cover the feet at low. Inside the park, walk a wide trail through tall forest or along South Espadilla Beach. Toward the far end of the beach, enter the forest and cross over to gentler Manuel Antonio Beach or take a path to Cathedral Point, which separates the two beaches. From there, see Mogote Island rising up sharply from the sea, its high cliffs crowned with vegetation. Both Mogote and Cathedral Point are sites where traces of prehistoric peoples can still be found.

These two white-sand beaches are lined with lush vegetation almost to the high-water line. Espadilla is steeper, with bigger waves. Farther down a trail through low mountains is Puerto Escondido, rockier and not as kind to the feet—its beach disappears at high tide. Allow time for a leisurely walk along Perezoso Trail, named for frequently seen sloths.

At Manuel Antonio Beach, face the sea and look to the far right end near the rocks for a prehistoric turtle-trap built by the Quepo people. The trap is a semicircular rock barrier that forms a pool at

Ree Strange Sheck

Squirrel monkey (mono tití) *at Manuel Antonio*

beach's edge. Turtles drawn toward shore for nesting could be trapped as the tide went out and the water level dropped below the barrier. Both green and olive ridley turtles lay eggs here, though not in masses.

In addition to primary and secondary forest and beaches, there are marshes, a mangrove swamp, lagoons, and woodland. Warning signs point out manzanillo trees along the beach; their leaves, bark, and apple-like fruit secrete a toxic white latex that stings the skin.

Dry season is January to March, with wettest months August to October. Even in rainy season, mornings are usually clear, permitting hours of quiet beach enjoyment. Annual rainfall is 153 inches (3,875 mm). Average temperature is 81°F (27°C). Manuel Antonio, protects 1,698 acres (687 ha) of land; 135,905 acres (55,000 ha) marine habitat.

Please do not feed the monkeys; some are becoming aggressive because of this practice. Picnic tables, latrines, and a small visitor center, where you can buy cold drinks, is beside Manuel Antonio Beach. For a guided walk, inquire at the park entrance or book through your hotel.

A major concern for this small, beautiful park is that owners of almost half of the park have never been paid. Without payment, the government legally cannot expropriate. Land prices have skyrocketed since 1972 when the park was created, and owners' patience is wearing thin. Donations designated to help purchase the land can be directed to the National Parks Foundation through The Nature Conservancy in the United States.

Details: Four miles (seven km) south of Quepos; telephone hotline 506/192, 506/777-0644, fax 506/777-0654. Open 7 a.m. to 4 p.m., closed Monday; admission is $6. Daily express buses run between San José and Manuel Antonio, local Quepos/Manuel Antonio shuttle buses makes frequent runs on a main road that passes most hotels. Daily scheduled flights from San José land near Quepos.

Punta Leona Hotel and Reserve

Exquisite forest, white sand beaches, nature programs, and a full range of water sports plus a scarlet macaw conservation program make Punta Leona a rich nature/adventure destination. The 741-

Ree Strange Sheck

Manuel Antonio Park from Hotel La Mariposa

acre (300-ha) private wildlife refuge protects one of the few remaining forests in the transitional zone between the dry forest and rain forest. From the gated entrance on the coastal highway, guests travel 2.5 miles (four km) to hotel and beaches through a fairyland forest.

This is scarlet macaw country. Since 1996 Punta Leona has been involved in a macaw conservation project to increase numbers of these spectacular yellow, blue, and red birds in the wild. Lack of adequate nesting sites as more and more habitat is destroyed and danger to chicks from nest robbers who sell them for pets are threats to survival of this endangered species. The protection strategy? Artificial nests are placed in this protected environment. Already chicks are being born in these nests.

See macaws on a 2.5-hour Early Bird Walk, along with toucans, trogons, manakins, hummingbirds, three-wattled bellbirds and others among 330 migrating and resident species. Visit a different location every day for five days if you wish: Limoncito Beach road, Pipra Trail, Paso de los Monos Trail, Los Cusingos (collared aracaris)

Road, and near the Insect Observatory. Twice daily a two-hour guided walk in the refuge focuses on stories of flora and fauna, with possibilities of seeing white-faced or spider monkeys, sloths, coatis, iguanas, and morpho butterflies. All walks are free to Punta Leona guests. Enjoy hummingbirds at two feedings stations. Evening slide shows feature birds and other animals, insects, and use of medicinal plants and naturalists lecture on Costa Rican culture, history, and ecology.

A full range of off-site tours is available, from diving, canopy tours, sunset cruises, and wildlife river trips to day visits to Carara (15 minutes away), Manuel Antonio (two hours), Arenal, and even Monteverde.

Punta Leona has three white-sand beaches ringed with lush vegetation and three swimming pools. The complex has restaurants and snack bars that offer everything from international and Costa Rican cuisine to pizza, hamburgers, and hot dogs. There are tennis and basketball courts, a gift shop, and a small grocery store. Lodging options include rooms, chalets, bungalows, and condos, many with the conveniences of a small house—full kitchen, washer/dryer. Rooms are at pretty Selvamar, set among the trees, doubles $82. Chalets are from $74 to $100. Arenas condos are $150. LeonaMar stands on a cliff above the ocean: gorgeous views of the Pacific from rooms and pool, steps lead to Playa Blanca, from $140—coatis show up at private terraces. A shuttle runs from 7 A.M. to 10 P.M. around the complex and to beaches on either side of the rocky outcrop known as Punta Leona.

Details: 90 minutes from San José, 15 minutes past the Tarcoles River on the coast road; 506/231-3131, fax 506/232-0791, info@hotelpuntaleona.com, www.hotelpuntaleona.com.

Rainmaker Nature Refuge

Not your ordinary trek through the forest, Rainmaker trails weave through glorious rain forest, along rushing streams, past jungle-surrounded waterfalls, and finally, to a series of three small and six spectacular canopy bridges totaling almost 600 feet (250 m). Anchored to giant hardwood trees, the suspended wooden walkways have waist-high protective nets secured to metal cables, all constructed to U.S. safety standards. Metal platforms around trees where sections of these hanging trails converge are also incredible way stations for contemplating the awe-inspiring panorama of a canopy ecosystem that includes more than 2,500 plants. Lianas a hundred feet long (30 m) hang from tree branches, colors of delicate-looking flowers adorn a landscape of greens. Monkeys live here, and jaguarundis (sleek, dark, long-backed wild cats), along with toucans, peccaries, coatis, anteaters, parrots, and tiny green-legged poison dart frogs that may be endemic to this area.

The 1,500-acre (600-ha) private reserve is in the Chonta mountain range, highest point 4,200 feet (1,700 m), the largest area of primary rain forest without government protection in the central Pacific region. The range and this private reserve form part of the Quepoa Biological Corridor, crucial habitat for fauna that migrate north and south between Manuel Antonio and Carara and east-west migrants between the Damas estuary system and the Talamanca Mountains. Rainmaker's goal is to conserve and protect this corridor in conjunction with sustainable development that involves community involvement and ecotourism.

For those with a fear of heights, the river walk alone is worth more than the price of admission. Trails are excellent (some stairs) and well-trained guides share stories of forest interrelationships and individual species. See a Jesus Christ lizard and learn about orange cup mushrooms. Definitely bring a bathing suit for a dip in one of the Eden-like pools. A look up at tiny people on hanging walkways lends dimension to the height of forest trees. Try to be one of those tiny people, however, for the canopy-bridge experience will be a highlight of your Costa Rica trip.

Entrance is only by guided tour, starting in Manuel Antonio/Quepos. In the buffer zone to the refuge, pass through fields of rice, plantains, watermelon, vanilla, and African palm. Hear history of the company towns, built in United Fruit days. At the visitor center, have a breakfast of delicious empanadas, tropical fruits, homemade tortillas, and maybe some *picadillo de papa* before taking to the trails. Not to worry about crowds: groups are small, only three persons on a bridge at a time, only six on a platform.

Details: *25 minutes northwest of Quepos; 506/777-0850, fax 506/777-1093, rainmkr@racsa.co.cr, www.rainmaker.co.cr. Tours leave* *from Manuel Antonio/Quepos at 7:30 A.M., in dry season added afternoon tour: canopy walk $65, river walk $42.*

GUIDES AND OUTFITTERS

Check "Air Tours" in Chapter 3 for ultralight flights with **Skyline of Costa Rica.**

In Quepos, **Canopy Safari** of Outdoor Expeditions, tel/fax 506/777-0100, cynthia@racsa.co.cr, has five platforms in primary rain forest above spectacular waterfalls; the intrepid zoom between platforms attached to a steel cable. Then take a nature hike to the bottom of the falls and swim in a huge pool; $80, including breakfast and lunch. Ask about a half-day tour to Villa Nueva for $50. Owners Diego and Cynthia promise small groups and experienced guides.

Near Jacó, **Chiclet Tree Tours,** 506/643-3222, fax 506/643-3424, terraza@racsa.co.cr, www.terraza-del-pacfico.com, has a three-hour canopy tour, moving between eight platforms from 66 feet (20 m) to 131 feet (40 m) via harnesses and pulleys on steel cables, with the longest transverse 492 feet (150 m), $55. Transfers are available, as well as packages with Terraza del Pacífico Beachfront Hotel.

Equus Stables, 506/777-0001, havefun@racsa.co.cr, between Quepos and Manuel Antonio, has guided horseback tours for all levels of experience. Its beautiful stables make it a kind of horse heaven—good horses and good saddles. A beach ride is $35, a four-hour waterfall ride is $60, including lunch. Open daily 7 A.M. to 7 P.M. You can also rent snorkel equipment and find e-mail service.

In Quepos next to the soccer field, **Iguana Tours,** tel/fax 506/ 777-1262, iguana@racsa.co.cr, www.iguanatours.com, offers white-water rafting on the Parrita River (class II-III), $85; on the class II-IV Savegre River rapids (also kayak), $90; and the Naranjo River (class III-IV), half-day with rapids like Robin Hood and Twister, $65. Sea kayak at Damas Island to explore mangrove and see wildlife or along Manuel Antonio's coast past islands where boobies and frigates nest, each $65. A boat tour through mangroves gives a chance to see caimans, crocodiles, sloths, boas, white-faced monkeys, and more; $60 including lunch or dinner. Go on a half-day horseback ride through countryside and forest, with a swim at a waterfall and lunch or dinner, for $60. Take a sunset sailing cruise along the coast of Manuel Antonio, $70. New is a tour to Carara, $75, and a visit to gorgeous Nauyaca Falls, involving a horseback ride to the falls, $90. Ask about transfer service (from San José, Golfito, Liberia, Monteverde, Puntarenas, and a host of other places) and half-day or full-day car rental, $55 and $90.

At Punta Leona, **J.D.'s Watersports,** 506/257-3857, fax 506/256-6391, 800/477-8971, jdwater@centralamerica.com, www.jdwatersports .com, offers cruises, scuba diving, beach water sports, and sportfishing. On the Jungle River Cruise on the Tarcoles and through a mangrove estuary see crocodiles, scarlet macaws, parrots, roseate spoonbills, herons, pelicans, ibis, and Jesus Christ lizards. No, this group doesn't feed crocodiles to lure them close to the boat. The tour includes lunch at the company's riverside farm and a swim in the pool, $55 (from San José $79). Take a three-hour sunset cruise on a 44-foot yacht for $35; perhaps you'll observe dolphins, whales, or giant manta rays. A PADI-certified center, J.D.'s offers certification courses, one-day resort courses for beginners for $85, and two-tank dives for certified divers, $65. Owner Pat Hoyman recommends January and February as the best months for viewing giant mantas and, for the adventurous, a white-tip shark dive. Not much coral is here, but the variety of colorful fish will astonish you—20 dive sites are offered. Go sportfishing for sailfish, marlin, tuna, and dorado, the best months December to May.

Kayak Joes, tel/fax 506/787-0049, is at Playa Pinuelas, 19 miles (31 km) south of Dominical. Try a half-day guided kayak tour that explores sea caves, $50 per person for two. Or go snorkeling at Ballena National Marine Park for $10 per hour or $30 for the day. Jungle/waterfall adventures available. Either fax or reserve at the Yak Shak in Domincal.

Planet Dolphin in Quepos, tel/fax 506/777-1647, dolphncr @racsa.co.cr, www.planetdolphin.com, has a super-duper half-day boat tour: mysterious islands, nesting sites for marine birds, blow holes, swimming, and snorkeling. Help count dolphins, whales, and turtles as part of marine studies projects. See colorful tropical fish, lobsters, starfish, seahorses, sand dollars, pelicans, dorado, wahoo, sailfish, marlin. Learn about history of Quepos people and Manuel

Antonio park, $55. Sign up for a learning week and study terrestrial and marine species and habitats, including horseback trips, canopy tour, mangrove trip, and ocean forays; $880 includes lodging, in-country transport, breakfasts and lunches, and research guide book. Check out the website for information on water conditions by month along with sightings of marine species.

CAMPING

At **Hacienda Barú,** spend a night in the jungle, camping in tents next to a shelter with flush toilets and shower. Observe nocturnal animals; take a night hike, and go bird-watching in the morning, $60. Located one mile (two km) north of Dominical, 506/787-0003, fax 506/787-0004, sstroud@racsa.co.cr, www.haciendabaru.com.

Oro Verde Biological Reserve south of Dominical allows camping for $5 per person per night. See description under "Lodging."

LODGING

Lodging possibilities are grouped by area: Carara/Manuel Antonio Areas and Dominical/Points South. Most have considerably reduced rates from May to November.

Carara/Manuel Antonio Areas
Costa Verde, 506/777-0584, fax 506/777-0560, U.S./Canada 866/854-7958, costaver@racsa.co.cr, www.costaverde.co.cr, has wide tiled balconies with classy leather rocking chairs, terraces, gardens, big, sliding wood-framed glass doors. See *tití* monkeys moving through the trees and enjoy a panoramic view of forest, sea, and Cathedral Point. The 46 rooms built on hillsides above Manuel Antonio open to the forest just outside the door, many with canopy-level views. All have kitchenettes, balconies, and ceiling fans, some with air conditioning. Doubles are efficiencies, $79, studio apartments $99, studios-plus (with dazzling ocean views) $119. The Anaconda Bar and Restaurant emphasizes fresh seafood and tropi-

cal fruits. At 4 P.M., come for Monkey Hour. Relax with camera and a drink while you wait for squirrel monkeys to drop by. Bring camera and binoculars to breakfast, for that matter—a sloth rested in an eye-level treetop not 10 feet from the open-air dining room. La Cantina is a steak, chicken, and seafood place next to an old train car, where you can send and receive e-mails. Two pools with ample sun decks are surrounded by lush vegetation. Costa Verde's own 30 acres (19 ha) of forest reserve form part of a corridor for wildlife, with a two-mile (three-km) nature trail open to guests. Other tours arranged include a guided park walk, horseback tour, rafting, and an estuary boat trip.

El Mono Azul, a mile from Quepos on the road to Manuel Antonio, 506/777-1548; tel/fax 506/777-1954, monoazul@racsa .co.cr, www.costaricanet.net/monoazul, is a small hotel with big heart. Eight bright, tidy rooms are $40 for two, continental breakfast included. There is a sparkling pool with a miniature waterfall (candlelight dinners beside it) and nightly movies—the first to arrive gets to choose movie channel. The restaurant, open to the public 7 A.M. to 10 P.M. daily, features salads, 10 kinds of pizza (delivered anywhere in Manuel Antonio), barbecued chicken, hamburgers, fish, pastas, and homemade bread and pastries, VISA accepted. The big heart? Eleven-year-old daughter of owner Jennifer Rice and her young friends create bookmarks, cards, coasters, painted rocks, even candleholders to preserve rain forest—100 percent of sales goes to a project that has already purchased two acres (0.8 ha) of forest and a small plot where children can name and plant trees. Stop by and get some of these delightful handicrafts.

Hotel California, between Quepos and Manuel Antonio, 506/777-1234, fax 506/777-1062, hotelcal@racsa.co.cr, www.hotel-california.com, is fun. Wall-sized murals by local artist Eric López decorate 22 spacious rooms, each celebrating one of Costa Rica's national parks. Colors are fabulous, matched in vibrancy by bright spreads, tall forest, and tropical plants around the multi-level hotel. All have refrigerator, stove, coffeemaker, satellite TV, balcony, and air conditioning; double from $120. Budget bamboo cabins are steps away, with cold-water showers. Enjoy the jungle-ensconced pool, snack bar, and cool-water Jacuzzi and a roof terrace for great ocean and sunset vistas. The restaurant specializes in fish. The surrounding forest is monkey habitat, but also explore the 173-acre (70-ha) private wildlife refuge Hotel California, Plinio Hotel, and others have created: six miles (10-km) of hiking trails leading to an observation tower and waterfalls. Offsite tours are arranged.

Hotel Club del Mar, tel/fax 506/643-3194, www.jacobeach.com, is tucked away on a peaceful cove at the south end of Jacó Beach. Light, nicely furnished rooms nestle among trees and tropical gardens. Views of surf and headland are fantastic. The 18 rooms offer a cool respite from the coastal sun—all have ceiling fans, some have air conditioning. Carved wooden lintels, floor-to-ceiling louvered doors, rattan furniture with deep cushions, and balconies or porches are among attractive features of superior rooms. Standard and economy rooms have equipped kitchenettes and colorful cushioned furniture; doubles are $82 to $96, taxes included. There is a sparkling swimming pool and a library. Philip and Marilyn Edwardes, gracious owners and hosts, along with son Simon, help guests with custom trips. The hotel offers a horseback safari to forest, beach, and waterfalls for $35, and kayak lessons and tours, from $35. A private guide is available, and snorkeling, fishing, and massages can be arranged. If you can't stay at Club del Mar, treat yourself to a gourmet meal at its Las Sandalias restaurant.

At **Hotel Verde Mar,** on Playa Espadilla in Manuel Antonio, 506/777-1805, fax 506/777-1311, verdemar@racsa.co.cr, rooms and pool have a forest setting with ocean views from the pool deck, and surf sounds lull you to sleep at night. Deep-yellow walls are accented at the ceiling with coral borders that feature turquoise iguana motifs—turquoise-colored doors and drapes unite it all. Twenty rooms feature one or two queen beds, most have kitchenettes and air conditioning, $55 to $85. Near the inviting pool, a walkway takes off through the trees to the beach—it is raised to minimize disturbance to plants and animals. At least once a day white-faced and squirrel monkeys play here. Verde Mar has no restaurant, but at least ten are a short walk away and cold drinks and bottled water are available in the office. Friendly staff and resident owners provide exceptional personal attention.

Hotel Villa Lapas, 506/667-0232, fax 506/663-1516, hvlapas @racsa.co.cr, is next door to Carara National Park on a former cattle ranch whose pastures have been returning to forest for more than ten years. The modern, 48-room hotel is in forest beside Tarcolitos River. Large air-conditioned rooms with high ceilings face the river. A flock of scarlet macaws may squawk in a nearby tree as you eat in the pretty, open-air dining room, also open to the public. One birder spotted more than 75 species of birds in 30 minutes. There is a gift shop, TV and video room, swimming pool, and mini golf. A guided two-hour walk in the Villa Lapa forest is on well-maintained trails, while a six-hour trek goes to a nearby spectacular three-tiered waterfall. Enjoy the butterfly garden, with species such as the morpho, monarchs, zebras, and "crackers," which get their name from the sound they make. Tours are available to Carara and Manuel Antonio. Day visits are $35 for lunch, butterfly garden, and pool time. Doubles are from $220, all inclusive.

Time seems suspended at **La Mariposa Hotel,** between Quepos and Manuel Antonio, 506/777-0355, fax 506/777-0050, 800/416-2747, htlmariposa@msm.com, www.lamariposa.com. Maybe it's the view of forest, sea, and white-sand beach curving out to Cathedral Point. Or perhaps it's the aura of seclusion, or the quiet attention to detail. The 36 rooms, suites, and villas, refined in their simplicity and tasteful decor, are woven into the greenery of the hillside: red tile roofs, white walls, bright colors in art and fabrics, bathrooms that incorporate tropical gardens, big windows, ceiling fans, king or double beds, and telephones; all suites have private terraces with stunning ocean views and air conditioning, some have hot tubs. Suites start at $190, deluxe rooms $150, standards $130. The dining room has an elegance about it—views of Pacific sky, gardens, and sea views framed by open arches and columns—and offers international cuisine. A palapa bar is by the swimming pool. Transfers and a full range of tours are arranged.

Makanda by the Sea, 506/777-0442, fax 506/777-1032, makanda @racsa.co.cr, www.makanda.com, is as elegant as its name. Located halfway between Quepos and Manuel Antonio, it encompasses almost 12 acres (five ha) of gardens, tall forest, and extraordinary rooms. Squirrel monkeys like it here, and sloths and coatis come to call. The secluded beach is down a short jungle path. Each of nine studios and villas has an ocean view. Colorful purples and greens contrast with gleaming slate-gray tile. Louvered doors open up rooms to the natural world. Cushiony sofas, king- or queen-size beds gracefully draped with mosquito netting, kitchenettes or full kitchens, ceiling fans (some with air conditioning), reading lamps, split-level rooms, balconies or terraces, hammocks and lounge chairs, individual Japanese gardens—these are some of the features. The large infinity pool and hot tub are set in the forest on a 45° hillside, with expansive decks that become canopy-viewing spots on the downhill side of the pool. Peace is palpable. Studios are $175, villas $230, including tropical style continental breakfast. Poolside Sunset Restaurant, open noon to 9 P.M. (reservations advised) turns out delectable seafood, beef, and poultry dishes, with herbs and coffee from the zone. Tours arranged.

Plinio Hotel, 506/777-0055, fax 506/777-0558, plinio@racsa .co.cr, www.hotelplinio.com, attracts people from all over the world. It's the kind of friendly place where you hear, "If you're ever in Sweden, look me up." The restaurant is a favorite with locals and visitors alike and features cooking with a European flair. Accommodations vary. Jungle House has a king-size bed, living area, kitchen facilities, a loft with queen-size bed and a deck, $115. Three-story family suites feature a rooftop sun deck, big living room, balcony, beds, and sofa beds, $100. There are two-story ocean-view studio suites for $80 and rooms from $55 to $65, double occupancy, breakfast buffet included. All units have ceiling fans or air conditioning. Rooms overlook a swimming pool and small poolside restaurant. Plinio, in cooperation with Hotel California and others, has a private wildlife refuge with six miles (10 km) of nature trails, one that leads to a 60-foot (18-m) wooden outlook tower with canopy-level views; on clear days see the Talamancas, Dominical, and Nicoya Peninsula. Isolde and Roger are wonderful hosts who invite you to experience the canopy tower whether you stay here or not. Afterwards, drop by the restaurant and order a natural *piña* (pineapple) drink or a banana daiquiri. Plinio Hotel is one mile (1.5 km) south of Quepos.

Si Como No Hotel Resort, between Quepos and Manuel Antonio, 506/777-0777, fax 506/777-1093, sicomono@racsa.co.cr, www.sicomono.com, is an experience. From the swimming pool with its waterslide and waterfall-fed hot tub to a laser theater/conference center (full-length feature film nightly) and nature trails through forested property, Si Como No reveals thoughtful planning by owner Jim Damalas. Energy-efficient air conditioners, a water management system that processes gray waters for landscaping and turns hotel sewage into fertilizer, and insulated roofs and windows that conserve energy are noteworthy features. Each attractive hillside suite has unobstructed views of forest and/or sea and sunsets; deluxe suites are $195, superior $175, standard $160. Breakfast included. All have ceiling fans and air-conditioning, kitchen or wet bar, and stocked minibar. Built-in sofas have brightly colored cushions—purples, reds, and oranges. Accents of cane adorn cabinets and furniture. Rates include buffet breakfast. The large atrium lobby incorporates tall trees that took root long before Si Como No was even a dream. A poolside snack bar is the place for breakfast and light lunches, while Claro que Sí Restaurant, open evenings, features authentic Costa Rican cuisine. Sign up for day tours or fishing at the concierge desk. Si Como No is a member of Small Distinctive Hotels of Costa Rica.

From the top of the hill, the octagonal roofs of **Tulemar Bungalows,** between Quepos and Manuel Antonio, 506/777-0580, fax 506/777-1579, tulemar@racsa.co.cr, www.tulemar.com, seem to hover among trees like visiting spacecraft. Each of the 14 delightful, spacious bungalows has an air of privacy and indisputably dynamite views of the blue Pacific. Half of the walls are full-length glass, with sliding screened windows. High wooden beams radiate from a bubble skylight. Peach and blue are the colors in sofas in the large living area, comforters on the two queen beds, and upholstered wooden chairs at the low breakfast bar. Each has air conditioning and ceiling fans, TV, VCR, hair dryer, and telephone. The equipped kitchen has microwave, cooktop stove, and refrigerator; doubles are $235, full breakfast included. Dine in the open-air restaurant next to the infinity-type pool. Nature trails wind through 33 hillside acres (13 ha) of lush forest and gardens. Where forest meets the sea is an intimate, secluded beach where squirrel monkeys pass through treetops and birds sing. Daily afternoon guided nature tours in the private reserve are open to guests and nonguests, $25; on Monday, when the park is closed, morning tours are added. Squirrel monkeys also play right outside bungalow windows, studying spectators as intently as spectators study them. Kayaks are free to guests. Off-site tours arranged.

WATER SAFETY

Basic rules apply for coastal swimming: Do not swim alone, on a full stomach, or while intoxicated. Do not swim at the mouth of a river, where currents can be treacherous. For the same reason, be careful around rocky points. Look before you leap. How deep is the water? Are people standing? Is the slope gradual or is there a steep drop-off? Ask local people how safe the water is.

Most of those who drown each year in Costa Rica are victims of riptides. Some rips are always in the same place, others come and go. Telltale signs are discoloration of the water—brown spots where turbulence is kicking up sand— and areas where breakers don't return directly to the surf but run parallel to the beach. Take a few minutes to watch the action of the sea before you go in. If caught in a rip, remember that it will only take you out, not drag you under. Panic is a factor in drowning. Don't fight the current. See if you can use the energy of a big wave to push you toward the beach. Motion to shore for help, but while help is coming, swim parallel to the beach; then, as the rip weakens, swim at a 45-degree angle toward shore. Don't try to swim directly toward the beach. If you can't swim, float; keep your legs and body close to the surface. If the water is shallow enough that you can walk when you feel yourself being pulled out, quickly go parallel to the shore to try to get out of current.

Some dangerous beaches are Playa Bonita near Limón; near the downtown entrance to Cahuita National Park; Doña Ana and Barranca Beaches near Puntarenas; Jacó; and south Espadilla Beach at Manuel Antonio.

Dominical/Points South

Villas Río Mar in Dominical, 506/787-0052, fax 506/787-0054, in San José 506/231-4230, fax 506/231-4254, info@villasriomar.com, www.villasriomar.com, is a short walk east of town along the Barú River. The 40 rooms in thatched bungalows are a delight, with bedrooms opening via double louvered doors to a terrace-like living area with a wet bar, small refrigerator, breakfast bar, bamboo coffee table and comfy cushioned bamboo armchairs. Sheer mosquito-net curtains and the thatched overhang of the roof lend an intimate privacy to this open-air living space. Ceiling fans cool bedroom and terrace; double $80. The jungle and beach resort has a large pool, swim-up bar, hot tub, and tennis court, all set in lush tropical gardens against a backdrop of 16 forested acres (6.5 ha). Nature trails lead to a viewpoint with spectacular coastline vistas, and birding is good from your own terrace. The distinctive *palenque*-style restaurant features fresh fish and meat entrees—try the Flying Dutchman rendition of red snapper over pasta. Yum! Breakfast is $5, lunch or dinner $10, taxes included. It is open to the public only for dinner, 7 to 9 P.M. Villas Río Mar offers guided walks or horseback rides in the forest. Off-site tours include snorkeling in Ballena National Park, tubing on the Barú, fishing, and visits to Canó Island, Corcovado, Manuel Antonio, and Nauyaca Falls. The hotel has mountain bikes, kayaks, surfboards, and snorkel and fishing equipment.

Cabinas Punta Dominical, 506/787-0016, fax 506/787-0017, is three miles (five km) south of Dominical. The spectacular setting, high on the point at Punta Dominical, puts the sea on both sides. Four spacious cabins of tropical hardwood, nestled discreetly among trees, have tremendous ocean views. Rooms have louvered, floor-length shutters on three sides, polished wood floors, two double beds and a bunk bed, ceiling fans, and screened windows. Each has a porch with a hammock. It's a peaceful, private place; doubles are $50, each additional person $12, taxes included, VISA accepted. The thatched, open-air restaurant, open to the public, has excellent food; it's worth a trip just to sit here and drink in the panorama of sea and coastline, with Ballena National Marine Park at center stage.

Hotel Villas Gaia, 22 miles (35 km) south of Dominical at Tortuga Beach, tel/fax 506/256-9996, at hotel tel/fax 506/788-

8676, hvgaia@racsa.co.cr, www.centralamerica.com, is a real find. Don't miss it. Twelve hilltop bungalows of rich tropical woods are nestled in the forest for private, intimate contact with nature. Each has orthopedic queen and single beds, reading lamps, ceiling fans (two with air), and solar hot water; sliding wood-framed glass doors open onto a spacious terrace with chairs to laze in as you watch wildlife and listen to sounds of waves from below; doubles are $60. Sloths, white-faced monkeys, anteaters, armadillos, kinkajous, frogs, even jungle cats have been seen in hotel gardens: it's a bird-watcher's paradise, 450 species identified so far. Watch spectacular ocean sunsets from the pool, sundeck, or charming poolside bar. The restaurant is gourmet: fried fish in macadamia crust, stuffed eggplant, Italian carpaccio, bananas with grated almonds and chocolate sauce. Order from the menu or choose a $30 meal plan, including taxes, that features daily specials. A tour desk arranges visits to Corcovado National Park or Caño Island, Ballena National Marine Park for diving or snorkeling, horseback riding, mountain and rain forest guided hikes, sea kayaking to Ventanas Caves, river rafting, ultralight flights, and sportfishing. You can come from Dominical or fly to Palmar Sur, with a 15.5-mile (25-km) transfer to the hotel; $25 up to four persons.

Oro Verde Private Biological Reserve, 506/771-4582, fax 506/771-1903, selvamar@racsa.co.cr, above Uvita, managed by the Duarte family, offers day visits as well as overnight stays in decidedly rustic houses. This rural cultural/ecological tour lets you experience something of life on the Duarte farm. The reserve itself is 356 acres (144 ha), about 70 percent in primary forest. You may see an anteater, howler or spider or white-faced monkeys, and two- or three-toed sloths—you will see birds, agoutis, butterflies (four morpho species), coatis, and waterfalls. Birding is good: fiery-billed aracaris, parrots, squirrel cuckoos, pale-billed woodpeckers, blue-crowned motmots, red-capped and orange-collared manakins, chestnut-mandibled toucans, five species of trogons, pied puffbird, and more. A three-hour forest tour is $20, including a guide from the family and lunch; a two-hour river tour takes in a pre-Columbian petroglyph and waterfalls for $10 per person; and a six-hour horseback tour to the top of the mountain, including lunch, is $96 for two. The houses, no electricity, are down the road from the

Duarte family home where five brothers and three sisters were raised. You'll be invited in. Cabins are $10 per person, another $10 per day for meals. Camping is permitted. Entrance to Oro Verde is 7.5 miles (12 km) south of Dominical and two miles (3.5 km) in from the main road (four-wheel drive here, or come in by horseback with advance notice).

Rancho La Merced, 506/771-4582, fax 506/771-1903, selvamar @racsa.co.cr, is near Punta Uvita, adjacent to Ballena National Marine Park. The working cattle ranch has 988 acres (400 ha) protected as a private wildlife refuge: primary and secondary forest, mangroves, and habitat on both the Morete River and along the beach. The rustic hillside farmhouse has two bedrooms, no hot water (but owner Walter Odio explains that it isn't cold, either), living room, equipped kitchen with gas stove, a hammock on the porch, and sounds of the sea below; doubles are $45, $10 each additional person. Monkeys come to eat from the mango tree in front. A generator gives electricity for three hours at night. Meals can be provided. Play cowboy for a day; take a five-hour hike and horseback tour including river, mangrove, beach, and forest; or take a horseback trip to Punta Uvita. Two hiking tours in the refuge include either river and beach habitats or forested mountains, with a view of the Morete River canyon and good birding. These tours, from $10 to $55 per person, are also available to day visitors. Horses can be rented.

FOOD

Carara/Manuel Antonio Areas
Barba Roja has been the place to eat in Manuel Antonia for years—shrimp, lobster, steak, nachos— and offers a quiet atmosphere with a nice view and good service. Open Tuesday to Sunday 7 A.M. to 10 P.M., Monday 4 to 10 P.M.

Look for **Café Milagro,** 506/777-1707, as you enter Quepos and also across from Karolas on the Manuel Antonio road; open 6 A.M. to 10 P.M. Coffee is roasted on-site daily. Get bagels and homemade baked goods and desserts along with iced coffee, espresso, or cappuccino; the brownies are to die for. Unique gifts are for sale.

The **Plinio Hotel**'s restaurant, 506/777-0055, between Quepos and Manuel Antonio is a favorite for its nice atmosphere and consistently excellent food from appetizers to desserts, specializing in Italian/ German cuisine but with Costa Rican dishes and Thai specialties. Open 7 A.M. to 10 P.M.

Karolas, 506/777-1557, open 7 A.M. to 10 P.M., has full breakfasts (including banana pancakes or *huevos rancheros*), light lunches, and dinner that includes dishes from enchiladas and chicken cacciatore to fish. Try the chocolate macadamia nut pie.

La Tortuga Floating Restaurant, 506/382-6378, is a floating restaurant on the waters of Isla Damas estuary 1.5 miles (five km) northwest of Quepos. Try seafood specialties while water birds fly by and monkeys possibly hang out nearby. Open 11 A.M. to 10 P.M., closed Monday.

About 2.5 miles (four km) south of Carara is **Steve and Lisa's** oceanside restaurant, with a menu from BLT's to shrimp and lobster. Open 6 A.M. to 10 P.M.

Dominical/Points South

In Dominical, stop in at **Gringo Mike's,** a restaurant, bakery and delicatessen, on the main street through town, 506/787-0032. Find bagels, cinnamon rolls, hash browns, Texas-style French toast, pizza, and great desserts. Open 7 A.M. to 10 P.M.

San Clemente Bar and Grill in downtown Dominical, 506/787-0026, serves Mexican food, cheeseburgers, blackened chicken, brown rice, and nightly seafood specials and unusual desserts. It's a picnic-table place with old surfboards on the ceiling—a local gathering place.

Ten minutes south of Dominical at Punta Dominical, enjoy a superb seaside setting and good food at the **Restaurante Punta Dominical,** 506/787-0016: huevos rancheros, shrimp and lobster, sandwiches, rice dishes. Open 7 A.M. to 9 P.M.

Villas Gaia, 22 miles (35 km) south of Dominical, 506/788-8678, has a gourmet restaurant well worth the drive. Under Dutch management, the restaurant features international, Latin American, and Caribbean cuisine: French toast with honey-lime syrup, spaghetti carbonara, fish with dill cream sauce, stuffed eggplant, and scrumptious desserts.

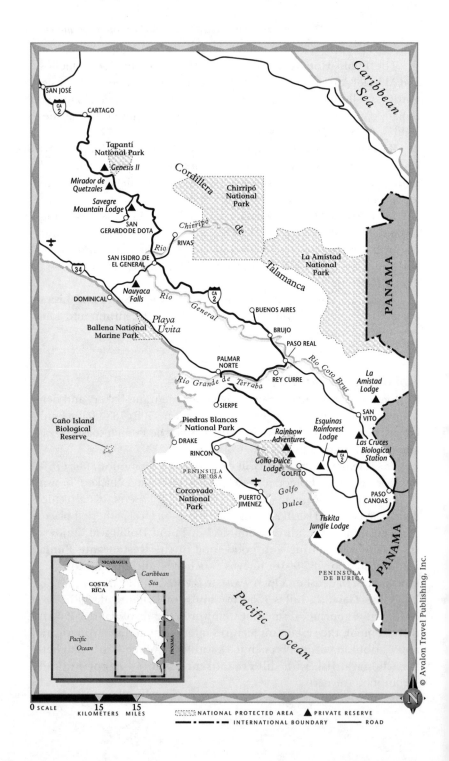

CARIBBEAN Sea

SAN JOSÉ

CARTAGO

CA 2

Tapantí National Park

Genesis II

Mirador de Quetzales

Savegre Mountain Lodge

SAN GERARDO DE DOTA

Cordillera

Chirripó National Park

Río Chirripó

RIVAS

de

La Amistad National Park

Talamanca

SAN ISIDRO DE EL GENERAL

34

CA 2

Nauyaca Falls

DOMINICAL

Río General

Playa Uvita

Ballena National Marine Park

BUENOS AIRES

BRUJO

PASO REAL

Río Coto Brus

PALMAR NORTE

REY CURRE

La Amistad Lodge

Río Grande de Térraba

SAN VITO

SIERPE

Caño Island Biological Reserve

Piedras Blancas National Park

Rainbow Adventures

Esquinas Rainforest Lodge

Las Cruces Biological Station

DRAKE

RINCON

PENÍNSULA DE OSA

Golfo Dulce Lodge

GOLFITO

CA 2

PASO CANOAS

Corcovado National Park

PUERTO JIMENEZ

Golfo Dulce

PANAMA

Tiskita Jungle Lodge

PENÍNSULA DE BURICA

PANAMA

NICARAGUA

Caribbean Sea

COSTA RICA

Pacific Ocean

PANAMA

Pacific Ocean

© Avalon Travel Publishing, Inc.

0 SCALE   15   15
KILOMETERS MILES

░░░░ NATIONAL PROTECTED AREA   ▲ PRIVATE RESERVE

▬ ▬ ▬ INTERNATIONAL BOUNDARY   ▬▬▬ ROAD

N

CHAPTER 14

South: Cerro de la Muerte to Golfito and La Amistad

The Talamancas Mountains, the highest range in the country, are in this biologically and scenically rich region, along with beautiful southern-Pacific beaches, impressive rivers, pineapple plantations, virgin forest; reforested pastures; virgin forest; and lands that knew only indigenous peoples and a trickle of pioneers until the Inter-American Highway to Panama pushed back the frontier in the 1950s.

Two big beautiful national parks are here, along with superb private nature reserves, and adventure/nature options galore in off-the-beaten track destinations.

LAY OF THE LAND

Centers of nature/adventure tourism described here are clustered in the Cerro de la Muerte area, San Isidro de El General/Chirripó area, and Golfito/La Amistad area. By land, the ribbon of highway through mountains and valleys known the Inter-American Highway is the lifeline. Scheduled airline service to Golfito on the Golfo Dulce cuts travel time to southernmost destinations.

The overland journey from Cartago to San Isidro de El General is one of the most spectacular in the country. The road winds up through Cerro de la Muerte and descends to the General River Valley. From the highest point on the Inter-American Highway, 10,938 feet (3,334 m), the road drops to 2,303 feet (702 m) in 28 miles (45 km). Highest point is near km 89: when conditions are right (not often), see both oceans.

As the road climbs out of the Central Valley after Cartago, fields of agave plants called *cabuya* (hemp) cover hillsides; then small farms with dairy cows dominate the landscape. The elevation increases and the temperature drops. Enter the recognizably different stunted vegetation of the *páramo*, then pass into forest once dominated by tall oaks whose remaining specimens are adorned with red bromeliads. Next come tree ferns, vines, and *sombrilla del pobre* (poor man's umbrella)—walls of greenery on both sides of the road. Lower, the vista of the General Valley opens. An early start is recommended; fog or rain becomes likely at higher elevations as hours pass.

Cerro de la Muerte got its name, Mountain of Death, because crossing it in early days on foot or horseback meant exposure to storms and frigid nighttime temperatures. This is the northernmost true *páramo* in the hemisphere; its plants and temperatures associated with Andean climes. Bird-watching is fabulous—quetzals live here year around, and some premier private nature lodges are down narrow roads off the Inter-American, including those in the Dota Valley.

The very mountains that formed a barrier until the last half of this century are an attraction for today's travelers. Chirripó National Park brings the hardy hikers, while an abundance of birds delights others. Some visit this area on their way to or from the Dominical/Uvita area and Central Pacific beaches (see Chapter 13), allowing travelers to make a loop that combines mountains and sea.

San Isidro de El General (population 44,369), some 85 miles (137 km) south of San José, lies in valley between the awesome Talamanca Range and coastal mountains. A center for shopping and transportation in a largely rural landscape, it is a pleasant place for wandering and absorbing flavors of a small Costa Rican town. I stumbled onto a double wedding in the church on the plaza one evening. Shortly after, a dog ambled in through the open door and made its way down the aisle, sniffing and looking, and ambled out

Striking paramo *landscape of Cerro de la Muerte*

again. Nobody seemed to mind. Chirripó trekkers turn east at San Isidro; the Dominical-bound go west. Two nearby nature/adventure options are high-adventure **Nauyaca Falls,** described under "Nature and Adventure Sights," and **Los Cusingos,** famous as the farm of noted naturalist, ornithologist, and author Alexander F. Skutch. About 30 minutes from San Isidro in Quizarrá, the farm is open to naturalists and bird-watchers from 6 A.M. to 4 P.M., but by reservation only; 506/253-3267, fax 506/253-4963, cusingos@cct .or.cr, www.cct.or.cr. In 1993 this 178-acre (72-ha) farm was purchased by the Tropical Science Center (TSC), which maintains it as a bird sanctuary for Neotropical migrants and resident endemic species. Dr. Skutch is coauthor of *A Guide to the Birds of Costa Rica.* Read about the farm in his *A Naturalist in Costa Rica.* Trails lead through a forest that somehow radiates the special energy of the man who has cared for it since 1942. Admission is $10. Area lodges and hotels arrange visits.

From San Isidro the Inter-American Highway passes through farm and ranch country and then mile after mile of pineapples.

Past the cutoff at Paso Real (the route to San Vito/La Amistad area), the road winds along the Térraba River. The airport at **Palmar Sur,** where scheduled flights land daily, is often the jumping-off place for travelers to the Sierpe River or Drake Bay (see Chapter 15).

At Río Claro, turn west off the Inter-American for the 14-mile (22-km) trip to **Golfito,** the only commercial port for the southern Pacific region. A long way from San José, 211 miles (340 km)

GOING BANANAS

Costa Rica is the world's largest exporter of bananas after Ecuador. Native to Asia, bananas got their start in Costa Rica in the 1880s. Each trunk in a banana plant produces one bunch and then dies; but a continuous supply of new trunks emerges from the plant's base. It takes nine months from start of a trunk to cutting of fruit, three months from flower to harvest. Blue plastic bags impregnated with insecticide and fungicide are placed over a bunch at about two weeks; they concentrate heat, quickening growth.

At harvest time, the still-green stalk of bananas is cut from the trunk and pulled on a cable to the packing plant. The plastic is removed, and "hands" of bananas cut from the bunch soak in water to allow latex to drain from the stem. Fruit that survives a selection process is washed, labeled, sprayed with fungicide, loaded in a box, and put aboard a container ship for the United States, Germany, Belgium, Italy, or the Netherlands.

The banana industry has been criticized for cutting of forests to create plantations and for the eco-impact of pesticides and the plastic bags, which often end up in rivers and oceans. Banana companies are making changes under the ECO-O.K. program based on environmental improvement by the industry (see Chapter 2).

to be exact. Golfito (population 14,980) is on the Golfito Gulf, which opens into really big Golfo Dulce (Sweet Gulf). As a port town, it was a busy center for banana exportation from 1938 to 1985 when the Bananera Company, a United Brands subsidiary, operated here. African palms have replaced bananas on much of the land, though bananas are being planted again. Now, with port improvements, Golfito receives cruise ships and is a land, sea, and air transportation hub for travelers to and from lodges on the Golfo Dulce or southern Osa Peninsula across the gulf. The town itself is along a narrow strip between water and mountains. Approaching by air, you may wonder where there is enough level land for a runway. Getting around is no problem. Taxis ply the major street from one end of town to the other, picking up passengers for about $1; the public bus is even cheaper. Water taxis at the public dock near the gasoline station get you to **Zancudo,** a popular laid-back beach area, and elsewhere in the gulf.

San Vito (population 14,357) is a small place with some big names around it: La Amistad National Park and two top private nature reserves. Italian immigrants helped settle the area in the early 1950s. You will find Italian restaurants and may hear Italian spoken on the streets. Near the border with Panama, San Vito is 168 miles (271 km) south of San José. Access is via Paso Real from the northwest or Ciudad Neily from the south. Drive carefully: cowboys and cattle travel the paved road, along with the usual menagerie of bicycles, dogs, chickens, and pedestrians.

NATURE AND ADVENTURE ACTIVITIES

Bring a spirit of adventure. Here there are peaks to climb, rivers to raft (camping on overnight trips), forests to explore, secluded beaches to enjoy, spectacular waterfalls, and bird-watching par excellence. Kayak and snorkel in the gulf. Fish in the ocean or trout fish in streams. Plant life is incredible: travelers not only experience it in the wild but can visit not one but two botanical gardens to see special collections and learn about tropical plants. Exciting macaw and cat release projects are underway on the Golfo Dulce. The quetzal quest brings many to the Cerro de la Muerte region, where these resplendent birds are almost always to be seen. Chirripó National Park is a mecca for hikers, and the area around the park, especially after pavement ends, is a diamond in the rough, wild and beautiful and little visited. It is magnificent country. A few visitor facilities are finally making La Amistad National Park a viable destination for the hardy.

FLORA AND FAUNA

Oak forests in the Cerro de la Muerte area are magnificent. Both plant and animal life are diverse in this region, with mountain, lowland, river, and coastal habitats. You can see quetzals and caimans, coatis and cuckoos, dolphins and dacnises. Frogs and felines and four species of monkey roam this territory.

VISITOR INFORMATION

Primary sources of information are park headquarters, private nature reserves, lodges, and tour operators.

GETTING THERE

From San José take the Inter-American Highway through Cartago. Turnoffs go to destinations such as San Gerardo de Dota (km 80), Chirripó (at San Isidro), San Vito and La Amistad (at Paso Real), and Golfito at Río Claro. Direct buses go from San José to San Isidro, Golfito, and San Vito. Scheduled daily flights go from the capital to Golfito, an hour's flight. See Appendix A for bus and airline information. From the Osa Peninsula, access can be by car around the Golfo Dulce to the Inter-American or from Puerto Jiménez by air, a daily passenger launch (90 minutes), or a hired boat. Access from the Central Pacific area is via the road between Dominical and San Isidro de El General.

NATURE AND ADVENTURE SIGHTS

Casa de Orquídeas

This botanical garden on the eastern shores of the Golfo Dulce is a marvel. Displays of gingers, heliconias, bromeliads, palms, and aroids such as anthuriums, philodendrons, diffenbachias, and elephant ear plants are spaced along paths under forest trees. The 4.5-acre (1.8-ha) garden is in the Golfito National Wildlife Refuge. Owners Ron and Trudy, residents for more than 20 years, give a dynamite two-hour tour, with fascinating facts about these tropical species, both native and exotic. See a walking palm, find out which tree has a connection to Chanel No. 5, and marvel at more than 100 species of orchids (namesake of the garden). Did you know that vanilla is the only edible orchid? Did you know vanilla comes from an orchid? See and hear about unusual plants such as miracle fruit, cannonball tree, gourd tree, and toilet paper plant.

See trees that bear fruits such as mango, mangosteen, star fruit, *guanábana* (sweetsop), and water apple. There are breadfruit and macadamia trees. Ron will probably open a cacao pod and let you taste the sweet pulp around the seed that gives us chocolate. A spice garden includes tumeric, basil, lemon grass, allspice, and cinnamon. See what some of the vegetables you will hear of or eat in Costa Rica look like: *ñampi, tiquisque, yuca*. Among exotics are Egyptian spinach, jícama, and a yard-long bean. With all these plants, see lots of birds and butterflies.

Details: *On San Josecito beach, 30 minutes from Golfito by boat. Tour at 8:30 A.M., closed Friday; admission $5.*

Chirripó National Park

Geologists, botanists, mountain climbers, biologists, adventure-seekers, and just plain nature lovers make their way to Chirripó National Park. Its 123,921 acres (50,150 ha) contain the country's highest peak—12,529 feet (3,819 m), glacial lakes, rivers, and habitats ranging from mixed forests, fern groves, and swamps to oak forests and *páramo.*

Look down on rainbows; on a clear day see both oceans from the peak. There are cloudy and clear days throughout the year, but February-March is driest. Annual rainfall is 138 to 197 inches (3,500 to 5,000 mm). Take warm clothes. Though maximums reach the 80s, count on cold nights, and there can be strong winds. Extremes between day and night can vary by 43°F (24°C); lowest temperature recorded is 16°F (-9°C). You could wake up to a frosty world, finding ice on lakes and stream banks.

Names like Savanna and the Lions, Valley of the Rabbits, and Moraine Valley hint of what early explorers found when they scaled these heights (the "lions" were actually pumas). Endangered species protected at Chirripó include margay, puma, ocelot, jaguar, tapir, and quetzal. Birds and animals are more abundant in the forest zones, though there are hummingbirds even in high *páramo*. Plants seem to cover every inch of trees in the cloud forest: orchids, bromeliads, mosses, and ferns. The way to the summit passes through seven distinct forest types. The higher you climb, the more stunted the vegetation.

Trails are marked. The large refuge at the Crestones base is an 8- to 11-hour hike up the mountain from the entrance. With a capacity for 40 persons, it offers bunks with foam mattresses, a wood-burning cookstove, dining area, solar-system lighting, and shared baths. Bring a warm sleeping bag and carry enough liquids and food. Cooking is not permitted outside of the refuge because of fire danger. Tent camping is allowed only at Paso de los Indios on the Herradura-Uran route only with a local guide and only for persons in excellent condition with mountain-climbing experience. Rock climbing is allowed only at Crestones and only for the experienced who bring their own gear.

Independent travelers must call the conservation area to reserve shelter space and for information about guides and bearers or horses (permitted only from January 1 to April 15). Reserve early, especially December to May. A day visit is possible without a reservation, hiking on the main trail as far as a small refuge at Llano Bonito.

Details: Ranger station12 miles (20 km) northeast of San Isidro de El General at San Gerardo de Rivas; open 5 A.M. to 5 P.M., latest departure to Crestones at noon. Admission is $6, lodging at shelter $6 per night. Telephone hotline 506/192. Reservations 8 A.M. to 4 P.M., 506/771-4836, tel/fax 771-3297. Take a bus from San Isidro to San Gerardo. Tour operators and lodges arrange treks. Blankets, sleeping bags, and gas stoves for rent.

Esquinas Rainforest Lodge

From the lodge we walked the trail in a steady rain, experiencing the wetness as well as the magic and mystery of this rich forest in Piedras Blancas National Park north of Golfito. Guides from nearby La Gamba pointed out a tree that exudes a flammable liquid. They explained the medicinal qualities of trees and other plants and pointed out miniature orchids and kingfishers and hummingbirds. This sector of the park is known as Rainforest of the Austrians, recognizing donations from Austrian people that purchased more than 6,000 acres (2,428 ha) of endangered forest, including the jungle around Esquinas Rainforest Lodge, which is operated by an Austria-Costa Rican foundation. The land was given to the Costa Rican government to be included in the national park.

The ecotourism component is an integral part of the foundation's conservation goals: it provides an alternative income source to former loggers in the area, and profits support agricultural and

Esquinas Rainforest Lodge, a private reserve in Piedras Blancas
National Park north of Golfito

social programs in the La Gamba community. A small biological station completes the picture. A station tour is $15.

Take one of the marked trails for a three- to five- hour hike into the park, using either printed trail guides or going with a La Gamba guide, at no charge, or a bilingual biologist from the research station ($20 for two hours). Waterfall Trail is a two-hour moderate trail, steep in places—bamboo walking sticks provided. This is a wild world of 2,500 plant species, 250 bird species, poison dart frogs, monkeys, and ocelots.

The main lodge is set in a former cattle pasture, transformed into spectacular gardens showcasing heliconias, palms, gingers, and tropical fruits and vegetables, surrounded by tall forest. Its immense conical thatched roof covers reception, gift shop, lounge area, and open dining room. Tiffany-style stained-glass hanging lampshades and bamboo chairs with brightly colored cushions provide a pleasant setting for delicious meals. Harvests from garden and nearby banana and cacao groves find their way to the table: *guanábana*, cas, papaya, star fruit, *mamones*, water apples, *yuca*, breadfruit, lemongrass tea, or chocolate in a heavenly dessert. Lodge elevation is 787 feet (240 m), average temperature 91°F (33°C).

Ten rooms in five bungalows are built of natural rock and wood, with curtained windows on three sides. Rooms have bamboo furniture, reading lamps, and ceiling fans. Each room has a veranda with comfortable chairs to lounge in while you observe golden-hooded tanagers (in Spanish called *siete colores*, seven colors), scarlet-rumped tanagers, and hummingbirds. Parrots and toucans abound. See the flash of orange and blue as a Baird's trogon flies by. Hear howler monkeys. A stream meanders through the grounds, flowing into a naturally filtered swimming pool. Doubles are $75 per person, including lodging, meals, taxes. A three-day/two-night package from San José also includes round-trip air and guided walk, from $280 per person double occupancy. Ask about Rainforest Adventure Week: hiking, canyoning, birding, horseback riding, kayaking, mountain biking, swimming. Off-site tours include adventure tours all the way to the Pacific on horseback and by foot, boat trips on the gulf, mangrove tours, kayaking, and fishing.

Details: *North of Golfito on the Inter-American, at km 37 turn west and follow signs, about 2.5 miles (four km); 506/293-0780, fax 506/293-2632, cellular at lodge 506/382-5798, gasguis@racsa.co.cr, www.regenwald.at.*

Genesis II

Walking through the cloud forest at Genesis II, a national private wildlife refuge, is like moving through a hanging garden in the mist. Bromeliads crowd every inch of space on stately oaks; mosses, mushrooms, and miniature orchids abound. Fallen blossoms from the canopy high above decorate the forest floor.

In the Talamanca Mountains, elevation 7,546 feet (2,300 m), this forest has an air of eternity about it. Bird songs echo through the trees. A collared redstart, known as the "friend of man," usually follows along the trail. Mixed feeding flocks pass by in rapid succession. Birds bring many visitors to this 104-acre (42-ha) private wildlife refuge: 153 species on current list. The resplendent quetzal is no stranger here and is easily seen March to June. Canadian owners Steve and Paula Friedman report seeing nine quetzals one day from the balcony. Distinctive sounds of the three-wattled bellbird are sometimes heard here. There are collared trogons, black guans, emerald toucanets, long-tailed silky flycatchers, silvery-fronted tapaculo, and hummingbirds—fiery-throated, magnificent, volcano, purple-throated, and gray-tailed mountain gems. Mammals include armadillos, tayras, squirrels, and rabbits; tracks of the tapir have been seen.

A two-mile (3.5-km) trail network is color-coded. Watch for glass ferns in Fern Gully, and devil's pitchfork. There's a bamboo walk and quetzal corner. Trail conditions are so good you can actually walk and look at the same time. Butterflies abound. The new canopy walkway includes a suspension bridge, three platforms, and two zip lines—open to day visitors. All platforms have views of canopy and river below; $45, including guided walk with Steve. Optional side trips go to Dominical, Los Cusingos, or Tapantí National Park.

Lodging is in the main house, nestled like an aerie in the trees. Five simply furnished rooms, with room heaters and flannel sheets, share two baths. Facilities are humble, but attention is first-class: chocolate on your pillow, hot water bottle at night, orchids or other tropical blossoms gracing napkins at mealtimes. Paula turns out marvelous meals served family style and featuring garden-fresh fruits and vegetables: lemon chicken, lasagna, and corvina with a lemon and dill sauce, Costa Rican dishes, and in season an omelet with chanterelles. Doubles are $85 per person for lodging, meals, and one guided walk per day, rain gear available. No credit cards.

A covered platform for camping has been added on a forested hillside—bring your own gear, $2 per person. Flush toilets are next to the platform. Bring your own food and use the facilities for cooking or eat at the lodge. If there are no campers, it's a great perch for bird-watching. Volunteers and interns are welcome, one-month minimum. Activities include trail work, reforestation, research, or even illustration for Genesis projects.

The name Genesis II? Steve and Paula chose it to signify a "second beginning," where they would attempt to live on the land in a more proper, peaceful way. Plant a tree to honor someone in the Memorial Grove; the $10 donation helps buy adjoining land, be it forested or pastures to be reforested.

Details: *90 minutes south of San José on the Inter-American, 2.5 miles (four km) east on unpaved road from turnoff at Cañon; tel/fax 506/381-0739, info@genesis-two.com, www.genesis-two.com. Take a San José/San Isidro de El General bus, get off at yellow Cañon church—pickup with advance notice. San José transfers.*

Golfo Dulce Lodge

Looking like a tiny village in a big forest, Golfo Dulce Lodge is a dream destination for adventurers and naturalists. Walk in remote Piedras Blancas National Park, observe birdlife from a 30-foot-high (nine-m) observation tower with a field of heliconias at its base and glorious forest around, explore swamps of the Esquinas River by boat, snorkel off a secluded beach, take the six-hour guided La Selva hike to the mountain ridge, go sea kayaking, visit a botanical garden at the far end of the beach, or get an insider's tour of release sites for two important wildlife projects just steps away from the lodge.

Esther and Markus Grether of Switzerland have created this unparalleled opportunity. To start with, they purchased more than 750-acres (300 ha) to protect rain forest and its denizens (donating part of it to the park), and then they built this small, attractive haven for fellow nature and animal lovers. With support from the

Grethers, **Zoo Ave** (see Chapter 5) now has an impressive site for reintroduction of scarlet macaws into Piedras Blancas, and other species such orange-fronted parakeets, mealy parrots, and white-faced monkeys. Guests get a tour to learn about captive breeding and release. Depending on when you visit, you may see dozens of macaws being prepared for release. Steps away is a release site for **Wildcat Rehabilitation Center Profelis,** which releases mainly ocelots, margays, and jaguarundis and involves long-term research on felines, a project initiated by biologist Siegfried Weisel.

On spacious lodge grounds, just steps away from a good

Ree Strange Sheck

Ron tells about vanilla orchid and vanilla bean at Casa de Orquídeas.

swimming beach in clear gulf waters, wildlife is at home, including Sheila, an injured white-tailed deer who has taken up residence. See toucans, coatis, squirrel monkeys, squirrel cuckoos, hummingbirds, trogons, honeycreepers, and tanagers.

Five detached bungalows have large covered verandas with hammocks and comfortable-cushioned bamboo furniture. Spacious, light-filled rooms have sitting areas. Three attractive rooms are near the small freshwater pool and thatched open-air dining room/bar. Delicious meals are European with a local flavor. Hydropower supplies the electrical energy and water is from a natural spring. Doubles are $105 per person, including air, taxi, and boat transport from San José, meals, lodging, and taxes—minimum two-night stay. Four-day, three-night packages start at $355 per person, including some tours.

Details: *San Josecito Beach 30 minutes north of Golfito by boat; 506/222-2900, fax (506)222-5173, aratur@racsa.co.cr., www.golfodulce-lodge.com.*

La Amistad International Park

Amistad (friendship) was created in connection with a sister park across the border in Panama to protect a vast forested corridor. It's a gigantic park, 479,692 acres (194,129 ha) in Costa Rica alone, big enough to sustain a healthy population of animals that require large areas for hunting and reproduction, such as tapir, jaguar, puma, and harpy eagle. It is a World Heritage Site and within La Amistad Biosphere Reserve.

Probably the largest population of quetzals in the country resides in this refuge of rain forest, cloud forest, and *páramo*, along with at least 400 other bird species. Epiphytes abound; more than 130 varieties of orchids are in the southwest corner of the park alone. There are 263 species of amphibians and reptiles. Spread across the rugged Talamanca Mountain range, Costa Rica's highest, the park protects not only endangered plants and animals but also important watersheds.

Though much of this fantasy land of geology and wildlife has yet to be explored, camping facilities and trails exist in the Altamira sector, elevations from 4,593 feet (1,400 m). Platforms for tents, covered picnic areas, toilets, and cold-water showers are at two camping areas. Choose from among three trails: Valle del Silencio, 12 miles (20 km), offers oaks and quetzals, panoramic views, a moss garden, another campsite; Altamira-Sabanas Esperanzas crosses Platanillal River, natural savannas, the tombs of an indigenous people, and, with luck, you'll see deer, spider monkeys, guans, quetzals, peccaries; and Gigantes del Bosque, almost two miles (three km) (allow three hours), visits primary forest, park limits, and trees 130 feet tall (40 m). Ask about possibilities in the Las Colinas sector, which can include a five-day trek to Cerro Kamuk, elevation 11,644 feet (3,549 m). All cooking must be done on gas stoves—no wood fires.

Annual rainfall is 138 inches (3,500 mm). Temperatures vary according to elevation, 64-77°F (18-25°C).

Details: *Las Tablas entrance to Altamira sector is three hours south of San Isidro: (15 km) south of Paso Real on the road to San Vito, turn east at Las Tablas to Altamira Ranger Station (four-wheel-drive in rainy season); telephone hotline 506/192, tel/fax 506/771-5116, 506/771-3155. Altamira sector open 7 A.M. to 5 P.M.; admission $6, camping $2 per day* *per person. Pay charges at office in San Isidro and then check in at Altamira station. By bus, take San José/San Vito bus and get off in Las Tablas, then travel by small bus to Altamira.*

La Amistad Lodge and Rainforest Reserve

The bird list for this place tells the story of incredible biodiversity—more than 400 species: 23 species of hummingbirds alone. A short walk before breakfast with the resident naturalist revealed crimson-fronted parakeets, fiery-billed aracaris, acorn and lineated woodpeckers, a double-toothed kite, white-ruffed manakin, boat-billed flycatcher, green hermit, Vaux's swift, boat-billed flycatcher, blue-gray tanager, and rufous-collared sparrow.

La Amistad Lodge is on Hacienda La Amistad, elevation 4,100 to 7,218 feet (1,250 to 2,200 m). It includes 37,065 acres (15,000 ha) of rain forest within Las Tablas Protected Zone, which is part of La Amistad Biosphere Reserve and a World Heritage site. To walk in this forest is to walk in a sacred place; one trail even has a cathedral—an immense, awe-inspiring fig tree. A 28-mile (37-km) circuit of trails is suited to different energy levels and physical abilities. Howler monkeys, spider monkeys, and peccaries are among 215 mammal species. Watch for dead man's finger among the incredible mushrooms along paths.

Owner Roberto Montero, whose grandfather owned this land, relates area history and his ideas for conservation through sustainable development. Guests get more than rain-forest ecology; they also see the largest organic farm in Costa Rica: coffee, vegetables, cardamom, jalapeños, fruit orchards, beef production.

The lodge is a three-story marvel of tropical woods. In the downstairs dining room, delicious buffet-style meals are served by friendly local people. Beautiful pre-Columbian pieces from the property are on exhibit (petroglyphs can be seen on some trails). The high-ceilinged, second-floor lounge has a big stone fireplace and opens onto an ample balcony. Five rooms, shared baths, are off the lounge. Across a walkway in back are five additional rooms with ceiling fans and private baths. Radio, computer, and telephone operate on solar power, and a hydroelectric plant provides other electricity.

Stay at a campsite deep inside the forest. Cotoncito, with six rustic cabins, shared baths, and a dining/common room, is the first of several planned. From this base, venture out into this secluded retreat's surroundings. Cotoncito is an hour from the lodge via four-by-four pickup.

Optional guided tours from the hacienda include half-day and full-day activities, mostly $20 to $35: natural history walks, horseback riding, bird-watching, trout fishing, a hike for the hardy to the Río Negro waterfall, a hacienda tour (including coffee milling). Off-site day tours go to Wilson Botanical, $70, and to Bambito in Panama, $100.

Doubles are $65 per person, including accommodations in either lodge or campsite, three meals, and a forest walk.

Details: *At Las Mellizas, 16 miles (26 km) northeast of San Vito, seven hours south of San José near Panamanian border; 506/289-7667, fax 506/289-7858, at lodge 506/773-3193. Take bus to San Vito; lodge transfers also to other destinations.*

Las Cruces Biological Station (Wilson Botanical Garden)

Sunshine, mountain mists, tropical birds, a tapestry of color that only nature can weave, a sense of peace—all of this is at Las Cruces Biological Station plus terrific food and tasteful rooms.

Nature travelers have made pilgrimages to the botanical garden here since it was established by Robert and Catherine Wilson in the 1960s. The 25-acre (10-ha) Wilson Botanical Garden contains an internationally known collection of some 5,000 tropical and subtropical plants. The palm collection is one of the largest in the world, many on delightful Tree Fern Hill Trail. Walk on Heliconia Loop Trail; Bromeliad Walk (see birds drinking from the big bromeliads in dry season), Orchid Walk (with more than 200 native and exotic species), Fern Gully (Costa Rica has 800 species of ferns), Maranta Trail; and Bamboo Walk. The Natural History Loop winds through Hummingbird Garden. Costa Rica has 54 species of hummers; the garden has 24. This self-guided trail has 15 stations; the trail booklet, on sale in the gift shop, is packed with interesting facts.

With purchase by the Organization for Tropical Studies and

birth of Las Cruces Biological Station, nature travelers and local folk were joined by scientists and students from Costa Rica and around the world. Guests have a chance to mingle with students or get a glimpse of leading-edge research underway here and in the surrounding rural landscape.

Trails in a forest reserve of 633 acres (256 ha) allow appreciation of orchids and palms and heliconias growing in their natural habitat. The reserve has 2,000 species of flowering plants, 330 species of birds, 80 species of reptiles and amphibians, and 80 species of mammals, including bats. The garden and forest reserve are habitat for more than 326 species of birds (including local aquatic species) and more than 3,000 kinds of moths and butterflies.

Twelve light-filled rooms have hardwood floors and a glass wall onto a balcony with garden and mountain views. Each room is furnished with a cushioned bamboo chair, bamboo nightstands, twin beds, a desk, and in-room telephone (one handicapped accessible). You are practically guaranteed to see fiery-billed aracaris from your balcony; from a large terrace near the dining room see scarlet-thighed dacnis, violaceous trogons, blue-headed parrots, turquoise cotingas. Meals are served family style both in the dining room and on an outdoor terrace. Student groups and researchers have separate quarters, but everybody comes together at mealtimes for interesting conversation. A small gift shop has good publications about the garden and Las Cruces.

In this mid-elevation rain forest, there's little rainfall January to March, but the rest of the year brings heavy fog and afternoon rains. Rainiest months are September to November. Annual rainfall is 158 inches (4,000 mm). Daytime temperatures average 70ºF (21°C), at night, 60ºF (15°C). Las Cruces is part of the Amistad Biosphere Reserve.

Day visitors are welcome; admission $8, lunch $8 (prior reservation). Overnight rates are $75 per person double occupancy, including lodging and three meals.

Details: *3.5 miles (5.6 km) south of San Vito; for reservations 506/ 240-6696, fax 506/240-6783; reservas@ots.ac.cr, www.ots.ac.cr. At Las Cruces 506/773-4004, fax 506/773-3278. No reservation needed for day visit without lunch or guide. Take direct San José/San Vito bus, taxi to Las Cruces. From Golfito, go to Ciudad Neily; turn north to Agua Buena.*

Mirador de Quetzales

Quetzals you will see here, and much more. A pair nested not 50 yards from the cabins on my last visit. Perched in a nearby tree ready to take his turn on the nest, the male had almost cobalt blue on his head, turquoise on his back, and a glorious red breast. Then, as it clung on the trunk for seconds in early-morning sunlight before entering the nest, its head and back feathers were brilliant green.

Later, along a trail, a black-billed nightingale thrush gathered lichen and moss for a nest. Walk with one of the Serrano brothers in their 74-acre (30-ha) forest to see mountain cypress, oaks, fossils near a waterfall, trogons, hummingbirds, parakeets, tanagers, woodpeckers, finches. It's a marvel. Enjoy the company of young men who have grown up on this land homesteaded in 1948 by their father, Eddie, who first cut wood to feed his large family and then moved to dairy farming and cheese making (still going on). One fine day while waiting for the bus to take cheese to San José, he noticed tourists stopped by the highway to look at *páramo* plants and watch for quetzals. He had both on his farm and invited them to come, launching the family's venture into tourism and a profound change in their view of nature. Eddie is gone now, but his wife, eight children, and their children carry on, reforesting and protecting wildlife.

The rustic retreat looks like a tiny village, with family houses also on the hillside. The lodge has six bunk bed rooms and two spotless baths. Good smells emanate from the kitchen, with fresh milk, cheese, blackberries (*mora*), and rainbow trout from the farm on the menu, along with homemade bread. The dining room has a fireplace and wooden tables and benches, an eclectic décor of family photos, bird photographs, a chain saw, ox yoke, and paintings done by son Jorge. A bright flower garden of fuchsias, pansies, and hydrangeas decorates the entrance. Nearby are five A-frame cabins with private baths. Overnight is $34 per person, including lodging, dinner, breakfast, and guided walk. No credit cards.

You can look down on clouds here, and across Valley of the Saints. On a clear day, see Irazú and Barva Volcanoes—perhaps even the top of Arenal. Watch milking and cheese making, fish for trout. Guided forest walks on a two-mile (three-km) loop trail take about two hours, $5. Come on a day visit: Jorge offers express service for the hurried who just want to see a quetzal. My advice? Don't hurry.

Details: *700 meters from the Inter-American turnoff near km 70, then a half mile (one km) to farm; 506/381-8456, ciprotour@racsa.co.cr, www. ecotourism.co.cr. Take San José/ San Isidro bus and get off at km 70, pick-up by prior arrangement, $5.*

Nauyaca Falls

For a waterfall adventure, this one is tops. Mount up at the office on the road between San Isidro and Dominical and take off on a 3.5-mile (six-km) horseback ride to the falls. Stop for breakfast at Don Lulo's home down the mountain, usually natural fruit drinks, breads, delicious *tortas de maiz y queso* (a fried cheese/cornmeal delicacy). Visit a menagerie of toucans, *tepezcuintles*, parrots, and scarlet macaws near the outdoor dining area before you climb in the saddle again.

Don Lulo, whose real name is Braulio Jiménez Rojas, wife Ruth, and five children have called this home for almost 40 years, with about two-thirds of the 150 acres in tropical rain forest or areas reforested with native species. The trail goes through some of that forest, populated with birds, poison dart frogs, and monkeys, and crosses some pretty rivers. Leave horses at the hitchin' post and walk on a narrow trail for an upper view of the spectacular two-tiered falls: one 148 feet (45 m) high, the other 66 feet (20 m). At the bottom is a huge pool, 3,000 square feet of surface (1,000 sq. m), up to 20 feet deep (six m). Change into your bathing suit behind some of the huge boulders along its banks or in changing rooms. Float in inner tubes, use ropes to pull yourself under the falls for a vigorous massage—very vigorous—or venture behind them. The truly adventurous can dive from rock ledges beside the falls into the pool.

On the way back, stop again at the farmhouse for a tasty lunch of homemade Costa Rican food. The tour runs six to eight hours, $35 per person. Reservations must be made the day before so the right number of horses will be saddled up. Tours leave daily by 7:30 A.M.

Details: *13 miles (22 km) west of San Isidro, eight miles (13 km) east of Dominical; 506/771-3187, fax 506/771-2003, www.ecotourism. co.cr/NauyacaWaterfalls. Transport daily from Dominical.*

Rainbow Adventures

The approach to secluded palm-lined Cativo Beach from the sea is stunningly beautiful. Rainbow Adventures is nestled against the backdrop of a forested hillside. It looks like a painting, a tropical destination of dreams and daydreams. Can reality measure up to this vision? Yes.

The lodge is unique and the 800-acre (324-ha) private reserve species rich. Green honeycreepers perch on tree branches next to rooms, brilliant reds of scarlet-rumped tanagers flash in landscaped gardens, howler monkeys move through hillside trees, *pizotes* (coatis) roam the grounds. On one visit I witnessed five chestnut-mandibled toucans perched in a single tree and a continuing, stubborn battle between a red-lored parrot and a yellow-naped woodpecker over a hole in a tree trunk. On another, hiking with manager John Lovell, we came upon the biggest, most beautiful fer-de-lance snake either of us had ever seen. A growing bird list numbers more than 260 species. I regret to report that the resident scarlet macaw that posed for pictures met his demise in an unexpected encounter with an ocelot.

Pleasant surprises are more often the order of the day at Rainbow Adventures. Would you expect to find stained-glass windows and turn-of-the-century antiques in the main lodge? The first floor of the wooden structure has a lounge and dining room open to gardens, and an impressive air-conditioned library with thousands of books related to natural history. The second has three double rooms that open onto a large veranda. The third, the penthouse, is open on three sides, with stained-glass panels suspended in the open space between chest-high walls and the roof. Bidets in baths. Antiques were collected by owner Michael Medill of Oregon. Two secluded cabins have handwoven silk rugs in their open living areas and two bedrooms. Furniture is handmade by resident craftspeople. You'll find a tropical flower on your pillow when you arrive.

Gourmet meals are generally buffet-style, with herbs and vegetables from the organic garden and fruits such as pineapples, papayas, bananas, plantains, water apples, star fruit, and *anona.*

Fill your days with a variety of activities. Swim in the lovely freshwater pool or the warm, usually gentle beach waters. John can give you a good description of the trails, which range from one- to six-hour hikes, some easy and some for the fit. Trek to a 50-foot (15-m) waterfall, through forest to the small hydro project that supplies electricity, to a big swimming hole above the falls. Guided tours are $5 per hour, boots provided. Animals commonly seen include agouti, banded anteater, coati, kinkajou, raccoon, tayra, iguana, Jesus Christ lizard, armadillo, collared peccary, and howler, spider, and white-faced monkeys. Boating is $40 an hour per boat, including guide, snorkeling gear, and safety equipment, with options of birding on the Esquinas River, a dolphin tour, fishing, and snorkeling at a number of sites, where you may see parrot fish, angelfish, triggerfish, starfish, moray eels, octopus, sharks, sea turtles, or dolphins. Rent a kayak, visit a botanical garden. Linger on strategically placed forest benches and the platform at Sunset Point.

Per person rates, double occupancy, are $155 for second-floor lodge rooms, $165 for the penthouse, $175 for individual cabins. Included are round-trip transfer from Golfito, meals, snacks, snorkeling gear, jungle tour, nonalcoholic drinks, beer and wine at meals, and taxes. A portion of profits goes to the local school.

Details: *45-minute boat ride north of Golfito. Reserve in U.S. if possible; 800/565-0722, 503/690-7750; fax 503/690-7735; telephone/fax in Golfito, 506/775-0220, where John checks for messages on trips into town to meet guests; info@rainbowcostarica.com; www.rainbowcostarica.com.*

Savegre Mountain Lodge

Here they don't talk about "if" you see a quetzal, they say "when." Roland Chacón, one of owner Efraín Chacón's 11 children, told me where we would see one on our early morning tour, and we did. These resplendent birds are here year-round, but best months to see them are February through May. The Chacóns' place is famous for quetzals and for hospitality. Efraín, who has lived here 45 years, started out with a dairy farm. Then when people began to come for trout fishing in the Savegre River that flows through his property, he and his wife let visitors stay overnight in their home. Eventually they built a guest cabin. In 1980, ecotourists began to arrive in search of the quetzal.

The lodge, also known as Cabinas Chacón, now has 20 comfortable, simply furnished rooms, some with sitting rooms. A spacious restaurant/bar is popular not only with overnight but also day visitors and local folks. Bring your appetite: fresh trout on the menu. A glassed-in lounge next to the dining room looks out to the river and a dazzling display of hummingbirds. Most nights a fire blazes in the fireplace.

About three-fourths of the 740-acre (300-ha) Chacón farm is in primary forest. A five-mile (eight-km) hiking trail affords fabulous views of forest canopy and hundred-year-old oaks; ask about the thrilling six-hour, six-mile (10-km) Cerro de la Muerte trek from the Inter-American. Shorter, easier trails exist, one to a waterfall, and walks along the rushing river on the country road are terrific: flowering trees, squirrels, birds galore: quetzals in roadside trees along with woodpeckers, trogons, emerald toucanets, and iridescent hummingbirds (more than 169 bird species). You might see rabbits, porcupines, white-faced monkeys, white-tailed deer, frogs, and foxes. Local bilingual guides lead tours. Horseback riding and fly fishing for trout are options. Guests can visit apple, peach, and plum orchards and packing plant on the farm.

Rainiest months are generally October and November; little rain falls from December to June. Precipitation is 120 to 150 inches (3,046 to 3,807 mm) per year; temperatures rarely exceed 76°F (24°C). Bring insect repellent for hikes and a jacket for cool evenings.

Lodging, meals, and taxes are $70 per person. A three-day/two-night package from San José includes lodging, meals, bird-watching and waterfall tours, horseback riding, and fishing, $331 per person. If you are in the area, stop by for breakfast, lunch, and a tour, $22, or come on a one-day tour from San José, $77. VISA accepted.

Details: *In San Gerardo de Dota, 55 miles (89 km) south of San José. Turn west off the Inter-American at km 80 and continue 5.5 miles (nine km) on a steep, attention-getting road with hairpin curves and beautiful views; tel/fax 506/771-1732, ciprotur@racsa.co.cr, www.ecotourism.co.cr. Take San José/San Isidro bus and get off at km 80; the Chacóns can pick you up; $5 each for two. Transfers throughout Costa Rica.*

Tiskita Jungle Lodge

If Robinson Crusoe had come ashore here, he would never have wanted to leave. Birders and nature photographers can have a field day without leaving the lodge's landscaped grounds, to say nothing of treasures that wait along beach and in tide pools or in the surrounding 247-acre (100-ha) biological reserve. Hundreds of tropical fruit trees draw birds like a magnet. I watched three chestnut-mandibled toucans casually eat a fruit breakfast. In the same tree were blue-crowned manakins, a lineated woodpecker, and blue-gray and scarlet-rumped tanagers. A bird book left handy helps identify birds, and a bird list of more than 300 species lets you know if anyone has seen it before you. As you explore, take advantage of a butterfly list, illustrated booklets on Tiskita Rain Forest Trail and tide pools, and trail maps.

The tropical fruits trees are part of an experimental station that encompasses the most extensive collection of tropical rare and exotic fruits in Costa Rica. Since 1980 manager Peter Aspinall, who owns the lodge with brother John, has gathered plants from around the world. Birds and guests alike can have their fill of more than 100 varieties, tasting such delicacies as star fruit (*carambola* in Spanish), passion fruit (*maracuyá*), guava, *guanábana,* custard apple (*anona*), jackfruit, araza, abiu, and dozens of others not yet household words. Once, he reminds you, bananas and pineapples were considered

Tiskita Jungle Lodge dining room

393

rare and exotic.

At Tiskita you may cross paths with four species of monkeys (including the small squirrel monkey), coatis, pacas, white-lipped peccaries, anteaters, or cats such as the ocelot, jaguarundi, and margay. Well-marked trails go through farm and forest, and to the beach at the bottom of the hill. Choose a walk through orchards or rain-forest with a naturalist who helps you find and identify plants, mammals, birds, reptiles, and butterflies as well as learn about importance of each to man and environment. Trail maps facilitate later exploration on your own. Walk to pristine waterfalls and bathe in small pools in company of kingfishers and hummingbirds beneath a canopy of giant forest trees. Ocean swimming and snorkeling is best at low tide, which reveals tide pools with colorful fish, anemones, and other sea creatures. Go horseback riding, fishing, or surfing—not far is the longest left-breaking wave in the country, a 1,600-yard (1,440-m) run at Punta Pavones. Take a day trip by air to Sirena in Corcovado National Park, across the Golfo Dulce.

A reserve for indigenous peoples borders Tiskita, which is the Guaymi name for fish eagle. Dashing hats, shell jewelry, painted gourds, and attractive bags made by Guaymis are for sale in the gift shop. Profits go to Tiskita Foundation, which supports land preservation and school and health projects in neighboring villages.

The Aspinalls describe Tiskita as five-star rustic. Sixteen rooms have fans, reading lamps, and an electric plug in private bathrooms. Constructed of wood and natural stone, all have ocean and jungle views from porches and verandas. Semi-outdoor bathrooms allow bird-watching while you bathe—water at ambient temperature. Support columns in rooms are polished tree trunks; door handles are pieces of naturally sculptured wood. Furnishings are simple and comfortable, perfect for this natural setting. No smoking is allowed in lodge facilities.

From a covered hillside lookout furnished with lounging chairs and surrounded by heliconias and palms, the sounds of sea and land mix—lots of parakeets and hummingbirds. Swim in the nearby free-form pool. Look across the Pacific to the Osa Peninsula. Watch the sun slide into the ocean in the evenings and fireflies flash in the dark.

The impressive original farmhouse, built in 1979, has character.

It houses a small reference library, lounge area, and dining room/bar. Meals are served buffet-style—delicious, varied, and generous. Boots and umbrellas are available. Bring a flashlight for nighttime walks. Lights out at 9 P.M.

Though remote—radio contact only—it is possible to drive in; it's an interesting three-hour trip from the Inter-American into a frontier region, crossing the Coto River by ferry and fording streams.

Per person double rate is $120 for lodging, meals, guided walk, and taxes. A three-day/three-night package is $455 per person (double occupancy) including round-trip flights from Golfito or Puerto Jiménez.

Details: 37 miles (60 km) south of Golfito on Pacific coast; 506/296-8125; fax 506/296-8133, tiskita@racsa.co.cr, www.tiskita-lodge.co.cr. Daily Golfito/Punta Banco bus passes Tiskita entrance. It leaves Punta Banco at 5 A.M., Golfito at 2 P.M.; $3 (plus small fee for river ferry). Check about road conditions in rainy season.

GUIDES AND OUTFITTERS

Brunca Tours in San Isidro de El General, 506/771-6096, fax 506/771-2003, ciprotour@racsa.co.cr, www.ecotourism.co.cr, has joined southern destinations in an exciting array of tours from San José. A three-day/two-night includes a quetzal trip to San Gerardo de Dota, rafting on the General River, and hiking and birding in private Las Quebradas Reserve, which has 413 bird species and a butterfly garden, $535 per person for two. Combine San Gerardo with Chirripó in a four-day trip for $595 per person. In a six-day tour, visit San Gerardo, Nauyaca Falls, Wilson Botanical Garden, the mangroves of the Sierpe River, and Corcovado, $1,222 each. A three-day rafting adventure includes overnight camping, $340 each, minimum three.

For camping gear in the Chirripó area, contact **Proyecto Visión al Futuro,** a small women's group that has U.S. equipment: sleeping bags, $2 a night; four-person tents, $4 a night; backpacks, $3; gas stoves; canteens; and ponchos. Get directions at the San Gerardo Park station: Virgita Mora's house is about a block north of the *pulpería* in

Herradura. Spanish speakers can call 506/771-1199, at the *pulpería,* and someone will fetch Virgita. She also rents rustic rooms, $7.

Selva Mar is in San Isidro de El General on the road to Dominical, 506/771-4582, fax 506/771-1903, selvamar@racsa.co.cr, does an admirable job of arranging lodging and tours, especially to destinations without telephones such as lodges south of Dominical and in Chirripó and Cerro de la Muerte; radio communication is still a lifeline. Caño Island and Corcovado tours are arranged, and Selva Mar has excellent Chirripó adventures, from three days/two nights for $368 per person for two to five-day/four nights for $529. Included are round-trip transfers from San Isidro, bilingual guide, males, lodging, park fee, sleeping bag, porter service, and taxes as well as guided hikes in the park. Loads of good park information on Selva Mar's website at www.chirripo. com. Combine Chirripó with rafting on the General River and/or Corcovado and Caño Island. Friendly, knowledgeable staff do custom trip planning.

Ree Strange Sheck

Mushroom artistry on the Osa Peninsula

Zancudo Boat Tours, tel/fax 506/776-0012, loscocos@ loscocos.com, www.loscocos.com provides water taxi service to and from Golfito and Puerto Jiménez and a number of half-day tours in the $40 range. One is a Coto River wildlife trip through farmland to tidal estuaries in pure jungle: see birds, crocodiles, monkeys, otters, orchids, heliconias. A Golfo Dulce boat trip includes Casa de Orquídeas, the botanical garden. Susan and Andrew arrange Osa Peninsula and Corcovado trips from basic to deluxe from the Golfito/Zancudo area. They also have delightful

Los Cocos cabins; see under "Lodging."

Check out Chapter 3 for other operators with river trips on the General and Chirripó adventures (Ocarina and Camino Travel are good).

CAMPING

For camping at **La Amistad** and **Chirripó National Parks** and at the private reserve of **Genesis II,** see descriptions of these destinations under "Nature and Adventure Sights."

In San Gerardo de Dota, land of rivers and quetzals, **Los Ranchos,** 506/771-2376, has delightful campsites in landscaped gardens around a small lake, with covered picnic areas that include grills, sink, and water, even an electric outlet. The bathhouse is spotless: toilet, sink, and hot-water shower. Three trails go through surrounding forest; hike 30 minutes to a beautiful waterfall. Socorro and Fernando Chacón own this piece of paradise: check in at their house (white with orange trim) across the road and up the hill. Four-person tents rent for $7 per night; for about $10 get the tent, use of a boat for the lake, and a horseback ride. Los Ranchos is just beyond Savegre Mountain Lodge.

LODGING

Avalon Private Reserve, cellular 506/380-2107, tel/fax 506/770-1341, avalonreserve@yahoo.com, is two miles (3.5 km) west of the Inter-American at Division, just past km 107. What awaits are 375 acres (152 ha) of cloud forest, fantastic mountain views, lodging, hiking trails, and a hillside hot tub with daytime views that stretch to the Osa Peninsula and Caño Island; the nighttime panorama is star filled. Entertainment here is provided by nature. More than 100 species of birds here include collared trogons, quetzals, three-wattled bellbirds, sulfur-winged parakeets, black-faced solitaires, sooty-capped bush tanagers, black-cheeked warblers. Expect to find beautiful orchids and butterflies in this high land. A two-hour guided tour is $5 per person. Rooms in two mountain cabins with porches and shared baths are $35 and $45, double occupancy; nearby are two private cabins, $55. All have heat. Ask about low-budget packages in shared rooms and about volunteer opportunities. Meals are served family-style: breakfast $5, lunch $4, dinner $9. Day visits are $3. No credit cards. The two miles of unpaved road is accessible year-round, gorgeous country.

At Zancudo Beach on the Golfo Dulce, **Cabinas Los Cocos,** tel/fax 506/776-0012, loscocos@loscocos.com, www.loscocos.com, has four terrific cabins on a long, palm-lined beach. Cabins have kitchens, fan, and a deck with hammock and handmade chairs. Choose either a quaintly restored banana company house, $40, or a thatched bungalow with polished tropical hardwood floor, $52. Owners Susan and Andrew Robertson can suggest restaurants on Playa Zancudo when you don't want to cook, and small grocery stores are nearby. They also offer free use of bicycles and boogie boards, and free laundry. Kayak in an estuary, half day for $40. They operate Zancudo Boat Tours: see under "Guides and Outfitters." Boat transfer from Golfito, 30 minutes, is $20 for two. Zancudo is accessible by car from Golfito.

Hotel del Sur, 506/771-3033, fax 506/771-0527, htlsur@racsa .co.cr, www.ecotourism.co.cr/hotelsdelsur, is 2.5 miles (four km) south of San Isidro on the Inter-American Highway. Sit by the large pool and gaze at the impressive Talamanca Mountains above the trees and enjoy colorful landscaped grounds. The 48 rooms are on two floors around a pretty garden with a fountain; 10 cabins for up to five persons each are farther back on the property. Deluxe rooms, two queen-sized beds and air conditioning, have carved wooden doors, white tile floors, and pretty watercolors; doubles $40 to $65 (two are handicapped accessible). Carpeted standard rooms —plainer, double and single bed—are $35. Cabins, with refrigerators, are $55. In addition to swimming pools, there are tennis and volleyball courts and bicycles for rent. A full-service tour operator is on-site. Airport pickup is available.

Las Gaviotas, 506/775-0062, fax 506/775-0544, lasgaviotas@hotmail.com, www.lasgaviotashotel.com, is on the main road into Golfito. Pleasant open-air restaurants and good food and swimming pools for children and adults are next to the gulf. The 21 rooms and suites and three bungalows are in tropical gardens with ocean views. Rooms, a bit dark because they open onto covered individual porches, are brightened by quilted bedspreads; doubles $42 to $54. Bungalows have two bedrooms and a living room/kitchen area with a hot plate and refrigerator, $84. All have telephones and cable TV. Near shore are remains of a World War II minesweeper that now serves as a picturesque roost for land and sea birds. Fishing and nature tours arranged.

In Canaan de Rivas, beautiful back country, is **Río Chirripó Pacífico Mountain Lodge,** 506/771-6096, fax 506/771-2003, ciprotour@racsa.co.cr, www.ecotourism.co.cr/ChirripoPacifico. Eight rooms are in a two-story hillside building above the Chirripó River. Only an hour from San Isidro, this place feels a peaceful million miles from anywhere. Rooms have windows on two sides to bring in the fantastic outdoors. Visit thermal waters in Herradura, a 30-minute walk away; hike in the mountains; go horseback riding; sign up for five area tours. Doubles are $45 including breakfast. The dining room is spectacular—see for yourself.

Talari Mountain Lodge, tel/fax 506/771-0341, talaripz@racsa.co.cr, is five miles (eight km) northeast of San Isidro on the road to Chirripó. Gracious and attentive hosts Pilar and Jan describe themselves as a *tica*-Dutch blend. Eight cabins are named for different area birds, with a painting of that bird decorating an outside wall. More than 176 species of birds have been identified on Talari's 20 acres (eight ha). The eight rooms are light and comfortable; double $48, including breakfast and taxes. Walk-ins with this book get 10 percent off if payment is in cash. Color-coded short trails go to the General River, through orchard (35 varieties of fruit) and secondary forest to an area being reforested with native species. The garden pool has an area for children; The pleasant restaurant has expansive views and good food, some grown at Talari: corn, beans, *yuca*, and a variety of fruits, including star fruit and cherimoya (*anona*). Don't miss the guava ice cream. On Fridays, enjoy music with dinner—Jan plays their Russian piano. The restaurant is open to the public Friday and Saturday from 6 to 9 P.M. and Sunday and holidays from noon to 7 P.M. Jan and Pilar offer a five-day Talari/Chirripó package for $215 per person and provide a great printed description of area attractions: they arrange visits to Nauyaca Waterfall and horseback riding along fantastic Blanco River. Free San Isidro/Talari transfer with advance notice.

At San Gerardo de Dota, **Trogon Lodge,** 506/223-7490, fax 506/255-4039, at lodge 506/771-1266, mawamba@racsa.co.cr, www.crica.com/mawamba, has mountain air, a rushing river, forest, flowers, cabins, and trout ponds, creating a living landscape painting. Nights can be chilly at 7,000 feet (2,134 m), so each room has an electric heater and the dining room has a cast-iron woodstove that radiates warmth. Twenty cozy rooms are in 10 cabins on slopes above the Savegre River. Striped comforters, reading lamps, and glass windows with louvered shutters make for comfort in this highland retreat; double $58. Meals are served family style: breakfast is $7, lunch or dinner $9. While eating, watch seven species of hummingbirds feed outside. Quetzals are seen on the landscaped grounds. A walk on trails within the 74-acre (30-ha) property may allow glimpses of acorn woodpeckers, collared and orange-belled trogons, black guan, emerald toucanets, or flame-colored tanagers. A guided walk is $10 for guests. Bikes and horses are $10 an hour. Try fishing in trout ponds or hike and ride horses to a waterfall. A one-day package from San José is $72. A three-day/two-night is $237 per person. Packages include transport, meals, guided walk; multiday tour adds lodging. Trogon Lodge belongs to Grupo Mawamba.

Between San Isidro and Domincal is delightful **Villas Paraíso Tropical,** 506/771-8182, paraisot@racsa.co.cr. Seven two-room bungalows are set in landscaped ground, and have big baths, good mattresses, and a pleasant living area; doubles $45 to $55. Régulo González and family are caring hosts. Go to Nauyaca Waterfalls (office is across the road), beaches, or horseback riding. Small trails on the mountainside behind the lodge have good views. On the property, see chestnut mandibled toucans, spider and white-faced monkeys, tanagers, and free-flying macaws that live at Nauyaca. Whether you stay here or not, don't miss eating in the pretty openair restaurant: *tico*/Mexican food, filet mignon, fruit shakes, pasta, a great club sandwich. The hotel is 5.5 miles (nine km) from Dominical, 14 miles (23 km) from San Isidro.

At **Zancudo Beach Club,** 506/776-0097, fax 506/776-0052, zbc@costarica.net, www.zancudobeachclub.com, you can go parasailing, waterskiing, sportfishing or take jungle tours horseback rides or day trips to Pavones to surf. Gary and Debbie are friendly, helpful hosts. Three cute two-room cabins have refrigerator, microwave, and coffeemaker, bright tropical murals on exterior walls, double $50; each of two rooms is $30 for two. Bicycles free. A terrific restaurant has pizza, fresh fish, fajitas, pasta, and nightly specials that might be Thai, French, Japanese, Korean.

FOOD

As you cross Cerro de la Muerte, typical restaurants offer *gallo pinto*, papusas, *gallos* (tortillas filled with whatever—usually meat, potatoes, or *arracache*), or cheese or bean empanadas. Top a meal off with a glass of stout Costa Rican coffee or *agua dulce*. At km 60 and km 77, rub shoulders with local folks at **Chesperitos. Las Georginas** (km 95) also has good food, buffet-style.

In Golfito, **Samoa del Sur,** 506/775-0233, is the place to eat; you'll spot its huge, distinctive, thatched roof on the shores of the gulf. The open-air restaurant/bar is a gathering place, fresh seafood a specialty, but there's a full range of offerings. It also offers attractive lodging.

In Zancudo, have the famous fish burger at **Sol y Mar,** 506/776-0014, or tempura dishes, nachos, tropical fruit shakes, nightly specials, and home fries for breakfast.

In San Isidro, **El Tenedor,** 506/771-0881, has local flavor and good food,; open 11 A.M. to 11 P.M., closed Monday. Find pastas, pizza, steaks, and rice dishes. Its half a block north of the plaza. If you crave Chinese food, **Bar-Restaurante Excelente** at the corner of the plaza, 506/771-8157, is a good choice. Try the Canasta de Mariscos, a seafood "basket." Nice atmosphere, open 11 A.M. to 11 P.M.

On the road to Chirripó, colorful **Rancho La Botija,** 506/382-3052, specializes in typical Costa Rican and Mexican food. The open-air restaurant is open from 8 A.M. to 5 P.M. Décor focuses on items from a traditional sugar mill *(trapiche)*.

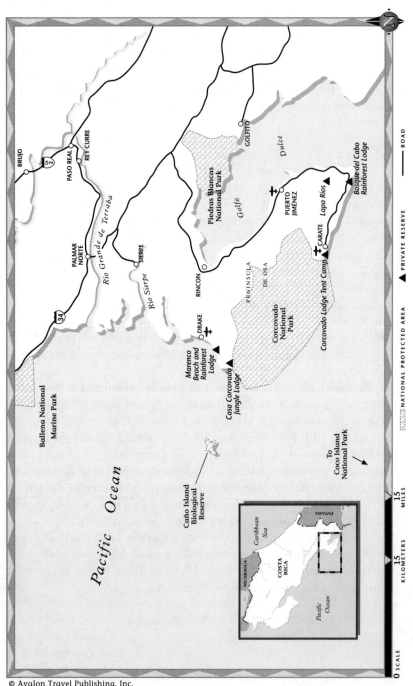

BRUJO

PASO REAL

REY CURRE

PALMAR NORTE

SIERPE

Rio Grande de Terraba

Rio Sierpe

DRAKE

Marenco Beach and Rainforest Lodge

Casa Corcovado Jungle Lodge

Ballena National Marine Park

Caño Island Biological Reserve

Pacific Ocean

Piedras Blancas National Park

GOLFITO

Golfo Dulce

RINCON

PUERTO JIMÉNEZ

Lapa Rios

Bosque del Cabo Rainforest Lodge

CARATE

PENINSULA DE OSA

Corcovado National Park

Corcovado Lodge Tent Camp

To Coco Island National Park

NATIONAL PROTECTED AREA   PRIVATE RESERVE   ▲   ROAD

0 SCALE   15 MILES   15 KILOMETERS

NICARAGUA   Caribbean Sea   COSTA RICA   PANAMA   Pacific Ocean

© Avalon Travel Publishing, Inc.

CHAPTER 15

Osa Peninsula, Caño Island, Coco Island

Large expanses of lowland tropical rain forest remain in this remote area that juts out from the southern Pacific coast, though inroads are creeping in to both forest and former isolation. It feels plenty remote, however—if cellular telephones don't work, radio is the main communication—and the forest is rich habitat for a spectacular array of fauna. Roads peter out along the edges, with access to many destinations limited to boats, hiking, horseback, or small planes. Fabled Corcovado National Park is here, along with wilderness lodges from rustic to tropical elegant set in extraordinary private nature reserves. Mountains, ocean, gulf, estuaries, and rivers—the natural wildness of the place—make for a nature/adventure paradise. Caño Island Biological Reserve, off the shore of the Osa Peninsula, and Coco Island National Park, which lies 331 miles (532 km) to the west, are also described in this chapter.

LAY OF THE LAND

For travelers, there are two main ports of entry to the Osa: Puerto Jiménez, on the southeastern shore across the Golfo Dulce (Sweet Gulf) from Golfito and the mainland, and Drake Bay, on the northwestern Pacific shore. Most visitors choose either a southern Osa experience or a northern one, both with access to the peninsula's centerpiece, Corcovado National Park.

Puerto Jiménez (population 7,267) is the largest town on the peninsula and has phone service, which makes it both a communication and transportation hub (access by road, sea, and air) for the southern region; think about it—the first car arrived here in the mid 70s. It is a jumping-off place for exceptional natural history/ adventure destinations. The Osa Conservation Area has an office here with information on Corcovado National Park. South of town and around the tip of the peninsula are some fabulous private nature reserves. You'll find restaurants, a bank, post office, tour operators, and small hotels in and near town. The passenger ferry from Golfito docks here.

Drake Bay, named for Sir Francis Drake, who sailed these waters more than 400 years ago, is a center for visits to Corcovado's San Pedrillo area, to Caño Island, and the Sierpe mangroves. Devote your time to snorkeling, diving, fishing, hiking, boat trips,

Ree Strange Sheck

Crystal-clear tide pool at Drake Bay

and horseback rides. Though the Drake Bay area is remote, accessible by charter flights or boat, a growing number of nature/adventure sites exist from the Sierpe River to the northwestern edge of Corcovado National Park. A road inching its way from Rincón now reaches as far as Drake's small landing field at the tiny town of Drake. Some see the road as a benefit to allow easier access; others fear it will increase logging and disrupt the peace of this special place. Time will tell. In the meantime, mountain bikers and hikers take advantage of it. Don't attempt to drive that road without checking on conditions first.

Most travelers still arrive via the Sierpe River, a destination in itself, with the chance to see kingfishers, tiger-herons, crocodiles, turtles, parrots, monkeys, blue herons, Muscovy ducks, and perhaps a roseate spoonbill. On one trip, a hard rain in the mountains had brought an avalanche of water hyacinths downriver, transforming the water into a floating garden—beautiful but tricky for navigation. The mouth of the Sierpe is treacherous at times, but lodges have seasoned boatmen. Be aware that boat landings on beaches will be wet—few lodges have docks—so come prepared to wade ashore. Once here, you can move about the area by boat and by foot. From Drake there is a path through forest and along beach to areas south, best attempted at low tide. I have walked as far as Marenco. Whether you do the long hike or not, don't miss the picturesque hanging bridge over the Agujitas River.

NATURE AND ADVENTURE ACTIVITIES

Adventure begins with getting here, and it doesn't stop till departure. From bases in the northern or southern regions of the peninsula, you can hike for hours or days, snorkel and dive in spectacular waters around Caño Island, enjoy birding (400 species), go horseback riding on beaches and through forest to secluded waterfalls, camp out, fish, surf, mountain bike, explore pristine beaches and interesting tide pools, try sea kayaking, visit a butterfly farm, take a canopy tour, meander through mangrove canals, see dolphins, and whale watch (humpbacks migrate

Hanging bridge over the Agujitas River, near Drake

Ree Strange Sheck

December through April). There's lots to do, but the pace here is relaxed. Sunset is an event, so don't miss it. At Coco Island, hike trails through beautiful forest and snorkel and dive to observe stunning undersea life.

A word to the wise: peninsula trails are up and down, with numerous streams and rivers to cross. Check about tides before setting off on coastal treks; the beach disappears in places at high tide, and river mouths easy to wade at low tide can be dangerous or impassable hours later.

FLORA AND FAUNA

All four species of monkeys found in Costa Rica are on the Osa Peninsula, along with crocodiles, sea turtles, agoutis, coatis, poison dart frogs, boa constrictors, more than 500 species of trees, pumas, army ants, sloths, orchids, and more, much more. Large mammals such as Baird's tapir and jaguar live here, and groups of white-lipped peccaries, uncommon elsewhere, still move through these forests. As for birds, prepare for a visual feast: toucans, trogons, hummingbirds, kingfishers, honeycreepers, antbirds, caracaras, elainias, hawks, herons, kingbirds, manakins, and tanagers. The black-cheeked ant-tanager is found only in Costa Rica and only in lowlands around the Golfo Dulce.

The most famous bird here is perhaps the scarlet macaw (*Ara macao*), *lapa roja* in Spanish—the largest of the Neotropical parrots. Once plentiful in lowlands along both coasts, these showy red-, blue-, and yellow-plumed creatures are now on the endangered species list due to destruction of lowland forest and capture for the pet trade. Often raucous, the birds can be fairly silent when feeding in the canopy. With large, powerful bills they extract nuts and seeds from unripe fruit, their main food, though they also eat leaves and fruit pulp. They are seed predators, not seed dispersers, since they digest plant embryos. Listen for sounds of discarded pieces of seeds or fruit falling from the canopy to the ground as you walk on a trail.

Macaws reach sexual maturity at five years, and a macaw pair may remain monogamous for years. Nesting is from December to July, with the female laying one or two eggs high in cavities in tall trees. They tend to reuse the same trees year after year. Along with preservation of habitat, another strategy for macaw protection is placement of boxes to serve as artificial nesting sites in areas that lack sufficient nesting trees—boxes are put in protected areas to reduce poaching of chicks. Captive breeding and release programs are also underway in Costa Rica.

Other places to see scarlet macaws are around the Tarcoles River and Carara National Park. Some are being reintroduced into Piedras Blancas National Park on the Golfo Dulce, and a few still exist in dry forest around Palo Verde National Park.

VISITOR INFORMATION

Ranger stations at Corcovado are good sources of information for park activities. Another is staff at private reserves, lodges, and tour companies.

GETTING THERE

Puerto Jiménez has access by air, boat, and road. Scheduled airline service is daily from San José and Golfito. A passenger launch makes a daily round trip between Golfito and Puerto Jiménez. If driving, turn west off the Inter-American Highway at Chacarita and follow the paved road through Rincón around the Golfo Dulce to Puerto Jiménez. A four-wheel-drive dirt road continues to Carate on the southwestern Pacific shore, passable most of the year.

Access to Drake Bay and points down the western shore of the peninsula is by air charter to Drake (40 minutes), by boat from other Pacific ports or from via the Sierpe River. To get to Sierpe, fly to Palmar Sur on daily scheduled flights or take a bus; then go by taxi to Sierpe, nine miles (15 km).

Most private reserve and hotel packages include transfers. Refer to Appendix A for bus and airline schedules.

NATURE AND ADVENTURE SIGHTS

Southern Osa

Bosque del Cabo Rainforest Lodge

If you like nighttime by candlelight, scarlet macaws flying overhead, a private outdoor garden shower, enchanting bungalows, sandy beaches, tall forest, and the sound of the sea, then Bosque del Cabo is for you. Perched on a cliff above Matapalo Beach, where the Golfo Dulce meets the Pacific, this small wilderness lodge and 400-acre (162-ha) private reserve has a winning combination of creature comforts and adventure. For the naturalist, there's a continuous parade of scarlet macaws and other tropical birds easily seen (350 species); monkeys, coatis, and agoutis appear on forest trails; whales and dolphins traverse neighborhood waters. From my veranda I once counted a feeding flock of 15 chestnut-mandibled toucans while howler monkey howls mixed with the sounds of the surf and a hummingbird whispered by my ear.

For full-fledged adventure, there are trails from easy to challenging that lead to the beach, tide pools, caves, and a tidal lagoon, or to a 75-foot (23 m) waterfall hidden in dense rain forest, or to a creek—poison dart frogs, gorgeous primary forest, waterfalls. View the canopy via zipline to a 110-foot (33.5 m) high platform. Go horseback riding, sailing, surfing (instruction available), sportfishing. Sign up for the sunset kayaking trip in the Golfo Dulce, for snorkeling at gulf reefs to see parrot fish, snapper, flag fish, small sharks, rays, flying fish, moray eels, oysters, or for sea kayaking. Boat trips go up the Tigre River or across the gulf to a botanical garden. Guided trips go to Corcovado, either the La Leona entrance or via a charter flight to Sirena. On a night walk, you may observe kinkajous, wolf spiders, tree frogs, glowworms, and fireflies ($10 per person). Guides are available for standard hikes or custom hikes, $5 per hour per person.

Creature comforts? This *is* Shangri La. Nine thatched bungalows above the sea are set in gardens of tropical fruits and flowers with forest as a backdrop. Mosquito netting drapes gracefully over comfortable beds, doors fold back to open the inside to sea and forest, a modern bath adjoins the outdoor shower. Four deluxe bungalows have king-size beds, wraparound decks, one with a stunning Santa-Fe style outdoor living area, and solar electricity with candlelight backup. Candles or lanterns warm the darkness in the other four—no electricity. Standard bungalows are $109 per person, double occupancy; deluxe, $129 per person, meals, service, and taxes included. An attractive two-bedroom house with furnished kitchen is $1,100/week, three-day minimum.

In a secluded forest studio nearby, let Fia give you a massage, $50 for one hour. And you can also relax in the pool or in a hammock at the poolside bar.

Food is outstanding, served in an open-air restaurant. Because of solar-powered electricity and lantern backup, there are no noisy generators. Local fruits and vegetables are incorporated in the meals, which include both typical Costa Rican and international fare with flair. Owner Philip Spier and staff give first-class attention to guests.

Details: *10 miles (16 km) south of Puerto Jiménez; tel/fax 506/735-5206, fax 506/735-5043, phil@bosquedelcabo.com, www.bosquedelcabo. com. Roundtrip transfer from Puerto Jiménez, $25.*

Corcovado Lodge Tent Camp

Fantasies of camping in the rain forest? Here's a chance to do it with enough challenge to satisfy an adventurous spirit and the surprise of some earthly comforts. The trip usually involves a flight in a small plane to Carate and a 30- to 45-minute walk along a forest-fringed beach on the southern Pacific coast to the tent camp. That's for openers.

But then new arrivals at Corcovado Lodge Tent Camp, owned by Costa Rica Expeditions, discover the campsite in a clearing between jungle-like forest and palm-fringed beach; 20 roomy 10-by-10-foot tents (with straight walls for plenty of headroom) are pitched on wooden platforms. Furnished with two single beds—a welcoming tropical flower on the pillow—each has chairs on a covered front porch only steps from the surf. Two bathhouses have four showers, four toilets, and four hand basins in each. A screened-in thatched dining room and a thatched hammock house and bar a few steps up the hill complete this jungle enclave. Electricity from a small generator is limited to certain hours in dining area and bath houses, so this is flashlight country after dark—along with moonlight.

Neighbors on this 400-acre (162-ha) private reserve contiguous to mammoth Corcovado National Park include magnificent scarlet macaws, coatis, tayras, scarlet-rumped tanagers, snakes, hermit hummers, colorful poison-dart frogs, four species of monkeys, cats, tapirs, sea turtles, butterflies, banaquits (watch for them in gardens drinking from heliconia blossoms), and toucans.

A self-guided loop trail is free to guests. On the two- to three-hour, mainly easy hike, my group saw a granddaddy of a howler, white-faced monkeys, spider monkeys with a baby, a chestnut-backed antbird (strikingly blue eyes) performing eye-catching flights to draw us away from its trailside nest, a black-hooded trogon, coatis, poison dart frogs. Other hiking tours range from easy to difficult. Two take trekkers into Corcovado: one a strenuous four-hour hike through La Leona entrance to the Madrigal River and beach for $25 plus park fee; another two hours farther through forest and along the beach to Salsipuedes, where visitors relax in tidal pools and sometimes see flocks of scarlet macaws, for $40 plus park fee.

An afternoon horseback ride to the tip of the peninsula offers breathtaking views of macaws squawking in flight overhead or feeding in almond trees, as well as of roosting sites for egrets, herons, and roseate spoonbills. Top it all off with sunset on the Pacific, $35.

If the tent doesn't offer enough adventure, spend the night on a platform the equivalent of eight stories above the forest floor. Observe diurnal creatures winding down and nocturnal ones moving onto the stage. Maximum is two people plus the guide for this extraordinary experience, $125 per person. If you are more of a diurnal creature yourself, ascend into the canopy by day to enjoy its incredible biodiversity—still a frontier for scientific research, $69. The platform is in a 200-foot (61-m) guapinol tree. Spider monkeys swing noisily through the trees to feed. Toucans, masked tityras, honeycreepers, hummers, hawks drop by. A personal platform highlight was the flight of a turquoise cotinga across the "arboreal pasture" in front and of a white morpho butterfly. Participants in a canopy expedition are hoisted to the platform and brought back to the forest floor in a bosun's chair—plenty of adventure with a level of comfort. Don't pass up leisure time on the deck of the bar, where birdlife is astounding—red-legged honeycreepers an arm's length away—and where we watched a seven-foot-long (two-m) boa constrictor shed its skin as it rubbed against plants in the garden below. Guided walks are available on-site and at Corcovado. La Leona entrance is a 10-minute walk, offering a fabulous opportunity for solo or guided exploration.

For a tent and two meals a day, arriving on your own, it is $57 per person double occupancy. A three-day Rain Forest Odyssey is from $699 per person, double occupancy, including lodging, meals, half-day canopy platform trip, hikes in Corcovado and at lodge, round trip air from San José, transfers, and park fee. With a bilingual naturalist guide, the rate is $999.

Details: A half-hour hike north of Carate; 506/257-0766, fax 506/257-1665, ecotur@expeditions.co.cr, www.expeditions.co.cr. Dirt road from Puerto Jiménez to Carate, where cars stop and hiking begins; taxis available in Puerto Jiménez. Charter flights to Carate airstrip. Packages include air charters or ground transport.

Corcovado National Park

Corcovado is a remote park. It's big—103,258 acres (41,788 ha) of land; 5,930 acres (2,400 ha) of marine habitat—and it is marvelous.

A park administrator reported counting 150 scarlet macaws flying in two groups near the Madrigal River. Five hundred species of trees are here, including probably the tallest in the country, a ceiba or kapok tree that soars to 230 feet (70 m). Eight habitat types exist: montane forest, cloud forest, alluvial plains forest, swamp, palm forest, mangrove, and rocky and sandy vegetation.

Trails link four major park stations: Sirena, La Leona, and San Pedrillo, on the Pacific coast; and Los Patos, inland near the Rincón River. They range from 4 to 15 miles long (6 to 24 km). Two popular routes are Los Patos to Sirena, 11 miles (18 km), and La Leona to Sirena, 10 miles (16 km). The hike from San Pedrillo to Sirena is not advisable except from December to April (drier months, when rivers are lower). Shorter trails fan out from stations. At Sirena, seven trails offer half-mile to three-mile (one- to five-km) forays into the forest. With advance notice, visitors can eat at ranger stations; breakfast is $4, lunch or dinner $7.

On trails or at stations, particularly Sirena, you can encounter scientific researchers studying everything from how jacamars know not to eat toxic butterflies to life habits of the squirrel monkey. Research findings are key to long-term protection of species and habitats.

Many visitors experience Corcovado on day trips: by boat to the San Pedrillo entrance from the Drake Bay area and to La Leona from the southern end of the peninsula, about a two-mile (three-km) hike from Carate. Some charter flights make Sirena a day-visit possibility.

The Pacific adds a marine component. Sperm whales pass by, marine turtles nest on its beaches, dolphins play, and there's a live coral reef at Salsipuedes. Among endangered species protected at Corcovado are five species of cat (including jaguar), giant anteaters, sloths, and the harpy eagle. Identified so far are 367 species of birds, 500 of trees, 104 of mammals, and 117 species of amphibians and reptiles. Visitors sometimes see the elusive tapir and herds of white-lipped peccaries. Near the Madrigal River, a park ranger and I came upon a group of coatis eating turtle eggs from a raided nest, and crabs munching on turtle hatchlings; along the trail white-faced monkeys fed from a wasp nest. Be quiet as you walk; be ready for the unexpected.

Corcovado has interesting human history. Local lore holds that Cubans trained along its beaches before the Bay of Pigs and that Sandinistas briefly used it for training before the overthrow of Nicaragua's president Anastasio Somoza in 1979. Miners invaded its confines to pan for gold in the 1980s but were evicted in 1986. Again in 1995, park personnel evicted miners. Before the park was established in 1975, hardy pioneers carved out small farms in the virgin forest.

Much of the terrain is hilly, rising from deserted coastal beaches. Mid-December to mid-April is the driest period; average annual rainfall in the mountains is 217 inches (5,500 mm). Average temperature is 79°F (26°C), and elevation goes from sea level to 1,932 feet (782 m).

Get information about Corcovado at the Osa Conservation Area office in Puerto Jiménez. Camping is permitted in designated areas next to park stations, by reservation only, and Sirena has dorm-style rooms for visitors. Bring repellent and, for overnights, mosquito netting.

Details: *Telephone hotline 506/192, 506/735-5282,/fax 506/735-5276. Open daily 8 to 4 P.M., office in Puerto Jiménez 8 A.M. to 4 P.M. Monday through Friday; admission is $6, camping $6 per person per day. Reservations essential for camping or meals at stations. The southeastern sectors of the park are entered through Los Patos, a 7.5-mile (12-km) trek from La Palma north of Puerto Jiménez and south of Rincón, or at La Leona ranger station, a 30-minute walk from Carate. From Drake Bay, access is by boat to the San Pedrillo station. Charter flights land at Sirena station. Area lodges and private reserves arrange tours; agencies offer packages.*

Lapa Ríos

Owners of this 1,000-acre (405-ha) private reserve, John and Karen Lewis, have proven that luxury and wilderness can mix in a thoughtful, conscious way. They set out to protect this piece of rain forest through a small, upscale ecotourism project designed to have minimal impact on the environment and to contribute to local development, education, and employment. It is working.

A spectacular main lodge houses reception, restaurant, bar, and an outdoor terrace. Guests look up at the underside of the 50-foot

(15-m) thatched palm roof. The intrepid can climb a hardwood circular stairway that makes four complete turns to an observation walkway three stories high. A 360-degree view encompasses forest and the sea 350 feet (107 m) below. A cliffside swimming pool has dynamite ocean views.

Fourteen striking bungalows are on three ridges below the main lodge. The first two are accessible to lodge and pool by wheelchair ramp. My secluded bungalow was 100 steps down. Each has a peaked thatched roof and gleaming floors of tropical hardwood. Double louvered doors open onto a large, very private deck, patio garden with an outdoor shower, and sea and forest views beyond words. A large indoor shower is open to forest views. Locally made furnishings are primarily of bamboo. Each room contains two double beds draped with mosquito netting, a desk, chairs with bright cushions, and ceiling fans.

Carbonara Beach down from the lodge is safe for swimming and has tide pools. Surfers find good waves nearby, and surf instruction is available. Among species here are small green-and-black poison-dart frogs, army ants and the birds that follow their marches, Costa Rica's four species of monkeys, woodcreepers and woodpeckers, boa constrictors, coatis, toucans and trogans, agoutis, euphonias, ocelots, and hawks. A self-guided trail free for guests features 18 points of interest. Local guides earn a living leading Lapa Ríos tours, tours with titles that help describe this place: Wild Waterfalls, Rain Forest Ridge (for the hardy), Early Birds (315 bird species), Starfish (beach and tide pools), Medicine Walk (led by a shaman guide). Take a night walk and see the shining eyes of nocturnal creatures. Ride a horse, fish (deep sea or shore), snorkel, or have a massage in a private forest overlook. Tours are $20 to $30 per person.

Plant a tree for $25, which helps support a Lapa Ríos reforestation program. On Tuesday and Thursday, accompany Karen to the Carbonara school to share songs and stories with the children, a school the Lewises helped start and continue to support as it makes a difference in lives of rural children. Lapa Ríos has received numerous ecotourism awards.

Off-site tours include a one-day visit via taxi and then chartered plane to Sirena in Corcovado ($550 for two), and trips across the

Golfo Dulce to visit a botanical garden or explore the Esquinas River.

Meals are a treat; they look and taste great. Desserts are scrumptious. Restaurant staff members are well trained and friendly. The restaurant is open to the public. Doubles are $182 per person including lodging, meals, service, and taxes.

Details: *10 miles (six km) south of Puerto Jiménez via unpaved road; 506/735-5130, fax 506/735-5179, info@laparios.com, www.laparios.com. Transfers are available.*

Northern Osa

Caño Island Biological Reserve

Caño Island is known for its marine life, but it is also an archaeological site. Rising above the Pacific, the land contains tall evergreen forest, a prehistoric cemetery, and mysterious round stones sculpted by the indigenous peoples who once walked here. Unfortunately, many graves were plundered before the island came under protection. The most abundant pottery dates from A.D. 220 to 1550.

Crystalline waters are a delight for snorkelers and divers. Five coral reefs, containing at least 15 species of stony coral, create a marine wonderland. Lobster and giant conch live here, as do eels, octopuses, sea urchins, brittle stars, and countless fish—jacks, grunts, and triggerfish. Manta rays, sailfish, sea turtles, humpback whales, and dolphins are here, along with soft and hard coral, though not as colorful or as abundant as on the Caribbean. Visibility averages 60 feet (18 m), temperature high 70s.

A trail climbs through the forest to points of archaeological interest. High cliffs rise from the coastline, with only a few small, sandy beaches that largely disappear at high tide. Island wildlife is scarce, consisting mainly of pacas, opossums, boa constrictors, a few species of bees, moths, butterflies, beetles, frogs, bats, rats, lizards, and ants. Among birds are ospreys, brown noddies, brown boobies, terns, and egrets. The forest is largely made up of locusts, wild figs, rubber trees, wild cacaos, and milk trees that exude a white latex that can be drunk as milk. The reserve protects 494 acres (200 ha) of land; 6,672 acres (2,700 ha) of marine habitat.

Most visitors arrive as part of a tour. Prior reservation is necessary, so independent travelers should contact Osa Conservation Area office.

Details: *12 miles (20 km) west of the Osa Peninsula from Drake Bay; telephone hotline 506/192, 506/735-5282, fax 506/735-5276. Open daily 8 A.M. to 4 P.M.; admission $6. Lodges and tour agencies offer tours from the Osa Peninsula, Golfito area, Dominical, and Quepos.*

Casa Corcovado Jungle Lodge

A secluded cove on the wonderfully wild Osa coastline marks the entrance to an extraordinary 170-acre (69-ha) private reserve adjoining Corcovado Park and a hilltop jungle lodge that makes one want to stay forever. Designed and built by owner Steven Lill, it reflects his long love affair with nature.

The perfume of an ylang-ylang tree drifts to the observatory bar situated at the edge of a canyon. Watch a coati feed on bananas, slaty-tailed trogons nesting in a nearby tree, and the astonishing colors of blue dacnis, shining honeycreepers, and red-legged honeycreepers. The bartender pointed out a tiny opossum resting in a palm, and interrupted lunch service to rescue a green honeycreeper from the web of a golden orb spider.

Species seen on a walk before breakfast with Felix, a local guide, included a buff-throated saltator, crowned woodnymph, long-tailed hermit, agoutis, spider monkeys, a red-capped manakin perched not three feet (one m) away, a chestnut-mandibled toucan, mealy parrot, both male and female blue seedeaters, white-faced monkeys, a cacique, red-billed pigeons, scarlet-rumped tanagers, and a rufous-tailed jacamar: a bird-watcher's heaven. When I took an afternoon trip down to the beach, spectacular blue shrimplike creatures darted in a pool at the base of a four-tiered waterfall. Get under it for a natural massage. Bats live in a big cave nearby, and turtles nest on the beach: remains of eggs from a nest raided by coatis were strewn on the sand. Guests can have picnic lunch served here and spend the day.

Well-maintained, color-coded trails loop around the reserve and go to the San Pedrillo entrance at Corcovado, about a half-hour walk, guides available. Go to Caño Island to snorkel or dive, go fishing, or kayak to San Josecito, a beautiful swimming beach. Meet at the *mirador* nightly for drinks and a memorable Pacific sunset. Meals are outstanding: manager Ricardo's experience as a chef shows: delicious and attractively served specialties every day. Lantern light glows at dinner, though electricity is available 24 hours in this remote place, from hydropower and solar systems. Drinking water is from a mountain spring, and the gorgeous pool in the river canyon, dwarfed by tall forest, is spring fed. Ten deluxe bungalows have beds gracefully draped with mosquito netting, walls as much window as wood, elegant tile floors, great bathrooms with huge showers.

A three-day, two-night package from San José is $640 per person, double occupancy, including air, land, and boat transfers, lodging, meals, tour to Corcovado or Caño Island , park fees, and taxes; or pick up the tour at Palmar Sur for $100 less. Add a day and go to both Corcovado and Caño Island, $795. Count on a wet landing—no dock; climb aboard a tractor-driven cart for a short ride up the hill to the lodge .

Details: *South of Drake Bay, bordering northern edge of Corcovado; 506/256-3181, fax 506/256-7409, in U.S. (888) 896-6097, corcovdo @racsa.co.cr, www.casacorcovado.com.*

Marenco Beach and Rainforest Lodge

This remote, laid-back tropical wilderness lodge and reserve is set in a hillside clearing amid lush premontane wet forest. Explore miles of beach and forest trails on the reserve's 1,977 acres (800 ha). Sit on your balcony and watch a parade of exotic birds—parrots, toucans with their outrageous beaks, scarlet macaws, brightly colored tanagers, and sometimes humpback and pilot whales in the ocean below.

On reserve trails, which vary from easy to challenging, you may encounter a slow-moving sloth or catch the scent of white-lipped peccaries. Lucia, the resident naturalist, can tell you about current research on spider and howler monkeys: watch for motion in the trees to spot them and the other monkeys that live here, the white-faced capuchins. She and others also study scarlet macaw populations (ask how to tell a male from a female) and bats: 27 bat species here. Learn that of the 103 bat species in Costa Rica, only three suck blood, and only one takes to humans—most feed on nectar, fruits and insects (a bat can consume 3,000 insects per hour). Perhaps you'll see the bat that makes tents.

417

Rent a horse to go along the beach or forest trails, and trek to the cool waters of the Claro River to take a dip in a freshwater pool next to the ocean, beneath towering forest giants. Make a day of it and continue to San Josecito to snorkel at the reef. At low tide, it's possible to walk north on the beach and forest trails all the way to Drake.

Snorkeling is good at coral gardens along Marenco's coastline, where you may see parrot fish, tangs, puffers, and angelfish. On a boat tour to Caño Island, 11 miles (17 km) west of Marenco, you'll probably see dolphins, maybe a manta ray. Diving safaris at Caño Island expose an underwater wonderland of octopus, lobster, moray eel, jack, damselfish, and triggerfish. A day trip to nearby Corcovado enters at San Pedrillo (25 minutes away by boat).

Marenco is a buffer zone that helps protect the park and employs local people. Eight rooms along the edge of the hillside have balconies open to a priceless view. Seventeen larger bungalows of wood and bamboo have tropical hardwood floors and floor-to-ceiling screened windows that let in lots of light and forest colors. Bird-watching from private verandas is superb. Delicious meals are served buffet or family style in a large, open dining room/lounge at the edge of the bluff: great ocean and treetop views. Check for after-dinner natural history slide shows. All-inclusive packages include airfare from San José, ground and boat transfers, meals, lodging, and specified tours: a three-night package with two tours is $528 per person; ask about a budget bus/boat package.

Marenco now has electricity, but bring a flashlight anyway. A radio telephone is powered by solar battery. Find crafts made by local people in the gift shop. No dock, so count on getting feet wet: luggage is transported up the hill to the lodge.

Details: *South of Drake Bay, 506/258-1919, fax 506/255-1346, in U.S. 800/278-6223, info@marencolodge.com, www.marencolodge.com. Packages include transfers from San José.*

Coco Island

Isla del Coco National Park

This beautiful green island was an early haven for explorers, privateers, pirates, and whalers because of its abundant fresh water, wood, fish, and coconuts; *coco* is Spanish for coconut. Today, it attracts divers, scientists, nature/adventure travelers, and treasure hunters: some believe that stories of buried treasure here fired the imagination of Robert Louis Stevenson for *Treasure Island.*

Scientists and tourists come in search of other riches: many endemic species—those found nowhere else—have evolved on this isolated island, a park since 1978 and a UNESCO World Heritage site since 1997, and sea life makes for incredible scuba diving. Seventy of 235 plant species are endemic, two species of lizards, 64 of the island's 362 species of insects, and three of the 85 bird species. An endemic palm is named for Franklin D. Roosevelt, who visited four times. This is an important nesting site for seagulls, noddies, and boobies. Another nesting bird is Espíritu Santo, or Holy Spirit. A small white bird, it often hovers in the air, unafraid, a few feet above a visitor's head. Its more prosaic English name is white tern. Eleven species of shark move through island's waters: huge whale sharks, hammerheads, and white-tips, among 200 fish species. Other underwater riches include 18 corals and 118 species of mollusks.

Coco's wild beauty encompasses spectacular waterfalls, dense vegetation, and underwater caves and coral gardens. A rugged coastline of high cliffs makes access possible only at Chatham and Wafer Bays. Upper elevations are covered by cloud forest, where epiphytes abound. Of volcanic origin, the island contains two-million-year-old rocks. Rainfall averages 276 inches (7,000 mm) a year. The park encompasses 5,930 acres (2,400 ha) of land and 240,268 acres (97,235 ha) of ocean.

This is a living laboratory for study of evolutionary processes. Threats to the delicate ecological balance here include introduced species (pigs, deer, rats, coffee, papaya) and fishing. Unbridled tourism would spell disaster. Historically, Coco's isolation minimized human impact; its inclusion in the park system is aimed at protecting it in a shrinking world. Permission is necessary for a visit —no overnight visitor facilities. Most travelers come via organized tours, mainly divers. A park station has radio contact with the mainland

Details: *331 miles (532 km) southwest of Cabo Blanco in the Pacific, 5° N, 8° W. Open 24 hours, admission $15. Telephone hotline 506/192, 506/283-8004, 506/233-4533.*

GUIDES AND OUTFITTERS

At Drake Bay, check with Brian and Gregory Chavez at **Costa Rica Ventures,** diving and rain forest adventure operators, tel/fax 506/385-9541, 800/317-0333, crventur@costaricadiving.com, www.costaricadiving.com. Diving and snorkeling at Caño Island is the main event. This certified PADI facility offers instruction from beginning open water to dive master. A two-tank dive is $85; a three-day PADI certification course is $280. A one-day resort course is $135 including instruction, equipment, lunch, park fees, and two-tank dive at Caño. Don't dive? Then take a guided walking tour of Corcovado or Caño, go day or night fishing, tube down the Agujitas River, go mountain biking, horseback riding, or sea kayaking, or take a whale- and dolphin-watching excursion, $50 per person or less. Multi-day dive and adventure packages are available. Brian and Gregory operate out of their Jinetes de Osa hotel.

Sierra Goodman at **Divine Dolphin,** located on Playa Caletas south of Drake Bay, offers environmentally responsible wild dolphin and whale adventures, 506/394-2632, sierra@divinedolphin.com, www.divinedophine.com. Spotted, bottlenose, common, and spinner dolphins are here; whales include humpback, pilot, sperm, false killer, and blue whales. These special sea creatures are never fed, chased, or harassed—the choice to interact is always up to them. Swimming with dolphins may be allowed, but no physical contact is permitted. A five-hour tour with lunch on the boat is $75. For more information on Sierra's Drake Bay Cetacean Foundation, ongoing research, and intern possibilities, check out the website. She operates from her Delfin Amor Eco Lodge, a tent camp.

At **Taboga Aquatic Tours** in Puerto Jiménez, contact Marco Loaicaiga, 506/735-5265, fax 506/735-5121. A Golfo Dulce trip includes stops at pristine beaches and forest exploration. Go surfing at Pavones, fish close to shore or out in the Pacific, snorkel at coral reefs, or take a mangrove boat tour to look for birds. Marco sets up charter trips to Caño Island, Sirena in Corcovado, and Drake Bay.

For diving at Coco Island, check out *Okeanos Aggressor* in Chapter 3 under "Scuba Diving and Snorkeling."

CAMPING

For camping at **Corcovado National Park** or at upscale **Corcovado Lodge Tent Camp** near Carate, refer to "Nature and Adventure Sights." **Drake Bay Wilderness Resort** also has tents, described below under "Lodging." Also at Drake, platforms for tents are available at **Jinetes de Osa,** $15, bring your own tent; contact information is under "Lodging."

Tent camping at **Delfin Amor Eco Lodge** on Playa Caletas on Drake Bay is $85 for two, including meals (mainly vegetarian and fresh fish). Three tent cabanas are next to an open-air restaurant, with 10 acres (four ha) of rain forest around and Pacific out front. Shared baths (three toilets and showers) have solar hot water. Owner Sierra Goodman operates Divine Dolphin tour company, and she offers multiday rain forest and dolphin/whale adventures, including visits to Corcovado, Caño Island, kayaking, diving, snorkeling, hiking, and horseback riding.

LODGING

Drake Bay Wilderness Camp, tel/fax 506/256-7394, at lodge 506/770-8012, in U.S. 561/371-3437, emichaud@drakebay.com, www.drakebay.com, is a relaxing, laid-back kind of place where you soon settle into tropical time: delight in antics of resident squirrel monkeys that cavort in fruit-laden gardens, make a date with a spectacular sunset, lounge in hammocks. A natural tide pool beckons at low tide.

Twenty rooms, solar hot water, are in seven buildings. All are simply furnished and have ceiling fans, luggage racks, even washcloths, for $85 per person double, including meals. Six 12-by-12-foot furnished oceanfront tents (twin beds, solar lights, fan) offer an alternative, with a shared two-shower, two-toilet bath bathhouse; $73 per person, meals included. Good food is served family style in a separate dining room, with complimentary *bocas* at 5 P.M. in the thatched, open-air lounge. A four-day/three-night packages is $710 per person double, including 40-minute flight to and from San José, landing at Drake Bay airport, lodging in cabin, meals, trip to Corcovado, either Caño Island or Claro River, and one more tour.

Guests can choose horseback riding, mountain biking, kayaking, diving, night fishing, offshore fishing, and tours to Corcovado or Caño Island. Four-day scuba diving, bird-watching, mountain biking, fishing, and kayaking packages available. On a Río Claro tour with Fernando, the terrific naturalist guide, 12 scarlet macaws fed in distant trees and a white hawk soared. Fernando explained that hawks follow white-faced monkeys, waiting for a chance to snatch the young, and then we saw the monkeys. Otters played in the river. You can swim up the river in life jackets and float down under a rain forest canopy. Use of snorkeling gear and canoes is free for guests.

Owners and hosts, Herbert and Marleny (Marleny's family homesteaded here), have a ranch across the bay; go by horseback, mountain bike, or canoe to visit the butterfly garden and green iguana project, to see white-lipped peccaries and deer in breeding programs plus free-flying toucans and scarlet macaws. If you don't see a butterfly emerge during the tour, you may be entrusted with a chrysalis to take back to the lodge so you can witness the event and be a part of the release program. Volunteers are needed. A four-bedroom furnished house at the farm is $580 per week.

Near Puerto Jiménez on Playa Platanares is **Iguana Lodge,** 506/735-5205, fax 506/735-5043, info@iguanalodge.com, www. iguanalodge.com. Charming two-story bungalows (one is wheelchair accessible) are down paths under tall trees with colorful tropical plants at understory level. Downstairs is a unique, open-style bathroom with plenty of privacy plus a couple of beds; the upstairs master bedroom has a definite tree-house feel with tropical woods, screens on open-to-the-forest walls and wooden louvers to keep rain out, and a hammock on the covered deck. Lights and fans are solar powered; solar-heated water doubles are $75 per person, including meals. Breakfast and lunch are served on the first floor of a dramatic, tall thatched building, with dinner in the impressive second-floor lounge and dining room with gulf views. The food gets good reviews: mango scones, ginger-chile grilled mahi-mahi. Owners Lauren and Toby Cleaver offer interesting tours: in addition to a jungle hike, kayaking, a tour on the Golfo Dulce, and sportfishing, guests can climb trees via ropes and pulleys and pan for gold, keeping what they find. Transfers from Puerto Jiménez, 10 minutes away, are $12 per trip.

Cerro de Oro Ecotourism Lodge is eight miles (14 km) northwest of La Palma; tel/fax 506/775-0033, 506/286-4203, cooprena @racsa.co.cr, www.agroecoturismo.net. Members of a small cooperative began this rustic lodge as an alternative to gold mining. The building, raised off the ground and with decorative rails of driftwood, has six double rooms, shared baths; $40, breakfast included. Eat in a rancho-style dining room. Only one mile (two km) from the Los Patos entrance to Corcovado, members offer guided walks in the park as well as its own reserve. Visit the Rincón River, where huge amounts of material were extracted in mining days, help harvest produce from the organic garden, see palm nurseries, share views of life with community members. Even do a little panning for gold. Ask about volunteer opportunities. Cerro de Oro is affiliated with COOPRENA, a consortium of small ecotourism cooperatives.

Jinetes de Osa is beachfront at Drake Bay, tel/fax 506/385-9541, 800/317-0333, crventur@costaricadiving.com, www.costaricadiving.com. Eleven simple, neat rooms have tile floors, ceiling fans, and solar-heated water; double $60 per person including meals. Coffee is delivered outside your room every morning. The open-air restaurant specializes in seafood, chicken, and pasta dishes, and fresh-baked bread. Service is family style. Raised tent platforms are available. Owners Brian and Gregory Chavez also operate Costa Rica Ventures; refer to "Guides and Outfitters." Ask about multiday dive and adventure packages. Round-trip Palmar transfers are $65.

La Paloma Lodge at Drake Bay, 506/239-2801, tel/fax 506/239-0954, info@lapalomalodge.com, www.lapalomalodge.com, is a delightful hilltop retreat with dramatic Pacific views and landscaped gardens that draw tropical birds. Fiery-billed aracaris feast on *almendro* trees. Their calls mix with those of chestnut-mandibled toucans, parrots, and macaws in appropriate jungle melodies, blending nicely with distant sounds of the sea. An agouti may cross your path on the 14 acres (six ha) of gorgeous gardens and forest. The large, thatched centerpiece of the complex, owned and managed by Mike and Sue Kalmbach, contains dining room, bar, lounge, and a marvelous veranda along the ocean side with lots of chairs for daytime bird-watching and for sunset watching at complimentary *boca* time. Excellent food (including fresh fish and shrimp) is served family style. Homemade bread is on the table at every meal, and nighttime brings rich desserts. A swimming pool and sun decks perched on the hillside have a dynamite ocean view.

Rooms are charming. Four large standard rooms near the dining room have sea-view terraces, rich tropical hardwoods, and colorful, cushioned bamboo furniture, double $120. Five thatched, two-story deluxe bungalows are set among trees and are very private: sleeping lofts, four-poster beds, sea views, polished floors, $145. All have hammocks, solar-heated water, ceiling fans, and orthopedic mattresses. Electricity is a combination of solar and generator power. Go horseback riding, diving, sportfishing, or to the Claro River. Accompany La Paloma's experienced naturalist guide to see and learn about toucans, manakins, scarlet macaws, parrots, monkeys, sloths, herons, and iguanas. Guests can kayak in the bay and the Pacific as well as the Agujitas River (highly recommended)—no charge. Staff is attentive and friendly. It's a dock landing but uphill to the lodge, luggage transferred. A four-day/three-night package, per person double, is $750 standard and $850 bungalow, including round-trip air and boat transfers, lodging, meals, and guided tours to Corcovado and Caño Island (on a 36-foot catamaran), park fees, taxes.

Río Sierpe Lodge on the Sierpe River, cellular 506/384-5595, fax 506/786-7366, in San José 506/283-7655, vsftrip@racsa.co.cr, is 15 miles (24 km) from Palmar by boat. Here the river is more than a half mile (one km) wide and 50 feet (15 m) deep; across it Violin Island has some of the tallest mangroves in the world. The rustic lodge, on a narrow bluff between river and mountain, consists of 17 rooms with passive solar hot water in private baths. Four rooms are off the dining room, others steps away; newer two-story rooms have a sitting area and bath downstairs and double and single beds upstairs. Furnishings are simple; all have fans, screened windows, reading lamps; doubles from $65 per person, including lodging, meals, soft drinks, Palmar transfers, and taxes. Electricity is from a generator; battery-powered reading lamps function when the generator is off. Water is from a mountain spring. Meals feature lots of fruits and vegetables, seafood, and pasta. Hike on trails behind the lodge and enjoy beaches at Boca Sierpe. Birds that are seen regularly—175 species—include the mangrove hummingbird, Baird's trogon, black-cheeked ant-tanager, yellow-billed cotinga, orange-chinned parakeet, riverside wren, and black hawk. White-faced monkeys eat mangoes near the dining room. Tours with local guides go to Corcovado or Caño Island, $55; a horseback trek to San Josecito Beach for hiking, swimming, and snorkeling is $75. Go scuba diving and tidal and ocean fishing. Leave time for interesting conversations with owner Mike Stiles, a naturalist and avid reader. A four-day/three-night naturalist package is $425 per person double, including San José/Palmar flight, boat transfer, lodging, meals, soft drinks, taxes.

FOOD

Since the private nature lodges and many of the hotels are in remote areas, with rates that include meals, you will probably take most of your meals where you stay. Try restaurants at hotels/lodges listed; here are a few other options.

In Puerto Jiménez, **Restaurante Carolina** serves pasta, ceviche, fish filet in ginger sauce, and rice dishes. **Pizzería, Ice Cream Parlor, and Restaurant Dominican Tica** has pancake or omelet breakfasts, hot dogs, banana splits, fresh-baked pastries. Both are on the main street, open 7 A.M. to 10 P.M.

At Drake Bay, **Aguila de Osa,** an upscale hotel, is known for great food. Fresh seafood and pastas are specialties, prepared with a unique tropical flair. Reservations recommended.

APPENDIX A
TRAVEL BASICS

WHAT TO BRING

Pack light. The rule of thumb is to get out what you plan to bring and then cut it in half. Traveling to a remote spot by small plane, boat, or jeep will limit what you can take on your in-country travels. Luggage is limited to 26 pounds per person on small aircraft, so bring a small bag to carry essentials for that leg of the trip and store your larger bag; most hotels and many tour operators offer storage service.

Consider these clothing tips. For forest hikes, long pants give more protection from insects and plants than shorts. Throw in cotton pants, especially in the rainy season, since it takes forever and a day for jeans to dry. A long-sleeved shirt is wise for protection from the sun—its rays are direct at 10 degrees from the equator—and from insects and scratches on narrow trails. Bring your bathing suit; nudity on public beaches is not acceptable in this culture.

Tuck in a sweater or light jacket for chilly evenings or wet, windy weather. Light clothes that can be layered will serve you well. A comfortable pair of walking shoes is paramount. Some prefer tennis shoes to hiking boots for forays into the tropical world. Whichever, they probably will get wet at some point—even in dry season a trail can lead through small streams—so have a backup. In rainy times, rubber boots are handy. Standard footwear for campesinos, rubber boots are inexpensive and available in markets and shoe stores, especially in rural towns. Many lodges supply boots, but don't expect extra-large sizes.

Rain poncho or umbrella? I pack both. A poncho, light weight and hooded, gives better protection to backpacks, fanny packs, binoculars, and cameras and is useful for boat rides or horseback trips. An umbrella is good for town time and for when you're not carrying twenty other things on the trail. In warmer areas, I suggest getting wet at least once, especially on a forest walk. Experience the elements. Protect your camera or binoculars and go for it.

Costa Ricans tend to dress on the conservative side. It has not been so many years since women did not wear pants or jeans, and shorts were only for the beach or sports. That has changed, though shorts are still not common in San José—mostly tourists wear them. Dress at nature lodges is casual, even in the evening, but for dinner at a nice restaurant in San José, local men may wear a coat and tie or at least a dress shirt; women, a dress or nice pants outfit.

Leave expensive jewelry at home. Much to Costa Ricans' dismay, thievery is on the upswing, especially in San José. I had a chain snatched from my neck on a downtown street at midday.

Though the electric current is 110 volts, same as in the United States and Canada, some places do not have three-prong outlets or outlets for the larger prong. So if you're bringing your computer on vacation (heaven forbid) or another appliance, bring an adapter that will fit in a standard two-prong outlet. When packing electric razors, hair dryers, and such, be aware that travel in the boonies may put you in a room without an electric outlet or in a lodge powered by a small hydro plant that will not accommodate their use.

A day pack is handy, even for city sightseeing. Be sure it closes securely. To further foil the light-fingered in heavy street traffic or on crowded buses, wear your fanny pack to the front or move your day pack to your shoulder where you can control access to it. A water-resistant pack helps.

You can buy Fuji, Kodak, Agfa, and other brands of film in San José and some outlying towns, but it's best to bring what you intend to use. Slide film is generally hard to find outside San José. You will not find the variety of ASA ratings and types of film you may be accustomed to. Don't forget spare camera batteries.

Keep any medicines you require with you, not packed in luggage to be checked.

Here is a checklist of other items:
• **Wide-brimmed hat** for rain or sun.
• **Flashlight** for nighttime hikes, to get from cabin to dining room in the middle of the forest, and when the power goes off unexpectedly or the generator is shut off before you're ready for bed at a remote reserve.

- **Sunscreen**
- **Insect repellent**
- **Pocket calculator** to simplify currency calculations, metric conversions
- **Moist towelettes**
- **Pocketknife**
- **Small mirror**—Some rustic facilities lack a bedroom mirror.
- **Anti-itch ointment**—an antihistamine cream for insect bites or even an antihistamine to take orally to reduce discomfort. If you do find yourself with bites and no ointment, juice from the stem of the impatiens (*china*) plant, abundant in many parts of Costa Rica, is an excellent natural remedy.
- **Antidiarrheal medicine,** just in case.
- **Washcloth**—Not all hotels supply them.
- **Reclosable plastic bags**—Small ones are ideal for passports or other important papers; a larger one is handy for a wet bathing suit or to keep camera or extra lens dry.
- **Plastic water bottle** or buy bottled water for hikes, bus rides, etc.
- **Binoculars**—You'll be sorry if you don't bring a pair.
- **Antifogging agent for eyeglasses,** especially during the rainy season, when putting binoculars or a camera to your glasses can result in one big blur.
- **Old tennies or sandals** for climbing over rocks at the beach to explore tide pools.
- **Tissues**—Public rest rooms in Costa Rica may not have toilet paper
- **Coin purse** to accommodate an ever-growing supply of change. (Unfortunately, only the small denominations seem to self-generate.)

Do not bring along impatience. Leave it at home. Who knows? After a time in Costa Rica without it, you may find you don't need to lug it around anywhere anymore.

ENTRY AND EXIT REQUIREMENTS

Requirements for Entry
- Passport or tourist card
- Ticket out of the country (air or bus ticket)

• Length of stay permitted: 90 days with passport, 30 days with tourist card

For U.S. and Canadian citizens no visas are necessary. If you don't have a passport, purchase a tourist card at the airline ticket counter on departure to Costa Rica; you will need a birth certificate or voter registration document along with photo identification, such as a driver's license. Citizens of other countries can check with the nearest Costa Rican consulate or the Costa Rican Institute of Tourism for entry requirements.

The law requires travelers to carry a passport or tourist card at all times while in the country. A photocopy of the passport will do, so leave the original in the hotel safe-deposit box. Be sure to copy pages that show your name, photo, passport number, and date of entry into Costa Rica. (Copy machines abound—signs advertise "*Copias.*")

Exit Requirements

• Airport departure tax (exit visa): $17

When leaving the country by air, tourists must pay a departure tax, which may be paid in U.S. dollars or colones (*not* traveler's checks, *not* credit cards). The exit visa can be purchased at a window inside the airport or from authorized agents who meet arriving taxis and cars—badges identify agents.

HEALTH AND SAFETY

Immunization Requirements and Health Precautions

No immunizations are required for entry. But even when staying at home, it is wise to have inoculations up-to-date. Is your tetanus booster current?

Malaria cases increased a few years ago in some parts of Costa Rica with the influx of refugees from neighboring countries, but it is not widespread. Dengue, carried by the *Aedes aegypti* mosquito, surfaces from time to time—both classic and hemorrhagic. Symptoms for dengue include sudden high fever, acute pain in head, muscles, joints, and eyes, and a rash on the chest and back. Mosquito eradication programs are in place as are education programs to reduce standing water. Check with your physician or local health office for advisory information. Contact the U.S. Centers for Disease Control for vaccine recommendations, 800/CDC-SHOT (800/343-7458).

Insects

I am well acquainted with two insects in particular: chiggers (*coloradillas*—co-lo-rah-DEE-lyahs) and ticks (*garrapatas*—gahr-rah-PAH-tahs). Chiggers are actually mite larvae. They live in grassy, bushy areas waiting to climb up the legs of passersby. Their bites itch like crazy, and the red bumps get worse if you scratch them. To discourage chiggers, dust sulfur powder on your socks, pant legs, feet, ankles, and lower calves before you walk in grass. Mosquito repellents are *not* effective. For bites, Caladryl or Eurax cream helps; some people take an antihistamine for severe itching. The effect of chigger bites can last for weeks.

Ticks hang out especially where horses and cattle are found. If you notice itching, look for the reddish-black tick under your skin when you undress. Be careful not to leave the biting end embedded because it can fester and cause infection. Dirk Schroeder, author of *Staying Healthy* (Moon Publications, 1999) recommends the following procedure: Remove ticks attached to your skin immediately with tweezers by grasping the tick's head parts as close to your skin as possible and applying slow, steady traction. Do not attempt to get ticks out of your skin by burning them or coating them with anything like nail polish or petroleum jelly. If you remove a tick before it has been attached for more than 24 hours, you greatly reduce your risk of infection. Afterwards, wash the bite with soap and clean water. Ticks can carry disease, so if you get a fever after being bitten, see a doctor.

In an area where mosquitoes are bothersome, use repellent and wear protective clothing. (A tip: don't forget to apply repellent on your hands and, when wearing sandals, on the arches of your feet.) Some places provide mosquito netting for beds; if not, inexpensive mosquito coils help. Find them in grocery stores.

Ants come in a wonderful assortment of sizes and colors. Don't stand still without first checking out the area. Sounds easy, but the advice is hard to remember when you freeze in place to observe a great green macaw or a coati. For hikes and trail rides, hats and long-sleeved shirts give some protection against ants that live in trees you might brush against.

If you are bitten by no-see-ums, the gnats known as *purrujas* in Costa Rica, use an antibiotic salve. You will not only be in more agony if you scratch the bites, but also risk infection. No-see-ums live near the coast, preferring areas near salt marshes. Repellents are not very effective; protective clothing works best.

African (killer) bees arrived in Costa Rica in 1982, and you would do well to assume that all bee colonies are now Africanized. Keep your distance from hives or swarms. The stings of Africanized bees are no more venomous than those of your garden-variety bee, but these insects are aggressive and attack with less provocation. The cumulative effect of many bee stings is dangerous. If you're attacked, move in a zigzag motion; you can probably outrun them. Head for water if any is nearby, and cover your head. If someone with you is attacked and cannot move, cover both of you with something light in color and get the person to safety. Remove stingers with a knife or fingernails, being careful not to squeeze more of the stinger's venom into the bite. Apply ice or cold water, and, if badly bitten, see a doctor.

Scorpion species in Costa Rica do not have fatal poison, but the sting can cause intense pain, itching, numbness of tongue and mouth, even vomiting and fever. Wash the bite with soap and water and disinfect it with alcohol. I routinely shake out boots or shoes before I put them on and shake and inspect my clothes, even folded towels. Anyone with allergies should seek medical help if the bite provokes breathing problems.

Snakes

Running on a path to catch a bus, I once came face-to-face with a snake racing to catch a gigantic frog. I had turned my head to glance at the frog as it leaped by and looked forward again to see a spectacular black snake with a luminous bright green stripe running the length of its long body about four feet in front of me. The top half of that body was reared in the air, the head at about the level of my knees. Startled, we stopped in our tracks and stared at each other for a timeless moment. Then in one graceful move, the snake melted to the ground and slid off into the leaves at the side of the trail. The lesson: if a giant frog passes you with incredible leaps and bounds, consider the possibility that something is in hot pursuit and headed your way.

Although seeing a snake in the tropical forest can be thrilling, be respectful and keep your distance. Minimize unpleasant surprises. First, running is not a good idea. Never sit on or step over a log or rock without checking the other side. Some snakes live in trees, with protective coloration, so watch where you put your hands and your head. Most bites, however, occur below the knees, so consider high boots. Two pairs of eyes are better than one, so walk with a friend. At night, carry a strong light.

Costa Rica has 135 species of snakes. Only 18 species are poisonous. Fewer than 500 snakebites—most affecting farmworkers—are reported each year, with fewer than 15 fatalities. The fer-de-lance, or *terciopelo*, accounts for almost half the bites.

Bite marks of venomous and nonvenomous snakes differ. That of a nonpoisonous snake shows two rows of teeth marks but no fang marks. If the bite was from a poisonous snake, keep the victim still (especially the affected part), and squeeze out as much venom as possible with your mouth or hands within the first 10 minutes after the bite. Tourniquets and incisions are not recommended for amateurs. Get medical attention as quickly as possible. There is a polyvalent serum for use against all venomous Central American snakes except the coral, which has its own serum.

Food and Drinking Water

Precautions make travel anywhere healthier. Give your body a break: keep to a diet it can recognize at first, adding a few new things each day. Get plenty of rest. If you would not eat in a greasy spoon or buy food from a street vendor at home, why risk it elsewhere in the world?

As for drinking water, reports of tap water contamination pop up from time to time though larger towns have regulated water systems. I tend to exercise more caution in coastal areas and try to follow the saying, "When in doubt, don't." When you stay at a hotel or reserve in a rural area, you have every right to ask about the source of water. Bottled water is now widely available, along with bottled carbonated drinks, beer, and packaged fruit juices. Contaminated ice continues to be a problem, mainly from the poor hygiene of those who handle it. And remember, if you don't trust the water as safe to drink, don't brush your teeth with it either.

A good substitute for water on a hot day on the coast is the liquid from a *pipa*, a green coconut. You can get *té de manzanilla* (chamomile tea) practically anywhere, with water that most likely has been boiled. Several companies offer a variety of delicious, packaged herbal teas. You can always get fine coffee.

The two largest dairy product companies are Dos Pinos and Borden; both are reliable and offer pasteurized products. Laser-treated milk that does not have to be refrigerated until opened is also available.

Peel fruits and vegetables (that's one reason you carry a pocketknife).

Street Crime

Theft is a worldwide phenomenon. Use common sense: don't wear expensive-looking jewelry or flash lots of cash when making purchases. Do watch your belongings. Don't leave cameras or binoculars lying unattended on the beach. Watch your pockets and bags on crowded buses and streets. Use a bag that closes securely and hold it tightly between arm and body. Carry your wallet in an inside coat or trouser pocket, not in a back pocket. Keep your passport separate from your money. Better yet, carry a photocopy of your passport (the photo and entry date pages) and leave the original in the hotel safe-deposit box, along with your airline ticket. Carry only the credit cards you need.

Be alert on the street if approached by an overly friendly person who claims to have met you somewhere. There are expert pickpockets around. I lost a watch while trying to explain to a man that I did not believe I knew him. I would know him now.

The Costa Rican Tourism Institute (ICT) has published a "Passport for Your Safety" brochure, distributed at airports, hotels, and other tourism businesses, with tips for travelers on how to have a safer vacation. In case of emergency, call 911.

Traffic Hazards

For a tourist in San José, there are easier ways to get around than by rental car: parking space is limited, car theft is a problem, and traffic is fierce. I would suggest you walk or take a taxi or bus.

In the countryside, roads are for cars, buses, trucks, cows, dogs, chickens, people, and landslides. Be careful out there. Some specific driving habits to look out for are passing on curves, use of climbing lanes by cars going downhill, and driving on whichever side of the road has the better pavement or fewer rocks or ruts. Tailgating is a national pastime.

Watch out for two-lane roads that feed suddenly into one-lane bridges and for lethal *huecos* (WAY-kos), holes in the pavement, which can knock passenger and vehicle for a loop. Tree branches laid across the road warn of trouble ahead, and when an oncoming car flashes its headlights, it usually means police ahead, an accident, or some other danger. Slow down.

Geography and climate team up to create landslides big and small. Fog is a permanent possibility on the highest section of the Inter-American Highway south of San José toward San Isidro de El General—the range known as Cerro de la Muerte. The earlier you get through that section, the better (and the scenery is magnificent). The same advice goes for the highway to Limón through Braulio Carrillo National Park.

On the San José-Puntarenas highway, you may find yourself in a string of cars, buses, and diesel-fume-belching trucks on a narrow, winding road. Adrenaline flows as vehicles jockey for position without a clue as to what may be approaching just around the curve. Avoid that road on weekends and after dark. In fact, avoid driving at night in general.

Even with road map in hand, you'll need to ask directions when traveling off main roads. Additional signs are going up along main tourism routes, but choices outnumber signs, especially on dirt roads. In the rainy season, always ask about the condition of the roads you plan to take before setting out each day.

Traffic police equipped with radar are on major roads. Watch the posted speed limit and buckle up. If you are stopped by transit police and cited, fines must be paid to a bank, or the rental agency will handle it for you. You should not pay the officer.

TRANSPORTATION TO COSTA RICA

Time, distance, and political considerations lead most tourists from the United States and Canada to opt for air travel to Costa Rica, which means landing at Juan Santamaría International Airport, 20 minutes from San José, or Daniel Oduber Quirós Airport, 15 minutes west of Liberia in Costa Rica's northwest sector.

Commercial carriers include American, Continental, and United (U.S. carriers); Aero Costa Rica and LACSA (Grupo TACA); and Mexicana (Mexico). Here are addresses and contact numbers (*all telephone numbers are area code 506*).

Airline	Address	Reservations	Airport
American	Across from Hotel Corobicí, Avenida 5b, Calles 40/42	257-1266	442-8800
Continental	From U.S. Embassy, 200 m south, 300 m east, 50 m north	296-4911	442-1904
Delta	Calle 42, Avenidas 2/4	257-4141	440-4802
LACSA	Calle 42, Avenida 5	296-0909	443-3555
Mexicana	Calle 5, Avenidas 7/9	257-6334	441-9377
United	La Sabana, Edificio Oficentro	220-4844	441-8025

Note: LACSA is now part of Grupo TACA, www.grupotaca.com.

TRANSPORTATION WITHIN COSTA RICA

Taxis, buses, rental cars, charter and scheduled airplanes, horses, ferries, bicycles, boats, balloons, helicopters, motorcycles, horses, foot power—many options exist for moving a traveler around the country. Most of you will experience the country's highways and byways. Potholes are a serious hazard on paved roads, and unpaved roads definitely add an element of adventure, especially in rainy months. The kilometers of paved roads grow yearly, always with greatest increases in election years (Costa Ricans say). Highway construction and maintenance are expensive in this mountainous, rainy nation, with added havoc wreaked by hurricanes and earthquakes. As you travel, you'll encounter superb highways, potholes, unpaved gutbusters, and charming country roads.

Planes

Two domestic airlines offer scheduled service: SANSA and Travelair. SANSA rates are generally lower, while Travelair prides itself on the level of service it offers. SANSA flights leave from Juan Santamaría airport near Alajuela; Travelair flights leave from the Tobías Bolaños airport, 15 minutes from downtown San José in the suburb of Pavas. Baggage is limited to 26 pounds (12 kilos) per person on each. Store extra luggage at your hotel or with the tour operator. Flights are generally less than one hour long. Because planes are small, it's advisable to reserve as far in advance as possible, especially in high season. Several charter companies provide air service. Look in the phone book under *"Aviación."* Don't schedule yourself too tightly since winds and bad weather can cause delays or cancellations, especially in rainy season.

SANSA: San José office, Calle 24, Avenida 5, 506/221-9414, fax 506/255-2176; sansa@lacsa.atlas-com.com; . Following are destinations and fares as of January 2000. All are to or from San José and are daily flights except for Nosara, which has only three flights a week. There is no reduction for round-trips. Reduced rates apply to children. Flights between La Fortuna and Tamarindo are $50 one way.

Destination	One-Way Fare (U.S. $)
Barra del Colorado	45
Coto 47	55
Golfito	55
La Fortuna	45

Liberia	55
Nosara	55
Palmar Sur	55
Puerto Jiménez	55
Punta Islita	55
Quepos	35
Sámara	55
Tamarindo	55
Tambor	45
Tortuguero	45

Travelair: San José office, Tobias Bolaños Airport, Pavas; 506/220-3054, fax 506/220-0413; reservations@travelair-costarica.com; . Following are destinations and fares as of January 2000. All are to or from San José except where noted, and are daily flights. Reduced fares apply to most round-trips. In addition to these scheduled flights, Travelair offers charter service. Aircraft are inspected before each flight according to Costa Rica Civil Aviation as well as the United States F.A.A.

Destination	One-Way Fare (U.S. $)
Carrillo (Sámara)	82
Golfito/San José	84
La Fortuna	59
Liberia	92
Quepos/Palmar Sur	63
Puerto Jiménez	90
Puerto Jiménez/Quepos	74
Puerto Jiménez/Golfito	35
Punta Islita	(on request, two or more)
Quepos	50
Tamarindo	92
Tamarindo/Liberia	34
Tambor	69
Tortuguero	51

Taxis

In the San José area, licensed taxis are red except for the orange airport vehicles. Take an unlicensed taxi at your own risk. Meters, called *marías,* are required for distances of up to 7.5 miles (12 km). Before you get in, don't be embarrassed to ask the driver if his *maría* works or to look to see if it's on. The meter will start with a minimum charge (at printing, 165 colones for the first kilometer); it goes up 90 colones for each additional kilometer in metropolitan areas. If you phone for a taxi, the driver can start the meter where he got the call. A driver who does not use the *maría* can be fined. To file a complaint at the Ministry of Public Works and Transport, be sure to get the taxi number and driver registration number and note the time. Drivers are generally courteous, though some will refuse to take you if they consider the distance too short or the traffic too fierce. Don't be surprised if this happens at the taxi stand on Avenida 2 in front of Gran Hotel Costa Rica. It gets my vote for the greatest percentage of surly drivers. Outside of San José, negotiate price with the driver first.

You can hire a taxi to go practically anywhere there is some kind of road. In outlying areas, taxis are often four-wheel-drive Jeep types. The fare for hired trips is based on distance and time, more if the trip is over bad roads. Set rates apply for some destinations: for example, from San José, the fare to Puntarenas is $50, to Cartago $12. Your hotel can call, ascertain fare, and reserve the taxi. Drivers will stop wherever you want to take a picture or soak up scenery; however, many drivers do not speak English. (Airport drivers usually speak English, but their rates are higher.)

Check yellow pages for taxi companies. Here are a few in San José *(all telephone numbers are area code 506)*:

CGT Taxi	254-6667
Coopetico R.L.	224-7979
Multiservicos Alfaro	221-8466, 223-3373
Taxis San Jorge	222-0025, 221-3434, 221-3535
Taxis Unidos	221-6865, 233-6637 (airport)

Buses

Bus service in Costa Rica is reliable and inexpensive. It offers a good opportunity to mix with local people. My bus travels have revealed a genuinely courteous people—helpful, friendly, good-humored, dignified. No pigs and chickens are in these buses. Vehicles are usually clean and so are the Costa Ricans who use them. I have encountered foreign tourists in Costa Rica who must have thought that going back to nature in the tropics meant going without a bath. Not so for Costa Ricans: for them, personal cleanliness truly is next to godliness.

Intercity fares from San José will not exceed $10 one-way; outside San José, local bus services can usually move travelers to other destinations without a return to the capital. Sometimes seats can be reserved with advance ticket purchase. If not, go to the bus stop an hour early. If the bus line has an office there, buy the ticket and get in line. If there is no office, buy a ticket from the driver or his assistant. Make sure you are in line for the correct bus. Verify that it's the right bus when you get on. Most buses carry only seated passengers but not always so in outlying areas. Check your ticket for a seat number; some routes assign seats, others don't.

Some buses have luggage compartments underneath; some have inside overhead luggage racks adequate only for a small pack or bag, and others allow luggage to be stored next to the driver. Newer long-distance buses have adequate legroom, while some of the old ones bring back memories of riding on a school bus: the seats are the same, but you are bigger.

If you end up standing in a crowded bus, watch your pockets. Even with those courteous, helpful, friendly, dignified people around you, a bad apple may be on board. Be especially careful with checked luggage. Get off the bus quickly to claim it at your destination. If you put a bag on an overhead rack, place it across the aisle from you so you can keep your eye on it, especially before the bus leaves and at intermediate stops.

On longer trips, carry bottled water and maybe a snack. Don't expect a restroom on board. If your destination is not the town itself, ask the driver to let you off as close as possible. In towns, taxis usually meet incoming buses.

Speaking some Spanish makes bus travel easier, but with politeness, persistence, and imagination, a non-Spanish-speaker can manage. Carry a map and point to destinations or write the destination down and show it when asking for guidance. Bus is spelled the same in Spanish but is pronounced "boos."

Destinations via public bus are listed below alphabetically, along with departure location, phone number, and duration of trip. Buses start from San José unless otherwise indicated. Some leave from terminals; others on the street with only a sign to indicate the bus stop. Schedules change and bus stops sometimes move; check at www.yellowweb.co.cr/crbuses for an online bus schedule; in San José check with the ICT information office.

Airport (Juan Santamaría): Calles 10/12, Avenida 2, 24-hour service leaving every 10 minutes 5 A.M.-10 P.M., then less frequently; 30 minutes; 506/222-5325

Alajuela: Calles 10/12, Avenida 2, (same as above); 506/222-5325

Arenal: See La Fortuna

Barva Volcano: Central market in Heredía (bus to Paso Llano) three times daily except twice on Sunday; then walk 3.8 miles (6 km) to park entrance

Boca Tapada: See Pital

Braulio Carrillo (via highway to Limón): Calle 12, Avenidas 7/9, every 30 minutes 5 A.M.-9:45 P.M. (this is the Guapiles bus; get off at the ranger station); 506/257-8129

Cahuita: Calle Central, Avenidas 13/15, express bus four times daily (advance ticket sales); four hours; 506/257-8129

Cahuita from Limón: 75 meters north of Radio Casino, eight times daily; 506/758-1572

Cañas: Calle 16, Avenidas 3/5, express bus five times daily (advance ticket sales), 3.5 hours. 506/222-3006

Carara National Park: See Jacó

Cartago: Calle 5, Avenidas 18/20, every 10 minutes 5 A.M.-midnight; after 8:30 the bus leaves in front of Gran Hotel, Avenida 2/Calles 3/5; 35 minutes; 506/233-5350

Chirripó: See San Isidro de El General

Ciudad Quesada (San Carlos): Calle 12, Avenidas 7/9, express bus every hour 5 A.M.-7:30 P.M.; 2.5 hours; 506/255-4318

Ciudad Quesada/La Fortuna: Municipal bus station six times daily, one hour; 506/460-0326

David, Panama: Calle 14, Avenida 5, once daily; four hours; 506/221-4214

Dominical: Calle 16, Avenida 3, express bus once daily; 506/777-0318

Dominical from San Isidro: Four times daily; 506/771-2550

Flamingo Beach: Calle 20, Avenida 3, express bus twice daily; six hours; 506/222-7202

Flamingo from Santa Cruz: Twice daily

Golfito: Calle 14, Avenida 5, express bus twice a day (advance ticket sales); eight hours; 506/221-4214

Guayabo National Monument from Turrialba: Twice daily

Heredía: Avenida 2, Calles 10/12, every 10 minutes 5 A.M.-10 P.M.; Calle 4, Avenida 5/7, every 15 minutes 6 A.M.-midnight; 25 minutes; 506/233-8392

Irazú Volcano: Avenida 2, Calles 1/3 (across from Gran Hotel), express bus 8 A.M. Saturday and Sunday only

Jacó: Calle 16, Avenidas 1/3, three buses daily; 2.5 hours; 506/233-1109

Jacó from Puntarenas: Three times daily; 1.5 hours

Junquillal: Calle 20, Avenida 3, one express bus daily; five hours; 506/221-7202

La Cruz or Peñas Blancas: Calle 16, Avenidas 3/5, five buses daily; five hours; 506/222-3006

La Fortuna: Calle 12, Avenidas 7/9, three times daily; 4.5 hours; 506/255-4318

La Fortuna from Tilarán: Twice daily; four hours

Lankester Garden from Cartago: south side of Central Park (bus to Paraíso) every 30 minutes 4:30 A.M.-10:30 P.M.; 15 minutes; 506/574-6127

Liberia: Calle 14, Avenidas 1/3, 11 express buses daily; four hours; 506/222-1650

Liberia from Puntarenas: From municipal bus stop, once daily; 2.5 hours

Limón: Calle Central, Avenidas 13/15, express bus hourly 5 A.M.-7 P.M., through Braulio Carrillo; 2.5 hours; 506/223-7811

Los Chiles: Calle 12, Avenidas 7/9, twice daily; five hours; 506/255-4318

Manuel Antonio: See Quepos

Manzanillo: Calle Central, Avenidas 13/15, express bus at 4 P.M. (advance ticket sales)

Manzanillo from Limón: Twice daily; 1.5 hours

Monteverde: Calle 14, Avenidas 9/11, express bus twice daily (advance ticket sales); four hours; 506/222-3854

Monteverde from Tilarán: From Santa Elena (3 km from Monteverde), 7 A.M. daily; three hours

Monteverde from Puntarenas: Once daily; 506/222-3854

Montezuma from Paquera: From Paquera dock when ferry arrives, 506/642-0219

Nicoya: Calle 14, Avenida 5, express bus seven times daily (advance ticket sales); six hours; 506/222-2750

Nicoya from Liberia: Every hour 5 A.M.-7 P.M.

Nosara (Garza and Guiones): Calle 14, Avenida 5; six hours; 506/222-2666

Nosara from Nicoya: Main terminal, 1 P.M. daily; 1.5 hours; 506/685-5352

Orosi Valley from Cartago: From Cartago church ruins every hour 8 A.M.-10 P.M.

Orotina: Calle 16, Avenidas 1/3, seven times daily

Palmar Norte: Calle 14, Avenida 5, seven times daily; five hours; 506/221-4214

Palmar to Sierpe: Six times daily

Peñas Blancas: Calle 16, Avenidas 3/5, six times daily; five hours

Pital: Calle 12, Avenida 9, twice daily, connection to Boca Tapada.

Playa del Coco: Calle 14, Avenidas 1/3, twice a day; five hours; 506/222-1650

Playa del Coco from Liberia: Three times daily

Playa Hermosa: Calle 12, Avenidas 5/7, at 3:20 P.M. daily; five hours

Playa Hermosa from Liberia: Five times daily

Poás Volcano: Avenida 2, Calles 12/14, 8:30 A.M. daily; two hours

Puerto Jiménez: Calle 12, Avenidas, 7/9, twice daily; 10 hours; 506/257-4121

Puerto Viejo de Limón: Calle Central, Avenidas 13/15, express bus four times daily; five hours; 506/255-1025

Puerto Viejo de Limón from Limón: from Radio Casino six times daily; 1.5 hours

Puerto Viejo de Sarapiquí via Braulio Carrillo: Calle 12, Avenidas 7/9, direct bus eight times daily (advance ticket sales); 2.5 hours; 506/258-2734

Puerto Viejo de Sarapiquí via Vara Blanca: Three times daily; four hours; 506/258-2734

Puerto Viejo de Sarapiquí from Ciudad Quesada: Municipal Terminal, twice daily; three hours; 506/460-0638

Puntarenas: Calle 16, Avenidas 12, every half hour 6 A.M.-7 P.M.; two hours; 506/233-2610

Quepos and Manuel Antonio: Calle 16, Avenidas 1/3, express three times daily from lot beside Hotel Musoc (advance ticket sales in adjacent market); 3.5 hours; 506/223-5567

Quepos from Puntarenas: From main bus terminal three times daily; 3.5 hours; 506/643-3135

Quepos from San Isidro: Twice daily; three hours; 506/771-1384

Sámara: Calle 14, Avenidas 3/5, daily express at 12:30 P.M.; six hours; 506/222-2666

San Isidro de El General: Calle 16, Avenidas 1/3, every hour 5:30 A.M.-4:30 P.M. (advance ticket sales); three hours; 506/771-0414

San Isidro to San Gerardo de Rivas (Chirripó): twice daily, 506/233-4160

San Vito: Calle 14, Avenida 5, (advance ticket sales), 506/222-2750

Santa Cruz: Calle 20, Avenidas 3/5, express bus nine times daily; five hours; 506/221-7202

Santa Cruz from Liberia: Every hour, 5:30 A.M.-7:30 P.M.

Santa Rosa/Peñas Blancas: Calle 14, Avenidas 3/5, six times daily

Sarchí: Three express buses on weekdays, noon on Saturday; 1.5 hours

Sarchí from Alajuela: Avenida Central/1, Calle 8, every 30 minutes 5 A.M.-10 P.M.; 1.5 hours; 506/441-3781

Sixaola: Calle Central, Avenidas 13/15, four express buses daily; 506/257-8129

Tamarindo: Calle 14, Avenida 5, once daily; 5.5 hours; 506/222-2750, 506/223-8229

Tilarán: Calle 14, Avenidas 9/11, five times daily except Sunday (advance ticket sales); four hours; 506/222-3854

Turrialba: Calle 13, Avenidas 6/8, hourly express 5 A.M.-10 P.M.; 1.5 hours; 506/556-0073

Uvita (Ballena National Marine Park): Avenida 3, Calles 14/16, weekdays 3 P.M., twice on weekends

Uvita from San Isidro: twice daily; two hours; 506/771-2550

A private bus option is **Interbus,** 506/283-5573, fax 506/283-7655, vsftrip@sol.racsa.co.cr, www.costaricapass.com. Nine routes go to beaches, mountains, volcanoes, and national parks: some routes interconnect. Here are examples: San José to La Fortuna or Manuel Antonio $29, San José/Monteverde or Monteverde to La Fortuna $45, San José to Cahuita is $30, and on to Puerto Viejo is $35. San José to Tamarindo is $35. Pickup is at your hotel, and travel is in air-conditioned vehicles. A weekly pass to be used on any routes is $175; 10 days is $210. The airport shuttle is $5—a bargain. Combine Interbus transport with lodging—more than 40 hotels to choose from—and you can even combine the bus with car rental.

Ferries

Ferries cross the Gulf of Nicoya from Puntarenas to Playa Naranjo and Paquera and cross the Tempisque River to join the mainland with the Nicoya Peninsula, an alternate to going through Liberia. Passenger launches cross between Puntarenas and Paquera and between Golfito and Puerto Jiménez (connecting the mainland with the Osa Peninsula). There's no advance purchase of tickets, so if you are driving, allow time for lines, especially on weekends. Here are specifics.

Puntarenas–Playa Naranjo Ferry: Between Puntarenas and the Nicoya Peninsula, at Playa Naranjo. Cost: car and driver $10.50, passengers $1.50 each. Leaves Puntarenas at 3:15 A.M., 7 A.M., 10:50 A.M., 2:50 P.M., 7 P.M. Leaves Playa Naranjo 5:10 A.M., 8:50 A.M., 12:50 P.M., 5 P.M., 9 P.M.; one hour; 506/661-1069, 506/661-3834, fax 506/661-2197.

Puntarenas–Paquera Ferry: Between Puntarenas and the Nicoya Peninsula at Paquera. Cost: car and driver $9, passengers $1.50 each or $3.50 first class. Leaves Puntarenas at 5 A.M., 8:45 A.M., 12:30 P.M., 2 P.M., 5 P.M., 8:15 P.M. Leaves Paquera 6 A.M., 8 A.M., 11:45 A.M., 2:30 P.M., 6 P.M., 8:30 P.M.; 1.5 hours; 506/661-2084, 506/661-2160.

Puntarenas–Paquera Launch: Between Puntarenas and the Nicoya at Paquera, passengers only, Cost: less than $1.50 each person. Leaves Puntarenas from behind the market at 6 A.M., 11 A.M., and 3:15 P.M. Leaves Paquera at 7:30 A.M., 12 P.M., 5 P.M.; 506/661-2830, fax 506/641-0241.

Tempisque Ferry: Across the mouth of the Tempisque River, connecting the mainland with the Nicoya Peninsula. Cost: car and driver about $2, passengers less than $.25 each. Leaves Puerto Níspero (mainland side) at 5 A.M. and Puerto Moreno (on the peninsula) at 5:30 A.M., with continuous service until 8 P.M.; 30 minutes; 506/685-5295.

Golfito Launch: across the Golfo Dulce between Golfito and Puerto Jiménez, passengers only. Cost: less than $3. Leaves Golfito at 11:30 A.M. and Puerto Jiménez at 6 A.M.; 1.5 hours

Car Rental

To rent a car, you need a valid driver's license, passport, and credit card. The minimum age is usually 21 to 25. All major car rental agencies have offices in Costa Rica, and there are several local companies as well. Offices are in San José and some towns, as well as some resorts. Few automatic transmissions are available.

Shop around. Deductibles can be high. Weekly rates are discounted, and travelers in the low season, May to November, may pay as much as 20 percent less. You may get better rates by reserving your car before you come, through international reservations. Ballpark figures for something like a Sentra or Tercel, based on current quoted rates, are $54 for one day and $330 for one week, including insurance and free mileage. Four-wheel-drives start at about $75 per day (Suzuki Sidekick), $475 for the week. There is usually a damage deposit up to $1,000. Ask for a map and a handout sheet on basic Costa Rican traffic regulations. Check the car for dents, scratches, or other damage before you accept it and have such damage noted in writing by the agent. Also check the spare and jack and such details as brake fluid, oil, water, and lights. I have had good luck with Prego Rent a Car.

Gas is sold by the liter. All petroleum is imported and refined in Costa Rica by RECOPE, the national refinery. Current prices per gallon are from $1.50 to $2, depending grade. In rural areas, watch the gas gauge: you will not find a service station in every town.

Speed limits are posted and the numbers are in kilometers, not miles. Before you rent a car, please read the "Traffic Hazards" above. Don't leave belongings visible even in a locked car, and don't leave luggage in the trunk at night or even unattended during the day. In fact, don't leave anything of value in an unattended car at any time.

Bicycles

Bicycle tourism is here. If you're going to do it on your own, remember that bike lanes do not exist. If this is your first trip to Costa Rica, you might consult one of the tour companies before you set off (see Chapter 3).

Hitchhiking

Hitchhiking is not common: bus fare is cheap. However, in rural areas where bus service is nonexistent or infrequent, local people wait by the road for a ride. Tourists do not generally hitchhike in Costa Rica except in an emergency.

Reservations

Reservations for hotels and for lodges at private nature reserves are highly recommended for visits from December to April and are increasingly advisable in the low season, now marketed as the Green Season. They are essential for Christmastime and Easter week—some hotels have higher rates at these times. Many hotels and reserves offer substantial discounts during off-season months, especially in beach areas.

Once in the country, call to reconfirm reservations you made from home; and bring copies of your confirmation. Prices listed are valid for January 2000; however, rates do change. Use these as guidelines. Taxes are not included in rates unless specified.

Tourist attractions also feel the impact of Costa Rican vacationers during school vacation from December through February and during a two-week midyear break in July. Beaches and parks are prime destinations.

At the Airport

When you arrive in Costa Rica at the San José airport, look for the Costa Rica Tourism Institute (ICT) airport information office after you make your way past *migración* (Immigration) and *aduana* (Customs). From 9 A.M. to 5 P.M. Monday to Friday, except holidays, ICT staff can answer your questions, help make hotel reservations, and give you a road map of Costa Rica. Pick up brochures published by ICT as well as by hotels and tour companies.

A bank at the airport is open for dollar transactions 5:30 A.M.-8 P.M. Monday through Friday, except holidays. It's across from the ticket counters on the ground floor near the airport information desk.

A taxi ride for the 11 miles (18 km) into San José is $10. You may be directed to a van, sharing with other passengers; ask the person assigning taxis what your fare will be. Fare on frequent public buses that pass in front of the airport is about $.50, but there are no luggage racks, so if you have big bags, forget it.

Outside the front door of the terminal are offices of half a dozen rental car agencies; near the passenger exit is a private tourist information and reservation agency called Travel Center. Open 9 A.M.-9 P.M. daily, the center has maps, books, lots of travel folders, and bilingual staff.

When you leave the country, you are asked to be at the airport two hours early. It's good advice; check-in lines can be long, and you need time to pay the departure tax and change remaining colones into dollars. Reconfirm your return flight at least 24 hours before departure.

COMMUNICATIONS

Language

Spanish is the official language of Costa Rica. English is taught in some public schools, so you will encounter *ticos* who want to speak English with you or try to help if you don't speak Spanish. Do not expect to find English-speakers wherever you go. Major hotels have bilingual staff, as do tour agencies and private reserves. However, the waiter, park attendant, or taxi driver may not speak English, and no one at the bus station may understand a word you say. But Costa Ricans will try hard to help as long as you are polite.

Ticos are delighted when you try out whatever Spanish you know, so learn a few words and phrases—at least *por favor* (pronounced por fah-VOR) and *gracias* (GRAH-see-ahs), "please" and "thank you." You will soon be saying *buenos días* (boo-EN-nos DEE-ahs), "good morning," with the best of them.

448

Telephones

International calls are easy, once you have access to a phone. From any phone in the country, you can contact an operator in Canada or the United States to place collect or credit card calls.

United States	Canada
AT&T	0-800/011-4114 0-800/015-1161
MCI	0-800/012-2222
Sprint	0-800/013-0123
Worldcom	0-800/014-4444

From a private phone you can dial direct, using the appropriate country code (001 for the United States and Canada), followed by the area code and the number. Call person-to-person collect, or charge a call to your credit card by dialing 09, the country code (1 for the United States and Canada), area code, and phone number. An operator will come on the line. You can also dial 116 for the international operator, but service is quicker and cheaper using the 09 service. At hotels where long-distance calls go through the switchboard, there may be a fee.

Prepaid telephone cards have arrived in Costa Rica. Buy a Servicio 199 card for international calls from a touch-tone telephone. Dial 199 and follow instructions. These cards, available from Costa Rican Electricity Institute (ICE) and stores displaying ICE signs, come in values of $10, $20, or 3,000 colones.

Two communications centers allow travelers to make international calls or send a fax or e-mail and pay on the spot (or call collect or use a telephone credit card). Radiográfica Costarricense in downtown San José, Avenida 5, Calle 3, is open 7:30 A.M.-9 P.M. daily. Comunicaciones Internacionales on Avenida 2 just west of the Gran Hotel Costa Rica and Plaza de la Cultura is open 7 A.M.-8:30 P.M. daily.

You can also buy a prepaid telephone card for in-country calls, which can be inserted in card-operated public phones. They come in amounts of 500, 1,000, or 2,000 colones. Coin phones require a supply of 5-, 10-, or 20-colón coins (look on the phone to see which it accepts). Place the coin in the slot; if the phone is working properly, it will drop only when your call goes through. If the phone starts beeping after you have talked awhile, feed it another coin or you'll be cut off. When calling a friend, give the person the number you are calling from (posted near the phone) so s/he can call you back and avoid the problem. For calls within Costa Rica, it is not necessary to dial an area code. Even local calls on private phones cost: the amount of time is added to a basic charge, which is one reason most businesses do not let the public use their private phones.

Notice the many public telephone signs as you travel around the country. Often they are in the local grocery or sometimes even in a private home. To call from one of these, give the person in charge of the phone the number to be dialed. Time is metered, and you pay when you finish.

NOTE: Numbers change regularly. If repeated calls to a hotel or lodge get no answer, assume the number has changed.

Mail

Some hotels sell postage stamps and will mail cards and letters for guests. However, it's fairly painless to do it yourself at the local post office, and Spanish usually is not necessary. Just hand the card to the person at the window, who will sell you beautifully colored stamps. Don't expect your cards or letters to get to recipients before you get home.

The line moves quickly at the Central Post Office in San José, Calle 2, Avenidas 1/3. Hours of window service are 7 A.M.-9 P.M. weekdays, 8 A.M.-noon on Saturday. Elsewhere, look for signs that say "CORTEL" to find the post office.

Fax, E-mail, Internet

If your hotel does not offer these services, go to Radiográfica or Comunicaciones Internacionales in San José, where you can both send and receive. Most post offices have telegraph services. Western Union has an office at Calle 9, Avenidas 2/4. A few hotels offer Internet access to guests.

Or watch for Internet cafes, found not only in San José but in Quepos, Dominical, Puerto Viejo de Limón and other areas around the country. There's even a McDonald's-MacIntosh combo.

MONEY MATTERS

Currency

The monetary unit is the *colón* (co-LONE). Its symbol is ¢. Take time to look at the coins—some are *colones* (co-LONE-ess) and some are *céntimos* (SEN-tea-mos). Each is clearly marked, but it pays to recognize that the coin marked "20" is 20 colones, not 20 céntimos. Bills come in denominations of 50, 100, 500, 1,000, 5,000. 10,000. (The 50- and 100-colon bills are being replaced with coins). Pretty 5- and 10-colón notes are rarely used now, though you can buy them as souvenirs. Coins are 1, 2, 5, 10, 20, 25, 50, and 100 colones: 10, 25, and 50 céntimos are still around but are an endangered species. Newer coins have a golden cast.

The colón floats in relation to the U.S. dollar; as of January 2001, the exchange rate was 318 colón to the dollar. Continuing mini-devaluations change the rate.

Expect to pay a premium for colones in a departure airport, so change a minimum or wait until you get to Costa Rica. You may change money legally at banks or at your hotel, though sometimes the hotel cash drawer is low, so don't wait until the last minute to ask. Do not change dollars on the street: it's both illegal and risky. The difference in the legal and black-market rate is only a few colones, and you risk receiving counterfeit money or being other-wise shortchanged or robbed.

Western Union has offices at Calle 9, Avenidas 2/4 and in San Pedro if you need to transfer cash. Telephone is 506/283-6336, toll-free inside Costa Rica 800/777-7777.

Hotels and banks usually charge a small amount for changing traveler's checks or give a lower exchange rate. Ask. Some have a minimum service charge whether you change $50 or $500 worth of checks. Do not assume that all hotels will accept credit cards, espe-cially in areas where telephone service is limited; inquire when you make your reservation. Also, some establishments add a surcharge for use of credit cards even though doing so is illegal.

Always have some smaller bills with you. Taxis or rural restau-rants or shops may not have change for a 5,000-colón note.

Banks

Hours vary but banks are open at least from 9 A.M. to 3 P.M., closed on holidays and weekends. A few have longer hours and are open Saturday morning. In San José the most efficient bank I have found for changing money is Banco Metropolitano (Avenida 2 between Calle Central and Calle 1), open weekdays 8:15 A.M.-4 P.M. But at any bank just tell the guard at the door that you want to change U.S. dollars (that much English everybody understands), and he will point you in the right direction.

Before you take a place in any bank line, ask to be sure you are in the right one. You sometimes must hand over your identification documents (passport, tourist card) at one window and complete the transaction at another. It can be a happy five-minute experience, or it can take 30 minutes or more. Non-U.S. currency is more difficult to change. Banks generally assess a small percentage for changing traveler's checks.

Credit Cards

More and more establishments accept credit cards, but ask before you spend if you're depending on plastic. Some establishments, hotels especially, add a surcharge for use of a credit card, even though it's illegal. You may want to check when you make your hotel reservation.

In downtown San José, an American Express office is on the third floor of the Banco de San José across from the Hotel Europa on Calle Central, Avenidas 3/5, open 8:15 A.M.- 4:15 P.M. weekdays. Call 506/257-1792 for information.

For VISA and MasterCard, automatic teller machines with 24-hour service (some for Plus and some for Cirrus) are increasingly available in the Central Valley, with at least one in places like Liberia, Limón, Ciudad Quesada, and Puntarenas (remember your PIN). A Credomatic office on Calle Central, Avenidas 3/5 deals with both of these cards. It's open 8 A.M.-7 P.M. weekdays, 9 A.M.-1 P.M. Saturday; for information call 506/257-4744.

You will be asked for your passport or tourist card for any credit card transactions at banks.

Taxes and Tipping

The sales tax is 13 percent. Currently there is a lodging tax of about 3 percent, so hotel bills will reflect 16.39 percent tax. (The 13 percent tax is also levied on the 3 percent). Efforts to eliminate the lodging tax have not yet succeeded. Rates listed in destination chapters do not include taxes except where specified, because the tax rate seems to change more often than the editions of my book. At restaurants you pay the 13 percent sales tax and a 10 percent service charge automatically added to your bill. Tipping beyond that service charge is at your discretion.

Tipping for services is a personal matter, of course, but here are some suggestions to guide you.

Taxi drivers: A tip is not expected, but if they load luggage or provide extra-special service, you may want to tip.

Bellboys, porters, etc.: At least $.50 per bag.

Housekeeping staff or cooks at private reserves: $.50 to $1 per person per day.

Naturalist and river guides: $3 to $5 per day, a little less for local guides without naturalist training.

Bus or van driver on a tour: $2 or $3 per person per day.

Riverboat captains: $2 or $3.

COSTA RICAN CUISINE

Gallo pinto is the staple of the Costa Rican diet: black beans and rice. Try to eat it somewhere other than a first-class hotel. A *gallo* is something with a tortilla wrapped around it—beef, cheese, beans, chicken, or pork. When faced with an unfamiliar menu in the countryside, you usually can't go wrong ordering one of the rice dishes such as *arroz con pollo* (chicken and rice) or a *casado*, which often comes with beef, chicken, or pork and vegetables such as *yuca* (cassava, a tuber similar to a potato), plantain, or squash with the ever-present rice and black beans. A vegetarian *casado* may also be available.

Olla de carne is a soup of beef and vegetables—chunks of *yuca*, squash, potato, corn on the cob, plantain, or whatever is in the house recipe. *Tico tamales*, traditional at Christmas, are wrapped in banana leaves; a filling of pork is most common, though it can be chicken. Try a *tortilla de queso*, a substantial tortilla with cheese mixed in the cornmeal. *Pupusas*, of Salvadoran origin, have found their way into typical restaurant menus in Costa Rica. Basically they are two tortillas fried with cheese inside—tasty and greasy.

Sea bass (*corvina*), prawns (*langostinos*), and lobster (*langosto*) are among fresh seafood available. An appetizer of ceviche, certain types of raw seafood "cooked" in lime or lemon juice and mixed with onion and coriander (*cilantro*) leaves, can serve as a great light lunch.

The big bunches of bright red or orange fruit you see for sale along roadsides are *pejibayes*, a palm fruit that has been harvested for food since ancient times. When boiled, it is often served as an hors d'oeuvre with a dollop of mayonnaise on top. Try it. You may not like it—the flesh is quite dense and on the dry side—but most *ticos* love it. Another product of the *pejibaye* palm is *palmito*, or heart of palm, served cooked or fresh. Some palm species do not resprout when cut for the "heart." The *pejibaye* does, and commercial plantations now supply the market, so you don't have to worry that your heart of palm salad cost a forest tree its life. Natives also make a fermented drink from the sap when a tree is cut. Have a guide point out the tree, a stately palm with hairy spines on the trunk.

Naturales, or natural fruit drinks, may come mixed with milk, in which case they will be listed as *en leche*, or with water (*en agua*). Popular fruits for the *naturales* include mora (a berry), *piña* (pineapple), papaya, mango, and cas. Let your surroundings guide you as to which is safest, or stick to bottled drinks. In the *campo* (country), you may find *agua dulce*, a hot drink made of boiling water and brown sugar. You can also have it mixed with milk (*con leche*). It's especially good in the mountains when there is a chill in the air. Cane-based *guaro* is the national liquor.

For sweets, try a dessert (*postre*, pronounced POS-tray) of flan, a sweet custard, or *tres leches*, a moist cake. *Cajeta* is similar to fudge.

HOLIDAYS

On official national holidays most businesses, including banks, close.

January 1—New Year's Day

Holy Week—Maundy Thursday and Good Friday rival Easter in importance. Banks and businesses close, some of them all week.

April 11—Day of Juan Santamaría, national boy-hero in the 1856 battle against William Walker and his filibusterers.

May 1—Labor Day

July 25—Annexation of the Province of Guanacaste, formerly part of Nicaragua.

August 2—Day of the Virgin de Los Angeles (Our Lady of the Angels), patron saint of Costa Rica.

August 15—Mother's Day

September 15—Independence Day (independence from Spain).

October 12—Day of the Cultures (Discovery of America).

December 25—Christmas (many businesses close from Christmas to New Year's Day).

TIME ZONE

Costa Rica goes by Central Standard Time year-round—no daylight savings time. A note on daylight hours: Since Costa Rica is only 10° north of the equator, it does not have seasonal variations in daylight hours that lands to the north have. If you get up with the sun, you will be getting up between 5 and 5:30 A.M. Darkness falls between 5:30 and 6 P.M.

APPENDIX B
ADDITIONAL RESOURCES

TOURIST INFORMATION

Costa Rican Tourism Institute (ICT)
800/343-6332 (8 A.M. to 5 P.M. Central Time)
E-mail: info@tourism-costarica.com
Website: www.tourism-costarica.com

ICT Information Office, San José
Calle 5, Avenidas Central/2
9 A.M. to 5 P.M. weekdays, closed for lunch
506/223-1091

National Chamber of Tourism (CANATUR)
E-mail: info@tourism.cr
Website: www.tourism.co.cr

Emergency Number
For emergencies within Costa Rica, call 911.

CURRENT HAPPENINGS

The *Tico Times* is an English-language newspaper published every Friday. It's an excellent source of information on what's going on in Costa Rica and is widely available in downtown San José and in some outlying areas. Website: www.ticotimes.co.cr.
506/258-1558, fax 506/233-6378.

Costa Rica Outdoors is a bimonthly magazine with excellent information for nature/adventure travelers. Check it out online: www.costaricaoutdoors.com.
800/308-3394.

For weather, in English, check out www.costarica.com/weather. A "forecast" button brings up a five-day forecast, and temperatures are even given in Fahrenheit.

For Spanish speakers, check out the Costa Rican daily newspaper *La Nación* online: www.nacion.co.cr.

PARKS AND RESERVES INFORMATION

Telephone Hotline: 506/192
Operates 7:30 A.M. to 5 P.M. Monday to Friday. English- and Spanish-speaking staff give information on how to get there, weather, entrance fees, and hours and days each area is open—some protected areas are closed one or two days a week. You cannot make reservations at this number, but staff can give you the appropriate number to call. Information can also be sent by fax.

CONSERVATION AREAS

Contact appropriate conservation area for overnight reservations or for answers to more detailed questions about individual parks, reserves, and wildlife refuges. The Ministry of Environment and Energy (MINAE) oversees the National System of Conservation Areas (SINAC) and protection of the country's natural resources. Go to www.minae.go.cr for more information on parks and reserves.

Amistad Caribbean Conservation Area:
Cahuita National Park, 506/755-0302, tel/fax 506/755-0060
Gandoca-Manzanillo Wildlife Refuge, tel/fax 506/754-2133
Hitoy-Cerere Biological Reserve, tel/fax 506/758-3996

Amistad Pacific Conservation Area:
La Amistad National Park, 506/771-4836, tel/fax 506/771-3297
Chirripó National Park, 506/771-3155, tel/fax 506/771-3297
Tapantí National Park, tel/fax 506/771-2970

Arenal-Huetar Norte Conservation Area:
Juan Castro Blanco National Park, 506/460-1412
Caño Negro National Wildlife Refuge, 506/661-8464,
  fax 506/460-0644

Arenal-Tilarán Conservation Area:
Arenal National Park, 506/695-5180, fax 506/695-5982
Tenorio Volcano National Park, 506/695-5908, fax 506/695-5982

Central Volcanic Range Conservation Area:
www.minae.go.cr/accvc
Braulio Carrillo National Park, 506/290-1927, fax 506/290-4869
Guayabo National Monument, 506/290-8202, tel/fax 506/556-9507
Irazú Volcano National Park, 506/290-8202, fax 506/290-4869
Poás Volcano National Park, 506/442-7041, fax 506/232-5324

Guanacaste Conservation Area:
www.acguanacaste.ac.cr
Guanacaste National Park, tel/fax 506/666-5051, 506/666-5020
Junquillal National Wildlife Refuge, tel/fax 506/661-8150
Rincón de la Vieja National Park, tel/fax 506/666-5051,
  506/666-5020
Santa Rosa National Park, tel/fax 506/666-5051, 506/666-5020

Central Pacific Conservation Area:
Carara, 506/383-9953, fax 506/416-7402
Manuel Antonio, 506/777-0644, fax 506/777-0654

Coco Island Conservation Area:
Coco Island National Park, 506/283-8004

Osa Conservation Area:
Ballena National Marine Park, tel/fax 506/786-7161
Caño Island Biological Reserve, 506/735-5282, tel/
  fax 506/735-5276
Corcovado National Park, 506/735-5282, tel/fax 506/735-5276

Tempisque Conservation Area:
Barra Honda National Park, 506/685-5667, fax 506/685-5276
Cabo Blanco Absolute Natural Reserve, tel/fax 506/642-0093
Las Baulas National Marine Park, tel/fax 506/653-0470
Ostional National Wildlife Refuge, tel/fax 506/680-0241
Palo Verde National Park, 506/671-1290, fax 506/671-1062

Tortuguero Conservation Area:
Barra del Colorado National Wildlife Refuge, tel/fax 506/710-2929,
  506/710-7673
Tortuguero National Park, tel/fax 506/710-2929, 506/710-7673

EMBASSIES IN SAN JOSÉ

Canada
Oficentro Ejecutivo La Sabana, Sabana Sur (Building 5, 3rd floor);
506/296-4149, fax 506/296-4270
France
Road to Curridabat, 200 m south, 25 m east of Indoor Club,
506/225-0733, 506/225-0933
Germany
Rohrmoser, 506/232-5533, 506/222-6671
Great Britain
Edificio Centro Colón, 11th floor, Avenida Colón, Calle 38,
506/221-5566, 506/221-5816
Holland
Oficentro Ejecutivo, La Sabana, Sabana Sur (Building 3, 3rd floor);
506/296-1490
Italy
Los Yoses, Avenida 10, Calles 33/35; 506/234-2326
Japan
Residencial Rohrmoser, 400 m west, 100 m north of La Nunciatura;
506/232-1255
Mexico
Los Yoses; 506/225-7284
Spain
Calle 32, Paseo Colon/Avenida 2; 506/222-1933, 506/222-5745

Switzerland
Centro Colon, 10th floor, Paseo Colón, Calle 38; 506/221-4829
United States
Rohrmoser, road to Pavas in front of Centro Comercial (any taxi driver can take you); 506/220-3939, fax 506/220-2305. Consulate: 506/220-3050, fax: 506/231-4783

METRIC CONVERSION TABLES

To change	to	Multiply by
Hectares	Acres	2.471
Meters	Feet	3.2808
Meters	Yards	1.094
Kilometers	Miles	.6214
Millimeters	Inches	.0394
Centimeters	Inches	.3937
Square kilometers	Square miles	.3861
Liters	Gallons (U.S.)	.2642
Liters	Pints	2.113
Kilograms	Pounds	2.205
Grams	Ounces	.0353

TEMPERATURE CONVERSION

Celsius to Fahrenheit: multiply by $9/5$ (or 1.8) and add 32.
Fahrenheit to Celsius: subtract 32 and multiply by $5/9$ (or .56).
Here are some reference points to save some of the math:

Celsius	Fahrenheit
0°	32°
10°	50°
20°	68°
30°	86°
35°	95°
40°	104°

FAUNA: ENGLISH AND SPANISH NAMES

English	Spanish
agouti	*guatusa*
anteater, silky	*serafín*
anteater, tamandua	*oso hormiguero*
armadillo	*cusuco*
bat	*murciélago*
bird	*pájaro, ave*
butterfly	*mariposa*
caiman	*caimán, lagarto*
coati	*pizote*
cougar, mountain lion	*puma, león*
crocodile	*cocodrillo*
deer, brocket	*cabra de monte*
deer, white-tailed	*venado cola blanca*
frog	*rana*
gopher	*taltusa*
hummingbird	*colibrí*
jaguar	*jaguar, tigre*
jaguarundi	*león breñero*
kinkajou	*martilla*
macaw	*lapa*
margay	*caucel, tigrillo*
monkey, howler	*mono congo*
monkey, squirrel	*mono tití, mono ardilla*
monkey, white-faced capuchin	*mono cara blanca*
ocelot	*manigordo*
opossum	*zorro*
otter, river	*nutria, perro de agua*
paca	*tepezcuintle*
parrot	*loro*
peccary, collared	*saíno*
peccary, white-lipped	*cariblanco*
raccoon	*mapache*
skunk	*zorro hediondo*
sloth	*perezoso, perica*
snake	*serpiente, culebra*

spider monkey	*mono colorado, mono araña*
squirrel	*ardilla, chisa*
tapir	*danta*
tayra	*tolomuco*
toad	*sapo*
turtle	*tortuga*

BIBLIOGRAPHY

Beletsky, Les. *Costa Rica: The Ecotravellers' Wildlife Guide*, San Diego: Academic Press, 1998.

Biesanz, Mavis Hiltunen, Richard Biesanz, and Karen Zubris Biesanz. *The Ticos: Culture and Social Change in Costa Rica*. Boulder: Lynne Rienner Publishers, 1998.

Boza, Mario A. *Costa Rica National Parks*. Madrid: Incafo (for Fundación Neotrópica de Costa Rica), 1996.

DeVries, Philip J. *The Butterflies of Costa Rica and Their Natural History*. Princeton: Princeton University Press, 1987.

Emmons, Louise H. *Neotropical Rainforest Mammals: A Field Guide*. Chicago: University of Chicago Press, 1997.

Forsyth, Adrian. *Journey through a Tropical Jungle*. Toronto: Greey de Pencier Books, 1988.

Janzen, Daniel H.., ed. *Costa Rican Natural History*. Chicago: University of Chicago Press, 1983.

Mayfield, Michael W., and Rafael E. Gallo. *The Rivers of Costa Rica: A Canoeing, Kayaking, and Rafting Guide*. Birmingham, Ala.: Menasha Ridge Press, 1988.

Reid, Fiona A. *Field Guide to the Mammals of Central America & Southeast Mexico*. Oxford University Press, 1998.

Sekerak, Aaron D. *A Travel and Site Guide to Birds of Costa Rica, with Side Trips to Panama & Nicaragua*. Edmonton, Alberta: Lone Pine Publishing, 1996.

Skutch, Alexander F. *A Naturalist in Costa Rica*. Gainesville, FL: University of Florida Press, 1971.

Skutch, Alexander F. *Trogons, Laughing Falcons, and Other Neotropical Birds*. College Station: Texas A&M University Press, 1999.

Stiles, F. Gary, and Alexander F. Skutch. *A Guide to the Birds of Costa Rica.* Ithaca: Cornell University Press, 1989.

Wallace, David Rains. *The Quetzal and the Macaw: The Story of Costa Rica's National Parks.* San Francisco: Sierra Book Club, 1992.

Wilson, Bruce M. *Costa Rica: Politics, Economics, and Democracy.* Boulder: Lynne Rienner Publishers, Inc., 1998.

GLOSSARY

aguacero - a downpour

arco iris - rainbow

arribadas - arrival or large numbers of turtles

avenida - avenue

banco - long seat

cajuela - basket

calle - street

campesino - farmer

cordillera - the Spanish term for mountain range

corvina - sea bass

casitas - little houses

casona - ranch house

costa rica - rich coast, the name given to the area during the times of the Spanish explorers

ensenada - cove or small bay

farmacia - pharmacy

gallo pinto - rice and beans wrapped in a tortilla

haga fila - get in line

hermosa - beautiful

invierno - (winter) for wet months, generally from May through November

lapas - macaws

maiz - corn

maría - taxi meter

metros - meters

mirador - viewing point

New World - North, South, and Central Americas

Old World - Europe and Africa

pailas - mud pots

palenques - round, thatched open-sided structure, often used for informal outdoor dining

paperos - potato farmers

páramo - treeless subalpine habitat with grasses and shrubs

peónes - day laborers

pequeñito - small

perezoso - three-toed sloth; lazy

playa - beach

postres - desserts

quebradas - ravines

reductor de velocidad - speed reducer

sabanero - cowboy

sodas - small, inexpensive cafes

teléferico - aerial tram

temporal - a continuous rain lasting for several days

ticos - the name Costa Ricans call themselves, said by some to come from a colonial saying: "We are all *hermaniticos* (little brothers)."

tijeras - scissors

verano - (summer) for dry season months, generally from December through April

INDEX

ABOUT THE AUTHOR

Ree Strange Sheck lived and worked in Costa Rica for more than eight years, notably working with nonprofit conservation organizations, such as the Monteverde Conservation League and the Organization for Tropical Studies. She returned to Santa Fe, New Mexico, in 1999.

She is an award-winning writer who has traveled throughout Latin America and lived in Guatemala, Ecuador, and Mexico. Her background in Latin American studies, including a Fulbright grant to attend the Universidad Central in Ecuador, and her first-hand experience provide her with a broad knowledge and appreciation of the Latin culture as well as the formidable pressures on the natural world in developing countries.

Her interest in conservation and nature is matched by a commitment to projects centered on human needs, having initiated a project to provide books for rural schools in Costa Rica, formerly helping in nutrition centers in rural Guatemala and working as liaison for Central American refugees in New Mexico.

She makes no bones about her love for Costa Rica and its people.

AVALON
TRAVEL
publishing

BECAUSE TRAVEL MATTERS.

AVALON TRAVEL PUBLISHING knows that travel is more than coming and going—travel is taking part in new experiences, new ideas, and a new outlook. Our goal is to bring you complete and up-to-date information to help you make informed travel decisions.

AVALON TRAVEL GUIDES feature a combination of practicality and spirit, offering a unique traveler-to-traveler perspective perfect for an afternoon hike, around-the-world journey, or anything in between.

WWW.TRAVELMATTERS.COM

Avalon Travel Publishing guides are available at your favorite book or travel store.

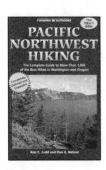

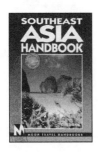

FOR TRAVELERS WITH SPECIAL INTERESTS

GUIDES

The 100 Best Small Art Towns in America • Asia in New York City
The Big Book of Adventure Travel • Cities to Go
Cross-Country Ski Vacations • Gene Kilgore's Ranch Vacations
Great American Motorcycle Tours • Healing Centers and Retreats
Indian America • Into the Heart of Jerusalem
The People's Guide to Mexico • The Practical Nomad
Saddle Up! • Staying Healthy in Asia, Africa, and Latin America
Steppin' Out • Travel Unlimited • Understanding Europeans
Watch It Made in the U.S.A. • The Way of the Traveler
Work Worldwide • The World Awaits
The Top Retirement Havens • Yoga Vacations

SERIES

Adventures in Nature
The Dog Lover's Companion
Kidding Around
Live Well

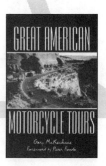

MOON HANDBOOKS

provide comprehensive coverage of a region's arts, history, land, people, and social issues in addition to detailed practical listings for accommodations, food, outdoor recreation, and entertainment. Moon Handbooks allow complete immersion in a region's culture—ideal for travelers who want to combine sightseeing with insight for an extraordinary travel experience.

USA

Alaska-Yukon • Arizona • Big Island of Hawaii • Boston
Coastal California • Colorado • Connecticut • Georgia
Grand Canyon • Hawaii • Honolulu-Waikiki • Idaho • Kauai
Los Angeles • Maine • Massachusetts • Maui • Michigan
Montana • Nevada • New Hampshire • New Mexico
New York City • New York State • North Carolina
Northern California • Ohio • Oregon • Pennsylvania
San Francisco • Santa Fe-Taos • Silicon Valley
South Carolina • Southern California • Tahoe • Tennessee
Texas • Utah • Virginia • Washington • Wisconsin
Wyoming • Yellowstone-Grand Teton

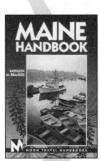

INTERNATIONAL

Alberta and the Northwest Territories • Archaeological Mexico
Atlantic Canada • Australia • Baja • Bangkok • Bali • Belize
British Columbia • Cabo • Canadian Rockies • Cancún
Caribbean Vacations • Colonial Mexico • Costa Rica • Cuba
Dominican Republic • Ecuador • Fiji • Havana • Honduras
Hong Kong • Indonesia • Jamaica • Mexico City • Mexico
Micronesia • The Moon • Nepal • New Zealand • Northern Mexico
Oaxaca • Pacific Mexico • Pakistan • Philippines • Puerto Vallarta
Singapore • South Korea • South Pacific • Southeast Asia • Tahiti
Thailand • Tonga-Samoa • Vancouver • Vietnam, Cambodia and Laos
Virgin Islands • Yucatán Peninsula

www.moon.com

Rick Steves

shows you where to travel and how to travel—all while getting the most value for your dollar. His Back Door travel philosophy is about making friends, having fun, and avoiding tourist rip-offs.

Rick's been traveling to Europe for more than 25 years and is the author of 22 guidebooks, which have sold more than a million copies. He also hosts the award-winning public television series *Travels in Europe with Rick Steves*.

RICK STEVES' COUNTRY & CITY GUIDES

Best of Europe
France, Belgium & the Netherlands
Germany, Austria & Switzerland
Great Britain & Ireland
Italy • London • Paris • Rome • Scandinavia • Spain & Portugal

RICK STEVES' PHRASE BOOKS

French • German • Italian • French, Italian & German
Spanish & Portuguese

MORE EUROPE FROM RICK STEVES

Europe 101
Europe Through the Back Door
Mona Winks
Postcards from Europe

WWW.RICKSTEVES.COM

ROAD TRIP
USA

Getting there is half the fun, and Road Trip USA guides are your ticket to driving adventure. Taking you off the interstates and onto less-traveled, two-lane highways, each guide is filled with fascinating trivia, historical information, photographs, facts about regional writers, and details on where to sleep and eat—all contributing to your exploration of the American road.

"Books so full of the pleasures of the American road,
you can smell the upholstery."
~ BBC radio

THE ORIGINAL CLASSIC GUIDE
Road Trip USA

ROAD TRIP USA REGIONAL GUIDE
Road Trip USA: California and the Southwest

ROAD TRIP USA GETAWAYS
Road Trip USA Getaways: Chicago
Road Trip USA Getaways: New Orleans
Road Trip USA Getaways: San Francisco
Road Trip USA Getaways: Seattle

www.roadtripusa.com

TRAVEL ✦ SMART

TRAVEL ✦ SMART® guidebooks are accessible, route-based driving guides. Special interest tours provide the most practical routes for family fun, outdoor activities, or regional history for a trip of anywhere from two to 22 days. Travel Smarts take the guesswork out of planning a trip by recommending only the most interesting places to eat, stay, and visit.

"One of the few travel series that rates sightseeing attractions. That's a handy feature. It helps to have some guidance so that every minute counts."
~ San Diego Union-Tribune

TRAVEL SMART REGIONS

Alaska
American Southwest
Arizona
Carolinas
Colorado
Deep South
Eastern Canada
Florida Gulf Coast
Florida
Georgia
Hawaii
Illinois/Indiana
Iowa/Nebraska
Kentucky/Tennessee
Maryland/Delaware
Michigan
Minnesota/Wisconsin
Montana/Wyoming/Idaho
Nevada
New England
New Mexico
New York State

Northern California
Ohio
Oregon
Pacific Northwest
Pennsylvania/New Jersey
South Florida and the Keys
Southern California
Texas
Utah
Virginias
Western Canada

Foghorn Outdoors

guides are for campers, hikers, boaters, anglers, bikers, and golfers of all levels of daring and skill. Each guide contains site descriptions and ratings, driving directions, facilities and fees information, and easy-to-read maps that leave only the task of deciding where to go.

"Foghorn Outdoors has established an ecological conservation standard unmatched by any other publisher."
~ Sierra Club

CAMPING Arizona and New Mexico Camping
Baja Camping • California Camping
Camper's Companion • Colorado Camping
Easy Camping in Northern California
Easy Camping in Southern California
Florida Camping • New England Camping
Pacific Northwest Camping
Utah and Nevada Camping

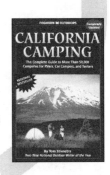

HIKING 101 Great Hikes of the San Francisco Bay Area
California Hiking • Day-Hiking California's National Parks
Easy Hiking in Northern California
Easy Hiking in Southern California
New England Hiking
Pacific Northwest Hiking • Utah Hiking

FISHING Alaska Fishing • California Fishing
Washington Fishing

BOATING California Recreational Lakes and Rivers
Washington Boating and Water Sports

OTHER OUTDOOR RECREATION California Beaches
California Golf • California Waterfalls • California Wildlife
Easy Biking in Northern California • Florida Beaches
The Outdoor Getaway Guide For Southern California
Tom Stienstra's Outdoor Getaway Guide: Northern California

WWW.FOGHORN.COM

CiTY·SMaRT ™

The best way to enjoy a city is to get advice from someone who lives there—and that's exactly what City Smart guidebooks offer. City Smarts are written by local authors with hometown perspectives who have personally selected the best places to eat, shop, sightsee, and simply hang out. The honest, lively, and opinionated advice is perfect for business travelers looking to relax with the locals or for longtime residents looking for something new to do Saturday night.

*A portion of sales from each title
benefits a non-profit literacy organization in that city.*

City Smart Cities

Albuquerque	Anchorage
Austin	Baltimore
Berkeley/Oakland	Boston
Calgary	Charlotte
Chicago	Cincinnati
Cleveland	Dallas/Ft. Worth
Denver	Indianapolis
Kansas City	Memphis
Milwaukee	Minneapolis/St. Paul
Nashville	Pittsburgh
Portland	Richmond
San Francisco	Sacramento
St. Louis	Salt Lake City
San Antonio	San Diego
Tampa/St. Petersburg	Toronto
Tucson	Vancouver

www.travelmatters.com

User-friendly, informative, and fun:
Because travel *matters.*

Visit our newly launched web site and explore the
variety of titles and travel information available
online, featuring
an interactive *Road Trip USA* exhibit.

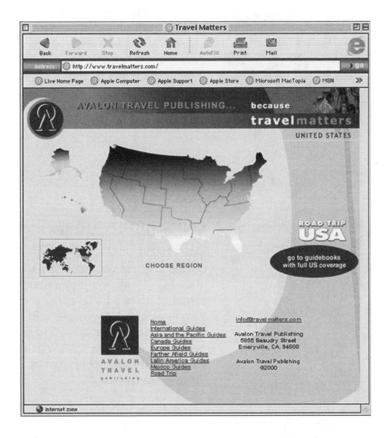

www.ricksteves.com

The Rick Steves web site is bursting with information to boost your travel I.Q. and liven up your European adventure. Including:

- The latest from Rick on what's hot in Europe
- Excerpts from Rick's books
- Rick's comprehensive Guide to European Railpasses

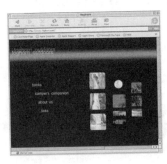

www.foghorn.com

Foghorn Outdoors guides are the premier source for United States outdoor recreation information. Visit the Foghorn Outdoors web site for more information on these activity-based travel guides, including the complete text of the handy *Foghorn Outdoors: Camper's Companion*.

www.moon.com

Moon Handbooks' goal is to give travelers all the background and practical information they'll need for an extraordinary travel experience. Visit the Moon Handbooks web site for interesting information and practical advice, including Q&A with the author of *The Practical Nomad*, Edward Hasbrouck.